From the Courtroom to the Classroom

)12345

shing Group

ne Sans and ITC Stone Serif

Library of Congress Control Number 20

Paperback ISBN 978-1-934742-20-4

Library Edition ISBN 978-1-934742-21-1

Published by Harvard Education Press,
an imprint of the Harvard Education Pu

Harvard Education Press
8 Story Street
Cambridge, MA 02138

Cover Design: Nancy Goulet

The typefaces used in this book are ITC

Contents

Acknowledgments

This project began with the generous support of the W. T. Grant Foundation. The Foundation funded our research on the implementation and effects of unitary status in Nashville, Tennessee, and a comprehensive review of national desegregation trends. We acknowledge Robert Granger, president of the foundation, for his deep interest in this topic, and in our project from the start. A recent grant from the Vanderbilt Center for Nashville Studies was essential in developing this volume, and in supporting our interest in emerging desegregation policies beyond Nashville. We thank Dan Cornfield, director of the Vanderbilt Center, for embracing the significance of this book, and its central arguments and themes, in the ongoing agenda of the center.

We also acknowledge the contributions of the authors in this volume. With good spirits and a sense of commitment, they worked with diligence and determination under a tight timeline, revising drafts and responding to reviews. Finally, we are grateful for the enthusiasm and guidance of our editor, Douglas Clayton, at Harvard Education Press. His steady hand and good judgment enriched the experience and the final product.

Foreword

Ronald F. Ferguson

In this book, Claire Smrekar and Ellen Goldring have assembled a timely and insightful collection of research-based essays on issues related to segregation, integration, and re-segregation in America. Beginning with *Brown v. Board of Education of Topeka*, the contributing authors analyze ups and downs in our national quest for equal opportunity in American public schooling. Segregated schools favored whites over blacks in the allocation of resources, thereby helping whites maintain economic, political, and social supremacy. This was most true in the South, where segregation was the law, but even in the North, social and cultural forces caused unequal access to a quality education. Beginning with *Brown*, plaintiffs in a series of court cases fought over four decades to integrate schools and equalize opportunity. Their efforts changed laws and transformed institutions.

In the second half of the twentieth century, state and federal courts, legislatures, and executive branch offices integrated schools and helped expand educational opportunity. Facing fear and resistance, civil rights organizations, elected officials, researchers, and regular citizens have kept the agenda alive—sometimes thriving, sometimes not. With special attention to federal court decisions that have removed desegregation orders, the chapters in this volume document changing patterns of racial isolation and suggest how future patterns may depend on the actions we as a society take going forward.

This book reminds us that Americans are fellow travelers on a long racial journey, each generation going along for part of the ride but none for the whole trip. Every family has its personal story of the trek. In my own family, one great-great-grandfather was the mulatto child of a white slave owner in Tennessee. Free himself, he taught slaves to read while hiding under the house. His grandson was my maternal grandfather, John (he insisted that we call him John, not Grandpa). John married Katherine, my maternal grandmother, whom we called Nana. Nana's father had disappeared while on a work trip in the rural South when she was about fourteen. Officials reported to Nana's mother that they found his tools and car, but never his body. I believe he was lynched and they just did not have the heart to tell her.

In the summer of 1962, I was twelve years old. John and Nana took my brother and me on a round-trip automobile excursion from Cleveland, Ohio, to Denver, Colorado. Nana and John were light skinned; John in fact could pass for white. My brother and I, however, were clearly "colored kids." So, when it was time to rent a motel room, my grandfather would go alone to check for availability. Nana stayed with us in the car, making sure we crouched on the floor of the back seat, out of sight. I wondered why, but did not ask. A few minutes later, John would return with a room key. At one stop the motel had a swimming pool. White families left when we entered the water. I assumed it was just a coincidence. However, I recall that Nana and John later laughed about how quickly the whites had pulled their children from the pool.

One year before that trip, my family and I had moved from an all-black community to an all-white neighborhood of small, owner-occupied, single-family homes. At age eleven, I became the early morning paper boy, delivering the *Cleveland Plain Dealer* at around 6:00 AM, before school. Curiously, half my customers cancelled their subscriptions the first time I tried to collect the weekly fee. No one explained why. A few months later, my new best friend Tony was not allowed to play with me anymore. The last time I tried to visit him, I could see him through the screen door, sitting on the living room floor watching television. His mother answered the door and said, "Tony isn't here." I did not know what to say, so I left and never went back. We remained in the same class at school and played together at recess, but never again after school. A few months later his family moved out of the neighborhood. Four years later, the neighborhood had "tipped"—it was all African American or, as we said back then, it turned all colored. By then a high school student, I had begun to understand the role of race in my earlier and ongoing experiences.

So much has happened since then. By the late 1960s, man walked on the moon and the rulings in *Brown* from the previous decade were finally being enforced. Only a few years earlier, both had seemed unlikely prospects. Around the same time, elite colleges reached out to increase the representation of blacks on their campuses. I and my fellow black students at Cornell University showed our appreciation by staging a building takeover in the spring of 1969, *after* being given almost everything we had requested. Today I teach at Harvard University, my hair is turning gray, a black person has been elected president of the United States, and white Americans are a minority group in California. By mid-century, the whole nation will have a nonwhite majority.

Am I dreaming? These are certainly very different times from when I grew up, but new questions are emerging. What type of society are we becoming? With whom will our progeny live and associate? In what ways might race matter? Race and social class remain distinctly salient but are confounded as never before. In many ways, middle-class Asians, Hispanics, and African Americans have more in common with white middle-class colleagues than with the poor. An African American man, I can teach in the Ivy League and feel welcome living in a suburban community where 95 percent of my neighbors are white. My children can go through the public schools with mostly white classmates and then attend colleges where the racial compositions are much the same. Their prom dates can be randomly drawn from among all racial groups and, at least for the young, race seems no barrier to friendship. It will not surprise me if one or more of my children marries outside the black race.

At the same time, Professor David Thomas, my black colleague from the Harvard Business School, says that if we fail to live up to our generation's responsibility, inner-city black neighborhoods may someday resemble the most isolated American Indian reservations—places where few outsiders visit and only the very poorest live—and other Americans will speak nostalgically about what percentage of their bloodlines can be traced to such origins.

We are not powerless to avoid such a future. We are time travelers whose footsteps reshape the racialized terrain through which we pass. As individuals, we may feel restricted to the beaten path. However, in mass, we can clear the way for new trails that will become wide roads as future generations travel along them with little knowledge or concern for the labors that produced them. For today's children, the struggles of more than half a century ago that led to *Brown v. Board of Education* seem like ancient history. Which of today's struggles will seem like ancient history fifty or sixty years from now? What place should racial justice and equality play in our contemporary struggles? Toward what outcomes should we strive?

Gross inequities in education remain. Although few American children of *any* race routinely achieve excellence, the human potential of some young people goes unrealized to a greater degree than for others—youth from disadvantaged homes, in the weakest schools, with the least affluent peers. And race is still a predictor. Average test scores, even among black and Hispanic children whose parents are college educated, remain substantially below those of white and Asian peers whose parents have similar schooling.[1]

So much work remains. Fortunately, the chapters of this volume help us understand both the past and the present and provide some key ideas for shaping the future. They describe the importance of court cases from the 1950s, 1960s, and 1970s that pressed school districts to desegregate, as well as later rulings that relaxed or removed the pressures that the earlier courts had imposed. Beyond legal rulings, these chapters provide social, demographic, and political explanations for why students in some districts are becoming more racially isolated. For example, parents make decisions based on their beliefs (some right, some wrong) about the consequences of placing their children in schools and classrooms with particular racial mixes. Some such decisions may be privately rational in the short term but socially counterproductive, especially from a long-term perspective.

This unique collection of case studies provides both quantitative and qualitative evidence from "inside the black box" of school assignment processes. It deepens our insights about the causes of racial isolation and the associated difficulty of achieving excellence in schools across society. It reviews and illuminates options for public policy and private behavior but offers no easy answers. It helps us respect the past, understand the present, and imagine possible futures. It presses us to clarify and fulfill our generation's responsibility for this part of the journey away from racial isolation and toward racial justice, social equality, and academic excellence. It is a welcome and timely contribution.

Unitary Status, Neighborhood Schools, and Resegregation

Claire E. Smrekar and Ellen B. Goldring

In the early 1950s, the U.S. Supreme Court heard a series of significant school segregation cases, the most notable among them, *Brown v. Board of Education of Topeka*. The unanimous *Brown* opinion in 1954 set the stage for racial desegregation in American public schools, striking down the use of race as a constitutionally impermissible (de jure, or based on law) mechanism to segregate black and white children.[1] It took more than twenty years for the promise of *Brown* to be realized—partly because of organized resistance among elected officials and education leaders in the South that was exacerbated by the famously ambiguous directive in *Brown II* (1955), in which the Court instructed states and school districts to "move with all deliberate speed" to dismantle their dual (or separate) educational systems.[2] In 1968, the Court's opinion in *Green v. County School Board of New Kent County* placed the imprimatur of desegregation monitoring with the federal courts and outlined a set of specific standards that districts had to meet in their efforts to eliminate segregated school systems. Districts that removed the vestiges of segregation (known as the *Green* factors) throughout the specified aspects of school operations, including staff and faculty assignments, transportation, facilities, and extracurricular activities, would be considered to have converted from a dual system to a "unitary" one.[3] In a subsequent landmark legal opinion, *Swann v. Charlotte-Mecklenburg Board of Education* (1971), the U.S. Supreme Court ruled that districts could implement crosstown busing and student reassignment strategies to ameliorate the combined effects of segregated housing patterns and neighborhood school attendance zones (known as de facto segregation).[4]

The pressing issues of timing and termination—or when court supervision and monitoring of desegregation orders would cease—was clarified twenty-three years after *Green* in a momentous pair of Supreme Court rulings, *Board of Education of Oklahoma City Public Schools v. Dowell* (1991) and *Freeman v. Pitts* (1992).[5] Together these rulings have established a road map for school districts to seek unitary status, based on the following three elements: compliance with court orders, elimination of the vestiges of segregation "to the extent practicable," and incremental relief as *Green* factors are met.

THE ERA AND THE AFTERMATH OF UNITARY STATUS

Over time, more and more school districts have returned to federal district court seeking a grant of unitary status. The pace of unitary status awards has quickened considerably since 2000, when the U.S. Department of Justice docket of elementary and secondary school desegregation cases numbered 430.[6] Today that number is 266. More than half of the districts that have been released from court supervision and declared unitary over the last twenty-five years have done so since 2000.[7] What factors explain this accelerated pace and pressing priority? What is the impact of court-ended desegregation policies on academic, demographic, and social outcomes? How does unitary status affect racial balance in school districts formerly operating under court-ordered desegregation plans? Do districts tip toward racial concentration and resegregate immediately following a grant of unitary status?

Surprisingly, only limited data are available that relate to the impact unitary status has had on the racial and socioeconomic composition of schools, or on the concomitant issues of academic achievement, graduation rates, and students' attitudes toward diversity and racially balanced schools. Critics of unitary status predict resegregation that results in increased inequality, reduced opportunity, and a flight from diversity. Others argue that academic achievement, reduced costs (e.g., those associated with crosstown busing), expanded parental choice, and closer neighborhood-school-community connections are among the benefits associated with unitary status. A report published in 2007 by the U.S. Commission on Civil Rights, an independent, bipartisan agency established by Congress in 1957, examined for the first time the impact of unitary status on racial balance across seven states in the South—a region with a historically large number of districts under court order and, subsequently, unitary status. The report offered mixed results, suggesting that "unitary districts have greater levels of racial concentrations than districts that remain under court order."[8] The commission concluded, however, that when the racial balance data were adjusted for the size of the districts' student populations, the percentage of white student enrollment, and the state in which the districts were located, the differences between unitary status districts and districts that remained under court order were not statistically significant. The report also underscored the effects of other demographic factors on increasingly diverse student populations, including the rapidly growing populations of Hispanic students in schools across the South.

These findings contrast with case study research on the impact of unitary status on racial integration in selected urban school districts in the South and other regions of the United States operating under grants of unitary status, and with the national data that indicate growing resegregation in urban school districts. National trends suggest that the degree of cross-racial exposure (or racial integration) in public schools has declined since the 1990s as a pronounced pattern of resegregation has emerged with increased momentum across the nation, but most rapidly in the South.[9] Frankenberg, Lee, and Orfield assert that U.S. schools are resegregating due to two concurrent trends: changes in the racial composition of neighborhoods, and the end of court-ordered desegregation.[10] Resegregation trends are evident in the most recent public school data (2005–06) reported by the U.S. Department of Education. These data indicate that black and Latino students are slightly more isolated—or segregated—from white students than they were in 1993–94.[11] Approximately three out of ten minority students attended schools in 2006 in which fewer than 5 percent of the students were white.[12] White students, in contrast, are slightly less segregated or less isolated from black and Latino students than they were in 1993–94, due to the growing proportion of students of color in public education generally. To what degree are these shifts in racial concentration related to the unitary status movement? Do larger demographic shifts between urban and suburban districts, as well as the influx of other ethnic and racial groups, provide persuasive evidence for other explanations?

The complex issues surrounding the end of court-ordered desegregation may reflect a general downplaying of race and ethnicity as criteria for the allocation of public resources, as well as a weakening of the political forces that support crosstown busing to achieve racial integration and a reevaluation of the neighborhood as a potential source of school improvement and school quality. Against the backdrop of federally mandated sanctions in No Child Left Behind, some argue that desegregation policies have not significantly improved achievement levels for minority students, leading many to advocate for goals of improved school quality and increased achievement in place of racial integration. Indeed, a number of black leaders have also called for an end to traditional desegregation policy for much the same reason—that minorities have borne an undue share of the integration burden and that school quality, not racial composition, should be the central policy criterion.

The Move to Neighborhood Schools

The removal of mandatory desegregation strictures and approval of unitary status are often associated with a return to neighborhood schools, or "encouraging racial diversity within a neighborhood school philosophy."[13] As noted by Goldring, Cohen-Vogel, and Smrekar, the end of decades-old, court-ordered desegregation plans typically involves a retreat from closely controlled diversity targets and the reduction of crosstown busing intended to integrate public schools in residentially segregated urban systems.[14] Unitary status allows a district to implement new student assignment plans that largely reassign students to neighborhood schools or schools that are closer to home; as a consequence, the length of time spent on a bus ride to school decreases for most students.

The return to neighborhood schools has generally been met with public enthusiasm; parents, black and white, have expressed the desire for their children to be schooled closer to home, even if it means they attend more-segregated schools. These opinions date back to public polls conducted on the subject almost ten years ago. For example, in a 1999 poll, 82 percent of respondents opposed busing, although there were significant racial differences. Eighty-seven percent of white parents said that students should go to their local schools even if it means that most of the students would be the same race, compared to 48 percent of African Americans.[15] Results from a public opinion poll conducted in a southern city that had been declared unitary indicated similarly, "Those who view busing as deleterious policy strongly support sending children to neighborhood schools, even if a higher quality school existed elsewhere."[16]

The return to neighborhood schools is embedded in widespread assumptions about the power of the neighborhood as a potential source of school improvement and school quality. First, neighborhood schools are expected to boost community attachment to schools, encourage resource sharing, and increase parental involvement and social capital.[17] In theory, schools closer to home should provide more time and opportunities for extracurricular and afterschool activities. The neighborhood schools might also become more knowledgeable about their students and parents, thus enhancing their ability to target social services through community outreach. These community and school conditions are viewed as a much-needed reversal of troubling trends linked to the loss of community in the era of school desegregation. As Morris writes,

> African American schools once served as the centers of close-knit communities, and in many instances, desegregation policies adversely affected African American students' and families' connections with their formerly all black schools. . . . Low-income, predominantly black communities especially need stable institutions and for many urban communities, schools can serve this function.[18]

However, Goldring and colleagues found that "geographic proximity does not necessarily translate into structurally supportive community contexts for children, and black children are much more likely to be reassigned to schools in high-risk neighborhoods as crosstown busing is eliminated."[19] Poor neighborhoods with high concentrations of poverty and limited community capacity certainly existed under earlier court-ordered crosstown busing arrangements, but busing moved and merged groups of students so that racially and socioeconomically diverse student groups were situated in these community contexts. Now, with new student assignment plans and the reduction of crosstown busing, that is no longer the case. Poor minority students are more likely to go to schools located in poor, impoverished communities, as these are the communities closer to their homes.

In some states, legislatures have enacted laws that require districts to devise student assignment plans that are consistent with the principle and policy of neighborhood schooling, further weakening the prospects for assignment strategies linked to diversity goals. For example, in 2000, Delaware enacted the Neighborhood Schools Act, which stated that districts

> shall develop a Neighborhood School Plan for their districts that assigns every student within the district to the grade-appropriate school closest to the student's residence without regard to any consideration other than geographic distance and the natural boundaries of the neighborhoods. . . . No student shall be assigned to any school on the basis of race and school assignments shall be made without regard to the racial composition of the schools.[20]

The law, which pertained to four Delaware districts, dismantled a court-ordered desegregation plan that had been in place since 1978. Reacting to similar sentiments, South Carolina enacted the Neighborhood and Community Schools Act of 2003. The General Assembly asserted that "rather than walking or biking to a neighborhood school, many students spend more time on a bus than they do with their families. One of the keys to improving education is a sense of community where teachers, students and parents feel as sense of ownership in their school."[21]

Certainly, these new policies affecting neighborhood schools reflect imperatives that privilege close proximity between home and school, often at the cost of socioeconomic and ethnic diversity. These trends raise important questions about the role and relative significance of "the total ecology of schooling" in a postdesegregation (or postbusing) era that reproduces the corrosive conditions of neighborhood poverty in newly rezoned, socioeconomically isolated, high-poverty neighborhood schools.[22]

New Legal Ruling, New Policy Challenges

Unitary status, neighborhood schools, and desegregation policies converged on June 28, 2007, in one of the most consequential U.S. Supreme Court rulings on race and education since *Brown* in 1954. In *Parents Involved in Community Schools v. Seattle School District No. 1* (*PICS*) and *Crystal D. Meredith v. Jefferson County Board of Education*, the Court limited the use of race in student assignment and school choice plans.[23] The decision has a direct impact on districts operating under unitary status but does not affect those functioning under existing court-ordered desegregation plans. The case has critical significance for districts that are planning to pursue unitary status, since these districts would be subject to *PICS* restrictions on the use of race in voluntary plans designed to create racial diversity under post-unitary status. Justice Kennedy's concurring and controlling opinion underscored the fact that a district may consider it a compelling interest to achieve a diverse student population, and he offered the following "race-conscious" mechanisms designed to achieve the aims of racial diversity: (1) devising student attendance zones to encompass racially defined/segregated neighborhoods; (2) building new schools in racially mixed neighborhoods or in areas that straddle racially identifiable neighborhoods; and (3) developing special or unique programs. The problems (or challenges) associated with these approaches are well known and well understood.

The first remedy is often associated with crosstown busing plans that assign students from racially segregated city neighborhoods to schools many miles away. This plan is antithetical to most parents' priority of close proximity between school and home and is one of the central reasons that districts seek relief from costly, court-ordered crosstown busing arrangements. Moreover, the burden of busing is almost always borne disproportionately by African American families. The second proposal bumps up against the reality of scarce resources for building new schools on real estate other than those parcels priced at the lowest end or in the least desirable sections of town. Third, special programs as conceived by Justice Kennedy already exist in magnet schools (and charter schools), but the patterns of resegregation are clear and compelling in districts like Charlotte-Mecklenburg that were once desegregation success stories but are now obligated to use race-neutral admissions in these choice schools.

The NAACP Legal Defense and Educational Fund and other groups assert that Kennedy's controlling opinion keeps racial diversity aims viable for districts nationwide, and they have published guides for districts to follow that meet the *PICS* criteria.[24] Other scholars argue that the recent Supreme Court ruling represents a steep—if not insurmountable—challenge for public school districts committed to maintaining racial integration among students in kindergarten through high school.[25] Whatever the short- and long-term outcomes of the *PICS* opinion and subsequent district diversity policies, this volume is designed to inform the debate regarding the context of (de)segregation and the consequences of new student assignment strategies.

THE FOCUS AND ORGANIZATION OF THE BOOK

This book offers a unique contribution to the research and policy debates on school desegregation by providing in-depth analyses of the legal and educational issues surrounding a sweeping change in the educational landscape: the end of court-ordered busing and a return to neighborhood schooling. The book is designed around four key objectives:

- Identify a set of important trends in the sociodemographic composition of schools following the end of court-ordered desegregation. How have districts responded to the end of court-ordered desegregation plans in terms of student and staff assignments? What priorities drive the new district policies on racial and socioeconomic desegregation and student assignment? How will the *PICS* opinion shape district policies in the future?
- Explore the implications of new policies on race and school choice across multiple levels and contexts, including classrooms and schools, and at the school district and national levels. What do patterns of achievement

among white, African American, and Latino students suggest in terms of the impact of these new policies?

- Scrutinize the conditions in school districts that served as landmark legal cases in the march toward desegregation in the United States. What is the impact of new student assignment plans on racial and socioeconomic segregation/integration patterns in these historically significant districts?
- Examine the aftermath of desegregation, including both social and academic outcomes, against the growing evidence of resegregation across urban school districts in the United States. Does race matter? What is the role of expanded school choice programs (e.g., magnet schools) under these conditions?

Unlike previous works that analyze a single school district, focus on "white flight," or reconsider the black-white achievement gap, this book integrates multiple case studies and empirical analyses with legal and political insights on race and education. After a court order is lifted and a district is declared unitary, priorities often focus on expanding choice options and creating neighborhood schools to improve student performance. These case studies probe the specific elements of districts' post-unitary status plans linked to these goals, with specific reference to the racial composition and student performance indicators that measure the outcomes of these policies. The analyses are derived from data released by state education officials, school districts, or, in some cases, collected as part of scholars' independent research projects. The district-level focus of each case is designed to punctuate the point of impact relevant to changes in student assignment policies. A state-level case (North Carolina) amplifies the collective consequence of district-level decisionmaking in a state with one of the most historically significant desegregation/unitary-status cases—*Swann v. Mecklenburg*. A national-level analysis paints a broad but detailed portrait of the trends in the racial composition of schools at three levels: states, counties, and districts. Collectively, the analyses are broadly representative of the ethnic diversity (African American, Anglo, Asian American, and Latino) found in public schools across various regions of the United States. Our intent is to highlight the multiple contexts impacted by desegregation issues and trends.

The book is divided into three sections. Section One (chapters 1 through 3), The Postbusing Era: Does Race Matter? provides the foundation for linking the key objectives of the edited volume with the studies that follow in the remainder of the book. In chapter 1, Jomills Henry Braddock II provides a detailed review of the social and academic effects of desegregation over the past several decades. Most of this research focuses on student outcomes, such as enhanced learning, higher educational and occupational aspirations, and greater social interactions among members of different racial and ethnic backgrounds. Research in developmental psychology has documented the social and developmental benefits of intergroup contact and school diversity, and these findings suggest that school diversity leads to positive social interactions that reduce stereotypes among racial groups. The chapter concludes with insights that may move policymakers' attention beyond achievement and attainment outcomes of integrated schooling and on to additional, sustaining purposes of educational diversity: civility, social equity, and the sustainability of a democracy. The author raises new questions regarding the role of diversity in society in light of the decline of court-ordered desegregation arrangements and new restrictions placed on the use of race in the pursuit of districts' diversity goals. If social science research points to the benefits of desegregated schools and the most recent data indicate trends toward resegregration, what are the implications for school districts that are declared unitary?

In chapter 2, Brian P. An and Adam Gamoran unpack school segregation trends to examine the mechanisms responsible for changes observed in the racial composition of schools between and within districts. The authors also provide new insights to explain segregation patterns across public and private schools—a new and important contribution to the research on school desegregation patterns. Given that the number of districts operating under unitary status is very small in comparison to the number of districts that are not (this is true even in the South, where most unitary districts are located), and, consequently, that broad national trends may mask the conditions and trends in unitary districts, the focus in this chapter is on changes in the school racial composition of sixty-five districts declared unitary, including both southern and nonsouthern districts. The findings suggest that the decline nationally in residential segregation has not been coupled with a similar decline in school segregation, despite the strong relationship between the two conditions. The reason for this rests with the changing demographic portrait of American public schools, in which an increasing proportion of black students attend majority nonwhite schools, due to the increasing number of Latino and Asian students in American public education. Furthermore, the analyses indicate that school segregation increased for districts after unitary status was declared, particularly in nonsouthern districts. The chapter underscores the need to move carefully across the national terrain of state-, district-, and school-level data to understand the discrete influences of unitary status, geographical and demographic shifts, and new policy levers on student racial composition in schools.

In chapter 3, Kevin G. Welner and Eleanor R. Spindler pursue the question of possible policy levers by exploring the social and legal implications of the recent Supreme Court opinion in the Seattle and Louisville cases (the *PICS* decision). This chapter identifies the limitations of policy options designed to mitigate racial segregation in public schools for districts operating under a grant of unitary status. The authors underscore the trends that are identified across the subsequent studies, scrutinizes the social context and legal landscapes that have shaped new policy imperatives, and considers the implications of new policies on race and schooling for public education in the United States.

Section Two, Unitary Status: Policy Levers and Legal Landscapes (chapters 4 through 7) presents case studies that explore the policy and legal contexts of new student-assignment and school-improvement plans following the dismantling of districtwide desegregation plans in demographically and legally distinctive school districts declared unitary. How do these new plans vary by context and dimension? What are the implications of these differences for students, families, and educators? This section focuses on the challenges of achieving social and educational equity in unitary status districts, each bounded by a distinctive legal and social framework. In sum, the section articulates the ways that local context matters.

In chapter 4, William S. Koski and Jeannie Oakes explore the role of the courts in pursuing educational equity goals in the context of desegregation litigation. Specifically, the authors examine the institutional limitations and opportunities created by the U.S. District Court in the San Jose, California, desegregation litigation. This case was initially aimed at creating ethnic balance among schools in this primarily white and Latino school district and later focused on fostering high-quality educational programs for all students. The chapter asks a pivotal question: What was the role of the court, if any, in creating equity-oriented educational policies, and what were the consequences of those policies, including detracking and a "college-for-all" policy in the schools? The authors suggest that although judicial intervention alone cannot bring about educational change, it may facilitate change by placing a legal imprimatur behind those who seek to implement broad-based school reform, thus providing leverage for leaders to advocate for additional resources and creating normative pressure (including the will and capacity) necessary for relevant constituencies to work toward school reform. More important, the San Jose case shows that courts can alter the structural conditions of political conflict and bargaining to facilitate the participation of traditionally disadvantaged communities that would not otherwise occur.

In chapter 5, Jack Dougherty, Jesse Wanzer, and Christina Ramsay explore the unique context and consequences of legal and political processes involved in desegregation aims that are anchored to a state's constitutional requirement for equal educational opportunity. This detailed account of state-level desegregation litigation in the state of Connecticut, *Sheff v. O'Neill* (1996) and *Sheff II* (2008), highlights the challenges associated with building political will, consensus, and capacity around educational policy goals associated with diversity and equity. Voluntary arrangements anchored to new magnet schools in the Project Choice plan have proved ineffective in reshaping school enrollments around goals of diversity. Issues of city-suburban demographic cleavages persist and continue to undercut efforts to reduce the socioeconomic and racial isolation in Hartford and the surrounding area's public schools. The case of Hartford and state-level involvement underscores how clarity in governance and accountability matter in adjudicating and implementing desegregation policies. The analyses further highlight the limitations of magnet school policies that use residence-based lotteries—presumed to pass constitutional muster under the recent *PICS* opinion—to remedy residential segregation patterns across urban and suburban areas. Finally, the chapter provides new insights regarding disincentives for suburban districts' (voluntary) desegregation efforts that are linked to No Child Left Behind's academic achievement mandates and sanctions.

In chapter 6, Roslyn Arlin Mickelson, Stephen Samuel Smith, and Stephanie Southworth present the legally and historically significant case of the Charlotte-Mecklenburg Schools (CMS) in North Carolina. CMS is perhaps unparalleled in terms of establishing new ground rules for desegregation orders across the nation following the *Swann* litigation in 1971. In this case, the U.S. Supreme Court approved crosstown busing in CMS as a legally permissible remedy to school segregation that was rooted in residential patterns across a metropolitan area. The impressive gains in academic performance and racial diversity achieved in CMS under court-ordered crosstown busing are contrasted with the district's rapid resegregation following a grant of unitary status in 2002 and the adoption of a race-neutral student assignment and magnet school plans. An array of contributing factors, including the district's changing demographics and persistent patterns of neighborhood segregation, are examined in this portrait of increasing racial concentration and achievement disparities among African American and white students in CMS.

In chapter 7, Claire Smrekar and Ellen Goldring explore the consequences of a common cornerstone of district policy following a grant of unitary status: a return to neighborhood schools. This chapter focuses on Nashville, Tennessee, and the social equity implications of assignment plans that provide schools closer to home for students who live in neighborhoods of concentrated poverty. The new policies on neighborhood schools reflect imperatives that privilege having close proximity between home and school, often at the cost of socioeconomic and ethnic diversity. The findings from the Nashville case study suggest that despite the additional social, health, and academic services provided at newly rezoned, inner-city neighborhood schools, an array of debilitating and distracting conditions may overwhelm efforts to address the social and academic needs of children and their families who live in racially and socioeconomically isolated neighborhoods. This chapter raises important questions regarding the role and relative significance of "the total ecology of schooling" in a postdesegregation (or postbusing) era that reproduces the corrosive conditions of neighborhood poverty in the newly rezoned high-poverty neighborhood schools. The authors explore the ways neighborhoods matter in the school lives of teachers and their students, and argue for rethinking the post-unitary student assignment plans against the backdrop of public housing initiatives linked to socioeconomic diversity.

Section Three, Consequences of Court-Ended School Desegregation (chapters 8 through 10), addresses the impact of resegregation on student achievement and future life choices. The focus of each case study rests with the consequences of new student assignment and choice plans. What do we know about achievement and attainment outcomes in districts declared unitary? How are these outcomes linked to policy changes following the grant of unitary status and new student assignment plans that privilege neighborhood schools and parental choice? The case studies involve different levels of analysis, from the classroom and school dimensions within a single district to state-level data. This broad analytical spectrum is designed to explore the implications of unitary status comprehensively and strategically, allowing for scrutiny across the array of pivotal policy points associated with desegregation policy.

In chapter 8, Charles T. Clotfelter, Helen F. Ladd, and Jacob L. Vigdor respond to this challenge by constructing a careful analysis of classroom-level segregation across North Carolina. The chapter suggests that recent increases in school segregation can be attributed to some combination of three basic trends: reduced judicial scrutiny, increased minority enrollment, and increased white tolerance. The chapter examines evidence on school segregation derived from a rich administrative dataset covering thousands of individual classrooms in roughly two thousand schools in all 117 North Carolina public school districts. The findings suggest that the forces determining segregation between schools differ from those determining segregation within schools. Specifically, consistent with an administrative effort to reduce the potential for segregation across schools, the authors find that the greater the racial diversity of a district, the lower the district's propensity to build new schools in response to population growth. At the same time, schools in racially diverse districts that have managed to achieve low degrees of segregation across schools are more likely to employ academic tracking, a policy that exacerbates segregation in classrooms within schools. Highlighting the need to examine local political processes and structures as they impact desegregation policies beyond the courts, this chapter provides evidence to suggest that district and school administrators actively manage the degree of interracial contact in public schools in order to accommodate the competing desires of their constituents.

In chapter 9, Catherine L. Horn and Michal Kurlaender return to the historic U.S. Supreme Court case of *Keyes v. School District No. 1, Denver, Colorado*, to examine the patterns of segregation and academic achievement among Latino students following the grant of unitary status in the district in 1995. The significance of the 1973 *Keyes* opinion was twofold: the decision extended to Latino students the same right to remedies extended in desegregation cases involving black students, and it made clear and compelling the fact that school desegregation issues and efforts extended beyond the South. This chapter describes achievement patterns relative to changes in racial/ethnic composition as a result of the end of court-mandated desegregation and uses a unique historic dataset of school-level data from 1994 to 2004. The authors characterize schools by the extent to which racial/ethnic shifts occurred after the 1995 unitary-status decision. The data indicate that the largest shifts in the racial composition of Denver's public schools occurred shortly after the end of court-ordered busing. This chapter provides important descriptive evidence of persistent academic achievement gaps between white and Asian students as compared to black and Latino students. Moreover, the changes in desegregation policies are coupled with new demographic shifts in Denver. Consistent with other urban districts, Denver has experienced a decline in white student enrollment while the Latino enrollment numbers have grown substantially, and suburban growth has shrunk the size of the city school population as a proportion of the district enrollment. As a result, white students are more racially isolated today in Denver than before unitary status.

In chapter 10, Kristie J. R. Phillips, Robert J. Rodosky, Marco A. Muñoz, and Elizabeth S. Larsen address the long-term impact of school desegregation in the district—Jefferson County Public Schools (JCPS) in Kentucky—that was the focus of the *PICS* Supreme Court ruling in 2007 that severely limited the use of race in student assignment plans. The new JCPS student assignment plan, slated for implementation in 2009–10, uses neighborhood (not individual student) income and education levels, coupled with neighborhood racial diversity figures, to assign students to schools. After a brief review of this new plan and the district's desegregation efforts that led to the Court's ruling, the authors examine the effects of attending an integrated school on future life choices—including where to live. The findings suggest that the racial mix of the neighborhood where students grow up and the diversity of their high school are strong predictors of the racial diversity in their neighborhoods five years after graduation. This second influence—high school racial diversity—represents a key lever that can be implemented and influenced through new diversity policies consistent with the *PICS* opinion. This chapter provides a bookend to the entire volume by connecting this legally significant, district-focused data to the long-term effects of desegregation addressed in chapter 1, and the policy approaches available to amplify diversity under the precepts of *PICS*, as outlined in chapter 2.

In the Conclusion, Jerome E. Morris outlines the collective impact and contribution of the findings presented in this volume and offers a compelling and insightful argument regarding policies on diversity and education against the landscape of place and neighborhood.

The significant contribution of this volume rests with the empirical data and the conceptual and historical analyses that offer pointed evidence of resegregation in the aftermath of unitary status at a time when more modestly expansive racial criteria related to magnet school admissions and transfer plans were allowable under pre-*PICS* court rulings and guidelines. These data may provide essential guideposts for districts considering the consequences of unitary status under the more restrictive *PICS* legal constraints regarding the use of race.

School choice, unitary status, and the return to neighborhood schools have headlined the national and education reform agendas for the past decade. These issues resonate with a cultural orientation, a mass media focus, and a public interest that coalesce in the demands for improved public education and the recognition of the historical precedents established by *Brown* in 1954 and the *PICS* opinion in 2007. This book makes a compelling argument for the need to connect the imperatives of new policies on race and schooling to the practices of educational leaders facing the demands of diversity, equity, choice, and excellence for all students. Student assignment policies represent some of the most complex and controversial decisions made by local school boards across the country. This book is designed to highlight the short- and long-term implications of these decisions for schoolchildren, their families, and their communities. As the return to neighborhood schools accelerates, schools resegregate, and magnet programs assume new roles, this book will provide timely information on critical social and academic outcomes for children. In sum, the significance of this book is rooted in the need for a better understanding of new policies on race and schools, the social and political context of choice, and the consequences of these reform strategies for school systems in urban America and for the lives of educators, students, and their families.

The Post-Busing Era

Does Race Matter?

CHAPTER ONE

Looking Back

The Effects of Court-Ordered Desegregation

Jomills Henry Braddock II

The recent fiftieth anniversary of *Brown v. Board of Education of Topeka,* sparked widespread celebration. It also provoked critical assessments, as social scientists and legal scholars debated the significance of this historic U.S. Supreme Court decision.[1] Academic assessments of school desegregation have examined the role and adequacy of social science evidence in shaping education policy, and in informing the judicial process on matters of educational equity.[2] These analyses reveal mixed assessments of the effectiveness of *Brown* in achieving educational equity, and of the role social science evidence has played in furthering that cause. Nevertheless, it is undeniable that the *Brown* decision had a tremendous impact on the education of African American and other minority student populations. In the pre-*Brown* era, unequal educational access and outcomes were not only commonplace, they had the sanction of law. As recently as 1940 in the South, for example, per-pupil expenditures for African American students averaged only 45 percent of that for white students.[3]

From the outset, the structure of educational opportunities for African Americans was understood to be related to school segregation. African Americans framed educational inequality in structural terms—as a matter of differential access to equitable learning opportunities. An example of this structural emphasis was reflected when, during oral arguments before the Supreme Court in *Brown v. Board of Education*, NAACP lead counsel Thurgood Marshall contended, "Equal means getting the same thing, at the same time and in the same place."[4] Thus, *Brown* established a legal framework and educational reform movement whose mission was the creation of equal educational opportunity for diverse student populations.

While the relative import of the evidence has been debated, it is undeniable that social research played a significant supportive role in *Brown v. Board of Education*. For example, much has been written about the importance of the well-known brief or social science statement, sometimes referred to as "footnote 11," that was submitted to the Supreme Court in 1952.[5] Following *Brown*, social scientists continued to provide expertise in developing and assessing the effects of district desegregation plans and educational programs. However, the role of social science research in advancing the plaintiff's original goals in the post-*Brown* era appears mixed, at best. Numerous studies of school desegregation's impact on student outcomes, such as achievement tests, intergroup attitudes, and the like, have produced mixed results. For example, the vast body of research examining short-term outcomes has typically focused on students' cognitive and social developmental outcomes in a decontextualized fashion. Specifically, this body of research has generally (1) measured achievement outcomes without examining how student learning opportunities are differentially structured by school practices, such as tracking and ability grouping, or (2) measured the outcomes of intergroup relations without considering the social contexts—that is, supportive versus hostile environments—in which they are embedded.

As a result, the net impact of most of the social science research in the post-*Brown* era has been to undermine public support, education policy, and judicial commitment to school desegregation. In contrast, the handful of studies focusing on the long-term effects of school desegregation, including improved life chances and social integration, have shown a consistent pattern of positive outcomes. This research, however, only began to appear in the literature in the late 1970s and early 1980s, and as a result it has played a less significant role in shaping dominant public perceptions and public policy. Nevertheless, even one of school desegregation's strongest opponents, David Armor, concedes that evidence on the long-term effects of school desegregation represents the "only justification for encouraging legislatures and school boards to overcome the very obstinate if not intractable condition of residential segregation."[6]

Building on previous reviews,[7] this chapter argues that because most research has focused mainly on equality in educational outcomes, the fundamental goals of *Brown*—the equalization of educational opportunities—have gone largely ignored. This chapter presents a critical review of the literature on both the short- and long-term effects of desegregation and examines important consequences of the apparent disconnection between the problem of segregation (unequal opportunities), the aims of *Brown* (equal educational opportunities), and the major emphasis of post-*Brown* research on school desegregation (attitudes and achievement).

DESEGREGATION RESEARCH IN THE POST-*BROWN* ERA

Post-*Brown* research on the effects of school desegregation on student outcomes can be distinguished by their focus on either short- or long-term effects.[8] Although both theory and empirical research suggest that any meaningful assessment of the impact of schooling on student outcomes should also consider the effects later in life,[9] including career attainment and adult social roles, research on adult outcomes has been limited. Studies examining the short-term effects of desegregation (i.e., achievement, attitudes, and aspirations) examine what happens to students while they are still in school as a result of intergroup contact.[10] Such studies comprise by far the most voluminous body of research on the impact of school desegregation.[11] In contrast, studies examining desegregation's long-term effects have focused on what happens to students as they move into adulthood (i.e., improved life chances and lifestyles) as a result of their intergroup experiences in elementary and secondary school.[12]

Recent attention to these long-term effects has expanded our understanding of school desegregation. Specifically, these studies have called attention to the importance of examining not only how school desegregation may improve people by increasing human capital (e.g., student test scores) or reducing social distance (e.g., prejudice and stereotypes), but also how it may open opportunities for career success by reducing structural or institutional barriers (e.g., access to important social networks, contacts, and sponsorship, or negative stereotypes associated with "black" institutions that may lead to statistical discrimination and the like) that often exclude minorities from fair competition.[13]

Short-Term Effects of School Desegregation

Academic achievement

Early studies of school desegregation typically focused on whether African American and white students' achievement test scores rose or fell following desegregation. Extensive evidence suggests that the academic performances of whites and African Americans are not harmed in desegregated schools, and that African Americans typically show achievement gains—especially in reading—as a result of school desegregation.[14] Despite debates regarding the relative size of the achievement gains, the research results are almost universally in a positive direction, whether they were drawn from case studies of schools and school districts or from comparative studies across large numbers of schools or school systems.[15]

Crain and Mahard conclude that although the evidence is mixed, desegregation is generally associated with modest gains in African Americans' academic achievement, especially among students who attended desegregated schools in the early grades.[16] Crain and Mahard's review, despite finding few empirical studies, concluded that desegregation also enhances Hispanics' academic achievement.[17] Like Schofield,[18] Crain and Mahard found virtually no evidence that the achievement of whites was affected in any way by desegregation. In 1982, the U.S. Department of Education commissioned seven politically diverse researchers representing different disciplines to examine a subset of rigorously designed studies. This expert panel concluded that desegregation had a small positive effect on African American students' reading achievement but no consistent effects on math achievement.[19]

Regrettably, the dwindling of government and foundation funding since the early 1980s has severely limited research on the academic consequences of school desegregation. Nevertheless, a handful of more recent studies reported findings that are generally consistent with the earlier research. For example, Pride and Woodward and Carsrud found that African American achievement was enhanced by desegregation.[20] Arias found that the achievement of both African American and Hispanic students in San Jose, California, was enhanced by desegregation, but only if desegregation raised the overall socioeconomic status of the student body.[21] However, two studies that examined the busing of African American students from Hartford, Connecticut, to suburban desegregated schools found that the desegregation had little impact on achievement test scores.[22]

A comprehensive review of research on racial and socioeconomic integration in schools and neighborhoods by Mayer and Jencks concluded that (1) the first year of attendance at a desegregated school usually has a small positive effect on the reading skills, but not on the math achievement, of African American elementary students; (2) twelve years in a predominantly white northern school probably has a substantial effect on African American students' academic achievement; (3) the effects on African American students of attending desegregated schools in the South and the effects of desegregation on white students in the North and South are uncertain.[23]

Recent studies at the district, state, and national levels provide further evidence that student achievement outcomes are enhanced in racially diverse schools. For example, Mickelson's analysis of school segregation and student achievement in the Charlotte-Mecklenburg school district in North Carolina found that the proportion of students' elementary education spent in racially identifiable African American schools had direct negative effects on end-of-course test scores and high school track placement, holding constant students' sixth-grade test scores and other variables associated with achievement.[24] Moreover, she reported that segregation in elementary school also had indirect effects on academic success as measured by sixth-grade standardized test scores and high school track placement, and on later academic outcomes like Scholastic Aptitude Test (SAT) scores and high school grade point average. While this pattern was observed for both African American and white students, African American students are more likely than whites to experience disproportionate harm from this form of racial isolation because they are more likely to attend racially identifiable African American elementary schools.

Other district-level evidence is offered by Ludwig, Ladd, and Duncan's analysis of Baltimore data from the U.S. Department of Housing and Urban Development's Moving to Opportunity housing mobility experiment.[25] These researchers found that despite some evidence of increased problem behavior among teens in the treatment groups, African American elementary school children from low-income families who moved from high- to low-poverty neighborhoods increased their achievement test scores. Similarly, studies of the Gautreaux program in Chicago, which relocated African American public housing residents into different parts of the metropolitan area, found that those who moved to suburban areas had lower dropout rates and higher rates of college attendance than those who moved to other parts of the city.[26]

At the state level, Bankston and Caldas's analysis of Louisiana data concluded that, holding constant the family, individual, and school-level influences on achievement, both African American and white students scored lower in schools with high concentrations of minority students, and that African American students' achievement was positively associated with the proportion of their schoolmates who were white.[27] Additionally, Grissmer, Flanagan, and Williamson's examination of changes in state test scores on the National Assessment of Educational Progress (NAEP) attributed significant increases in the academic achievement of African American students in some states but not others to school desegregation.[28]

At the national level, Schiff, Firestone, and Young's analysis of NAEP math and reading scores found that both African American and white students who attended desegregated schools where whites were in the majority outperformed students who attended predominantly African American schools.[29] Furthermore, Brown's analysis of data from the National Educational Longitudinal Study concluded that schools with the highest academic achievement overall and with the smallest gap between students of different races and ethnicities were between 61 percent and 90 percent white or Asian American and between 10 percent and 39 percent African American and Hispanic.[30] Further indirect support is suggested by evidence showing that during the 1980s, for example, improved test performance among African Americans accounted for roughly 40 percent of overall gains in SAT scores.[31] And, although improvement in African American student test scores occurred nationwide, as then-president of the Educational Testing Service Gregory Anrig noted, the most significant gains were achieved in the South, where school desegregation probably had its greatest impact.[32]

Because these desegregation studies are often based on different theories, employ quite diverse methods, and define desegregation in different ways, the results are difficult to summarize. Moreover, as Schofield points out, most studies occurred in the first years of program implementation; nearly all studies focused only on African American and white students; and little attention has been given to school- or district-level contextual factors (e.g., whether students were resegregated at the school level or whether the district desegregation plan was voluntary or mandatory).[33] Nevertheless, research on the effects of desegregation on student academic achievement, as measured by standardized tests, seems to support the proposition that African American and Hispanic students learn somewhat more in schools that are majority white than in schools that are predominantly nonwhite.

Unfortunately, research in this area has often been guided, implicitly or explicitly, by cultural deficit theories, which assume that mere exposure to white classmates would create the possibility for lateral transmission of values that might raise African American achievement.[34] As such, studies of achievement have often lacked any theoretical basis linked to the rationale for *Brown*. Thus, this vast body of research has typically not examined access to learning opportunities or other mediating mechanisms (high teacher expectations, positive school climate, etc.) that are related to academic success.[35] Surprisingly, this remains true for many recent studies as well (Mickelson represents a notable exception).[36]

Wells et al. argue that the Equality of Educational Opportunity study had a huge impact on the conceptualization of equal educational opportunity by sharpening the focus on the distinction between educational resources and educational outcomes.[37] Before the 1960s, equal opportunity meant equal access to equivalent schools, but after the Coleman Report the definition meant access to equal outcomes, the result being that better educational opportunity became associated with closing the achievement gap between blacks and whites.[38] Coleman's study also had a huge impact on deemphasizing the role of schools and resources in accounting for the achievement gap. Research then turned to other factors, often assumed to be related to sociocultural deficits and differences, and led to an emphasis on compensatory education rather than a reconfiguration of schools and learning opportunities.[39]

The Coleman Report's findings were inconsistent with African Americans' understanding that desegregation or racial balance—that is, merely being in the same building—does not ensure integration, acceptance as equals, or lead to equal treatment. Rather than focusing on the learning opportunities and educational climates provided African American and Latino students in desegregated schools, which have been shown to be inequitable,[40] most social science studies instead focus almost exclusively on academic outcomes, which are, at best, indirectly linked to desegregation policy. In the end, school desegregation per se was not pursued as an educational program or treatment, but as a vehicle to provide access to equitable learning contexts.

Moreover, researchers have shown that differential access to equitable learning opportunities remains a persistent and pervasive problem, both between and within schools.[41] For example, schools with predominantly low-income and African American or Latino students offer fewer high-track classes and greater numbers of low-track, remedial, and vocational classes than schools serving middle-class or predominantly white student populations.[42] Even within racially mixed schools, African American and Latino students are disproportionately overrepresented in low-level courses and underrepresented in college-prep courses.[43] These patterns of over- and underrepresentation extend beyond levels that might be predicted based on measured achievement.[44]

Numerous studies have documented the extent of tracking in desegregated schools, its effects on students, and alternative classroom organizational/instructional practices for addressing the problem of heterogeneity in the classroom.[45] In seeking to understand the impact of schooling, evaluation experts emphasize the importance of asking the right questions. More specifically, they argue that evaluation outcomes should be clearly rooted in the particular objectives of the programs being assessed.[46] Thus, given the *Brown* plaintiff's focus on equal educational opportunity and the subsequent legal ruling, it might be expected that post-*Brown* desegregation researchers would more appropriately have focused on trends toward parity in African American representation across schools, classrooms, and courses as critical educational equitable outcomes, rather than, or at least in relation to, the cognitive and affective outcomes that came to dominate the desegregation research agenda. Such systematic inattention to differential access to learning opportunities seems especially ironic, given that, even in the 1950s, the social scientists who wrote the famous social science statement that led to the *Brown* decision—"Effects of Segregation"—clearly understood that school desegregation had to be accompanied by changes in school organization and practice.[47]

Intergroup relations

Beyond developing academic skills, schools at both the elementary and secondary levels play an important role in transmitting society's culture and values to its young, as well as giving them the appropriate knowledge and skills for leading productive and fulfilling adult lives. It is in this realm that the effects of school desegregation have been especially impressive, and it is where schools have provided the most important context for American youth to learn how to deal with diversity. It is largely through intergroup interaction in school that young people learn the dispositions and skills that result in positive intergroup perceptions, attitudes, and behaviors.

Several studies of the contact hypothesis focused on schools as the setting for studying intergroup contact.[48] Pettigrew and Tropp's recent comprehensive meta-analytical review of more than two hundred empirical studies provides strong support for the hypothesis,[49] noting that face-to-face contact is importantly related to reduced prejudice, that prejudice reduction resulting from intergroup contact is generalizable across different situations, and that intergroup contact affects a broad range of outcomes. In this vein, Patchen suggests that the racial composition of the classroom is more important than the racial composition of the school as a whole in influencing cross-racial interaction.[50] Thus, to fully understand the benefits and outcomes of racially diverse schools, especially outcomes related to intergroup interaction, it is critically important to understand students' experiences in the classroom and other school environments.[51]

Nevertheless, research on intergroup contact between children of different racial and ethnic backgrounds in desegregated schools has also produced mixed results. Early reviews of the literature indicate that the majority of studies on interracial contact in desegregated schools show few positive effects on intergroup relations.[52] However, more recent studies of the impact of desegregated classrooms show that children exposed to racially diverse peers in the classroom exhibit reduced adherence to racial stereotypes and reduced racial prejudice.[53] Schofield and Sagar provide an important and striking example of voluntary cross-race peer interaction.[54] They observed student interaction in a prestigious middle school in which seventh-grade classes were racially mixed but eighth-grade classes were more homogeneous, due to tracking based on standardized test scores (one eighth-grade class group was comprised of 80 percent white students and another of predominantly African American students). During five months of observing voluntary peer interactions in the school cafeteria, the researchers found that the number of seventh graders who sat next to or across from students of another race tripled, while the number of eighth graders who sat next to or across from students of another race declined. They concluded that the daily classroom exposure to ethnically diverse students was directly related to students' willingness to engage in voluntary interactions with peers of a different race.

Desegregated classroom environments can also promote a range of positive cross-race attitudes and interactions, including tolerance, understanding, and positive intergroup attitudes; increased voluntary cross-race peer interactions; and interracial friendliness.[54] Because friendliness implies a more intimate form of engagement than voluntary cross-race interaction, it is noteworthy that researchers have found that racially desegregated classroom environments can positively impact interracial friendliness. These findings regarding friendliness fall into two groups—those relating to generally friendly interracial contact,[56] and cross-race best friendships.[57] In studying African American and white cross-race best friendships, Hallinan and Smith found that students of one racial group were friendlier toward students of another racial group as the proportion of the smaller racial group increased.[58] They conclude that racially balanced classrooms maximize the interracial friendliness of both African Americans and whites.

Long-Term Effects of School Desegregation

Research on long-term outcomes examines how desegregation contributes to the structure of opportunities in adult life. This research focuses on whether or not school desegregation, independent of social class and academic credentials, (1) enhances life chances for African Americans and Hispanics; and (2) contributes to more pluralistic and diverse adult social relationships and experiences in educational, housing, and workplace settings for all students.

Pluralistic outcomes: Affective

As noted, research suggests that elementary-secondary desegregation affects youth's interracial attitudes while they are still attending those schools. However, research also demonstrates the enduring effects of school desegregation on intergroup relations. For example, Sonleitner and Wood's study of 292 white adults who were children when desegregation plans were implemented in Oklahoma school districts found that interracial contact at an early age had significant negative associations with both anti-black prejudice and adherence to stereotypes.[59] Sigelman, Bledso, Welch, and Combs found that students from racially diverse school environments develop an increased likelihood of supporting continued and widespread desegregation initiatives.[60]

Braddock and Gonzalez's analysis of data from the National Longitudinal Study of Freshmen found that social isolation in elementary-secondary schools plays a more significant role than neighborhood isolation in diminishing social cohesion among young adults.[61] Three indicators of social cohesion were examined: social distance, preferring to have neighbors of the same race, and preferring that children have same-race schoolmates. Their findings show that the net effects of early (K–12) school segregation were found to be significant on at least two of three social cohesion outcomes for each racial/ethnic group (African Americans, Asians, Latinos, and whites).

Using longitudinal survey data collected at ten public universities, Saenz, Ngai, and Hurtado tested whether students' precollege racial environments (i.e., mostly segregated versus mostly integrated) have a lasting or limiting effect on their interactions with diverse peers in college.[62] The study assessed students' positive interactions with diverse peers, which served as a proxy for whether the cyclical effects of segregation could be interrupted. The study found that students' precollege racial environments and experiences had significant and lasting effects on important college diversity outcomes, including cross-racial interactions and attitudes about racial discrimination.

Pluralistic outcomes: Behavioral

Segregation in K–12 Schools and Colleges. Research has shown quite compellingly that racial segregation is self-perpetuating over the life course and across social contexts. Studies based on multiple datasets across several decades have produced strong and consistent evidence that both majority and minority individuals whose childhood experiences in schools and neighborhoods take place in largely segregated environments are likely also to lead their adult lives in largely segregated settings.[63] The earliest empirical documentation of the perpetuation of segregation showed that African Americans who attended desegregated schools were more likely to function in desegregated environments in later life.[64] As adults, they were more frequently found to live in desegregated neighborhoods, to have children who attended desegregated schools, and to have close friends of the other race than did adults of both races who had attended segregated schools. This research broke new ground in studying the long-term effects of school desegregation and in theorizing about important intervening causal mechanisms that may break down barriers to integration and assimilation.

Several subsequent investigations of the long-term effects of school desegregation have produced additional evidence that both minority and majority segregation tend to be perpetuated over stages of the life cycle and across institutional settings.[65] Much of this evidence is based on analyses of longitudinal studies that permit meaningful assessments of educational and early career attainments. Furthermore, the analyses in the later studies typically utilize national longitudinal data, and findings from these data have, to a large extent, ruled out one key alternative explanation that the results hold only for a certain subset of students—for example, students who are especially sensitive to the effects of desegregation or who were desegregated in some particular way.

Segregation in K–12 Schools and Postsecondary Outcomes. Research suggests that early desegregation is related to the type and quality of African American students' postsecondary experience. These studies concluded that African Americans who have been educated in desegregated elementary and secondary schools are more likely to attend predominantly white colleges and experience greater social integration than their counterparts who attended racially isolated K–12 schools.

Braddock analyzed survey data obtained in 1972 from 253 African American students attending two predominantly African American and two predominantly white colleges in a single southern state.[66] The results revealed a strong positive association between high school and college desegregation, after controlling for academic credentials, social class, and college inducements, such as offers of financial aid. This study, however, was geographically restricted and excluded two-year colleges.

More compelling evidence that early school desegregation affects attendance at predominantly white colleges was provided by a national study that included statistical controls for the students' region, social-class background, college admissions credentials (high school grades and test scores), and residential proximity to alternative colleges.[67] Using National Longitudinal Survey data from over three thousand black 1972 high school graduates, this study found both direct and indirect effects of early school desegregation on attendance at predominantly white colleges. This relationship was strongest for African American students who had attended desegregated elementary schools. In addition, it was found that among African American students who were enrolled in desegregated colleges, those who had also attended desegregated elementary and high schools, controlling for differences in social class and ability, were more likely to continue in college and fare better academically than students who had attended segregated schools.

Using data from the African American sample of the High School and Beyond survey, Braddock confirmed earlier findings of the effect of attendance at desegregated high schools on subsequent attendance at predominantly white colleges.[68] Braddock also found that in predominantly white two-year colleges, African Americans who had attended desegregated schools were more likely to major in the higher-paying technical or scientific fields than were graduates of segregated high schools. These results are consistent with earlier studies suggesting that high school racial composition has an impact on African Americans' aspirations to enter career fields where they have traditionally been underrepresented.[69]

Segregation in K–12 Schools and Labor Market Outcomes. Social scientists have noted that the racial employment and income gap is not solely due to differences in the level of education attained by African Americans relative to whites, especially in light of the dramatic closing of the gap relative to years of school completed. African Americans and whites who complete a similar amount of education continue to show substantial differences in earned income and employment rates. A key reason for these persisting disparities lies in the types of occupations in which African Americans are employed and the way employers fill, and workers seek, jobs.

Desegregation can affect the occupational attainment of African Americans and other students of color in two ways. First, school desegregation is positively related to the jobs and occupations to which African Americans aspire and have access. Second, school desegregation positively affects the resources that African Americans have available when seeking a job. Thus, desegregation in education directly affects not only the type of job obtained, but also whether or not any job is obtained. Specifically, desegregation can increase the pool of contacts from whom African Americans can obtain information about available jobs. Such informational networks are highly important not only for providing specific job information and referrals, but also for providing information about job-seeking strategies. Furthermore, desegregated education may provide credentials that are more likely to be accepted at face value by white employers.

Research indicates that school racial composition contributes to (1) African American students' developing and persisting in plans to enter professional and nontraditional occupations where they are underrepresented;[70] (2) employers preferring to hire African Americans from desegregated schools over similarly qualified African Americans from segregated schools;[71] and (3) the likelihood of students from all racial backgrounds being employed in ethnically diverse work environments.[72]

Green analyzed follow-up data collected in 1980 by the American Council on Education from a national sample of African Americans who had been high school freshmen in 1971.[73] He found that high school racial composition was positively associated with the racial composition of adult coworker and informal friendship groups. Braddock and McPartland used data from the National Longitudinal Survey's Youth Cohort (NLS-Y) to study the effects of high school racial composition on employment segregation.[74] They found that for African Americans in the North, high school racial composition was the strongest predictor of coworker racial composition. However, in the South, they found community racial composition to be the major predictor of coworker racial composition. They suggest that the strong association between community and school desegregation in the South make it difficult to disentangle the unique and joint effects of school and community desegregation.

Braddock, McPartland, and Trent used data from the African American and white subsamples of the National Longitudinal Study of 1972 (NLS-72) merged with survey data from their subjects' 1976 and 1979 employers.[75] They found that both African Americans and whites from desegregated schools were more likely to work in racially diverse firms than their counterparts from segregated schools. This finding was replicated by Braddock, Dawkins, and Trent, using data from three national surveys: the 1979–80 National Survey of Black Americans (NSBA), a 1987 follow-up of the NLS-Y, and a national survey of the 1976 and 1979 employers of NLS-72 participants.[76] They found that white, African American, and Hispanic graduates of desegregated schools were more likely than their ethnic peers from segregated high schools to be employed in ethnically diverse firms or coworker groups. In a related study, Crain examined employment decisions in a national survey of more than four thousand employers of NLS-72 respondents and found that employers gave preference in hiring decisions to African American graduates of desegregated high schools.[77]

LESSONS LEARNED

There are important lessons to be learned from post-*Brown* school desegregation research. While social scientists have unquestionably made substantial contributions to equity and social justice in American society through their studies of school desegregation, questions arise regarding to what extent current debates over the role and effectiveness of *Brown* may be related to social researchers asking the wrong questions in the aftermath of the decision.[78] If the *Brown* decision represented, as many people believe, a judicial ruling about African Americans' moral, ethical, and fundamental right to citizenship, one might argue that most of the post-*Brown* research on school desegregation should have been more appropriately framed as "assessments of the implementation" of an important new direction in education rather than "summative evaluations" of the efficacy and appropriateness of desegregation policies. Researchers have not generally evaluated other civil liberties in the same way they have assessed African American children's rights to attend any publicly supported school. Voting rights, for example, were not, nor should they have been, "assessed" in terms of whether racial gaps in registration or voter turnout declined. Historically, Americans' constitutional rights are fine-tuned where necessary in order to make them work well rather than "evaluated" to determine if they should exist. Arguably, in the case of *Brown*, support for and enforcement of the principle of equal educational opportunity has been diminished as a direct result of research-driven arguments that school desegregation has not worked to close the achievement gap.

In this sense, efforts to assess the efficacy of the *Brown* decision largely on the basis of test-score gaps have been functionally equivalent to attempting to assess Title IX on the basis of whether disparities in test performance disappeared between males and females in science and mathematics. Indeed, as a consequence of increased access to opportunities to participate in science and mathematics courses, many male-female performance gaps have significantly narrowed. Most Americans would find that a laudable outcome of Title IX. However, it is highly unlikely that women, or advocates of gender equity, would allow the nation's commitment to this particular dimension of educational equity to be tied to questions about achievement test performance gaps. In *Brown*, as in Title IX, the important research issues should involve questions of access with a focus on the implementation and fidelity of implementation of mandated policies and plans.

This chapter has argued that most short-term studies of school desegregation have been misguided in focusing largely on learning outcomes rather than on learning opportunities. It has also suggested that the long-term studies focused on educational returns in adulthood have generally been more useful, as this research has been grounded more appropriately in the broad aims of *Brown*. Nevertheless, even the long-term outcome research has been limited by its exclusive focus on the consequences for individuals of segregation and desegregation. As a result, the policy relevance of long-term desegregation research has diminished for the Supreme Court, which in several recent rulings has focused increasingly on state, rather than individual, harms and benefits in determining the acceptability of school district efforts to promote educational diversity.

As the United States rapidly becomes both more racially and ethnically diverse and increasingly segregated across racial/ethnic boundaries, there are compelling reasons for educational researchers and policymakers to be concerned about the future of school desegregation.[79] Both singly and in combination, growing diversity and increased segregation have important implications for the nation's stability and well-being. Diversity, and segregation, can undermine the social cohesion needed to bind American citizens to one another and to society at large.[80] As this chapter has noted, a significant body of research documents the critical role of school desegregation in preparing the nation's youth for living in an increasingly diverse society. Thus, a compelling argument could be made that America needs more, not fewer, opportunities for racially and ethnically diverse students to attend school together.

CHAPTER TWO

Trends in School Racial Composition in the Era of Unitary Status

Brian P. An and Adam Gamoran

Beginning in the mid-1950s, the United States experienced a marked decline in the number of minority students attending racially isolated schools. Between 1954 and 1972, the South witnessed a 75 percent decrease in black attendance at schools that were 90–100 percent nonwhite.[1] Since 1990, however, these decreases have halted and in fact have begun to reverse. Between 1991 and 2003, the proportion of minority students attending schools with 50 percent or more nonwhite students increased in every region for all minority groups. Nationally, a greater proportion of minority students now attends racially isolated schools (90 percent or more nonwhite) than before 1990. The largest increases for black students attending majority nonwhite schools have occurred in the South and in states bordering Mexico.[2]

At the same time, an increasing number of districts across the South have been declared unitary and freed from court-ordered desegregation (districts that removed the vestiges of segregation throughout the specified aspects of school operations would be considered "unitary"). Three important Court decisions in particular—*Board of Education of Oklahoma City Public Schools v. Dowell, Freeman v. Pitts*, and *State of Missouri v. Kalima Jenkins*—have contributed to the accelerating rate of school districts across the nation that have been declared unitary.[3] Since 1990, eighty school districts were declared unitary and/or had desegregation court orders dismissed.[4] Many writers identify this rollback in school desegregation as the major force behind the increase in racial isolation and "resegregation."[5]

There is no doubt that African American students today are less likely to attend majority-white schools than they were in the 1980s. However, whether these increases derive from changes in black-white segregation is less clear. Popular measures, such as the proportion of African American students that attend majority nonwhite schools, capture both the racial imbalance observed across schools and changes in the student population of a district. Some writers point out that the changing composition of schools attended by African American students mainly reflects changes in the U.S. population— that is, a larger portion of minority students overall—rather than increases in black-white school segregation.[6]

The increased proportion of African American students in majority non-white schools in no small measure reflects the increased representation of Latino students in the U.S. school population. Among public elementary students, the proportion of African American students increased 6 percent, from 17 percent in 1990 to 18.1 percent in 2000. Meanwhile, the proportion of Latino students increased 47 percent, from 11.5 percent in 1990 to 16.9 percent in 2000.[7]

In this chapter, we address these competing narratives by analyzing national and local trends in school racial composition. We use a measure that is insensitive to changes in the U.S. school population, thereby concentrating solely on racial imbalance. Examining national trends using this measure extends previous studies that focus on regional trends.[8]

This chapter contributes to previous research that examines national trends in that we decompose the contribution of segregation into three geographic components: states, counties, and districts.[9] Court-ordered desegregation decisions have their impact at the district level due to the *Milliken, Governor of Michigan v. Bradley* decision, which essentially limited court-ordered desegregation regulations to within districts.[10] Overall levels of school segregation may mask important trends at different geographic levels. Changes in racial composition may occur between districts as a result of changes in residential patterns, or from an increase in white families sending their children to private schools. Declarations of unitary status and the end of court-ordered desegregation may also alter the allocation patterns within a district, because where there are clear segregation patterns, districts have the option of assigning students based on characteristics such as residence. Consequently, one cannot make assumptions about the mechanisms that have created observed levels of school segregation and must instead examine the issue empirically.

Our analysis includes segregation patterns across public and private schools. Changes in segregation patterns may reflect an insurgence of white students into private schools, where desegregation regulations are less stringent than at public schools accepting federal funding. For example, Fairlie and Resch estimate that a 10 percent increase in the minority population of a county increases the probability that a white student will attend a private school by 0.013–0.015.[11] Reardon and Yun find that in the South, the white attendance pattern for private schools is directly related to the size of the black population at the county level.[12] Whereas the proportion of blacks in a county explained 25 percent of the variance in white private school enrollment in 1970, by 1980, the black population proportion explained 65 percent of the variance. Also, if unitary-status decisions lead to residential school assignment instead of busing, white students may return from private to public schools. By examining both private and public school enrollments, we are able to account for all students in the U.S. education system. As such, we are able to consider whether previous studies that included only public schools may have underestimated the level of school segregation.

While the national trends show whether school segregation patterns have changed across time, they do not necessarily show how changes in desegregation policies affect changes in racial composition because the number of districts that are no longer mandated by court order to desegregate their schools is small in comparison to the total number of districts across the United States. Even in the South, where a majority of unitary districts are found, districts that are declared unitary represent a small fraction of all public school districts. In other words, national trends may obscure the local effects of unitary-status decisions. Consequently, we turn to an analysis of the influence of unitary status on allocation patterns of students within districts. We explore changes in school racial composition for sixty-five districts that are no longer under court order to desegregate their schools, which includes both southern and nonsouthern districts.

Previewing our results, we find that national trends in school segregation did not grow over time. If anything, the evidence shows that school segregation decreased, especially between Latinos and whites. However, the trends in school segregation did not follow the marked declines in residential segregation. Because school racial composition is largely determined by residential composition, one would expect school segregation to follow a pattern similar to residential segregation. Contrasting trends for school and residential segregation suggest that, had it not been for declarations of unitary status, school segregation would have declined instead of remaining unchanged over time.[13]

We further find that the association between school segregation and residential segregation increased over time. This finding is consistent with the expected consequences of unitary districts, in that, as court-ordered desegregation ended, the relationship between school and residential segregation was decoupled to some degree. When school districts were freed from desegregation policies, they were able to allocate students based on other criteria, such as residential patterns.

Surprisingly, the inclusion of private schools in our analysis does little to change the overall levels of school segregation, suggesting that results from previous studies, which included only public school students, depict an accurate representation of the overall trends in school segregation. The results do show that within-county segregation increased by 14 percent to 37 percent after private schools were included, suggesting that school segregation exists across sectors. For the most part, however, the national trends remained consistent over time, irrespective of the inclusion of private schools.

While school segregation did not increase in the nation as a whole between 1990 and 2005, we find evidence that it did increase in districts after unitary status was declared, with the largest association for nonsouthern districts. Unitary-status decisions seem to increase school segregation by approximately 13 percent in southern districts and 39 percent in nonsouthern districts.

DATA AND METHODS

To analyze national trends in school racial composition, we used data from the Common Core of Data (CCD) and the Private School Universe Survey (PSS). Both the CCD and the PSS were provided by the U.S. Department of Education's National Center for Education Statistics. The CCD is an annual survey that provides demographic information for a census of public elementary and secondary schools, whereas the PSS collects school-level information biennially for a census of private schools in the United States.[14] For the national trends, we used data from the 1990–91, 1993–94, 2000–01, and 2005–06 academic years. The 1990–91 and 2000–01 academic years correspond closely to the 1990 and 2000 U.S. Census years. Therefore, we used

1990 and 2000 to examine the school racial composition as it relates to residential racial composition.[15]

The 1993–94 academic year was the first in which the PSS provided school-level information on private school racial composition. Coincidentally, the 1993–94 academic year is also the earliest in which the CCD provided school-level information on racial composition for all states—with the exception of Idaho, where information on racial composition was not collected until 2000–01. The 2005–06 school year is the most recent for which data is provided by CCD and PSS. To ensure comparability across years, we dropped Idaho and its schools from our analyses.

To analyze trends in residential patterns, we used tract-level census data from 1990 and 2000.[16] We restricted our sample to individuals from five to seventeen years of age, which is approximately the age range of individuals attending primary and secondary schools. We further matched the CCD and census data by county, which ensures that the counts of schools and residents used in our analysis are from similar geographic locations.

There is no comprehensive list of unitary districts in the United States. Therefore, we relied on prior studies to identify which districts have been granted unitary status. We used information from three sources in which we identified seventy unitary school districts.[17] Five districts were considered unitary before 1987—the earliest year of our sample—and therefore were dropped from the analysis. Among the remaining sixty-five school districts, four (6.2%) were from northeastern states, twelve (18.5%) from midwestern states, forty-five (69.2%) from southern states, and four (6.2%) from western states. Each school district has approximately eighteen years of data, yielding 1,176 district-by-year time points.

Measure of Racial Segregation

As a measure of racial segregation, we employed Theil's entropy index of segregation (H). Like other measures of segregation (e.g., dissimilarity index), H measures the evenness with which racial groups are distributed among geographic locations (e.g., schools, tracts). An advantage of H over other common measures of segregation (e.g., dissimilarity index) is that H allows for the decomposition of segregation into between- and within-group components. We decomposed overall levels of segregation into attributions to states, counties, districts, tracts, and school sectors. H does not rely on the racial composition of the population, but on how evenly the groups are distributed across schools or tracts (for the formula of H, see appendix 2A).

H ranges between 0 and 1, where 0 reflects racially balanced schools and 1 reflects complete separation by race. Reardon and Yun suggest that a 0.05 change in H reflects a significant change in segregation levels, as this amount of change corresponds to roughly a 10-point change in the dissimilarity index.[18] Reardon and Yun provide a useful guide to interpreting the values of H as it corresponds with the values of the dissimilarity index (D).[19]

RESULTS

In the past decade, the United States witnessed an increase in the proportion of minority students that attend majority nonwhite schools.[20] This increase may reflect changes in school segregation, or it may reflect changes in the U.S. population.[21] To address this question, we turn to national patterns in school segregation.

Changes in the Student Composition at Majority Nonwhite Schools

A concern of measuring racial isolation as the proportion of black students attending nonwhite schools is that this measure is sensitive to changes in the student population. An increase in the population of other minority groups, such as Latinos, would increase the representation of all students—including whites—that attend nonwhite schools.[22]

Between 1993 and 2005, the number of white students attending U.S. schools decreased slightly, from 31.5 million in 1993 to 30.5 million in 2005. However, their share of the U.S. student population decreased by 8.5 percentage points, from 67.3 percent in 1993 to 58.8 percent in 2005. The main reason for this is the upsurge of Latinos attending U.S. schools. In 1993, Latinos represented 12.1 percent of the nation's student population; by 2005, their representation increased to 18.9 percent.

As a result, students are attending schools with a greater exposure to other racial and ethnic groups. This is most notable in racially homogeneous schools (90–100 percent of one race). In 1993, approximately 52 percent of the nation's white students attended 90–100 percent white schools. By 2005, the percentage of white students attending racially homogeneous schools decreased to 39 percent.[23]

These results show that one cannot make inferences about school segregation from exposure rates. We therefore turn to analyses in which the measure of school segregation is insensitive to the racial composition of the population, focusing on the evenness of racial groups across schools.

National Patterns in School Segregation, 1990 and 2000

School segregation across states

In the United States, school segregation remains high. In 2000, for example, public school segregation between black and white students was 0.498 (table 2.1), which was labeled "extreme segregation."[24] To put this in perspective, a district with ten schools would have a value of about 0.498 in H if seven of the schools were completely segregated and three of the schools were fully integrated.

However, a significant portion of school segregation is due to the unequal distribution in the patterns of immigration and residence among members of different racial and ethnic groups at both the state and local (e.g., district or county) levels. Interstate segregation captures the unevenness in the distribution of racial and ethnic groups across states. In general, this measure represents differences in migration patterns across racial groups. Some states have a greater representation of minorities in their population and others have fewer. These uneven migration patterns inflate the figures for total school segregation because, while our measure of segregation (H) is insensitive to changes in the U.S. population, the overall measure is not immune to "natural" barriers that make it nearly impossible for all U.S. schools to have the same racial composition. Therefore, it is critical for measures of racial segregation to capture these state-level differences because not accounting for the racial makeup of states grossly overestimates school segregation patterns.

In 2000, 17 percent (0.085) of the total black-white school segregation (0.498) can be attributed to segregation across states. While this may be considered a meaningful portion, it pales in comparison to state-level segregation of other nonwhite students. Interstate segregation between Latinos and whites accounted for 44 percent (0.229) of the total Latino-white school segregation (0.521) in 2000. This finding is not surprising, considering that immigrant minorities, particularly Latinos and Asians, tend to live in a handful of states. For example, over half (57%) of all Latino students in the United States reside in two states, California and Texas. We observe a similar pattern between "others" (i.e., Asian Americans and Native Americans) and white students. These results demonstrate that accounting for interstate segregation is important because studies that do not account for this difference may misattribute segregation to other geographical locations, such as counties and districts.

Overall levels of segregation remain high for all regions. The lowest level of school segregation was between others and whites in the Midwest (0.256),

TABLE 2.1: School Segregation (H) between Whites and Nonwhites, 1990 and 2000

	Regions									
	Nation		Northeast		Midwest		South		West	
Blacks	1990	2000	1990	2000	1990	2000	1990	2000	1990	2000
Total Segregation	.494	.498	.602	.587	.597	.602	.379	.396	.420	.403
Between States	.096	.085	.052	.047	.053	.042	.057	.051	.075	.072
Between Counties	.183	.187	.255	.237	.246	.245	.159	.174	.112	.107
Between Districts[a]	.123	.132	.184	.210	.233	.248	.055	.056	.145	.135
Between Districts[b]	.187	.195	.292	.300	.250	.264	.144	.150	.157	.146
Within Districts	.092	.093	.110	.093	.065	.067	.108	.115	.087	.089

	Regions									
	Nation		Northeast		Midwest		South		West	
Latinos	1990	2000	1990	2000	1990	2000	1990	2000	1990	2000
Total Segregation	.549	.521	.606	.567	.463	.453	.578	.501	.412	.419
Between States	.246	.229	.085	.075	.109	.108	.295	.247	.134	.125
Between Counties	.148	.125	.267	.244	.156	.144	.180	.134	.095	.085
Between Districts[a]	.089	.099	.144	.166	.135	.140	.044	.049	.113	.126
Between Districts[b]	.139	.133	.320	.307	.139	.144	.109	.084	.117	.130
Within Districts	.066	.069	.110	.082	.063	.060	.059	.070	.069	.082

	Regions									
	Nation		Northeast		Midwest		South		West	
Others	1990	2000	1990	2000	1990	2000	1990	2000	1990	2000
Total Segregation	.358	.346	.300	.326	.270	.256	.278	.259	.337	.330
Between States	.148	.138	.033	.045	.045	.041	.070	.077	.113	.102
Between Counties	.100	.101	.138	.161	.110	.102	.119	.105	.090	.090
Between Districts[a]	.056	.058	.056	.060	.068	.071	.024	.023	.080	.086
Between Districts[b]	.087	.094	.138	.167	.076	.077	.071	.070	.097	.101
Within Districts	.054	.048	.073	.060	.048	.042	.065	.054	.053	.052

Source: Common Core of Data 1990, 2000.

Note: This analysis does not include schools from Idaho. Authors' calculations.

[a]Denotes interdistrict segregation within multidistrict counties.

[b]Denotes interdistrict segregation that includes multidistrict and unidistrict counties.

while the Northeast generally exhibited the greatest overall levels of school segregation. The region with the lowest level of school segregation depends on the racial group. Consistent with previous observations, school segregation between African American and white students was lowest in the South (0.396 in 2000), although the West was also comparably low (0.403).[25] School segregation of 0.419 in the West was the lowest between Latinos and whites, and others-white school segregation was lowest in the Midwest (0.256).

Interstate segregation is substantial for some regions and less substantial for others. In general, the lowest amount of segregation that is attributable to states is in the Northeast. In 1990, interstate segregation accounted for 0.085 or 14 percent of the overall Latino-white school segregation in the Northeast, which was the largest interstate share among all racial groups for this region. Consequently, at least 86 percent of the total school segregation found in the Northeast lies within states. The low levels of interstate segregation indicate that the distribution of minority students, relative to whites, is spread more evenly across states within the Northeast than in other regions. Therefore, the high and extreme levels of school segregation found in the Northeast is due to factors that occur within states—most notably racial differences in residential patterns.

The South exhibits the second largest amount of school segregation between Latinos and whites. However, approximately half (0.247) of the total Latino-white segregation (0.501) lies across states. This finding is largely because the vast majority (over 84 percent) of Latinos in the South reside in Texas and Florida. Once between-state segregation is accounted for, the South is among the lowest in within-state school segregation between Latinos and whites, with the West having comparably low within-state segregation levels. Latino-white segregation within southern states was 0.283 (0.180+0.044+0.059) in 1990 and 0.253 in 2000.

School segregation within states

Within states, we decomposed school segregation into attributions to counties, districts, and schools. Whereas interstate segregation generally captures differences in migration patterns across racial groups, interdistrict (and inter-county) segregation largely captures differences in residential patterns. In a county with two school districts, for example, if all black families reside in one school district while all white families reside in another, then school segregation for that county would be entirely attributable to differences across districts. In this example, policies that attempt to create racial balance within districts would be ineffective because these policies operate at a district-by-district level.

Within states, we focused on inter- and intradistrict segregation because court-ordered desegregation regulations are almost always limited to within districts.[26] However, school districts typically reside within counties, and not accounting for variations across counties would likely inflate the estimates of interdistrict segregation. An issue arises when decomposing school segregation across counties and districts in that a notable proportion of U.S. counties (34%) contain a single school district, most commonly in the South. States, however, typically contain many counties, and unidistrict counties are captured in intercounty estimates, thereby underestimating the levels of interdistrict segregation. We therefore report two estimations of interdistrict segregation. The first ("Between Districts[a]" in table 2.1) denotes the estimate of interdistrict segregation but assigns information from unidistrict counties to the county level—which occurs when decomposing school segregation across counties and districts. The second ("Between Districts[b]" in table 2.1) denotes an adjusted estimate of interdistrict segregation, where we assigned unidistrict counties to the district level.[27] The estimate of within-district segregation is unaffected by the assignment of unidistrict counties. Because we were interested in school segregation at the district level, we reported findings from the adjusted measure of interdistrict segregation.

Nationally, approximately 45 percent of the total within-state segregation lies across districts. To give an example, interdistrict segregation between black and white students (0.195) accounted for 47 percent of the total within-state segregation (0.187+0.132+0.093) in 2000. These results show clear racial differences in residential patterns across school districts. As a result, a substantially lower proportion of the total within-state segregation lies within districts. Nationally, the amount of school segregation that lies across counties and districts is approximately three times the amount of school segregation that lies within school districts. In 2000, for example, black-white segregation between counties and districts was 0.319 (0.187+0.132), whereas the degree of black-white segregation within districts was 0.093. Similar ratios exist for other racial groups. These results indicate that even if school districts fully integrated their schools, only a quarter of the total school segregation within states would be eliminated.

Although most of within-state school segregation lies across counties and districts, the magnitude of the contribution is not the same for all regions. For all racial groups, within-district segregation is lowest among midwestern states. In 2000, black-white segregation within midwestern states was 0.560 (0.245+0.248+0.067). About 12 percent of the total within-state segregation (0.067) was due to differences within districts. This implies that midwestern states experience the lowest levels of racial segregation across schools within their districts. However, this finding mainly reflects the racial homogeneity of students within a district because, relative to other regions, midwestern states exhibit the largest racial differences in residential patterns. At the other extreme, within-district segregation is largest for southern states. In 2000, for example, within-district segregation between African American and white students accounted for 33 percent (0.115) of the total within-state segregation (0.345) in the South. Because desegregation policies are almost always limited to within-district allocation of students, these results suggest that changes to desegregation policies—such as declarations of unitary status—have the greatest potential impact for the South, while the midwestern states would be the least affected by changes to desegregation policies.

These findings reiterate the importance of decomposing school segregation into its geographic components. For example, our results in the South are consistent with previous research by Reardon and Yun, who also report that the vast majority of total segregation lies across school districts.[28] However, we derived smaller estimates of interdistrict segregation because Reardon and Yun did not partition school segregation into its state and county components, so that the contributions of interdistrict segregation are also capturing segregation at other geographic levels. Nevertheless, their substantive conclusion remains the same where there are clear racial differences in residential patterns in the United States.

Changes in school segregation over time

To address whether schools are becoming increasingly racially imbalanced, we turn to changes in school segregation patterns between 1990 and 2000. In the South—where court-ordered desegregation was the most widely enforced—black-white school segregation modestly increased from 0.379 in 1990 to 0.396 in 2000. However, a 0.017 change in total segregation does not constitute a meaningful increase.[29] If anything, the national trends show moderate decreases in Latino-white school segregation. This was especially evident in the South, where Latino-white segregation dropped meaningfully, from 0.578 in 1990 to 0.501 in 2000. According to Reardon and Yun, a 0.05 change in H corresponds to a meaningful change in segregation.[30] This decrease in Latino-white segregation in the South was largely due to the increase in statewide residence patterns of Latinos. Between 1990 and 2000, about 70 percent of all southern states at least doubled their number of Latino students, and some states (e.g., Arkansas) increased their numbers by over 600 percent. The increasing number of Latino students in southern states therefore reduced total school segregation by reducing the interstate and intercounty levels of segregation.

The national trends show that within-district segregation—school segregation that is most affected by the rollback in desegregation policies—was stable across decades. Within regions the findings were inconsistent, in that there was some evidence of increased within-district segregation (e.g., black-white and Latino-white segregation in the South), but also decreases in within-district segregation (e.g., others-white segregation in the South). More importantly, the magnitude of the change is not large, countering the expectation that segregation within districts has increased due to the increasing number of unitary districts.

Although the national trends show general stability across time in levels of school segregation, these trends do not necessarily imply that changes in desegregation policies—such as declarations of unitary status—have no influence on school racial composition. Considering that there are approximately 16,000 school districts in our sample, it is not surprising that unitary districts do not have a marked influence on the national stage. Even if we assumed that all unitary districts were located in the South, these districts would comprise less than 3 percent of all districts in that region. In later sections, we examine changes in racial composition for districts that were granted unitary status.

The consequences of unitary status are not merely a reflection of school segregation, but may also reflect changes in residential segregation. In the era of desegregation, the relationship between school and residential segregation was loosely coupled—at least more so than in the era of unitary status—due to concerted efforts to bring racial integration to schools within a district. Once a school district was granted unitary status, districts were free to assign students—for example, to neighborhood schools. As more districts are becoming unitary, the association between school and residential segregation may increase as other allocation criteria are used to assign students to schools. To put it another way, if school segregation follows residential segregation, then patterns of school and residential segregation will converge. If school segregation is independent of residential segregation, then school policy may have resulted in different segregation paths than what would have occurred on the basis of residence alone.

National Patterns in Residential Segregation, 1990 and 2000

Overall and regional patterns

With the exception of others-white segregation, national trends show that residential segregation between whites and nonwhites has declined. Our national results are mainly consistent with previous studies that concentrated on southern states.[31] Although black-white school segregation remained relatively unchanged (see table 2.1), black-white residential segregation modestly declined, from 0.538 in 1990 to 0.509 in 2000 (see table 2.2). Because school segregation did not uniformly follow residential segregation, these results suggest that school segregation may have declined had it not been for unitary status.[32]

In addition, black-white residential segregation declined in every region, with the smallest decrease in the South and the largest decrease in the West. Whereas the South experienced a smaller decline in black-white segregation than other regions, it also witnessed the highest level of intercounty segregation. In 1990, intercounty residential segregation accounted for 0.133 or 30 percent of the total segregation in the South. By 2000, the share of intercounty segregation increased to 0.145. This indicates that African American and white families are increasingly living in different counties over time.

Residential segregation between Latinos and whites is also pronounced, although smaller than black-white segregation. Moreover, residential segregation between Latinos and whites was substantially lower than their degree of school segregation. In 2000, Latino-white school segregation was 0.521 (table 2.1) but their residential segregation was 0.341 (table 2.2), indicating that school attendance patterns between Latinos and whites are far more stratified than residence patterns. Consistent with patterns of school segregation, approximately half of the total residential segregation between Latinos and whites lies across states. A similar pattern holds between others and whites. As such, Latino-white and others-white residential segregation within states are substantially lower than black-white residential segregation within states.

Comparing school and residential segregation patterns

In 1990, the largest discrepancy in school and residential segregation was between blacks and whites. Intercounty school segregation accounted for 46 percent of the total within-state segregation between blacks and whites (0.183/[0.183+0.123+0.092]; see table 2.1). During this period, intercounty residential segregation accounted for 34 percent of the total black-white segregation within states (table 2.2). Therefore, intercounty school segregation

TABLE 2.2: Residential Segregation (*H*) between Whites and Nonwhites (5–17 years of age), 1990 and 2000

	Regions									
	Nation		Northeast		Midwest		South		West	
Blacks	1990	2000	1990	2000	1990	2000	1990	2000	1990	2000
Total Segregation	.538	.509	.611	.579	.669	.625	.445	.433	.406	.346
Between States	.087	.090	.039	.044	.050	.049	.056	.061	.056	.053
Between Counties	.151	.156	.199	.192	.215	.219	.133	.145	.088	.083
Within Counties	.299	.263	.374	.343	.404	.357	.257	.228	.263	.210

	Regions									
	Nation		Northeast		Midwest		South		West	
Latinos	1990	2000	1990	2000	1990	2000	1990	2000	1990	2000
Total Segregation	.371	.341	.409	.376	.336	.309	.360	.307	.250	.231
Between States	.187	.172	.049	.049	.082	.074	.210	.172	.085	.076
Between Counties	.076	.063	.138	.121	.108	.103	.084	.058	.050	.043
Within Counties	.108	.107	.222	.206	.146	.131	.066	.077	.115	.112

	Regions									
	Nation		Northeast		Midwest		South		West	
Others	1990	2000	1990	2000	1990	2000	1990	2000	1990	2000
Total Segregation	.297	.295	.188	.221	.227	.241	.216	.203	.288	.298
Between States	.121	.106	.022	.029	.036	.038	.055	.046	.077	.066
Between Counties	.073	.080	.056	.073	.087	.094	.085	.081	.078	.088
Within Counties	.103	.109	.110	.119	.104	.109	.075	.076	.133	.143

Source: U.S. Census 1990, 2000.

Note: This analysis does not include schools from Idaho. Authors' calculations.

accounted for 37 percent more of the total within-state segregation than did intercounty residential segregation. Although not definitive, this result is consistent with white flight, where white families in counties with substantial black populations are placing their children in private schools.[33]

By 2000, however, between-county school segregation had dropped so that it was now only 22 percent greater than between-county residential segregation. If the intercounty segregation of schools being greater than the segregation of residences is an indication of white enrollment in private schools, then this downward trend suggests that white flight may have decreased by as much as 11 percent. This finding is consistent with family behavioral patterns in a school district that is no longer under court order to desegregate its schools. A well-documented behavior that occurs in desegregated schools is that some white families pull their children out of the public school and send them to private schools.[34] When desegregation policies are terminated, white families have less incentive to send their children to private schools, and a potential consequence is the return of white students to public schools. Our evidence so far is consistent with this pattern. These results, however, infer public and private enrollment patterns based on the discrepancies in the observed segregation between schools and residential areas. They do not examine private school enrollments directly.

In the following sections, we directly examine whether changes in private school enrollments may account for the trends in school and residential segregation (see also appendix 2B, table 2B.1). The reason for including private schools is to assess whether white flight to private schools has diminished and whether our initial results that used only public schools were masking the actual levels of school segregation in the United States. PSS did not collect school racial composition before 1993–94, and we are therefore unable to examine years prior to 1993. We begin by estimating the school racial composition in 1993 and 2005 only for public schools. Including the results from table 7.1, we provide school composition estimates for 1990, 1993, 2000, and 2005. We then include private schools to see the extent to which racial composition has changed. Because private schools do not belong to school districts, we concentrate on county-level differences.

National Patterns in Public and Private School Segregation, 1993 and 2005

Including the results from table 2.1, we observe a significant downward progression in Latino-white school segregation between 1990 and 2005 (table 2.1). Nationally, Latino-white school segregation declined from 0.549 in 1990 to 0.501 in 2005—yielding a difference of 0.048 in H. For other racial groups, however, we continue to observe the level of school segregation remaining relatively unchanged over time.

We expected that the inclusion of private schools would lead to higher estimates of overall school segregation, due to the overrepresentation of whites in private schools. Surprisingly, the inclusion of private schools does not alter the overall level of school segregation for the nation or within states. As expected, black-white school segregation was larger in the private than in the public school sector. In 2005, black-white segregation in private schools was 0.56, compared to public school segregation of 0.49, resulting in a 0.07 difference in H (results not shown). However, students who attend private school comprise just 8 percent of all students who receive formal schooling in the United States. The low share of students who attend private schools was the main reason for the relatively unchanged patterns of school segregation.

Although the inclusion of private schools does not change our estimates of overall segregation, it does alter our findings for within-county segregation. For 2005, we find estimates of within-county school segregation that are between 14 percent and 37 percent higher after private schools are included. These results show that prior estimates that include only public schools underestimate school segregation due to racial differences across sectors.

In general, differences in school attendance across sectors are most pronounced between black and white students. Nationally, 0.025, or 10 percent, of within-county segregation (0.250) between black and white students was attributable to segregation across sectors, and the contribution remained the same between 1993 and 2005. Southern states experienced greater levels of school segregation across sectors, where 16 percent of the total segregation within counties lies between school sectors. By contrast, western states exhibited the least amount of school segregation across sectors, where between-sector differences account for 3–4 percent of the total within-county segregation. The large sector differences in the South are likely due to the pronouncement of desegregation policies in southern states and the reaction of white families to desegregation.

In general, differences across school sectors accounted for 6.7 percent of within-county segregation among Latino and white students in 1993, but increased to 8.4 percent in 2005. This change was largely attributable to a 77 percent increase in between-sector segregation in southern states, where between-sector segregation accounted for 5.7 percent of the total within-county segregation in 1993 but increased to 10.1 percent in 2005. Nationally, a similar increase occurred for between-sector segregation among others and white students, but the increase was chiefly attributable to changes in northeastern states. In 1993, approximately 13.1 percent of total within-county segregation was due to attendance differences across sectors, but between-sector segregation increased to 17.2 percent in 2005.

Findings from the inclusion of private schools are not consistent with our earlier, tentative conclusion that unitary status leads to a return of white students to public schools. Sector differences between black and white students have remained consistent over time, despite the trend toward unitary status, and sector differences between Latinos and whites have actually increased in the South. Therefore, the anticipated reversal in the behavioral pattern of white families after the end of court-ordered desegregation appears to have been incorrect. However, attendance patterns at private schools may largely reflect patterns at nonunitary districts, considering that the relative share of unitary districts in the United States is small.

The Relationship between School and Residential Segregation

To determine whether the level of school segregation reflects residential segregation, we examined the correlation between school and residential segregation at the county level. If the association between school and residential segregation increased over time, then racial composition patterns at schools may be increasingly due to housing patterns. An increase in the association between school and residential segregation is consistent with a unitary-status explanation, in that unitary districts are more likely to allocate students based on residence patterns. If, however, the association has decreased over time, then factors other than housing patterns contribute more to school segregation. This association is consistent with desegregation policies where the efforts to racially integrate schools often lead to a bypass of neighborhood boundaries. Generally, counties with large numbers of minorities tend to exhibit the greatest school and residential segregation. In these analyses, we controlled for the size of the minority population for a county in order to estimate associations between residence and school segregation patterns that are insensitive to minority size.

Nationally, the association between school and residential segregation for blacks and whites increased 10 percent, where the correlation was 0.524 in 1990 and 0.575 in 2000 (table 2.3). This result is consistent with previous research that found an increase in the school-residential association.[35] However, our findings incorporated all counties in the United States, whereas previous research examined the relationship between school and residential segregation in heavily black southern counties.

Compared to other racial groups, the school-residential association is greatest between blacks and whites (with the exception of the West). Moreover, the school-residential association is greatest in the Northeast, where black-white school segregation is almost perfectly correlated with black-white residential segregation. By contrast, the school-residential association is weakest in western states, suggesting that the vast majority of school segregation is attributable to factors other than residential patterns. With the exception

TABLE 2.3: Relationship between Residential and School Segregation between Whites and Nonwhites

Blacks	Nation	Regions			
		North	Midwest	South	West
1990	.524	.880	.493	.525	.347
2000	.575	.915	.545	.581	.257

Latinos	Nation	Regions			
		North	Midwest	South	West
1990	.424	.772	.234	.261	.504
2000	.561	.832	.382	.514	.535

Others	Nation	Regions			
		North	Midwest	South	West
1990	.519	.619	.455	.375	.777
2000	.520	.801	.438	.371	.723

Source: U.S. Census 1990, 2000, and Common Core of Data 1990, 2000.

Note: This analysis does not include schools from Idaho. Figures are partial correlations, controlling for the size of the minority population in a county.

of the West, the evidence suggests that the connection between school and residential patterns has increased over time.

National trends also show a substantial increase in the school and residential association between Latinos and whites. In 1990, the school-residence correlation was 0.424. This association increased to 0.561 in 2000 (change of 32 percent). In particular, the Midwest experienced a 63 percent increase (from 0.234 in 1990 to 0.382 in 2000) in the correlation between school and residential segregation, and the South experienced an even greater increase of 97 percent. Although these increases are astonishing, the school-residential association for these states is lower than the national average. Like black-white segregation, the school-residential segregation between Latinos and whites was strongest in the Northeast, where the school-residential association was 0.772 in 1990 and 0.832 in 2000.

Whereas the results from school-sector analyses are inconsistent on the consequences of unitary status, the results that examine the relationship between school and residential segregation are consistent with a unitary-status explanation. In general, these findings indicate that school assignment patterns are increasingly based on residential patterns, particularly in the Northeast. Even in the South—where much of the desegregation efforts took place—there have been increases in the school-residential association for African American and Latino students.

The goal of this chapter is to shed light on the debate over the recent increase of African American students attending racially isolated schools. The proposed reason for this increase is that the retreat of desegregation policies is leading to school resegregation. The national trends show mixed support for the influence of unitary status on school racial composition. Overall, we find little evidence that school segregation grew between 1990 and 2005. These results are consistent with previous studies that used measures that capture racial imbalance, and they stand in stark contrast with studies that use measures that capture racial isolation.[36] If anything, there is evidence that school segregation decreased over time, especially between Latino and white students. We therefore conclude that changes in the national level of school segregation is attributed to changes in the U.S. population during the past several decades, which has led to the increase of minority exposure for all racial groups.

However, trends in school segregation did not follow trends in residential segregation. Although school segregation remained stable over time, residential segregation experienced a decline for blacks and Latinos. These findings suggest that the influence of unitary status, which should lead to an increase in school segregation, may be masked, due to the simultaneous decline in residential segregation. Moreover, we find that the allocation of students to schools is increasingly determined by residential patterns—a consequence of unitary status. In general, the association between school and residential segregation has increased in all regions. The increase in the school-residential association is particularly alarming in the South, considering that many of the desegregation efforts took place in that region.

While the national trends shed light on the debate of resegregation and its mechanism (i.e., unitary status), we contend that the consequences of unitary status emits too weak a signal to draw definitive conclusions, due to the small number of unitary districts. If writers concede that the national scope presents too large a landscape to evaluate the influence of unitary status, then scholars are able to move past the debate of which measures of school segregation accurately account for the national trends and instead focus on whether districts that were granted unitary status experienced a change in their school racial composition. Previous research has shown that unitary status transforms the attendance patterns of students within a district.[37] In the following sections, we analyze the changes in school segregation for districts that have been declared unitary.

Comparing School Segregation between Unitary and Nonunitary Districts over Time

In this section, we focus on changes to school segregation in districts that were granted unitary status. The major consequence of unitary status, as writers contend, is the increase in the level of segregation across schools for these districts. We match unitary districts to comparable nonunitary districts, based on several criteria from 1987 and 1988.[38] The results show that the levels of school segregation in 1987 and 1988 were similar between unitary (solid lines) and nonunitary districts (dotted lines), reflecting the deliberate design of forming comparable samples, although there was a modest initial gap of 0.027 in Latino-white school segregation (figure 2.1). This gap is

FIGURE 2.1: School segregation of unitary and comparable nonunitary districts over time

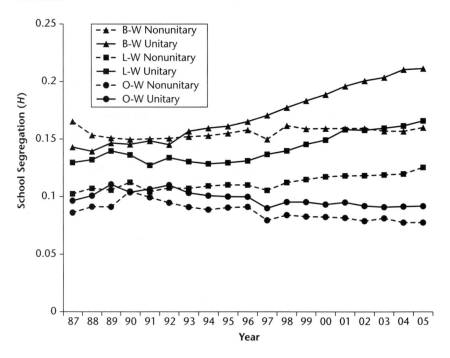

accounted for when examining changes in Latino-white segregation between unitary and nonunitary districts.

Relative to other racial groups, the influence of unitary status has its greatest impact on black-white school segregation. Historically, desegregation policies were put in place to remove the vestiges of the earlier dual (segregated) system. These policies had the greatest impact on southern schools, where a substantial proportion of the nation's black population resides. Therefore, districts that were declared unitary should mostly be located in southern states.[39] Indeed, southern districts are driving the overall trends in school segregation because approximately 70 percent of unitary districts in our sample are in this region.

Our results show that in unitary districts (solid lines), black-white school segregation increased steadily, from 0.143 in 1987 to 0.211 in 2005. By contrast, black-white school segregation in comparable nonunitary districts (dotted lines) remained relatively steady during this period, hovering around 0.156. This stable trend in school segregation is further observed in the national trends in within-district segregation (not shown). As such, the gap in school segregation between unitary and nonunitary districts increased over time.

Between 1987 and 1996, there was little difference in black-white segregation among unitary and nonunitary districts. During this period, the vast majority of districts in the sample (74%) were not yet granted unitary status. Over time, early adopters are better able to effectively implement school assignment patterns that counter the assignment patterns that were enforced under court-ordered desegregation. At the same time, more districts were granted unitary status, leading to an increase in the black-white segregation gap between unitary and nonunitary districts. A notable increase occurred in 2001, at which point two-thirds of the sample were declared unitary. By 2004, when all districts in the sample were granted unitary status, the black-white segregation gap between unitary and nonunitary districts was 0.054 in *H*—reflecting a significant change in school segregation.[40]

The end of court-ordered segregation did not lead to the same increase in school segregation for other racial groups. While the gap in Latino-white segregation between unitary and nonunitary districts was 0.042 in 2004, there was an initial gap of about 0.024 between 1987 and 1996. Therefore, figure 2.1 shows that unitary status increased Latino-white school segregation by 0.014 to 0.02 in *H*. The modest increase in Latino-white segregation in unitary districts partially reflects the historical context of desegregation policies. Court-ordered desegregation for Latino students did not fully emerge until several decades after *Brown* and was never strenuously enforced.[41] Furthermore, it is no coincidence that the vast majority of districts that applied for unitary status were in the South. The national trends reveal that, compared to other regions, within-state segregation between Latino and white students was among the lowest in the South (see table 2.1). The large proportion of unitary declarations occurring in the South and the lower levels of school segregation, compared to other regions, may have led to the modest changes in Latino-white school segregation in unitary districts. Unitary status had little impact in others-white school segregation, which is consistent with the conclusion of previous scholars that observed that Asian Americans (the major racial group in the "others" category) were the most integrated racial group in U.S. schools.[42]

With the exception of others-white school segregation, the results from figure 2.1 show that school segregation in unitary districts has increased over time, whereas school segregation in nonunitary districts has remained relatively consistent. This increase is modest between Latino and white students and substantial between African American and white students. This has led some scholars to conclude that, although black-white segregation remains among the lowest in the southern and border states, resegregation of black students is also greatest in this region.[43]

Impact of Unitary Status on School Segregation

Although the majority of unitary districts in our sample are from the South and therefore drive our overall trends, it remains unclear whether unitary districts from this region also witnessed the greatest changes in student assignment patterns across their schools. Moreover, while comparisons between unitary and nonunitary districts in figure 2.1 reflect the impact of unitary status, other factors unaccounted for in the comparisons may lead to the overall difference between these groups.

We therefore employ fixed-effects models to analyze the effects of unitary-status decisions on school segregation (see table 2.4). Fixed-effects models take advantage of the repeated observations available for each district. This approach controls for constant characteristics of districts in both observable and unobservable predictors. Fixed-effects models rely only on within-district variation over time, because they remove all variation that occurs across districts. We included two indicators that potentially account for the within-district variation: unitary status, and an interaction between unitary status and region. The interaction term was included to examine whether the effect of unitary status differs between the South and other regions.

In general, black-white and Latino-white school segregation increased after a district was declared unitary. Because an interaction term between unitary status and nonsouthern region was included in the models, the unitary indicator reflects the effect of unitary status in the South. Similar to the results found by Clotfelter et al., our estimates show that black-white segregation in southern districts increased by 0.023 after unitary status was declared.[44] Although a 0.023 change in H may appear modest, recall that within-district segregation constitutes a relatively small share of the total school segregation. The average black-white school segregation for southern districts in the sample was 0.175. Therefore, the increase of school segregation after unitary status corresponds to approximately 13 percent of the average level of black-white segregation in the South.

Similarly, Latino-white segregation in southern districts increased by 0.016, or by 12 percent of the overall Latino-white segregation (0.134), after unitary status was declared. The difference in the estimated unitary coefficient between blacks and Latinos was not statistically significant (p < 0.14), suggesting that southern districts altered their school assignment patterns similarly for African American and Latino students after they were granted unitary status. Surprisingly, others-white segregation slightly decreased after

TABLE 2.4: Fixed-Effects Estimates of Changes to School Segregation (H) between White and Nonwhite Students, 1987–2005

	Black		Latino		Others	
Unitary	.023	***	.016	***	−.011	***
	(.004)		(.003)		(.003)	
Unitary x Nonsouth	.041	***	.022	***	.000	
	(.006)		(.005)		(.004)	
Constant	.158	***	.133	***	.102	***
	(.002)		(.002)		(.001)	
Average School Segregation (H)						
Southern Districts	.175		.134		.083	
Nonsouthern Districts	.166		.160		.131	

Note: Standard errors are in parentheses.

* p < .05, ** p < .01, *** p < .001

a district was declared unitary, reflecting the observed decrease found in residential patterns between whites and others (see table 2.2).

Confirming prior concerns (e.g., Orfield and Yun), we find that school segregation increased after southern districts were granted unitary status. However, inconsistent with prior expectations, the impact of unitary-status decisions is greater in nonsouthern districts than in southern districts. In nonsouthern districts, unitary-status decisions increased black-white school segregation by 0.064 (0.023+0.041), which is approximately 39 percent of the overall black-white school segregation (0.166) in nonsouthern states. For Latino students, school segregation increased by 0.038 (0.016+0.022), or 24 percent of the average level of Latino-white segregation, in nonsouthern states.

Among the twenty unitary districts outside of the South, sixteen districts were in the Midwest and Northeast (twelve and four, respectively). Recall that the national trends (see table 2.1) showed that midwestern states exhibited the largest and northeastern states the second largest racial differences in residential patterns. As a result, schools within these districts tended to be the most racially homogeneous in the nation. In these regions, districts under unitary status are increasingly assigning students to schools based on patterns of residence, thereby increasing the level of racial homogeneity even further.

CONCLUSION

In this chapter, we addressed two competing narratives for school racial composition patterns in recent decades. The first is a return to resegregation engineered by a retrenchment of desegregation policies, which allowed districts to assign students based on characteristics such as residential patterns. The second is that the observed increase in minority students attending racially isolated schools is due to changes in both racial imbalance and racial composition.

Gary Orfield and colleagues proposed that U.S. schools are witnessing an increase in racial segregation due to the increasing number of districts across the South that have been declared unitary and freed from court-ordered desegregation. Therefore, districts under unitary status are able to assign students to neighborhood schools. Because the relationship between school and residential segregation was weaker in the era of desegregation, when these districts are granted unitary status, one would expect school segregation to more closely resemble residential segregation. Scholars from both sides of the debate have addressed this claim by focusing on two separate but inter-related questions. First, have the national trends in fact shown an increase in racial segregation over time, or are the observed trends a statistical arti-fact due to the sensitivity of the segregation measure to changes in the U.S. population? Second, do unitary-status decisions impact the assignment pat-tern of students to schools?

Regarding the first question, we found little evidence that school seg-regation has increased over time. Using a measure of segregation that was insensitive to changes in racial composition, we showed that national trends in school segregation did not grow between 1990 and 2005. Even in the South, where court-ordered desegregation was the most widely enforced, black-white school segregation did not significantly increase between 1990 and 2005. If anything, there was evidence that school segregation decreased over time, especially between Latino and white students. Moreover, within-district segregation—school segregation that is the most affected by uni-tary-status decisions—was stable across decades. These results suggest that the increasing proportion of black students attending majority nonwhite schools, for example, is largely due to the increasing number of other minori-ties (e.g., Latinos and Asians) that reside in the United States—which would lead to the impression of increased resegregation. As Clotfelter et al. point out, the common index of the proportion of black students attending major-ity nonwhite schools "may have lost much of its meaning as a measure of racial segregation."[45]

Regarding the second question, we found support for the view that uni-tary-status decisions impact the assignment patterns of students to schools. Trends in school segregation did not follow trends in residential segrega-tion (as residential segregation experienced a decline) for blacks and Latinos. While Latino-white school segregation declined between 1990 and 2000, the rate of decline was lower than the decline in Latino-white residential segrega-tion. In the South, where many of the desegregation efforts took place, black-white school segregation slightly increased over time while residential segre-gation slightly decreased. In general, these results suggest that the patterns of residential segregation do not fully explain the patterns of school segrega-tion. School segregation may have actually increased had it not been for the simultaneous decrease in residential segregation.[46]

Our study further revealed that the association between school and resi-dential segregation increased between 1990 and 2000. This finding is a con-sistent consequence of unitary status, in that school districts begin to lose its influence on integrating schools as other criteria (such as residence) take prominence in assigning students to schools. The school-residential associa-tion has generally increased in all regions, and even the South has witnessed an alarming increase in its school-residential association for African Ameri-can and Latino students.

Surprisingly, including private schools in the analysis did little to change our calculations of the overall levels of school segregation. There was some evidence that within-county segregation increased by 14 percent to 37 percent after private schools were included, suggesting that school segregation exists across sectors. However, with some exceptions, the national trends remained consistent over time, irrespective of the inclusion of private schools. These results lend little support to the hypothesis that white students would return to public schools in the era of unitary status.

In addition, we examined whether there were changes in school segrega-tion after a district was declared unitary. We found that school segregation did increased in districts after unitary status was declared. In general, uni-tary-status decisions affected school assignment patterns for African Ameri-can and Latino students. Others-white segregation did not increase after a district was declared unitary, and, in fact, it experienced a slight decrease. The results show that unitary-status decisions increased black-white school segregation by about 13 percent in southern districts. Contrary to prior expectations (e.g., Orfield and Lee), the largest impact of unitary status did not occur in southern districts, but in nonsouthern districts, where unitary-status decisions increased black-white school segregation by 39 percent and Latino-white segregation by 24 percent. This finding is especially troubling, considering the intense levels of residential segregation in midwestern and northeastern states. Schools within these districts tend to be more racially homogeneous than in other regions, and the consequence of unitary-status decisions are making these schools even less racially diverse.

We began this chapter with competing narratives: one stated that unitary status has led to the resegregation of our nation's schools, and a second that asserted that segregation was stable and that racial isolation reflects changing population patterns rather than school assignment policies. We find, in the end, that both narratives have a measure of truth. On the one hand, unitary-status declarations result in increased segregation. We found this in our anal-ysis of sixty-five districts that have been released from court-ordered deseg-regation. On the other hand, these policy effects are too small and too few to affect the broader patterns of increasing racial isolation, which are domi-nated by the changing face of the U.S. population. Nevertheless, these findings imply that unitary status does increase school segregation at the local level. As more districts abandon their desegregation efforts, these findings may yet reveal a significant impact on the national stage.[47]

APPENDIX 2A

As explained by Reardon, Yun, and Eitle,[1] the entropy index of segregation is expressed as:

$$H = \frac{\sum_i \frac{t_i}{T}(E - E_i)}{E},$$ (1)

where T represents the total enrollment of a population (e.g., district, metropolitan area, county) and t_i represents the enrollment for school i. Moreover, E is the entropy—the measure of diversity—for the population and E_i measures the diversity for school i. E is defined as:

$$E = \sum_r Q_r ln \frac{1}{Q_r}$$ (2)

Where Q_r represents the proportion of the population that is comprised of racial group r. H ranges between 0 and 1, where 0 reflects racially balanced schools and 1 reflects complete separation by race.

APPENDIX 2B

Table 2B.1. School Segregation (*H*) between Whites and Nonwhites, 1993 and 2005

			Regions							
	Nation		Northeast		Midwest		South		West	
Blacks	*1993*	*2005*	*1993*	*2005*	*1993*	*2005*	*1993*	*2005*	*1993*	*2005*
Public Schools only										
Total Segregation	.493	.485	.594	.568	.596	.573	.384	.395	.410	.381
Between States	.094	.083	.051	.043	.049	.035	.055	.045	.077	.077
Between Counties	.185	.184	.251	.233	.250	.233	.164	.178	.111	.100
Within Counties	.215	.218	.291	.292	.296	.305	.166	.172	.222	.205
Public and Private Schools										
Total Segregation	.501	.490	.593	.568	.600	.574	.397	.406	.420	.383
Between States	.086	.077	.048	.040	.048	.034	.049	.041	.073	.071
Between Counties	.163	.163	.212	.199	.223	.213	.142	.155	.102	.093
Within Counties	.252	.250	.333	.329	.328	.326	.207	.211	.245	.219
Between Sectors	.025	.025	.025	.024	.020	.019	.033	.034	.007	.008
Within Sectors	.228	.225	.309	.304	.308	.308	.173	.177	.239	.211

			Regions							
	Nation		Northeast		Midwest		South		West	
Latinos	*1993*	*2005*	*1993*	*2005*	*1993*	*2005*	*1993*	*2005*	*1993*	*2005*
Public Schools only										
Total Segregation	.542	.501	.592	.537	.458	.432	.563	.476	.412	.414
Between States	.246	.209	.083	.065	.113	.098	.285	.203	.137	.127
Between Counties	.143	.128	.261	.239	.154	.137	.173	.152	.092	.078
Within Counties	.153	.164	.248	.233	.192	.197	.104	.121	.183	.208
Public and Private Schools										
Total Segregation	.540	.504	.586	.538	.456	.432	.561	.481	.412	.418
Between States	.236	.204	.081	.062	.108	.093	.279	.202	.127	.119
Between Counties	.133	.119	.224	.209	.137	.126	.169	.146	.085	.074
Within Counties	.171	.181	.282	.267	.211	.212	.114	.134	.200	.226
Between Sectors	.011	.015	.026	.027	.009	.012	.006	.014	.013	.017
Within Sectors	.160	.166	.256	.240	.202	.200	.107	.120	.188	.209

Table 2B.1. *(Continued)*

Others	Nation		Regions							
			Northeast		Midwest		South		West	
	1993	*2005*	*1993*	*2005*	*1993*	*2005*	*1993*	*2005*	*1993*	*2005*
Public Schools only										
Total Segregation	.356	.332	.307	.320	.268	.241	.274	.250	.335	.324
Between States	.146	.133	.039	.045	.046	.038	.073	.074	.108	.109
Between Counties	.101	.100	.147	.169	.108	.096	.115	.102	.091	.084
Within Counties	.109	.100	.121	.106	.114	.107	.086	.073	.136	.131
Public and Private Schools										
Total Segregation	.360	.335	.313	.322	.274	.243	.277	.249	.338	.326
Between States	.142	.130	.035	.040	.042	.035	.064	.070	.105	.104
Between Counties	.090	.088	.115	.137	.098	.088	.106	.093	.084	.078
Within Counties	.128	.117	.163	.145	.134	.121	.107	.086	.148	.144
Between Sectors	.009	.010	.021	.025	.007	.008	.008	.007	.006	.007
Within Sectors	.120	.107	.141	.120	.127	.113	.099	.078	.142	.137

Source: Common Core of Data 1993, 2005, and Private School Universe Survey 1993, 2005.

Note: This analysis does not include schools from Idaho. Authors' calculations.

CHAPTER THREE

The Post-*PICS* Picture

Examining School Districts' Policy Options for Mitigating Racial Segregation

Kevin G. Welner and Eleanor R. Spindler

In the summer of 2007, in *Parents Involved in Community Schools v. Seattle School District No. 1* (*PICS*), the U.S. Supreme Court declared unconstitutional the policies of two school districts that used race as a component of their student assignment policies.[1] These affirmatively adopted, voluntary policies pursued integration in the absence of a court order. In fact, court desegregation orders had been in short supply since earlier Supreme Court decisions severely limited the authority of the federal courts to mandate desegregation.[2] Therefore, such voluntary actions had become one important remaining avenue for school districts hoping to avoid the harms of segregated schooling.

Although the *PICS* decision foreclosed this policy option, the underlying educational and social justifications for desegregation policies remain.[3] Educational leaders in school districts across the country are thus faced with a set of educational goals and a dearth of corresponding policy approaches for achieving them. After surveying the research and scholarship concerning the effects of racial diversity, this chapter explains the legal landscape in the wake of the recent *PICS* decision and then offers some policy guidance concerning future options for mitigating the sizable and increasing level of racial isolation in schools.

RESEARCH ON THE EFFECTS OF RACIAL ISOLATION

For centuries, America's schools have been starkly segregated, and that segregation continues.[4] Moreover, U.S. schools remain unequal in terms of both resources and outcomes.[5] There is—or should be—nothing debatable in these statements. What is controversial, however, is the significance of the separate and different educational experiences of American students. The policies adopted by the school boards in Seattle, Louisville, and elsewhere are premised on the belief that racial separation is harmful and contrary to American ideals—basic principles concerning the harms of a balkanized society. Others disagree with these principles, and while issues of ideals are largely nonempirical matters, many issues regarding schooling outcomes can be investigated empirically. As set forth below, the results of that research clearly demonstrate harmful effects of racial segregation in schools.

In 2007, the National Academy of Education convened a committee of experts to analyze the social science research referenced in the amicus curiae (friend of the court) briefs filed with the Supreme Court in the *PICS* case. The committee reached the following three primary conclusions:[6]

1. African-American students' achievement is higher in less segregated schools, and these benefits tend to be greater in earlier grades.[7]
2. Less segregated schools tend to have reduced levels of racial prejudice. Research has identified four conditions that, if present, help to achieve these positive effects in racially diverse environments: (a) equal status of all group members, (b) cooperative interdependence among group members, (c) normative support of positive relations and of equal status, and (d) interactions that disconfirm stereotypes and encourage understanding of other group members as individuals.[8]
3. For African American students, racial diversity in schools is associated with better long-term outcomes, such as college attendance, as well as greater tolerance and better intergroup relations among adults of different racial groups.[9]

Other research questions were not answered as clearly—most notably, the question of the effects segregated school environments have on Latino children. Despite the fact that Latino students are currently the largest and arguably the most segregated minority in the United States, most research addresses only black-white segregation.[10]

RACIAL ISOLATION AND POLICY REMEDIES: BEFORE *GRUTTER*

The United States has suffered a long history of racial prejudice and isolation.[11] Although the era of court-ordered desegregation brought some progress, schools have subsequently experienced resegregation over a period now

spanning almost two decades.[12] Patterns of urban-suburban housing segregation have been predictable, persistent, and ubiquitous.[13] School choice policies that do not include enrollment constraints fail to mitigate this segregation and, in fact, tend to result in an additional layer of segregation on
top of the housing segregation.[14] Below we briefly describe the court decisions that have shaped the context faced by school district policymakers
who might want to adopt a student assignment system to avoid or mitigate
racial isolation.

Beginning in the late 1980s, federal courts began applying the Fourteenth
Amendment's equal protection clause to strike down so-called reverse-dis-
crimination policies—race-conscious policies adopted by states and other
governmental bodies that were designed to mitigate segregation and help
members of groups that had been past victims of discrimination. Most prominent among these policies were those supporting affirmative action and
magnet schools.

The courts, while generally acknowledging the admirable goals of these
policies, applied "strict scrutiny" because the policies used race to determine
the allocation of benefits. When the government places burdens or advantages on people because of their race, ethnicity, or national origin, equal
protection jurisprudence demands that the government's policy be narrowly
tailored to pursue a compelling state interest.[15] That is, there must be a tight
fit between the policy and the compelling goal. This is known as strict scrutiny—a demanding inquiry that few policies survive.

Remediation of past intentional discrimination had long been considered
this kind of compelling governmental interest. Accordingly, Jim Crow segregation—which is a clear violation of the Fourteenth Amendment—could be
redressed by a court order mandating desegregative busing and other race-
conscious remedies. However, educational and social benefits associated with
racial diversity have remained in legal limbo. Might these also represent a
compelling governmental interest that could support a narrowly tailored
race-conscious policy? Could a governmental body, even in the absence of a
finding of past intentional discrimination, adopt race-conscious policies in
order to advance diversity goals?

These were the main questions underlying a series of decisions leading up
to *Grutter v. Bollinger* and *PICS*.[16] U.S. Supreme Court decisions in 1989 (*Richmond v. Croson*) and 1995 (*Adarand Constructors Inc. v. Peña*) addressed the
nature of acceptable affirmative action policies in government contracting,
striking down set-asides.[17] Lower federal appellate courts, taking their cues
from these cases, struck down higher education affirmative action programs

(e.g., *Hopwood v. Texas*, 1996; *Podberesky v. Kirwan*, 1994).[18] Still other federal courts struck down race-conscious K–12 student assignment policies (e.g., *Eisenberg v. Montgomery County Public Schools*, 1999; *Tuttle v. Arlington County School Board*, 1999; *Wessmann v. Gittens*, 1998).[19]

One of these ill-fated K–12 student assignment policies had been instituted at Boston Latin, a public high school with competitive admissions. The policy was characterized as "racial balancing" and was struck down by the First Circuit Court of Appeals.[20] Similarly, in *Tuttle*, the Fourth Circuit struck down a student assignment policy from Arlington County, Virginia.[21] That policy used a weighted lottery to decide admissions for a popular, oversubscribed alternative kindergarten school. The weighting formula included race as well as English-language ability and low-income status. In *Eisenberg*, the court— again the Fourth Circuit—also concluded that a racial-balancing policy, used for admissions at a magnet school, was unconstitutional.[22]

Other courts upheld the policies. The Second Circuit Court of Appeals, for instance, upheld a race-conscious urban-suburban student transfer policy in Rochester, New York (*Brewer v. West Irondequoit Central School District*, 1999).[23] The First Circuit upheld a policy in Lynn, Massachusetts, that placed race-conscious constraints on school transfers (*Comfort v. Lynn*, 2005).[24] In all these cases, the courts applied strict scrutiny, but in the latter two the courts found that the policies were narrowly tailored to advance a compelling diversity interest. Similar conclusions were reached by the appellate courts, which upheld the race-conscious student assignment policies in Louisville and Seattle—decisions that were ultimately reversed by the Supreme Court in *PICS*.

The *Comfort* decision and the appellate decisions from Louisville and Seattle were handed down after the Supreme Court's decision in *Grutter*, which rejected a constitutional challenge to the University of Michigan Law School's affirmative action policy. As discussed in greater detail below, the *Grutter* Court reasoned that an institution of higher education can have a compelling interest in securing the educational benefits of a diverse student body, and a critical mass of underrepresented minorities may be necessary to further that interest. In each of the cases following *Grutter*, the judges carefully considered the contextual differences between K–12 schools and institutions of higher education. While a university may have a compelling interest in diversity and may be legally allowed to use a "critical mass" policy to pursue that interest, the K–12 context is different, as it lacks direct parallels in terms of diversity interests and critical mass.[25]

Part of the context for the above decisions was provided by some earlier Supreme Court opinions concerning the termination of desegregation orders, particularly *Board of Education of Oklahoma City Public Schools v. Dowell* (1991) and *Freeman v. Pitts* (1992).[26] These opinions set forth guidelines that directed courts to end desegregation orders, explaining what school districts must do to satisfy their remedial obligations. In legal terms, the former "dual systems" (separate systems for blacks and whites) could be declared "unitary." A key feature of these unitary-status cases is that districts did not ever need to demonstrate that their schools had become integrated. Instead, the districts could point to their good faith efforts and contend that their current segregation was de facto, and that it was therefore sufficiently attenuated from past wrongdoing that it should not be considered a vestige of the former dual system.

As *Freeman* and *Dowell* were being applied by courts in cases that ended court supervision, several school districts across the country (primarily in the South) attempted to address segregation voluntarily. Out of these efforts arose cases like *Eisenberg, Tuttle, Wessmann, Comfort,* and the Seattle and Louisville litigation. Even though these districts were not—or were not any longer—under court orders to desegregate, they adopted student assignment policies designed to avoid the segregation that can result from residential segregation and parental choice. Their choice plans placed constraints on student assignments, using approaches such as racial tiebreakers for over-enrolled schools. These policies were intended to avoid the harms of racial isolation and gain educational and social benefits associated with racially diverse schools.[27]

THE *GRUTTER* DECISION

The *Grutter* Court focused on a variety of details that had the potential to eventually doom K–12 race-conscious student assignment policies. To understand these obstacles, consider the five key elements that the *Grutter* Court identified as part of a constitutional affirmative action policy: "(1) individualized consideration of applicants; (2) the absence of quotas; (3) serious, good-faith consideration of race-neutral alternatives to the affirmative action program; (4) that no member of any racial group was unduly harmed; and (5) that the program had a sunset provision or some other end point."[28] A K–12 policy could certainly comply with elements two though five, although "unduly harmed" (element four) is a tough standard to nail down.[29] But an individualized, holistic review of the "application" of a six-year-old child to be assigned to a given elementary school is much more difficult to envision than is such a review of a law school application. Applying *Grutter*, a federal court of appeals confronted these issues but concluded that the school district in Louisville, Kentucky, could keep its race-conscious policy.[30] As noted above, similar decisions were handed down in favor of voluntary race-conscious student assignment policies in Lynn, Massachusetts, and Seattle, Washington.[31] The plaintiffs in these cases had challenged the race-conscious policies based on the contention that they had violated the Fourteenth Amendment's equal protection clause because they allocated benefits to individuals based on their race. The school districts and their supporters characterized the policies as necessary and said they were carefully crafted to promote the same type of diversity interest that the *Grutter* Court recognized as compelling.

In each of these three appellate decisions, the court's majority found that the match between the district's compelling diversity interest and its race-conscious student assignment policy was narrowly tailored. Specifically, the courts were not deterred by the *Grutter* decision's requirement, in the higher education context, that each student's application be individually and holistically reviewed, with race never considered as a separate factor that could tip a decision in a rigid manner. The race-conscious admissions policies in these school districts did not systemically elevate a student's race beyond a variety of other important factors. Instead, a form of individualized attention was provided as part of the assignment plan that was "of a different kind in a different context than the Supreme Court found in *Grutter*."[32] For instance, students' files included their ranked preference of schools, along with information about whether they lived near a school and whether they had siblings at the school, as well as their racial background. Other individual-level factors could be considered to be embedded within a student's school rankings— academic interests, hobbies, test scores, or career plans could all influence students' choices. However, "if a public school makes no pretense of admitting only the most meritorious students, then it would be nonsensical to evaluate their files individually in search of merit."[33]

These appellate courts also confronted the reality that higher education institutions serve different purposes than K–12 schools, and that the two types of schools seek diversity for slightly different reasons. Specifically, the law school named in *Grutter* sought wide-ranging diversity, not just racial diversity, whereas the Seattle, Louisville, and Lynn school districts argued for the express benefits of racial diversity. Accordingly, while students' race was considered alongside other factors, those other factors focused not on merit or diverse experiences but on family choice and efficiency-related concerns, such as the proximity of a student's residence to the school. The appellate courts reasoned that the viability and sensibility of considering any given factor should depend on the district and its policy goals. For these districts, in the K–12 context, the goal was racial diversity, so an individualized examination would be little more than a pretense. As the court explained in *Comfort*, "Unlike the [University of Michigan] policies, the Lynn Plan is designed to achieve racial diversity rather than viewpoint diversity. The only relevant criterion, then, is a student's race; individualized consideration beyond that is irrelevant to the compelling interest."[34] In drawing such distinctions, the appellate courts pointed to language in the Supreme Court's *Grutter* decision, stressing that each situation had to be judged on its own merits: "Context matters when reviewing race-based governmental action under the Equal Protection Clause."[35] The ruling continued, "Not every decision influenced by race is equally objectionable and strict scrutiny is designed to provide a framework for carefully examining the importance and the sincerity of the reasons advanced by the governmental decision-maker for the use of race in that particular context."[36]

THE *PICS* DECISION

The U.S. Supreme Court chose two of these cases, Seattle's *PICS* case and Louisville's *McFarland* case, for review. The resulting decision, also known as *PICS*, clarified the law in some respects but also left ambiguity on several key questions. A five-justice majority—consisting of a concurrence and a four-justice plurality—struck down the specific policies of the Seattle and Louisville school districts. However, the concurring justice joined with the four dissenters in concluding that educational diversity and combating segregation are compelling governmental interests that districts may pursue under certain circumstances. Because the concurrence, written by Justice Anthony M. Kennedy, provided the crucial fifth vote, it should arguably be considered the controlling opinion (or "controlling concurrence"). That is, a school district looking to design a constitutional policy that would promote diversity would need to satisfy Justice Kennedy's concerns in order to build a five-justice majority to uphold the policy.[37]

The following sections of this chapter unpack Justice Kennedy's opinion and explain future constitutional options for districts seeking to achieve racial diversity. They also highlight lingering uncertainties not adequately addressed in the Court's opinion. Finally, we discuss what the Court's ruling means, in concrete terms, for districts that wish to pursue racial integration.

Background

The choice-based student assignment plans that were at issue in *PICS* allowed students to attend their neighborhood schools or transfer to other schools within the district. In both districts named in the case, the plans sought to mitigate racial isolation and prevent any school's enrollment from slipping too far away from the district's overall proportion of white/nonwhite (Seattle) or black/other (Louisville) students.

In Seattle, the assignment system was challenged only for the district's high schools. Each high school student was given the option to attend any school in the district and asked to rank the order of his or her top three choices. If a school they chose was oversubscribed, the student would first be assigned based on how close they lived to the school and whether they had siblings already attending the school. School officials could also deny a student's request to attend if that student's enrollment would exacerbate an existing racial imbalance at the chosen school.

Similarly, Louisville students could attend their neighborhood school or a school in their district-defined neighborhood cluster, or they could request a transfer to any other school in the district. The Louisville system applied at all levels—elementary, middle, and high school. School officials could deny the student's request on the grounds of available space or because the transfer would result in further racial segregation of either the sending or receiving school.

Justice Kennedy's Opinion

In his separate opinion, Justice Kennedy concluded—in agreement with the Court's plurality—that the methods used by the two school districts were unconstitutional because they were not narrowly tailored. He found that Seattle's assignment plans failed to "make an adequate showing," that its "blunt distinction" between white and "nonwhite" students furthered the district's interest in achieving racial diversity.[38] The concurrence expressed concern that under Seattle's plan, a school with 50 percent white students and 50 percent African American students would qualify as "balanced," while a school with 30 percent Asian American, 25 percent African American, 25 percent Latino, and 20 percent white students would not.[39] Louisville's assignment plans were similarly condemned as being "broad and imprecise" and employing a "limited notion of diversity" by considering race exclusively in terms of "black/other."[40] Bhargava, Frankenberg, and Le read this reasoning to suggest "that nuanced and pluralistic considerations of race will be more likely to pass the Court's narrow-tailoring inquiry."[41]

The key principle underlying Justice Kennedy's concurrence in *PICS* is that a governmental determination about an individual student should not hinge on that student's race. However, Justice Kennedy also concluded that school districts must be "free to devise race-conscious measures" to pursue their compelling interest in "avoiding racial isolation" and to achieve "a diverse student population."[42] School districts can therefore continue to take steps to promote diversity and avoid racial isolation in schools; it is the nature of those steps that is now the key question for lawyers and policymakers.[43] If these measures were to "address the problem in a general way without treating each student in a different fashion solely on the basis of a systematic, individual typing by race," strict scrutiny would not be required.[44] The concurrence advises that such race-conscious measures might include the following: strategic site selection of new schools, drawing attendance zones in recognition of neighborhood demographics, allocating resources for special programs, recruiting students and faculty in a targeted fashion, and tracking enrollment, performance, and other statistics by race. Justice Kennedy opined that each one of these mechanisms is "race conscious," but because they are all non-individualized none would "demand strict scrutiny to be found permissible."[45]

Moreover, Justice Kennedy suggested that if nonindividualized measures proved ineffective, a school district could constitutionally adopt a policy that considers an individual student's race during the school-assignment process. This possibility is set forth in several aspects of the concurrence. Perhaps the most notable passage begins with Justice Kennedy asserting that the goals in Louisville and Seattle could have been achieved "through different means," including the nonindividualized approaches mentioned above. He then stated that a school district could, "if necessary," use

> a more nuanced, individual evaluation of school needs and student characteristics that might include race as a component. The latter approach would be informed by *Grutter*, though of course the criteria relevant to student placement would differ based on the age of the students, the needs of the parents, and the role of the schools.[46]

Recall that the *Grutter* guidelines generally required that students be evaluated on an "individualized, holistic" basis, which called for a consideration of all the ways they might contribute to a diverse student body.[47] Although Justice Kennedy stated that an analysis of an individual K–12 student must be "informed by *Grutter*," his statement that the "criteria relevant to student placement would differ based on the age of the students, the needs of the parents, and the role of the schools" should be understood as consistent with the *Grutter* Court's emphasis on the fact that "context matters when reviewing race-based governmental action under the Equal Protection Clause."[48] Yet exactly how the narrow-tailored criteria from *Grutter* apply to K–12 student assignment policies is not fully explained in Justice Kennedy's *PICS* opinion.[49]

In short, districts may only pursue plans that include individualized consideration of race as part of a broader diversity plan after they have demonstrated that nonindividualized and race-neutral alternatives are ineffective at "achieving their precise, compelling interests."[50] It is unlikely that courts would require school districts to exhaust every race-neutral possibility before adopting a race-conscious plan. Rather, "they simply need evidence that the school district made a good faith effort to explore other alternatives."[51] Courts make factual findings of "good faith" in many different contexts, but limited precedents usefully defined boundaries in terms of student assignment policies. Accordingly, many school districts will undoubtedly hesitate, exhausting even those race-neutral and nonindividualized possibilities that are obviously futile before opting for race-conscious plans.

Future options

For school districts that are currently pursuing or want to pursue policies that mitigate racial isolation or foster a diverse student population, the effects of the *PICS* decision vary, depending on the district's legal status and on the type of policy pursued. Initially, it should be noted that districts remaining under desegregation decrees are not affected by the Court's decision, and race-conscious student-assignment policies made in accordance with such court orders may continue. This is because the *PICS* case concerned voluntary policies pursuing diversity as a compelling interest, not policies in place to remedy past discrimination.

Districts with voluntary school choice plans that rely explicitly on the race of individual students are most affected by the Court's decision. To pursue racial integration, these districts can initiate race-neutral and nonindividualized race-conscious options. The evidence about the effectiveness of such measures is, however, mixed at best. Some contend there is evidence suggesting that nonindividualized options have been somewhat successful in places like Seattle (potential benefits are discussed in the following section of this chapter).[52] Others claim these methods have been entirely unsuccessful in the same places:

As Justice Breyer shows, Seattle and Louisville are excellent examples of the ineffectiveness of these methods. As to "strategic site selection," Seattle has built one new high school in the last forty-four years. In fact, six of the Seattle high schools involved in the *PICS* case were built by the 1920s; the other four were open by the early 1960s. Louisville tried "drawing" neighborhood "attendance zones" on a racial basis. That method worked only when forced busing was also a part of the plan. Both Louisville and Seattle also tried "allocating resources for special programs." They both experimented with specially resourced "magnet school" programs, but the limited desegregation effect of these efforts extends at most to those few schools to which additional resources are granted. In addition, there is no evidence from the experience of these school districts that it will make any meaningful impact. Louisville and Seattle also tried "recruiting faculty" on the basis of race, but only as part of a broader assignment program.[53]

As Kaufman's argument suggests, one can accept the legal wisdom (and policy wisdom) of trying nonindividualized alternatives before moving to explicit, individual considerations of race and still have concerns about the practical applications of Justice Kennedy's listed options.

Nonindividualized options

Justice Kennedy listed five race-conscious but nonindividualized options for districts to consider in lieu of individual consideration of race: strategic site selection of new schools, drawing attendance zones in recognition of neighborhood demographics, allocating resources for special programs, recruiting students and faculty in a targeted fashion, and tracking enrollment, performance, and other statistics by race. These can be thought of as a "wholesale" or domain approach, rather than a "retail" or individual use of race.[54] They are blunt tools, which Justice Kennedy saw as preferable to scalpels, in part because he rejected the school district arguments that scalpels can be precisely utilized (recall the critique of categories like "white" and "nonwhite") and in part because refinements based on racial categorizations are anathema to the Constitution:

> In the administration of public schools by the state and local authorities it is permissible to consider the racial makeup of schools and to adopt general policies to encourage a diverse student body, one aspect of which is its racial composition. If school authorities are concerned that the student-body compositions of certain schools interfere with the objective of offer-

ing an equal educational opportunity to all of their students, they are free to devise race-conscious measures to address the problem in a general way and without treating each student in different fashion solely on the basis of a systematic, individual typing by race.[55]

The approaches listed by Justice Kennedy generally do have merit, some more than others.[56] For example, districts might create magnet programs to encourage students to travel outside their neighborhoods to attend school.[57] Dual-language Spanish magnet schools are, when successful, a particularly effective way of achieving racial integration through race-neutral methods. Although the immediate goal of such a school is language acquisition, it is also likely to foster racial diversity.[58] Nonetheless, there is little evidence that such magnet school programs alone can achieve racial integration; racial diversity is at best a collateral benefit of these programs.[59]

In addition to themed magnet programs, special programs such as the International Baccalaureate and Advanced Placement might attract a racially diverse group of students. Typically, a special program is started in a school with a high percentage of neighborhood students of color in an attempt to draw white students to that school.[60] However, even when such programs successfully create an integrated student body, they sometimes fail to achieve true integration because of resegregation within the school itself, through tracking.[61] An "integrated" school serves no purpose if mostly white students are enrolled in special programs while primarily nonwhite students are enrolled in the school's general programs.

Redrawing attendance boundaries is another approach districts might take to mitigate racial segregation. In many districts, attendance boundaries are typically redrawn every few years—each time districts plan to open, close, or consolidate schools, or to address significant changes in student enrollment. This provides an opportunity for districts to regularly consider student demographics.[62] Many districts today have sophisticated planning software that can consider district demographics and project the impact of a change in the attendance boundary on an individual school's enrollment. Although adjusting attendance boundaries can raise sensitive political issues, racial diversity can legitimately be among the many goals school officials consider during the process.[63]

A school or district might also try to attract a diverse group of students and faculty with targeted recruiting and outreach methods. Potential strategies include information and leaflets in multiple languages aimed at attracting a broad range of students, door-to-door outreach in particular communities, partnerships with local community centers or civil organizations, mentoring programs, and open-houses for students of designated racial groups.[64] These strategies might be particularly effective in attracting and retaining a diverse student body for new magnet programs or other special programs, as described above.

It should also be noted here that the aforementioned approaches (as well as the approaches used in Seattle and Louisville) are designed for school districts large enough to support more than one school at both the elementary and secondary level. Smaller school districts that have, for example, only one high school might pursue the involvement of and cooperation with neighboring districts to improve racial diversity. In 2007, for instance, Omaha Public Schools joined with the eleven surrounding school districts to form a metropolitan learning community.[65]

Without questioning the merit of any of these approaches, in many districts it seems unlikely that they, alone or in combination, will be sufficient to substantially mitigate racial isolation or achieve a diverse student population. We turn then to a race-neutral alternative that districts are increasingly considering: policies that take into account a student's socioeconomic status.

Race-neutral, socioeconomic integration strategies

With the movement away from race-conscious policies, a trend that long preceded the recent *PICS* decision, greater attention has been paid to the use of policies that integrate students according to socioeconomic status.[66] Such plans generally constrain parental choice to the extent that a given choice would increase socioeconomic segregation. If a predominantly biracial district has a sizable overlap between socioeconomic status and race, racial integration can become a collateral benefit of socioeconomic integration. Moreover, socioeconomic integration has benefits of its own.[67] However, integration by socioeconomic status has not succeeded in desegregating public schools, particularly in large, multiracial, urban districts, despite the strong correlation between race and socioeconomic status in the American population.[68] Kaufman states that it is significant that

> Justice Kennedy does not include socio-economic integration strategies among the methods that school districts must exhaust before using explicitly racial classifications. Perhaps . . . he is aware of the overwhelming data demonstrating that reliance on socio-economic status does not advance the goal of racial integration in schools.[69]

Furthermore, and notwithstanding Kaufman's correct statement that the concurrence does not include socioeconomic integration in the list of possible approaches, Justice Kennedy does include the following, which addresses the issues of proxies and, indirectly, socioeconomic integration policies:

> If it is legitimate for school authorities to work to avoid racial isolation in their schools, must they do so only by indirection and general policies? Does the Constitution mandate this inefficient result? Why may the authorities not recognize the problem in candid fashion and solve it altogether through resort to direct assignments based on student racial classifications? . . . If race is the problem, then perhaps race is the solution. [But this] argument ignores the dangers presented by individual classifications, dangers that are not as pressing when the same ends are achieved by more indirect means. . . . The idea that if race is the problem, race is the instrument with which to solve it cannot be accepted as an analytical leap forward.[70]

Reading the Kennedy concurrence as a whole, the door appears to be open for the constrained choice policies that use socioeconomic status, or for other decisionmaking using socioeconomic status, even if those individual characteristics are used for "indirection" as a proxy for race. Policy success, however, does not necessarily follow from legality; in many districts, a socioeconomic desegregation plan will likely do little to further the goal of avoiding racial segregation.

Louisville's revised plan

In late January 2008, the Jefferson County school board passed a temporary desegregation plan that uses geography instead of race and would apply to children entering first grade, those new to the district, those who have moved, and those requesting transfers.[71] These students would be assigned "so that elementary schools have at least 15 percent and no more than 50 percent of their enrollment from school residential areas with minority populations of at least 45 percent."[72] The superintendent was quoted as saying, "This is not much different than the way we have operated in the past. . . . We are just using the geographic area of a school's 'resides area' and not a student's race."[73] This plan was immediately challenged in court, but the judge rejected the plaintiff's request for a temporary injunction.[74]

More recently, the Jefferson County school board voted unanimously to make the temporary geography-based student assignment plan permanent. This plan attempts to integrate students by two other factors in addition to race: income level and parents' level of educational attainment.[75] Under this proposal, elementary, middle, and high schools must enroll at least 15 percent and no more than 50 percent of their students from designated neighborhoods—those that have income and education levels below the district average and that have above average numbers of minorities.[76] The plan is race conscious but nonindividualized and, in contrast to the temporary plan, race is only one factor in the general (nonindividualized) line drawing. This new geography-based plan will be implemented in the Jefferson County Schools in the 2008–09 academic year.

This proposal for a permanent plan seems in line with the Kennedy concurrence. Yet a legal challenge seems probable if the plan is adopted. Moreover, the geography-based plan will have a more attenuated link to race than the plan declared unconstitutional—meaning that racial segregation patterns may reemerge.

Individualized, holistic approach

If a school district can demonstrate that it has exhausted its race-neutral and nonindividualized race-conscious options, the Kennedy concurrence suggests that it can then legally implement an assignment system with an individualized, holistic use of race among other demographic (and nondemographic) factors. Some magnet high schools that have competitive admissions processes might, in particular, be able to imitate the affirmative action programs of colleges and universities.[77]

This step-by-step approach—first trying race-neutral and nonindividualized race-conscious measures, and then moving to individualized measures by holistic analyses of student applications—will demand a great deal of documentation (in anticipation of court challenges if the latter stage is reached). But it does leave open practical options for those districts with the political will and resources to walk through the steps and implement the sort of holistic review suggested by Justice Kennedy. In some districts, race-neutral and nonindividualized race-conscious approaches might be sufficient to achieve racial integration; other districts might be able to implement a school choice plan employing a nuanced, individualized assessment of multiple student characteristics, including race. As Ryan explains, "A lot would depend on the size of the district, the degree of residential segregation, the amount of economic diversity and the degree to which income and race correlate in that district, and the scope of the student assignment plan."[78] Although process details would vary between districts, the Court's decision has left tools in place for districts to use if they want to mitigate racial segregation.

San Francisco Unified School District (SFUSD) may be among the first school districts to pursue Justice Kennedy's conditional option—to implement individualized but holistic analyses of student applications, having tried and found lacking various race-neutral and nonindividualized race-conscious approaches. Several members of the SFUSD school board have in fact stated that they believe San Francisco could be a test case, given its recent attempts at nonindividualized policies.[79] SFUSD currently uses a "diversity index" to assign students if a school is oversubscribed. The index considers five race-neutral factors: language spoken at home, free or reduced-price lunch eligibility, public housing eligibility, academic performance, and the quality of the child's prior schools.[80] However, the race-neutral diversity index has not eliminated racially isolated schools; SFUSD general counsel David Campos explained: "San Francisco has [tried race-neutral options] . . . but [they] haven't worked and many schools have resegregated."[81] It is likely that other districts, including Seattle and Lynn, will also investigate their options down the line if they find that race-neutral and nonindividualized race-conscious policies do not adequately mitigate racial isolation or achieve a diverse student population.

Conflation of Compelling Interests

At one point, Justice Kennedy's concurrence clearly identifies two separate compelling interests: "A compelling interest exists in avoiding racial isolation, an interest that a school district, in its discretion and expertise, may choose to pursue. Likewise, a district may consider it a compelling interest to achieve a diverse student population."[82] But the discussion earlier in his concurrence of the race-neutral and nonindividualized race-conscious options that districts must pursue prior to using individualized, race-conscious criteria seems to conflate the two interests: "In the administration of public schools by the state and local authorities it is permissible to consider the racial makeup of schools and to adopt general policies to encourage a diverse student body, one aspect of which is its racial composition."[83]

This raises the question of whether these various steps outlined by Justice Kennedy are only necessary if a district is pursuing "diversity" rather than trying to mitigate racial isolation. Generally speaking, a narrowly tailored analysis is inextricably linked to the relevant compelling interest, so a compelling interest in mitigating racial isolation will require narrowly tailored policies that are different from the narrowly tailored policies required to pursue a compelling interest in diversity. Given that diversity concerns a variety of factors (including race) while racial isolation concerns only race, it would seem logical that a policy could be race focused if it is pursuing only the compelling interest of avoiding racial isolation.

Yet this logic must be tempered by Justice Kennedy's antipathy toward race-conscious, individualized policies. School districts would be well advised to pursue nonindividualized policies—like the one Louisville is now pursuing—before pursuing any policy that uses race for individualized decisionmaking.

Guidelines for Future Policies

According to Justice Kennedy's concurrence, school officials can take race-neutral steps to try to achieve their compelling interest in avoiding racially isolated schools.[84] They can also apply nonindividualized race-conscious policies in pursuing this goal. In fact, he concludes that such race-neutral and nonindividualized race-conscious policies should not trigger strict scrutiny. Finally, if these approaches do not, or cannot, adequately further the compelling interest, then districts can also take race explicitly into account in an individualized way, but "only if they are a last resort to achieve a compelling interest."[85] And these individualized race-conscious policies must be holistic; race can only be considered as part of a personalized, comprehensive review akin to the law school admissions process approved in *Grutter* and may not be used as a "tiebreaker" to determine a student's school assignment. But, as James Ryan notes, beyond those basic rules "it gets sketchy."[86] It is unclear, for example, how a district should demonstrate that race-neutral and nonindividualized race-conscious measures have not and will not work to achieve racial diversity. There are no guidelines suggesting how much or what kind of evidence is required before a district can legally consider individual students' race when assigning them to schools. Moreover, the task of proving that race-neutral alternatives failed is made harder by the fact that the district must prove a negative; at some point districts must demonstrate the very opposite of what they are hoping to achieve.[87]

Assuming that a district is in fact able to provide sufficient proof that race-neutral and nonindividualized race-conscious alternatives have failed, the question then becomes the exact nature of the allowed consideration of an individual student's race, which is not clear from the Kennedy concurrence.[88] Justice Kennedy suggests that such a consideration should be part of a broader assessment that includes "other demographic factors, plus special talents and needs."[89] However, no details or examples are provided as to what kinds of special talents or needs might be relevant.[90] And the concurrence acknowledges that consideration of special talents may be inappropriate for younger children. Finally, it is unclear what demographic factors may or should be considered alongside race and a child's special talents and needs. It would seem that a district may be allowed to seek policy remedies only to mitigate racial isolation, as opposed to pursuing an interest in broad-based diversity, since Justice Kennedy's *PICS* concurrence emphasizes the former as a compelling interest. But if that is the only goal, why should other demographic factors or elements of diversity be included in the consideration?[91]

What Justice Kennedy's concurrence clearly reflects is a dislike of any overt use of race not simultaneously accompanied by other demographic factors and his objection to using race as a decisive tiebreaker for oversubscribed schools.[92] Ryan cogently identifies this key point: "Justice Kennedy prefers the consideration of race to be obscured as much as possible."[93] This is one explanation for the ambiguity surrounding the consideration of race along with other, loosely described factors. It is also possible that this uncertainly could be designed to deter districts from pursuing policies that include individual consideration of race for fear of lawsuits alleging impermissible student assignment policies. From the concurrence in *PICS* as well as past opinions, it is reasonable to assume that Justice Kennedy would be most comfortable with the use of only race-neutral proxies to achieve racial diversity in schools.

Justice Kennedy's opinion was welcomed by some civil rights advocates for its rejection of the plurality's invocation of a "colorblind" society and for its acknowledgment of the importance of the nation's historical struggle to establish racial justice.[94] In fact, the *PICS* decision marked the first time that a majority of justices recognized compelling interests in promoting student diversity and avoiding racial segregation in K–12 schools.[95] Perhaps most important was Justice Kennedy's recognition of avoiding racial isolation as a compelling interest that school districts can pursue: "To the extent the plurality opinion suggests the Constitution mandates that state and local school authorities must accept the status quo of racial isolation in schools, it is, in my view, profoundly mistaken."[96]

However, his opinion lacks clarity concerning when and how a district can move beyond marginally effective race-neutral and nonindividualized race-conscious policies. As Nussbaum states, "This all-important opinion is a cipher: it did not announce a set of workable criteria that might possibly substitute for the Seattle criteria, which Justice Kennedy rejected on utterly unclear grounds."[97] While the *PICS* decision should be read as allowing districts to continue to pursue racial integration, it cannot easily be read as explaining exactly how they can legally do so. Implicitly recognizing that ambiguity, Justice Kennedy's concurrence ends by essentially calling on school districts to find creative ways of carrying out their policies within his guidelines:

> Those entrusted with directing our public schools can bring to bear the creativity of experts, parents, administrators, and other concerned citizens to find a way to achieve the compelling interests they face without resorting to widespread governmental allocation of benefits and burdens on the basis of racial classifications.[98]

CONCLUSION

The *PICS* case, and in particular the Kennedy concurrence, established guidelines for voluntary racial integration policies that districts should attempt to follow if they seek to mitigate racial isolation. Justice Kennedy's controlling concurrence concluded that the government can indeed have a compelling interest to mitigate racial isolation in our nation's public schools. However, the key guideline underlying Kennedy's concurrence is that unless other options have been exhausted, a decision about an individual student cannot hinge on that student's race.

As a practical matter, this means that school district leaders who choose to confront patterns of racial segregation should pursue race neutral and non-individualized race-conscious policies. They can draw attendance boundaries to mitigate the effects of housing segregation. They can, in a district using school choice, advertise extensively in minority communities, trumpeting the opportunities available at a school with few minorities currently enrolled—and vice versa. Another option not mentioned by Justice Kennedy but consistent with his reasoning would be the strategic placement of academic programs, such as providing resource teachers for English-language learners at a school currently enrolling few Latino students. The concurrence also appears to allow for the use of proxies, such as family socioeconomic status, that may help decrease racial isolation. Finally, the Kennedy concurrence suggests that if these efforts fail to adequately mitigate segregation, then the racial classifications of individual students might be used as a last resort, but only as one consideration in a broader diversity plan. It remains to be seen how the competitive law school model, holistically considering the merits of an applicant, would translate to the "application" of a K–12 student to a noncompetitive public school.[99]

The *PICS* plurality concluded by declaring that "the way to stop discrimination on the basis of race is to stop discriminating on the basis of race."[100]

It's a simple equation, with a superficial attraction. Court orders and race-conscious policies were always a Band-Aid on larger, endemic issues of race and poverty in the United States. Necessity being the mother of invention, perhaps educational leaders and others will answer Justice Kennedy's call for "creativity" and truly address some of those larger, endemic issues rather than resign themselves to the constantly increasing segregation of the past two decades.

Unitary Status
Policy Levers and Legal Landscapes

CHAPTER FOUR

Equal Educational Opportunity, School Reform, and the Courts

A Study of the Desegregation Litigation in San Jose

William S. Koski and Jeannie Oakes

In the aftermath of *Brown v. Board of Education of Topeka* and the struggle to achieve integration in our nation's schools, commentators have alternately bemoaned and celebrated the role of the courts in the quest for equal educational opportunity. Court critics have decried the "imperialist" judiciary's desegregation mandates, claiming that such intervention violates the hallowed principles of federalism, separation of powers, and local control.[1] Court advocates, however, have lauded such intervention as the only means to craft social policy that respects the rights of the politically powerless.[2] Ideological arguments aside, many pragmatic scholars and researchers have questioned, as a theoretical and empirical matter, whether courts are able to bring about social change and equal educational opportunities at all.[3]

This chapter enters the fracas between the courts and school reform by analyzing the desegregation litigation and efforts to create educational equality in San Jose, California. We provide an account of the 37-year-old San Jose Unified School District desegregation litigation and its effect on educational policy in the district. Specifically, we ask two related questions: What was the role of the court in setting the conditions for equity-minded educational policy reform? Did those policies result in greater equality of educational opportunity and outcomes?

Employing a detailed archival review of legal documents and press reports, as well as interviews with key policy players, we describe the political and institutional conditions under which the U.S. district court sought first to bring about racial/ethnic balance in the district and later to reform the district's educational policies to promote greater equality and high academic achievement for all of its students. We provide evidence that, although judicial intervention alone cannot bring about educational change, it may facilitate educational change in at least three ways: a judicial order can provide disentrenchment of powerful political interests, "cover" for policy elites who seek to implement equity-minded school reform, and the normative pressure necessary for relevant constituencies to work toward school reform. More important, the San Jose case shows that courts can alter the structural conditions of political conflict and bargaining to facilitate the participation of traditionally disadvantaged communities that would not otherwise occur in a majoritarian political process. Finally, the chapter studies the question of whether or not the litigation-induced policy reforms in San Jose actually resulted in greater equality of educational outcomes on the ground. Analyzing data collected during the litigation and publicly available data about the district after its release from court supervision, we seek to understand the extent to which the district's efforts to detrack its schools and provide college opportunities for all have been successful.

BEYOND THE "DYNAMIC" AND "CONSTRAINED" COURT: THE "NEW MEANING" OF JUDICIAL REVIEW

In his seminal work, *The Hollow Hope*, Gerald Rosenberg weaves together two competing paradigms of courts as change agents in social policymaking: the "dynamic" (or "strong") court perspective and the "constrained" court perspective.[4] The dynamic court view argues that because courts enjoy relative economic and institutional independence from the executive and legislative branches (collectively, the political branches), they can act when the legislative and executive branches are unable or unwilling to do so. Moreover, because federal judges are appointed to life tenures on "good behavior," they are shielded from electoral politics and from the public, constituency, and interest group pressures that the political branches face. Finally, because judicial decisions turn on legal rights and the quality of argument rather than political power, even weak and unpopular groups can prevail (i.e., courts provide a counter-majoritarian check on the political branches).

A constrained court perspective, on the other hand, posits that courts face three major hurdles that prevent them from making social policy that differs from that which the political branches would produce: (1) the rights constraint, (2) the independence constraint, and (3) the capacity constraint. Rosenberg succinctly describes the rights constraint as "the bounded nature of constitutional rights [that] prevents courts from hearing or effectively acting on many significant social reform claims."[5] This is the formal institutional component of rights and is embedded in the text of the U.S. Constitution and its interpretive case law, and it is given teeth by the doctrine of *stare decisis* (i.e., the rule that requires courts to abide by precedent laid down in previous cases). In school desegregation cases in particular and school reform cases in general, a long line of case law interpreting the Equal Protection and Due Process clauses of the Fourteenth Amendment to the U.S. Constitution places a formal constraint on district court judges who want to apply that law to a perceived educational wrong. This limited-nature-of-rights constraint is one institutional hurdle that prevented integration-minded plaintiffs and courts from attacking segregation in the North and West (including San Jose) until the U.S. Supreme Court's seminal decision in *Keyes v. Denver School District No. 1*, which provided guidance to plaintiffs seeking to demonstrate that school board decisions that would result in maintaining or exacerbating racial segregation could be evidence of segregative intent, even without a segregation policy on the books.

Beyond the rights constraint, Rosenberg argues, courts will not produce social policy that is meaningfully different from the political branches because they are not, in fact, politically or economically independent of the political branches. If the political branches disagree with judicial rulings, they can repeal statutes, amend the Constitution, or simply ignore the judicial interpretation.[6]

Having determined that a school system practice violates some legal right, the court is left to craft and implement an effective equitable remedy that will place the aggrieved plaintiffs in the position they would enjoy had they never been wronged. Such remedy should also prevent future constitutional violations. The capacity limitation is rooted in the simple notions that courts lack the social fact-finding tools to develop appropriate policies and that they do not run schools on a day-to-day basis and therefore cannot directly implement remedial decrees.[7] Many have argued, however, that the alleged inability of courts to discover the relevant social facts and design remedial policy in desegregation cases is overstated. With reliance on expert witnesses and court-appointed special masters, judicial fact-finding is no worse and may be better than legislative fact-finding.[8] Moreover, many courts have left the remedial decree design process to the local education officials or to both parties in the suit through consent decree bargaining.[9] Finally, courts have developed a variety of tools to assist them in remedial decree implementation, including task forces, magistrates, monitors, and masters.[10]

Just over a decade after Rosenberg proclaimed the promise of court-induced social change a "hollow hope," some scholars have begun to take a fresh look at public law litigation and the role of courts in restructuring public agencies. Among them, James Liebman, Charles Sabel, and William Simon have specifically considered the role of courts in school reform, and their assessment of the potential for judicial success is far less gloomy.[11] Rather than viewing the court as an institution that simply hands down remedial orders in a traditional "command-and-control" model of bureaucratic reform, courts are taking an "experimentalist" approach to school reform. Instead of issuing top-down, inputs-oriented, fixed-rule decrees, courts are now called upon to destabilize or disentrench embedded and powerful political interests that have systematically failed to meet their obligations to schoolchildren and remain immune to traditional forces of political correction. The role of the court, then, is to restructure traditional political bargaining so that all relevant constituencies may negotiate a settlement that reforms complex institutions, like schools. Significantly, courts are not charged with fixing schools; they are simply called upon to monitor the performance of schools (or states or school districts) against agreed-upon educational outcomes. When schools fail to perform as required, the court—prompted by litigation—can provide a forum for "new publics" of reform-minded constituencies, particularly those whose voices go unheard in traditional political fora, to restructure the school to achieve success. Like Rosenberg's thesis, the experimentalist model does not posit that courts alone are sufficient to bring about school reform. But, unlike Rosenberg's thesis, the experimentalist accepts a judicial role in a *political* process evolving toward the improvement of conditions for the traditionally politically powerless. As Sabel and Liebman put it, "These . . . developments suggest the possibility of a non-court-centric form of judicial review that preserves the capacity for constitutional deliberation as a form of reflection on the deepest norms of the political community, while substantially lessening the intrusiveness of the judiciary and so tempering the counter-majoritarian dilemma."[12] With this framework in mind, we turn to San Jose.

SCHOOL DESEGREGATION IN SAN JOSE: THE COURT AND EQUAL OPPORTUNITY

Situated in the South San Francisco Bay Area, the San Jose Unified School District stretches nearly sixteen miles in a banana-like fashion from the Bayshore Freeway in the north to the Almaden Valley in the south. The width of the district varies from its narrowest point in the south (one and one-half miles) to its thicker midsection (four miles). Since World War II, ethnic minorities— primarily Mexican Americans at first and later a much smaller Vietnamese American population—tended to settle in the northern downtown portion of the district. The Almaden Valley, which is parceled into tranquilly named suburbs like Willow Glen, is the home of a largely white and to a lesser extent Asian American population. The district currently boasts forty-one schools: twenty-eight elementary schools, six middle schools, and seven high schools. In 2006–07 it enrolled 31,097 students who are classified in seven different racial/ethnic groups: 1.0 percent American Indian; 12.7 percent Asian; 0.6 percent Pacific Islander; 1.8 percent Filipino; 51.3 percent Latino; 3.5 percent African American; and 28.0 percent white.[13] The district has not always been majority "minority." Indeed, until the 1990s, white students were the majority in the district. Like many California school districts, San Jose has witnessed a growing Latino population since the 1960s. How the district provided (or did not provide) equal educational opportunities to that growing population is at the heart of this chapter.

Early Warning Signs and the (Halfhearted) Effort to Stave Off History

Since at least 1964, San Jose district officials had known that their schools were ethnically segregated.[14] In 1962, the district's Board of Trustees (Board) publicly stated that de facto segregation was inherently harmful and in 1963 acknowledged the increasing balkanization of ethnic groups in the residential areas of the district. So concerned was the Board that it commissioned a study of racial/ethnic segregation in its schools and found in 1964 that the residential pattern was reflected in the district's schools. In 1966, the State of California found ethnic segregation in the district and urged the district to voluntarily take steps to desegregate its schools or risk losing some $1.25 million in state and federal categorical funding. Two years later, a report commissioned by the Santa Clara County Office of Education confirmed the state's findings and recommended busing as a strategy to alleviate the "deleterious effects" of ethnic imbalance in San Jose's schools. Foreshadowing the desegregation problem of the 1980s and 1990s, Superintendent George Downing expressed doubts that a busing plan would achieve integration because students tend to stay with their own ethnic groups in the hallways and classrooms of "desegregated" schools.[15] Although Downing and the Board supported efforts to beef up the educational services in the downtown schools, neither was willing to pursue busing as a remedy for ethnic imbalance in the schools.

By 1969, however, Downing and the all-white, five-member Board could no longer delay. In a February 10, 1969, board meeting, in response to another warning from the state and in an abrupt reversal of position, Downing "reaffirm[ed the district's] commitment to a high quality integrated education program."[16] Downing cited the district's efforts to improve educational services in the mostly Latino downtown schools.[17] "In spite of these and other efforts," Downing lamented, "we continue to face the problem of the minority student who finds himself isolated from the larger community and who feels almost total frustration in his attempt for positive self-identification."[18] Recognizing the potential for busing, however, the Board tapped the brakes by appointing a community advisory group to provide recommendations for what it called the "primary objective" of integrating the district's schools.[19]

This study group, known as the Quality Urban Education Study Team (QUEST), would prove to be the early flashpoint for the busing debate in San Jose. Initially, QUEST was composed of people dedicated to achieving the goal of integration—through busing if necessary. The Board remained cool to busing, however, and repeatedly discouraged QUEST from recommending it. In what is now a familiar story, the antibusing forces began to organize.[20] At a board meeting on February 5, 1970, busing opponents demanded that QUEST be opened up to antibusing advocates and pledged to organize to oppose busing. Just two months later, Parents for Better Education (PBE) was formed, claiming a membership of one thousand and calling for the seats of those Board members who would not oppose busing.[21] The Board acquiesced and not only opened QUEST's membership to PBE, but also altered QUEST's mission from the primary goal of integration to the "long-term priority" of integration.[22] Now more important to the Board was the maintenance of its neighborhood school policy—a policy under which the Board neutrally assigned its students without regard to race or ethnicity. As long as the policy was strictly followed, according to district theory, the district could not be deemed unlawfully segregated.

After nine months of wrangling, QUEST recommended that the Board and its new superintendent, Charles Knight, adopt a desegregation plan developed by San Jose State University professor Robert Sasseen, based largely on open enrollment/voluntary transfers, magnet schools, and the long-term plan of a large educational complex. Knight approved of many of the recommendations, but the Board was losing interest in desegregation and did not act on them. Instead, the Board's attention turned toward the extreme overcrowding in the Almaden Valley schools and the rebuilding of many schools that had been condemned by state law. Under California's 1933 Field Act legislation, school districts were required to build and maintain their school buildings so they could withstand an earthquake of a certain magnitude. Thirteen San Jose schools did not meet state standards and the Board voted to close, raze, and rebuild those Field Act schools. The combined result of continued residential growth in the Valley and Field Act condemnations was double sessions and unhappy, vocal, influential parents.

The Board's primary response was to ask the voters for money. To fund the school rebuilding effort, the Board held bond elections in 1971, 1972, and 1973, threatening double sessions and more busing should the bond measures fail. All three failed, despite the call to relieve overcrowding. The Almaden Valley responded by suggesting that its children be permitted to transfer to the nearby, below-capacity Cambrian and Union school districts. Superintendent Knight approved of the interdistrict idea and the Board adopted it unanimously in a vote on May 16, 1974. Four days later, however, the Board rescinded the measure on the advice of counsel. Such a breach of the district's neighborhood school policy could be perceived as a chink in the district's armored defense against busing.

The Almaden Valley parents were not the only parents concerned about how the district would deal with overflowing schools. Led by a Latino advocacy group called *La Confederación de la Raza Unida*, the Chicano Teachers Association, and the federally funded Model Cities employees, Latinos in the district fought in 1973 for the rebuilding of the condemned Wilson Middle School on the same downtown spot where it had previously been located. Model Cities and the *Confederación* had long pressured the district for better schools downtown. But the Wilson School had been located in a Latino neighborhood and would inevitably be opened as an ethnically imbalanced Latino school. Yet the coalition of Latino groups was unconcerned with ethnic imbalance—they wanted their neighborhood school back. More to the point, Wilson became the symbol of and rallying point for the growing dissatisfaction among Latinos with the district's perceived mistreatment of their children. Poor reading scores, poorly trained teachers, and almost no bilingual/bicultural education evidenced that educational mistreatment. But the litigation-conscious (certainly not integration-conscious) Board chose not to rebuild Wilson, instead expanding the nearby Hoover site on the grounds that it did not want to exacerbate ethnic imbalance.

The overcrowding issue was resolved by rebuilding eleven Field Act schools and a decline in student enrollment during the baby bust. As for the idea of using busing to alleviate ethnic imbalance, the district attempted to seal busing's coffin with an August 1974 poll of district parents that found busing to be unpopular. The poll found that 82 percent of all parents opposed "forced, mandatory busing," 74 percent of Mexican American parents opposed such busing, and 20 percent of all parents opposed even voluntary busing.[23] But the district's treatment of the QUEST recommendations, the busing issue, and the Field Act schools would have repercussions.

The Case That (Almost) Nobody Noticed

In the autumn of 1971 and in the wake of the QUEST maelstrom, two Mexican American families—the families Diaz and Vasquez—sued the district to stop it from rebuilding the condemned Field Act schools on their original sites because such school siting would only perpetuate and exacerbate the district's ethnic segregation. Arnulfo and Socorro Diaz were no activists.[24] They simply saw that the Almaden Valley schools were better than those their children attended and they felt this was the result of ethnic discrimination. They attended and spoke at meetings to find out why, but no one listened. Jose Vasquez was an activist. He was the leader of *La Confederación de la Raza Unida*. But in filing the lawsuit against the district, neither Vasquez nor the Diazes had the full support of the Latino community or even the *Confederación*. The Diazes were ridiculed at church for publicly challenging the district; they even received death threats. They felt, and may have been, only "three Mexican American parents" (neither the Mexican American community nor civil rights leaders), as the press consistently portrayed them.

Arguing on behalf of the families and all Spanish-surnamed parents and students in the district, attorneys from Santa Clara County Community Legal Services (Legal Aid) sued to obtain a restraining order from the federal district court that would halt the rebuilding of eleven Field Act schools. The Legal Aid lawyers asserted that rebuilding the schools would perpetuate ethnic segregation in violation of the equal protection clause and Title VI of the Civil Rights Act.[25] Judge Robert Peckham of the Northern District of California tentatively agreed and issued a restraining order that blocked reconstruction of the schools pending further hearings. In a statement issued by the Board of Trustees, however, the district vowed to "vigorously resist" the plaintiffs' effort to extend the order.[26] Two months later, the district prevailed, as Peckham lifted the order and refused to grant a preliminary injunction. Peckham found that the district had never segregated its students by law and the plaintiffs hadn't shown how the district acted to create ethnic imbalance in the schools. But he warned the district in that early hearing that if the district rebuilt the schools without regard to ethnic balance, "they might very well bring busing on their heads."[27] The district largely ignored the warning and rebuilt nine of the eleven schools on their original sites, hoping the Latino litigants would go away.

They didn't. In 1973, the Supreme Court handed down the *Keyes* decision and provided guidance to desegregation advocates on how to prove intentional discrimination in the absence of a segregating statute. In July 1975, the Diazes, Vasquezes, and Legal Aid dragged the district back into court for a ten-day trial on whether the district's policies were intended to isolate Latino students. Almost necessarily, the district admitted that its schools were ethnically imbalanced, but it maintained that it did nothing to cause the segregation. Rather, it hewed to its neutral neighborhood school policy—the de facto segregation resulted from the "uncontrollable" residential choices of ethnic groups in the district.[28]

Legal Aid, following the prescription of the *Keyes* decision, marched through nearly a dozen Board policy decisions that allegedly resulted in the perpetuation and exacerbation of ethnic imbalance. The plaintiffs pointed out that the district had known of the segregation since the mid-1960s, yet it had opened nine ethnically imbalanced schools since 1965. It raised the specter of busing in its 1971 probond election propaganda. It reconstituted QUEST under community antibusing pressure. It deviated from its neighborhood school policy, if only for a few days. Finally, it ignored warnings from the State Board of Education (SBE) that it had to take steps to integrate its schools.[29]

Peckham considered the plaintiffs' arguments but was not persuaded.[30] He rebutted each of plaintiffs' factual allegations with the two-pronged observation that (1) the extant ethnic imbalance was the product of the neutral and educationally sound neighborhood school policy, and (2) the district was under no affirmative duty to integrate, even if it had passed up opportunities to do so. In sum, the segregation was not intentional. Peckham again warned the district, however, that he did not "intend to brand the current allocation of students with a judicial imprimatur, or to discourage the school board from attempting to improve racial balance in the school system."[31] Nevertheless, the district ignored Peckham's admonition. The plaintiff families were not content with Peckham's decision and appealed it.

A three-judge panel of the reputedly activist Ninth Circuit Court of Appeals found in November 1979 that Peckham had applied the wrong standard for intentional discrimination and they remanded the case to Peckham for further consideration.[32] The judges' opinion suggests that Peckham improperly found that the district's ethnically neutral neighborhood school policy "constituted either a complete defense to a charge of segregative intent, or, completely dispelled the inferences of segregative intent that flowed from the proof."[33] The Ninth Circuit instructed Peckham to take a look at all of the evidence and draw inferences regarding intent. In response, Peckham issued a lengthy opinion in 1981 that did not change his initial conclusion: in light of all the evidence, the district did not intend to segregate students through its policies.[34] It was beginning to seem as though educational equity would not come to San Jose through judicial action.

Local Politics and External Pressures: San Jose's Tepid Response

It was no secret that San Jose's schools were segregated. Yet in the years since the Board had acknowledged such segregation in 1964, there was little grassroots political pressure to desegregate San Jose's schools. Up until 1979, press accounts identify only a few lonely voices calling for desegregation: former teacher and trustee Mary McCreath, the families Diaz and Vasquez, Legal Aid, and certain members of QUEST. More important, the south side families continued to resist desegregation that would require mandatory busing of their children. Despite the absence of meaningful internal pressure for desegregation, the Board was forced to consider desegregation as external pressure mounted.

Throughout the late 1960s and into 1971, the Board received periodic warnings from the State of California that the ethnic imbalance in its schools violated California policy. In the summer of 1975, the County of Santa Clara Human Relations Commission held sparsely attended hearings on segregation in the schools, while the education chair of the NAACP flew into town to condemn school segregation.[35] The district did nothing. Not until the SBE promulgated desegregation rules did the district reluctantly move. In April 1978, the SBE issued a directive that required all districts in the state, by July 1, 1979, to submit a desegregation plan, show that they are desegregated, or prove that they cannot be desegregated.[36] Not straying from its modus operandi, the Board did not publicly address the SBE rules until January 1979, when it authorized yet another citizens advisory commission to study the problem and make recommendations. The commission was not appointed until mid-March 1979 and did not have its first meeting until May. By then it was clear that the district would miss the July 1 deadline. This time the SBE would not permit the district to flout its order, as SBE president Michael Kirst threatened the district with financial penalties and possible court action. This prompted a fire drill. In a little more than three months, the sixty-five-member commission defined "desegregation" for San Jose schools and developed a five-year plan to "desegregate" the schools. Still, the plan was late and not implemented by a required September 1979 deadline, but SBE imposed no sanctions.

The five-year voluntary desegregation plan was again based on magnet schools. Under the plan's lenient definition of "segregated," only fourteen San Jose schools, all of which were downtown, were out of compliance and needed to be desegregated. The proposed special programs and magnets included gifted-and-talented programs, "back-to-basics" schools, creative and performing arts schools, and science/environmental programs (only some of which would be in downtown schools). The objective of the plan was the actual elimination of segregation in *all* district schools by 1985. The glitch in the plan, however, was its dependence on unsecured federal funding. In 1980, only $500,000 in district funds and another $710,000 from the Emergency School Aid Act (ESAA) had been committed to the plan (the ESAA would shortly be repealed by Congress). The district also sought an additional $1.8 million in funds from the choice-friendly, antibusing Reagan administration under a federal program that encouraged the development of magnet schools. Washington initially rejected that request because San Jose's plan was not as well-developed as other cities' plans, the district was moving too slowly, and it had been cited by the Office for Civil Rights (OCR) for violating the rights of limited English proficient (LEP) students. Hobbled from the outset by limited funds and hasty preparations and later wracked by the district's 1983 fiscal bankruptcy, the plan did little to create ethnic balance in the schools. In fact, by 1985, thirteen schools remained ethnically unbalanced under the commission's own definition.

More important, the desegregation plan did little to address the desires of the Latino students and families it was intended to benefit. Early in the citizens advisory commission's planning process, nine primarily Latino members defected from the commission and proposed their own desegregation plan. Calling themselves the Coalition for Downtown Schools and joined by educators from the downtown schools and Latino activist (and eventual plaintiff in the *Diaz* lawsuit), Jorge Gonzalez, the group advocated improved educational programs in downtown schools (both enriched courses and back-to-basics courses), bilingual/bicultural classes, and no mandatory busing. The coalition viewed the commission's definition of segregation as one that would disproportionately bus Latino children from their neighborhood schools, while white Almaden Valley children would more likely remain at home. The coalition's position was bolstered by a March 1980 OCR report finding that the district was violating the educational rights of LEP students under the OCR's Lau Guidelines.[37] The district's tepid response to external pressure was simply not enough.

The Courts Intervene: Remedying Unlawful Segregation (1985–2003)

Still not content with Peckham's 1981 ruling that the district had not intentionally segregated its students, Legal Aid and the Latino families again asked the Ninth Circuit to review the case. Initially, another three-judge panel voted two to one to uphold Peckham's conclusion,[38] but in May 1984, on the thirtieth anniversary of the *Brown* edict, an en banc panel of the Ninth Circuit reversed Peckham's decision in what would prove to be a watershed moment for San Jose's schools.[39] The Ninth Circuit noted that the district had catered to a public opposed to desegregation, had responded to overcrowding in the schools by instituting educationally disadvantageous double sessions to avoid transferring whites downtown, had assigned faculty and staff on the basis of ethnicity, had refused to respond to SBE admonitions to desegregate, and had sited new schools and rebuilt Field Act schools in a fashion that perpetuated and intensified ethnic imbalance. The court further opined that "an inescapable conclusion that the Board intended segregation emerges from a view of the evidence as a whole. The pattern of Board choices that consistently maintained or intensified segregation is apparent. . . . In almost every instance, the Board chose to 'turn toward segregation' rather than away from it."[40] In finding that the district acted with segregative intent, the Ninth Circuit did what Peckham would not; it aggressively interpreted the evidence against the district. The Ninth Circuit also did not do what Peckham had to do; translate this constitutional violation into an effective remedy.

Remedying unlawful segregation: Ethnic balance and
equal educational opportunity (1985–94)

Desegregation was coming to San Jose through Judge Peckham's courtroom, and the cast of characters before Peckham had changed to reflect the gravity of the matter. Though the Diazes and Vasquezes remained integral, important decisions regarding the plaintiffs' position in remedial proceedings were joined by an enlarged representative class of Latino plaintiffs, some of whom belonged to the Latino advocacy group *Raza Si*, headed by Jorge Gonzalez.

Strapped for resources and overwhelmed with its caseload, Legal Aid continued to be the lead attorneys on the matter, but it enlisted the support of the Mexican American Legal Defense and Education Fund (MALDEF) and its lead litigator (and former head of OCR) Norma Cantu to work through the remedial phase of the litigation. Perhaps most important to crafting a sensible and effective position on remedial issues, however, was the plaintiffs' decision to retain heavyweight desegregation expert, Charles Willie. Willie was a desegregation veteran and known for his support of ethnic/racial integration as a remedy for desegregation.

In the defendants' corner was also a new team. Hired in large part for his extensive and successful experience in desegregating Pasadena's schools, Ramon Cortines was appointed superintendent just prior to the commencement of the remedial phase. Cortines became instantly admired in San Jose and was perceived to be capable of making any desegregation plan work in the district.[41] The district also abandoned their local counsel, hiring Peter Collison, an experienced litigator and former big-firm lawyer to handle the remedial phase of negotiations and hearings. Finally, to go head to head with Willie, the district hired Christine Rossell to design their proposed remedial plan. Rossell too had testified in many desegregation matters and was known for her belief that "voluntary" desegregation plans were the most effective in attaining ethnic/racial balance and preventing "white flight."

Although the district had initially proposed a voluntary magnet program in July 1985, Peckham rejected that plan as inadequate and scheduled a ten-day hearing to develop a new plan.[42] The hearing was a classic battle of social science expertise and experienced conjecture. The two sides could not even agree on a definition of "desegregation," with the district proposing a definition that would result in far less ethnic mixing than the plaintiffs' definition. The district's plan continued to focus on voluntary desegregation through the establishment of four districtwide dedicated magnet schools and sixteen magnet programs. The plan was supported by Rossell's argument that mandatory student assignment and busing would prompt white flight, thereby leaving no white students to integrate in the district. Under the plaintiffs' "controlled choice" scheme, integration would not be left up to student and family choice. If a student chose not to attend a magnet, he would be permitted to rank his choice of school within his attendance zone but would only receive his preference if the preferred assignment met the ethnic composition goals. Otherwise, he would be mandatorily assigned a school. Finally, the plaintiffs proposed that an outside monitor oversee the implementation of the plan. This proposal and its threat of an accompanying loss of district control so incensed Superintendent Cortines that he threatened to quit his post if the monitor were appointed.[43]

Judge Peckham was largely sold on Rossell's thesis that mandatory busing caused white flight, and on New Year's Eve 1985, he basically adopted the district's strategy, save a few significant provisions. He maintained the district's focus on voluntary transfers, magnets, and enriched programs. Perhaps aware that the district itself would be charged with implementing the court's order, that significant portions of the Latino community were opposed to mandatory busing from their neighborhood schools, and that choice would likely result in greater parental and student satisfaction, Peckham refused to adopt the bulk of the plaintiffs' more rigid assignment plan. Though he feared white flight, Peckham did refuse to adopt the district's go-slow approach. Instead, he decided to set interim goals of having 60 percent of all students in desegregated schools by 1986–87, 70 percent by 1987–88, 80 percent by 1988–89, and 90 percent by 1989–90. Peckham finally insisted on establishing a court-appointed monitor to "function as the eyes and ears of the court, to ensure that the district carries out its desegregation responsibilities in compliance with [the] order."[44]

The plaintiffs nominated Beatriz Arias, a Stanford School of Education professor, to be the monitor. This was an educationally sound and politically savvy choice. Arias had served on the expert panel in the Los Angeles desegregation case, as court monitor in the Denver case, and, most important, as a teacher in the Pasadena district while Cortines was superintendent. "She's realistic, she's practical, and I believe that she will be objective with this community," Cortines said on the day of her appointment.[45]

On the first day of the plan's implementation—the first day of school, September 8, 1986—the biggest problems faced by the district were late buses, some longer-than-expected bus rides, a few missing crossing guards, and one or two students who didn't get picked up.[46] San Jose was a far cry from Little Rock (no official resistance), nor was it Boston (no organized and violent community resistance), nor was it Detroit (no significant white flight). The first day of busing was more media event than community crisis, as reporters poked microphones in students' faces and one district official took to the sky in a helicopter for a bird's-eye view of the yellow bus fleet. Before the first day, there had been some reason to be nervous, as one of the architects of the plan, Superintendent Cortines, resigned his post to take the superintendent's job in San Francisco and a handful of Almaden Valley parents calling themselves Save Our Schools threatened to disrupt the plan. But all went off pretty much without a hitch.

From that point forward, it was clear that Judge Peckham and company would be active in the ongoing implementation of his order. In addition to the semiannual reports, Peckham routinely requested that Arias study specific issues. Arias handled dozens of student appeals from the assignment system and her office grew into a $250,000-per-year operation. For the district's part, it tried to co-opt the monitoring process with its own office of integration and routine reporting. The relationship between the monitor's office and the district became something less than amicable, as the district ultimately sought limitations on the monitor's role. Peckham responded to that request with anger. "There has to be, during the life of this decree, continual and thorough monitoring by this court and by the court-appointed monitor," Peckham insisted, but "there's a hostility, almost, over the court having anything to do with this [plan] and the monitor having anything to do with this."[47]

How did the district perform? Money, for starters, was not a big issue. Most of the district desegregation expenses were reimbursed by the state—up to $3.1 million in first year alone.[48] By 1993, the district was receiving some $3.5 million in federal funds for magnet schools and up to $22.6 million in state reimbursements for busing, "direct and indirect costs of running the program," magnet programs and schools, dropout prevention, teacher training, and day care. "Desegregation has been our savior," proclaimed Norris Hill, the district's director of magnet programs in 1993.[49] As for the plan's ethnic-balancing provisions, the district performed better than anticipated. Faculty desegregation was achieved in the first year, 1986–87. Also in the first year, with some six thousand students on buses, 83 percent of the district's students were in desegregated schools, the district's third-year goal.[50] White flight was minimal, as district enrollment was within 1 percent of projections in the first year,[51] and only 3–6 percent of the white student population fled.[52] By the end of year two, 86 percent of the students were in desegregated schools;[53] by 1988–89, the district had met its 90 percent goal a year ahead of schedule; and by 1991, virtually all San Jose students were in desegregated schools.[54] The district was so confident about its success that it informally argued to Peckham in October 1990 that it had already complied with the *Dowell* (Oklahoma City) standard for unitary status.

Notwithstanding these successes, certain problems surfaced. The district's assignment system, which favored parents and students who signed up for schools in the spring before the following school year, disproportionately affected Latinos. Because Latinos tended to sign up and thereby rank-order their schools later than whites, far fewer Latinos received their first-choice schools.[55] Arias and others charged that the district's bilingual services were inadequate.[56] Latinos were bused more often than whites and typically spent more time on the buses. Arias (in 1988 and 1990) and the local newspaper (1991) also reported the rise of second-generation discrimination.[57] In 1991, Latinos were twice as likely as their classmates to be suspended, to drop out, or to be retained in grade.[58] Latinos scored roughly two grade levels below the district average on state achievement tests. Finally, within-school segregation, greater percentages of whites in advanced placement, college prep, and honors courses, and greater percentages of Latinos in remedial courses—became the norm.[59] Activists like Jorge Gonzalez of *Raza Si* lamented the inefficacy of the desegregation plan in bringing about educational equity. "I don't know exactly what we won," he mused.[60]

The failure to address the educational needs of Latino students was particularly glaring against the backdrop of changing district demographics. At the time Judge Peckham issued his initial remedial order, whites made up 57 percent of the student body and Hispanics made up 30 percent. By the 1992–93 school year, these figures had reversed: whites constituted only 30 percent while Hispanics had grown to 44 percent, and Asian Americans (13%) and African Americans (3%) accounted for the bulk of the remaining population. Ignoring the needs of the largest ethnic groups would be difficult.

Perhaps sensing plaintiff dissatisfaction with the busing aspects of the plan, probably emboldened by the Supreme Court's blueprint for unitary status in the *Pitts* and *Dowell* cases, and/or responding to pressure from white parents opposed to busing, the district finally filed a motion for unitary status on June 19, 1992. The decision to file was likely bolstered by the state's assurances that desegregation funds would not be cut off as long as the district continued to implement a desegregation plan.

Remedying unlawful segregation: School reform and
equal educational opportunity (1994–99)

Rather than acceding to the district's demands, the plaintiffs opposed the district's motion on the grounds that even if the ethnic balancing goals of the remedial decree were met, the "vestiges" of discrimination remained. Accordingly, they seized the unitary status motion as an opportunity to seek a modification to Peckham's remedial order that would correct the educational and second-generation discrimination problems that had arisen.

Within-school segregation was a particularly contentious issue because the desegregation efforts actually encouraged the practice of tracking. Successful desegregation of school sites depended on white parents' willingness to send their children to magnet schools in minority neighborhoods. Because white parents were considered more likely to participate in desegregation if their children were placed in separate, high-track classes, district officials readily embraced and accommodated tracking.[61] But in 1988, when Arias detailed the use of tracking to resegregate students within schools, the then-superintendent quickly replied, "As far as classroom segregation goes, this district has never segregated students ethnically."[62] Judge Peckham seemed to agree: "The limited classroom segregation that does exist appears to be justified by educationally and demographically valid considerations."[63]

However, the evidence would show otherwise. In preparation for the unitary status hearing, experts in tracking and ability grouping supplemented Arias's monitoring reports with extensive new analyses of the district's treatment of Latino students, drawing on the extensive database the district had been required to maintain. Particularly striking were the findings that the district's tracking system had the effect of creating racially imbalanced classes, with whites favored systematically in class-enrollment decisions. Statistical analyses revealed that this skewed enrollment pattern could not be explained solely by students' past achievement (as measured by test scores). Moreover, low-track placement was found to have a negative impact on students' academic achievement. For example, while only 56 percent of very high-scoring Latinos were in "accelerated" classes, 93 percent of whites and 97 percent of Asian Americans with comparable test scores were enrolled in these classes. Furthermore, students with "average" test scores who were placed in low-track courses lost ground on subsequent tests, while those with "average" scores who were placed in regular and accelerated classes gained. In other words, whether students began with relatively high or relatively low achievement, those who were placed in lower-level courses showed fewer gains over time than similarly situated students placed in higher-level courses.[64]

As the plaintiffs pushed for attention to such issues, the district itself was recognizing the urgency of addressing Latino students' needs. In 1991, the superintendent told the newspaper that the district was now focusing more on achievement than on desegregation alone. He claimed that he personally had encouraged the schools to give up tracking and pointed to the district's participation in "Equity 2000," a project intended to move Hispanic students into higher-level math courses.[65] The tide shifted even further toward an emphasis on education quality for the district's Latino students when, in 1993, Linda Murray became the superintendent. Murray brought with her significant experience with a desegregation order in Broward County, Florida, which had left her skeptical of the ability of student assignment plans alone to remedy educational inequality. She also recognized the unique needs of Latino students and English-language learners (ELLs). Symbolic of that recognition, her first acts included the appointment of a Latina to administer the desegregation office and an announcement to deploy the district's desegregation funds to address the inequities Latinos faced.

In February 1993, during the extensive preparations for the unitary status hearing, Judge Peckham died. Judge Ronald Whyte was selected to continue the case and he wasted no time in letting the parties know how he would manage it. Embracing an experimentalist perspective, Whyte stated, "This strikes me as the kind of dispute that cries out for settlement between the parties," he observed.[66] He added, "Hopefully, I'll see [a consent] order that is appropriate."[67] With that prodding, Whyte postponed the hearing and appointed a retired California superior court judge to mediate the dispute. Given the plaintiffs' desire to move toward improved neighborhood schools, the district's desire to diminish court oversight, and its representations about creating equal opportunities in the downtown schools, Whyte's decision to impose a mediated resolution created the opportunity for a "new public" to arise around reforming San Jose's schools.

For almost ten months, the parties, their attorneys, and their experts worked without the court to hammer out a mutually agreeable modification to the 1985 order. Superintendent Murray recalled later that the plaintiffs' interest in the achievement issues helped persuade her that the district should stay with the court order and use it to leverage their "doing the right thing" for Latino students.[68] She decided to use the negotiation process to craft something that would help close the achievement gap and jump-start the efforts to eliminate tracking that relegated Latino kids to lower-level classes. Murray reflected:

> It became obvious to me that we had huge achievement gaps—it was obvious to everyone—and that maybe we could use the negotiations process to recraft the court order into something that would deal with the primary issue of achievement gaps and opportunity gaps. So, I often say in retrospect [that] it was opportunistic to go to the table and say, rather than getting out of the court order right now, let's put a consent decree in place which would have a clock—it wasn't going to [go] on forever. . . . I just thought that this would really jump-start the efforts we need to make in dealing with tracking, low achievement, and [the fact] that so many Hispanic students were in classes that were getting them nowhere.[69]

In January 1994, the parties signed a sweeping overhaul of the remedial decree. The plaintiffs acknowledged the new spirit of cooperation. "If this agreement is followed by everyone involved, it will really build a partnership. I think the plaintiffs are on the way to developing some trust with the district," *Raza Si*'s Jorge Gonzalez told a reporter.[70]

This court-approved agreement (the 1994 consent decree) went far beyond what Peckham ordered, or perhaps could have ordered, in terms of educational components. Both parties touted the new direction of the order. "The new agreement addresses the educational progress of all students in San Jose Unified," announced Superintendent Murray. "Within every school, we are going to work very hard to make sure that every student is having equal access to all programs."[71] Gonzalez concurred: "To me, the most important thing is that [the plaintiffs] and the district have realized that we have the same goal. . . . This agreement is simply a tool to allow the district to be successful with all students."[72]

Reflecting the parties' new direction in "desegregation," the 1994 consent decree reads less like a judge's order and more like a chapter from a school reform text. First, the district committed to detracking its students and relying more on mixed-ability classrooms with high standards for all students. All elementary students were to be assigned to general classrooms; there would be no self-contained gifted-and-talented education (GATE) classrooms and all GATE instruction would instead be conducted in the general classroom or on a limited pullout basis. All middle schools were required to adopt the Accelerated Schools model developed at Stanford University by Henry Levin, with its high expectations and increased support for all students. In the high schools, ability grouping could continue in advanced grades, but the ninth-grade core courses would be mixed ability (except for bona fide course sequences like ninth-grade geometry, advanced algebra, trigonometry/precalculus, calculus). The district was also required to design an aggressive plan to get all students, beginning in elementary school, into higher-level course sequences.[73]

Second, specialized programs were being developed to target the success of Latino students. Foremost was the district's commitment to providing *bilingual* education for all ELLs who wanted it. This included identification of ELLs, placement in primary-language classrooms in schools where fifteen or more ELL elementary students at any grade level requested such instruction, and proper monitoring for making the transition to English classrooms. It should be noted, however, that the institutionalization of bilingual programming in the 1994 consent decree would be in tension with efforts to reduce ethnic isolation, at least at the classroom level, as ELL students would be concentrated in certain classrooms in order to receive primary-language instruction.

Third, the decree required extensive reporting of performance by the district and its individual schools along more than a dozen indicators, including retention rates, graduation rates, grade point average, and state assessment test scores. What is notable about this performance reporting is the decree's shift from external monitoring to internal monitoring of student outcomes and reporting to the plaintiffs and their counsel. Although the office of the court monitor continued to exist, it was clearly being phased out as "the parties agree that the district should begin to assume responsibility for self-monitoring, with an anticipated reduction in the cost of external monitoring."[74] Similarly, the parties agreed to eliminate judicial intervention to the extent possible, as they consented to informal alternative dispute resolution processes whenever disagreements arose.

Finally, the parties did not abandon ethnic balance as a remedy for intentional segregation. However, the requirements for such balance were relaxed through a change in the definition of a "segregated" school, as any school could have up to 70 percent Latino enrollment. Moreover, a half dozen of the district's schools were relieved from any ethnic-balance goals. By August 1994, this number increased to eight schools. This relaxation in ethnic-balance goals would set the stage for the return to neighborhood schools. The decree concluded with an agreement that should the district "fully comply" with the decree's provisions, the district will be, by definition, "unitary." The district agreed not to bring a unitary status motion before the end of the 1995–96 academic year, but, if the plaintiffs failed to raise an objection in writing to the district's compliance with the decree, the plaintiffs would be barred from contending that the district was not unitary.

Despite good intentions all around in using the consent decree to bring fundamental reform, implementation proved difficult. Superintendent Murray expected resistance from the district's white and affluent community members, particularly around detracking, and thought the court order would help:

> It's very hard to get through the attitudes and expectations of more affluent parents who want their children accelerated. . . . In their minds it's best to take the cream of the crop and put them in a curriculum all by themselves. . . . I thought I could use the court order if it mandated the elimination of tracks. It became a buffer for me and my Board to say that it is an order of the court.[75]

However, Murray and her colleagues failed to anticipate the vehemence of the opposition they would confront. Many white parents saw the decree as unfairly advantaging Latinos at the expense of their own children. Even some who saw themselves as supportive of desegregation feared that detracking would place their own children's education at risk by "dumbing down" classes. Fueling these fears, local media reported that teachers complained that the inclusion of "kids that used to be in remedial classes" made their classes hard to teach and lowered the level of instruction.[76] Parents in the southern, mostly white portion of the district also objected to adding bilingual kindergarten to an elementary school, mainly on the ground that all children should be taught in English. Making matters even more contentious, many Latino parents saw the district as not making a wholehearted effort. Some interpreted the district's use of the court order as the reason for the reform as a lack of commitment to the reforms. By using language that demonized the court order, the district administration quickly converted the consent decree into a lightning rod for all divisive issues and attitudes facing them.[77]

By January 1996, the school board that had hired Superintendent Murray had soured on her abilities, demanded her resignation, and then rescinded their demand.[78] The district's leadership was divided and in disarray. Nevertheless, at the end of the 1995–96 academic year, the district brought a motion for "partial" unitary status, over the plaintiffs' objections about the district's compliance. Judge Whyte never heard this motion either, as the district and the plaintiffs reached another modification to the decree that would ultimately return students to their neighborhood schools:

> The parties agree that now is the proper time for the San Jose Unified School District to make a fundamental change in its student assignment practices. In implementing the student assignment provisions of the 1985 Remedial Order and the 1994 Stipulated Modified Remedial Order . . . the District has fully complied with the numerical ethnic requirements for assignments to all of its schools. . . . In accomplishing this goal, the school board and the District have acted free of any intent to discriminate against any ethnic group in the [District].
>
> For the future, the parties believe that desegregation of the elementary schools can be achieved with a student assignment system that (1) does not employ numerical standards, and (2) combines neighborhood school assignments with voluntary Majority to Minority intradistrict transfers, magnet schools and targeted recruitment.

The parties recognize that by adopting these provisions, the racial composition of some or all of the District's schools may change from present levels. Plaintiffs agree not to seek any future modification in student assignment practices that would mandate that the District return to satisfying ethnic numerical ratios at its schools, or that would require the District to assign or reassign students to schools based on ethnic numerical ratios. Plaintiffs further agree that the racial composition of the District's schools will not be used as evidence of discriminatory intent with regard to the implementation of the District's student assignment program.[79]

This August 1996 accord put the finishing touches on the transition of the desegregation litigation, away from ethnic balancing as the central meaning of equal educational opportunity and on to the creation of good neighborhood schools as the meaning of equal educational opportunity.

Without explicit goals for ethnic balance, however, the district hoped to maintain some semblance of integration with continued magnets, voluntary majority-to-minority transfers, and targeted recruitment to encourage such voluntary transfers. Yet all seemed to recognize that the 1996 modification would result in racially isolated neighborhood schools.[80] Perhaps acknowledging this, the parties essentially breathed life into *Plessy v. Ferguson's* (1896) "separate but equal" doctrine by promoting vertical equity through additional funding to schools with greater than 75 percent Latino enrollment.

Undoubtedly wiser about the potential for a public backlash to thwart reforms, Superintendent Murray used a provision in the court order for parent outreach to spend desegregation funds on a concerted public engagement campaign. Employing Public Agenda, a public opinion research group, the district conducted focus group research with diverse sets of parents, students, teachers, and community members, asking for their views about the quality of San Jose's schools. Public Agenda also coordinated "community conversations," engaging hundreds of parents, teachers, and community leaders in talking about their aspirations for San Jose's children. Participation in these public conversations was managed carefully to ensure that large numbers of underserved Latino parents attended and were heard. Those meetings and a follow-up written survey of all high school parents, students, and teachers convinced district officials that the community would support higher standards and rigorous curriculum. Even teachers, they concluded, would support a policy that prepared all high school students for college, providing they were given the training and support to achieve this goal.

Moving on this apparent community consensus, the Board adopted a "college-for-all" policy requiring that, beginning with ninth graders entering high school in fall 1998, all students pass the sequence of fifteen courses required for University of California and California State University admission (the "A–G courses") in order to earn a diploma. This sequence includes three years of college preparatory math through algebra II, three years of college preparatory science including two lab sciences, and two years of a foreign language.

Looking back on the process, Murray sees the court order as helping them move toward this reform, even though it hadn't required it. The detracking ordered by the 1994 consent decree resulted in many more Latino middle and high school students being placed in challenging classes. That these students were doing at least as well academically as previous cohorts in lower-level courses helped dispel myths about Latino students' capacity to do well in challenging courses.[81]

Remedying unlawful segregation: ELLs and equal educational opportunity (1999–2003)

Partially motivating the return to neighborhood schools was the fact that many Latinos who were being bused to the largely white (and increasingly Asian American) schools on the south end of the district were also ELLs. Upon their arrival, they found that the bilingual courses to which they had access in the downtown schools did not exist, thus preventing equal access to much of the curriculum. This lack of language-appropriate instructional services was highlighted in the court monitor's 1991 "Five Year Summative Report."[82]

To address that lack of curricular access, recall that the 1994 consent decree specifically called for extensive interventions to meet the needs of ELLs. Put simply, equal educational opportunity in San Jose meant language access for ELLs through transitional primary-language programming.[83] But this attention to the language needs of ELLs was jeopardized with the 1998 enactment of legislation implementing California's voter-approved initiative, Proposition 227, which would virtually eliminate bilingual education in the state. That initiative, dubbed "English for the Children" by its supporters, sought to impose English-immersion programming on most California classrooms. But the new public comprised of plaintiff representatives and district leaders that had developed under Judge Whyte's supervision recognized the threat and also saw an opportunity to preserve (and improve on) the work of the 1994 consent decree. Because the U.S. district court was administering the consent decree pursuant to its powers under the U.S. Constitution, Judge Whyte could invoke the supremacy clause of the Constitution to ensure that a state law would not trump federal power. In other words, the desegregation litigation itself—once viewed as a burden imposed on the district—could now be used to shield the district (and plaintiffs) from what they viewed as the adverse consequences of state law.

By the end of the 1990s, much had changed in the district. Not only had Latinos become the largest ethnic group, "Latinos constituted a majority on the school board [including Jorge Gonzalez]—three out of five. In addition, the associate superintendent and three senior directors were Latino. Latinos were also better represented among the ranks of school principals."[84] The result of this change was the substantial alignment of interests between the plaintiffs and the district. Indeed, in October 1998 and March 1999 court filings, both the plaintiffs and the district seemed to agree that equal opportunity in the context of the desegregation case meant three things: (1) that the district should stay the school reform course it had charted in 1994 by targeting resources to Latino students in the downtown schools, detracking and desegregating classrooms, monitoring student outcomes, and phasing out direct court supervision; (2) that any efforts to achieve ethnic balance at the school-site level should be voluntary; and, significantly, (3) that San Jose's ELL students should have access to equal opportunities through a modified transitional primary-language program. The parties accordingly proposed a program for elementary ELLs that offered them a choice between transitional primary-language instruction in the district's Academic Language Acquisition (ALA) program at certain elementary schools or English-immersion instruction at their assigned elementary school. Essentially, the parties agreed that providing equal access to Latino children in the context of desegregation litigation meant offering families the choice to "opt out" of Proposition 227's English-only mandate and into transitional primary- language instruction. In all other respects, the modified consent decree reflected the school reform measures of the 1994 consent decree and the student assignment policies of the 1996 modification.

The End of Judicial Intervention and the Future of Equal Educational Opportunity

By May 2002, the San Jose desegregation litigation was some thirty-one years old, the district had met its racial balance goals some thirteen years earlier, and it had returned to neighborhood schools and demonstrated its ability to self-monitor for some eight years. It was probably no surprise, then, that at a May 8, 2002, status conference in the case, Judge Whyte, on his own accord, raised the question of whether the district ought to be declared unitary and judicial supervision concluded. A week later, Judge Whyte wrote to the parties, directing them to meet and confer on the court monitor's continued role and the issue of whether further court supervision was necessary at all: "The court anticipates a joint report summarizing any issues of dispute before a motion for unitary status is filed by the district. The court anticipates that the district will file a motion for unitary status (which, of course, may or may not be opposed by plaintiffs) within the next three to four months."[85]

Having presided over the desegregation litigation for nearly ten years and having created the forum for a new public made up of district officials and plaintiff representatives to define equal educational opportunity, Judge Whyte perhaps seemed satisfied that the disentrenching role of the court was unnecessary, especially given the shifting demographics of the district and the composition of the Board and administration. With his goading, the parties entered into protracted (May 2002 to April 2003) final settlement negotiations in the hope of avoiding a costly—and, for the plaintiffs, potentially risky—unitary status motion proceedings. After all, the plaintiffs had already essentially conceded that the district had fully complied with the 1986 remedial order, the district had been released from numerical balancing goals in 1996, and the plaintiffs would therefore be hard-pressed to demonstrate how the vestiges of the pre-1985 intentional segregation continued to exist. Even so, Judge Whyte provided one final forum for the new public to institutionalize the desegregation case's vision of equal educational opportunity.

With the children in both the Diaz and Vasquez families long since graduated from high school, the plaintiffs' attorneys decided to establish a plaintiffs committee for the purpose of advising counsel on how best to resolve the litigation and to authorize counsel to enter into a settlement agreement. Longtime plaintiffs' counsel Francisco Garcia-Rodriguez participated in monthly meetings of the committee from June 2002 to March 2003. The meetings were publicized widely and were well attended. Each meeting's focus was on the review of settlement proposals, recommendations for how the district could maintain the gains from desegregation, and proposed modifications to any settlement terms. At a March 3, 2003, committee meeting, more than one hundred class members and the committee voted to approve a proposed final agreement (with only one dissenting vote) and selected two committee members—Martha Barahona and Bertha Madero—to serve as named class representatives in place of the Vasquez family.

What did the new deal provide? Despite the turn away from a focus on integration and toward creation of equality in neighborhood schools, the centerpiece of the final settlement agreement (the Agreement) was a voluntary integration plan (VIP) and an ongoing process for involving the community in district oversight through a standing committee on integration. Notably, the VIP, which was developed by a district-led (with community participation) blue ribbon committee on integration, did not recommend mandatory ethnic balancing or even numeric goals. Rather, it focused on a race-neutral student assignment plan that looked to attendance boundaries, magnets, choice, and targeted recruitment of students. Students would be presumptively assigned to neighborhood schools, unless the student requested a voluntary transfer that would aid *socioeconomic* diversity. Specifically, students could transfer out of their attendance boundary schools if they were transferring from a low socioeconomic status (SES) school to a high SES school, or vice versa. Race neutrality became the watchword, as the district could have become subject to California's Proposition 209, which prohibited government agencies, like school districts, from providing any race-based preferential treatment. Whether Prop 209 applied to voluntary integration efforts in K–12 school districts was actually an open question, but the district was unwilling to tackle that issue and opted to create integration without race-based policies. Of course, it did not hurt that the state, under the Targeted Instructional Improvement Grant Program, began to provide funding for districts moving from court-ordered to voluntary desegregation plans. That program permitted the district to continue its voluntary desegregation efforts while receiving some $30 million in desegregation funds.

The district also committed to continue the 1994 and 1999 consent decrees' focus on classroom desegregation, access to advanced courses, and the ALA program for ELLs. The Agreement took those equity reforms a step farther and provided that the district would improve achievement and college readiness for underperforming (in addition to low-achieving) students. The plaintiffs' hope was that this Agreement would formalize and internalize equity norms that had been developed under judicial oversight because the court would no longer be available to the plaintiffs.

Judge Whyte signed off on the Agreement on August 22, 2003. In doing so, he dissolved the consent decrees and agreed to relinquish jurisdiction at year's end. District trustee and former plaintiff Jorge Gonzalez told a reporter that the judge's order "felt really good. . . . The bottom line was, I think he saw both parties were honest in keeping the goals of the original court order alive."[86] Gonzalez elaborated on this latter bit of historical interpretation a year later in a newspaper article commemorating *Brown's* fiftieth anniversary in San Jose: "The suit was never filed for desegregation. . . . We wanted equal opportunity."[87] Irrespective of its historical accuracy, Gonzalez's statement and his very involvement in the case exemplified the new public that had arisen in San Jose. From Latino community activist to plaintiff to school board member, Gonzalez became the voice of Latino children and the Board's own conscience in its efforts to eliminate the vestiges of past discrimination. And from mandatory busing and ethnic quotas to bilingual education, classroom desegregation, and vertical equity for downtown schools, the litigation created a forum for the new public to arise and enact its own version of equal educational opportunity. But did it make a difference?

SCHOOL REFORM IN FACT? THE IMPLEMENTATION OF DETRACKING AND "COLLEGE FOR ALL" IN SAN JOSE

Just as the consent decree both forced and enabled the district to adopt detracking at the elementary and middle schools and a "college-for-all" high school graduation policy, the funds triggered by the case provided essential support for the implementation of these ambitious policies. Between 1998 and 2002, teachers received intensive professional development in teaching demanding courses to diverse groups of students, and administrators received coaching on making fundamental changes in the schools' master schedules. Teacher-led committees developed new instructional materials and technologies to support their teaching, and they developed an array of "safety net" programs (Saturday academies, before- and afterschool instruction, "shadow" classes, summer "bridge" programs, etc.) for students struggling to meet the more stringent course requirements. New assessment systems provided frequent data that school administrators and teachers were expected to use to track student progress, flag students in need of extra supports, and to inform instruction. Annual "climate" surveys administered to teachers, students, and parents monitored satisfaction with the quality of education at the schools.

Because staff resistance threatened the successful implementation of these changes, a "golden handshake" early retirement incentive was offered to speed the departure of teachers and administrators unwilling to support the new direction. Hundreds took the deal. To replace them and ensure a full supply of qualified teachers, the district recruited vigorously, focusing especially on math, science, and foreign language teachers. At the same time, Murray met weekly with the teachers union president, seeking to solve problems as soon as they arose and providing extra resources and support in response to teachers' concerns. The district also mounted an aggressive and successful campaign to pass a bond measure that would allow the upgrading and expansion of the high school science labs. District leaders tapped business partners for resources and sought grants from foundations. Even with all of this strategic work, however, the court order continued to be a powerful lever. Murray recalls, "If people were unhappy, I had the hammer of the court to back me up—that this was not only in the best interest of the children, we really had no choice."[88]

The results have been quite impressive. Data from California's Basic Education Data System show that the overall graduation rates have remained steady, even with the far more demanding graduation requirements. More impressive is the increased percentage of students graduating who have earned grades of C or better in the rigorous college preparatory courses—from 37 percent in 2001, the class graduating just before the requirement was instituted, to 66 percent in 2006.[89] These gains pushed the district far above the state average, which was 40 percent in 2006. Although the increases have been most dramatic for white students—a jump of 34 percent (from 39 percent to 73 percent) between 2001 and 2006—Latinos have also made striking gains of 30 percent (from 19 percent in 2001 to 49 percent in 2006). Statewide, in 2006, Latinos graduated having earned grades of C or better in the rigorous college preparatory courses at a much lower rate of 26 percent. Notable, too, is that the gains on all of these measures have been most dramatic at the district's lower-achieving high schools that have larger percentages of Latinos and low-income students. The district's enrollment of Latino students in Advanced Placement courses more than doubled over the five years of implementation.

Despite these impressive gains, racial gaps remain, with Asian American and white students outscoring Latinos throughout the district and the high schools in the mostly white and Asian American southern part of the district outscoring the mostly Latino schools downtown.[90] Nevertheless, the shift to providing educational quality considerably narrowed the district's racial gaps on other measures, including scores on the state's standardized math and language arts tests.

It has been ten years since San Jose's school board adopted its college-prep-for-all policy. Beginning with the graduating class of 2002, all students earning diplomas from the district high schools have been required to complete the fifteen academic courses needed for admission to the state's four-year public universities. This policy has made San Jose's graduation requirements the most stringent in the state, a fact that has become an enormous source of pride in the district. Although the policy was spurred by the need to respond to the 1994 and 1996 consent decrees (and greatly supported by desegregation funds), the end of the case has not diminished the district's commitment.

THE COURT AND EQUAL EDUCATIONAL OPPORTUNITY IN SAN JOSE

Educational change happened and continues to happen in San Jose. No doubt the changing demographics of the district, public opinion, certain activists, and educators all had a hand in this change. The question remains, however, whether the court was essential or even contributed to the kind of change that occurred in San Jose, given the rights, independence, and capacity constraints it faced. Put simply, the district court, though slow in acting, was integral to such reform.

Overcoming Judicial Constraints in San Jose

As early as the 1973 *Keyes* decision, and clearly by 1979, the rights constraint should not have impeded judicial intervention in San Jose, but Judge Peckham was no judicial activist. For thirteen years (1971–84), Peckham refused to deviate from a restraint-oriented interpretation of the law. Of course, it is impossible to tell whether Peckham felt constrained by precedent, whether he was narrowly interpreting the law to justify his own policy ends, or whether community resistance to potential busing influenced him. But the Ninth Circuit easily found de jure segregation in 1984 and took the opportunity to excoriate the district for its longstanding resistance to addressing segregation. Then, in three short years, with the backing of the Ninth Circuit, state and federal dollars, and the early leadership of Superintendent Cortines, Peckham oversaw the desegregation of San Jose's schools.

Rosenberg postulates that on their own, courts cannot bring about social change. Nothing in the San Jose story would disprove the postulate—that the law, political elites, and the economic force of external actors, the federal and state governments, were necessary to Peckham's success. But what Rosenberg deemphasizes is the necessity of court action in the face of majoritarian politics. Indeed, courts can provide the moral coercion to act. The district was simply unwilling to tackle segregation until the Ninth Circuit told it that its segregation was unconstitutional. Once found morally culpable, the district hired an integration-friendly superintendent and proceeded with implementing a remedy. What is more telling is the public's passive response to the highly intrusive remedy of racial balancing. The court as agent of the values embodied in the Constitution was a necessary condition for educational change in the face of majoritarian politics in San Jose.

Judicial Experimentalism and School Reform in San Jose

Ethnic balancing did not ultimately meet the educational needs of the political and ethnic minority Latinos in the district. On the contrary, Latinos in the northern end of the district bore the brunt of the busing remedy, were concentrated in low-track classes, and were more likely to attend sub-par schools that did not provide primary language support. But the Constitution and law do not clearly recognize those concerns. In fact, because the district had achieved the goal of ethnic balance by 1989, it was entirely possible that the Supreme Court trilogy of *Dowell*, *Pitts*, and *Jenkins* could have released the district from judicial supervision had the district's first unitary status motion gone to a hearing.

Seeing a potential confluence of party interests in the early 1990s, Judge Whyte did not allow a unitary status motion to go forward and instead maintained jurisdiction (conceding some monitoring authority to the district), maintained the leverage behind the plaintiff class (but did not involve himself in the crafting of the remedy), and told the parties to bargain a remedy to past discrimination (but did not require that the remedy be ethnic mixing). What arose was a new public motivated to reform San Jose's schools, and the resulting remedial decree provided something for both sides: neighborhood schools, bilingual education, and improved and enriched programs in downtown schools for the plaintiffs; neighborhood schools, quality educational programs, state desegregation money, and reduced reliance on the monitor for the district. Both parties shared many of the decree's goals—indeed, one might argue that the consent decree provided "cover" to Superintendent Murray to implement the detracking reforms that were unpopular with some teachers and white and Asian American families on the south side—and the educational improvement aspects of the decree have reportedly become district ethos.

All this suggests another role for the judiciary in bringing about social change: that of superintendent in a counter-majoritarian political process. Not only did Judge Whyte's courtroom provide a forum for unconventional desegregation remedies to be discussed, it provided such a forum for previously disenfranchised constituencies to participate in that conversation. So successful were the plaintiffs in bringing their agenda of high-quality neighborhood schools to the table that they both won resource gains (think primary-language programming, desegregated classrooms, and additional funds for high-minority schools) and were also able to change the power dynamics in the district, as one-time activist and plaintiff, Jorge Gonzalez, became inside reformer. This is hardly the command-and-control model of judicial intervention that was so often criticized in the early days of desegregation.

The Meaning of Equal Educational Opportunity in San Jose

Equality of educational opportunity is neither a static nor uniform concept. Its meaning changes from town to town and time to time as politics, law, schools, and communities interact. In San Jose, the status quo ante distribution of educational goods largely prevailed for nearly two decades after de facto segregation was acknowledged in the district. A "neutral" neighborhood school policy and "nondiscriminatory" conduct were not only the district's defense to a desegregation lawsuit; it also defined educational equality among the students in the district. This district-imposed and -defended definition of equality was abruptly overridden by the Ninth Circuit's 1984 order and Judge Peckham's consequent decision to impose the traditional remedy for intentional segregation—ethnic balancing. Right from the outset of majority-to-minority transfers, magnets, and ethnic caps, however, it was not at all clear that this accommodation of the meaning of equality would be the one that would stick.

Desegregation usually conjures up images in black and white. Desegregation in San Jose, however, has meant remedying the past discrimination against Latino students and that remedy has a distinctly Latino flavor. Our evidence suggests that San Jose's Latino families wanted quality education in their downtown schools more than they did the sacrifice of hour-long bus rides to integrated and purportedly better schools in Almaden Valley. Throughout the 1960s and 1970s they demanded enriched and basic skills programs in the downtown schools. Latino advocates also wanted bilingual education programs. Despite the coalition's pressure and the admonishments of OCR, however, the district largely continued to ignore the demands for quality educational programs downtown.

This changed under court order. Facilitated by continued judicial supervision and fueled by Arias's reports, the newspaper's exposés, and pressure from *Raza Si*, Latinos attained two major goals—policies directed at quality education downtown and bilingual education. In the majoritarian political process, the mostly white district and Board could ignore with near impunity the demands of the political and ethnic minority Latinos. In consent decree negotiations, however, the district had to listen or face continued and costly litigation. Thus, in 1994, the desegregation case began to look more like a school reform initiative, as ethnic-balance goals took a passenger seat (but not quite a backseat) to educational goals. "We view this almost as an educational reform case," said Legal Aid's Francisco Garcia.[91]

From detracking to better funding downtown to accelerated schools to recruiting Latinos for GATE programs, the emphasis shifted to raising the academic achievement of Latinos. None of this is to say that the Latino community in San Jose opposes integrated education; it only suggests that the preferred goal of quality schools near home is currently incompatible with ethnic mixing in the sixteen-mile district. At bottom, educational equity in San Jose is multifaceted, fluid, and time and place specific. Only now, the court is no longer involved in this evolution.

CHAPTER FIVE

Sheff v. O'Neill

Weak Desegregation Remedies and Strong Disincentives in Connecticut, 1996–2008

Jack Dougherty, Jesse Wanzer, and Christina Ramsay

When word of the *Sheff v. O'Neill* decision hit the headlines in 1996, school desegregation advocates expressed a note of optimism. The Connecticut Supreme Court's 4–3 ruling in favor of the plaintiffs signaled an important victory for integrated education in one state, particularly at a time when Chief Justice Rehnquist and the U.S. Supreme Court were rolling back federal rulings across the rest of the nation (such as in *Missouri v. Jenkins*).[1] In a case that centered on the capital city of Hartford, Connecticut's highest court declared that "the existence of extreme racial and ethnic isolation in the public school system deprives schoolchildren of a substantially equal educational opportunity and requires the state to take further remedial measures," regardless of whether or not the segregation had been deliberate.[2] In contrast to most of the other case studies in this volume, Connecticut's judicial branch advanced the cause of school integration at a time when the federal government was retreating.

However, this local policy analysis traces how the story took a different turn over the next decade. First, it briefly reviews how Connecticut's legal and political process stalled on providing a meaningful desegregation remedy for seven years after the plaintiffs' courtroom victory (1996–2003). The chapter concentrates next on the limited results of the four-year legal settlement known as *Sheff I* (2003–07), with an analysis of the multiple reasons behind its failure and its meaning within the national context of the *PICS* decision.

Furthermore, it contrasts two consecutive attempts to build political consensus around the next phase of the legal remedy, *Sheff II* (2008–13), and its promise to meet the state's constitutional requirement for equal educational opportunity. Previous scholars have long debated the merits of voluntary versus mandatory approaches to desegregation.[3] This case study updates our current understanding of school desegregation policy and practice by illustrating what a voluntary plan—driven by weak policy tools and blocked by powerful disincentives—has not yet achieved in Connecticut.

A CITY, ITS SUBURBS, AND THE *SHEFF* CASE (1996–2003)

Nearly two decades ago, the *Sheff v. O'Neill* (1989) lawsuit gained national attention as an innovative legal challenge to city-suburban school segregation.[4] Filed on behalf of the lead plaintiff, an African American Hartford student named Milo Sheff, the suit challenged state officials, represented by then-governor William O'Neill. The *Sheff* plaintiffs included eighteen students, including both minority children from Hartford and white children from nearby suburbs, all of whom argued that their education was compromised by the lack of diversity. At that time, the Hartford Public Schools' population consisted of 91 percent minority students, surrounded by suburban districts comprised of 88 percent white students.[5] Furthermore, nearly half of Hartford's schoolchildren lived in poverty, while the broader metropolitan region was consistently ranked as one of the nation's wealthiest. But the federal court system offered no means for addressing metropolitan segregation. The U.S. Supreme Court's *Milliken v. Bradley* decision held that city-suburban desegregation remedies were valid only when there was evidence that multiple districts had deliberately acted to segregate.[6] As a result, rather than taking their case to federal court under the Fourteenth Amendment's equal protection clause, the *Sheff* plaintiffs filed their complaint in state court, arguing that segregated schooling violated Connecticut's constitutional guarantee of equal educational opportunity.

The Connecticut Supreme Court's 1996 decision in favor of the *Sheff* plaintiffs was remarkable for both what it did and did not say. On the one hand, the state's highest court challenged one of the fundamental causes of city-suburban inequality. The court's majority pointed specifically to Connecticut's school districting statute, which established "town boundaries as the dividing line between all school districts in the state," as a constitutional violation.[7] Although school district boundaries were not intended to be discriminatory when originally drawn by the state in 1909, they were "the single most important factor contributing to the present concentration of racial and ethnic minorities in the Hartford public school system."[8] Therefore, the court ruled that the state's maintenance of these boundaries, which separated Hartford schoolchildren from their suburban peers, violated Connecticut's constitutional prohibition against segregation, as well as its obligation to provide substantially equal educational opportunity for all.[9]

On the other hand, the court's 1996 decision did not specify any remedy, timetable, or goal for how this constitutional violation should be addressed. While mindful of the urgent plight of Hartford's schoolchildren, the judicial branch took a more cautious approach: "We direct the legislature and the executive branch to put the search for appropriate remedial measures at the top of their respective agendas."[10] Connecticut's Republican governor and the suburban-dominated Democratic legislative leaders immediately proclaimed that they would never invoke mandatory busing but would instead promote more gradual steps toward desegregation.[11]

In 1997, the legislature passed "An Act Enhancing Educational Choices and Opportunities," whose title clearly emphasized voluntary actions without mentioning racial integration. Although the law codified a state interest in diversity and contained some mandatory language—such as requiring all school districts to submit biannual reports on their activities "to reduce racial, ethnic, and socioeconomic segregation"—the main provisions encouraged voluntary participation in school choice programs, such as interdistrict magnet schools, to help achieve these goals.[12] Political scientist Kathryn McDermott and her colleagues emphasized that "the act was designed to *encourage* interdistrict programs, but not to require them."[13] A year later, the legislature also transformed Project Concern, a 30-year-old voluntary school transfer program for Hartford students wanting to attend suburban schools, into what is commonly known today as Project Choice.[14]

Some *Sheff* advocates followed the court's logic by proposing a more radical desegregation remedy: merge Hartford and its neighboring suburbs into a metropolitan school district. Naming their proposal "The Unexamined Remedy," these advocates sought to eliminate or greatly reduce the influence of the school district boundaries that had been described as the single most important factor behind the constitutional violation in the *Sheff* decision. But in the eyes of most state legislators, this metropolitan remedy entailed mandatory actions that would threaten local school governance in districts across the Hartford region, and it eventually disappeared from the political discourse due to lack of support.[15]

By March 1998, nearly two years after the *Sheff* ruling, the plaintiffs had seen very little progress by state officials in response to the court's "urgent" call for relief for Hartford schoolchildren. Only two interdistrict magnet schools enrolled Hartford students, both in substandard facilities, and only 469 participated in the suburban district transfer program, its lowest number ever.[16] The *Sheff* plaintiffs filed a motion for a court order for an effective remedy, but a year later the superior court declined, ruling that "the plaintiffs failed to wait a reasonable time" and that "the legislative and executive branches should have a realistic opportunity to implement their remedial programs before further court intervention."[17] After continued limited progress, the plaintiffs filed a similar motion in December 2000, which resulted in a three-week hearing in 2002, followed by settlement negotiations into the next year.[18]

THE *SHEFF I* SETTLEMENT AND FAILURE TO MEET THE GOAL (2003–07)

In January 2003, after several years of litigation, the *Sheff* plaintiffs and the Connecticut attorney general (representing the defendants) announced a legal settlement. This four-year remedy, known today as *Sheff I*, called for the expansion of voluntary desegregation measures, with the modest goal of enrolling 30 percent of Hartford minority students in reduced-isolation settings by 2007.[19] At that time, both parties estimated that 10 percent of Hartford minority students were already enrolled in its two key programs: interdistrict magnet schools and Project Choice city-suburb transfers. Under Connecticut statute, the attorney general must submit a legal settlement with financial appropriations to the legislature, but it requires a three-fifths majority vote in both houses to override it. When Connecticut's house of representatives voted 87–60 in favor of the $135 million resolution and the state senate did not object, the *Sheff I* settlement became law.[20]

Under this four-year agreement, the number of interdistrict magnet schools in the region rose to twenty-two, featuring a wide range of themes designed to attract both city and suburban students: the arts, character education, classics, Montessori, multiple intelligences, and science. Fourteen magnets were located within the City of Hartford, while the others were established in nearby suburbs with significant percentages of minority students. Most were managed by a regional service cooperative known as the Capitol Region Education Council (CREC), or directly by the Hartford Public Schools (HPS). All of the CREC magnets had been established before 2003 as partnerships between districts that reserved a number of seats in new buildings that were constructed primarily with state subsidies.[21] By contrast, the *Sheff I* settlement specifically called for creating eight additional "host" magnet schools, to be operated by HPS, over the four-year agreement. Most of these began by converting an HPS neighborhood school into a thematic magnet school, with long-term plans for major renovations or new building construction, using state subsidies.[22]

On average, interdistrict magnet schools were more racially balanced than most of the typical city or suburban school that students would have attended.[23] Yet the racial composition of magnet schools varied widely, particularly at the end of the four-year settlement. At one extreme, the Simpson-Waverly Classical elementary magnet school (operated by HPS) enrolled 95 percent minority students in a building that had previously been a regular neighborhood school by the same name. At the other extreme, the Greater Hartford Academy of the Arts high school resource center (operated by CREC) enrolled 26 percent minority students in a brand-new building with multiple spaces for rehearsals and performances. Accordingly, these two magnet schools served very different student populations. Simpson-Waverly Classical enrolled 154 Hartford minority students (or 74 percent of its magnet population) among all grade levels that had been phased into the magnet program. In contrast, the Greater Hartford Academy of the Arts enrolled only 49 Hartford minority students (or 12 percent of its magnet population), drawing a far larger percentage of suburban students in 2006–07.[24]

To the surprise of some desegregation planners, over 40 percent of all minority students who attended magnets lived in suburban school districts in 2006–07. When the *Sheff* case was filed in 1989, many people envisioned the "suburbs" as uniformly white towns and did not anticipate the growth of black and Latino student populations, particularly in inner-ring suburbs, during the 1990s and 2000s. Between 1989 and 2007, the minority student population rose sharply in nearly all suburbs, including those with previously sizable numbers of minority students (Windsor rose from 31 percent to 66 percent) and those that were previously nearly all white (Wethersfield rose from 4 percent to 20 percent). When Hartford-area magnet schools opened and began advertising for students, many planners anticipated that the suburbs would generate primarily white applicants. But when totaling all magnet enrollments in 2006–07, the share of suburban minority students (29%) surpassed that of suburban white students (25%). Most important, given the majority of white students in all Hartford-area suburbs, this means that suburban minorities are enrolling in magnets at significantly higher rates than whites.[25]

Initially, the highly favorable publicity surrounding new magnet schools may have led the public to mistakenly believe that all magnet schools counted toward reaching the *Sheff* goal of 30 percent Hartford minority students in reduced-isolation settings by 2007. But this was not the case. The "Missing the Goal" report by the authors of this chapter found a greater number of Hartford minority students enrolled in magnets that did not meet *Sheff* desegregation standards than in those that did. According to the 2003 *Sheff I* settlement, a magnet school meets the desegregation standard if the proportion of minority students does not exceed a specified limit, calculated as 74 percent in 2006–07. (The calculation is based on the percentage of minority students in the entire twenty-two-district *Sheff* region [44 percent in that year], plus thirty percentage points, to create the 74 percent standard.) To complicate matters, the settlement exempted magnet schools from meeting the desegregation standard during their first three years of operation, meaning a magnet would qualify for a period of time, then not qualify when its exemption expired. In addition, many Hartford students attended HPS magnet schools but were not officially enrolled in magnet programs, since converted elementary magnets typically phased in grades from kindergarten upward each year. Some older elementary students attended schools that were magnets in name only.[26]

The second major initiative of the *Sheff I* desegregation agreement called for expanding the Project Choice city-suburb transfer program, also operated by CREC. When the 2003 settlement was announced, Project Choice enrolled almost nine hundred students, the vast majority of them Hartford minority students who transferred to suburban school districts. (Officially, Project Choice permits transfers in either direction, but hardly any suburban students apply to enroll in Hartford neighborhood schools, and few of Hartford's remaining white students use the program to leave the city school district.) During settlement negotiations, both parties expected that suburban districts would agree to enroll seven hundred more Project Choice minority students from Hartford, for a projected total of 1,600. Despite these intentions, Project Choice remained stuck at 1,070 students in 2007, making only a fraction of the progress hoped for by desegregation planners.[27]

In comparing maps of the Hartford region, suburban district participation in magnet schools is nearly the opposite of its participation in Project Choice. Districts sending the highest percentage of students to magnet schools tend to be in the inner-ring suburbs with the largest proportions of minority students (see map 5.1). For example, Bloomfield, a suburban district with 95 percent minority students. has the highest magnet participation rate, with one out of five students (21%) attending an interdistrict magnet. Other suburban districts with high levels of minority students (East Hartford, 76 percent; Windsor, 66 percent; and Manchester, 46 percent) follow with the next highest magnet participation rates, ranging from 5 percent to 10 percent. Conversely, Project Choice participation rates are highest in outer-ring suburban districts with large proportions of white students, such as Canton and Granby, where magnet rates also rank among the lowest (see map 5.2).[28] Note that when students apply to the magnet program, they select one or more specific schools, but when students apply to Project Choice, they have little control over the suburban district they are assigned to.

By 2007, the *Sheff I* remedy had failed to meet its goal for 30 percent of Hartford minority students to be educated in reduced-isolation settings. When adding up all of the data permitted under the settlement, the percentage had climbed to only 17 percent, far short of the targeted goal for June 2007. The numbers became more troubling when broken down into two categories: legal compliance and actual students. The "Missing the Goal" report distinguished between the percentage of the goal attained from all factors ("legal compliance," which included all exemptions and part-time programs) versus those attained by Hartford minority students enrolled in full-time reduced-isolation programs ("actual students"). After subtracting 1,033 stu-

MAP 5.1: Magnet School Participation, as Percentage of Total District Enrollment, 2006–07

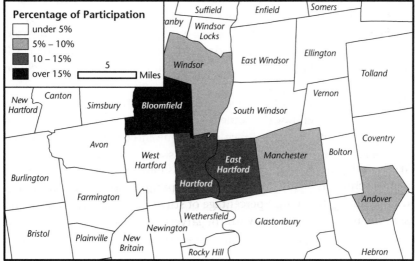

MAP 5.2: Project Choice Participation, as Percentage of Total District Enrollment, 2006–07

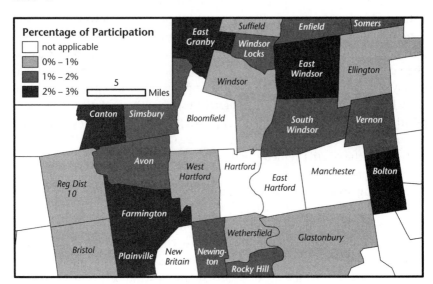

dents (4.7%) enrolled in racially imbalanced magnet schools (exempted due to being opened within the previous three years), and another three percentage points (based on full funding levels for part-time interdistrict cooperative grants, not full-time schools), the rate of actual Hartford minority students enrolled in reduced-isolation settings fell to 9.3 percent. In other words, the settlement began with an official estimate of 10 percent in 2002–03, but four years later the actual percentage of Hartford minority students in reduced-isolation magnet schools and Project Choice suburban districts had fallen slightly backwards, to 9.3 percent (see figure 5.1 and table 5.1).[29]

During the eighteen years between the original filing of the *Sheff* lawsuit in 1989 to the end of the settlement period in 2007, the racial demographics of students remained nearly the same in central city schools but rose dramatically in most suburbs. Minority students comprised 91 percent of the Hartford Public Schools in 1988–89, a figure that rose slightly to 94 percent in 2006–07. But during the same period, every one of the suburban school districts in the Hartford metropolitan region experienced substantially more growth in the percentage of its minority students. In some suburbs, the growth appeared small (like rural Suffield, from 3 percent to 6

FIGURE 5.1: Actual and Legal Progress toward *Sheff I* Goal, 2003–2007

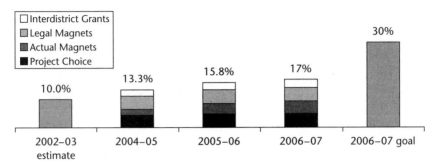

percent minority), while in many other suburbs, racial change was widely noticed (like West Hartford, from 12 percent to 34 percent minority, and East Hartford, from 23 percent to 76 percent minority). Overall, in the twenty-one suburban districts named in the original *Sheff* lawsuit (excluding the city of Hartford), the proportion of minority students rose from 12 percent in 1988–89 to 30 percent in 2006–07. Programmatic voluntary integration efforts such as magnet schools and city-suburban transfers did not change

TABLE 5.1: Hartford Minority Students in Public Schools, 2006–07

Magnet Schools	Students	Percentage toward Sheff Goal
Actually meeting *Sheff* standard (≤74% minority)	973	4.4
Legally meeting *Sheff* standard (≤3rd year of operation)	1,033	4.7
Not meeting *Sheff* standard (>74% minority and 3+ years)	1,043	
Grade levels not phased into magnet program	1,406	
Project Choice city-suburb transfers	1,070	4.9
Hartford neighborhood schools	16,412	
Total	**21,937**	
Interdistrict cooperative grants (calculated by level of state funding for part-time program, not actual students)		3.0
Total Percentage		**17.0**

Source: Connecticut State Department of Education, 2007.[30]

the circumstances for the vast majority of Hartford students who continued to attend racially isolated neighborhood public schools (over 16,400 out of nearly 22,000 students, or 75 percent).[31] But suburban districts did experience non-programmatic forms of voluntary integration, as minority families rented apartments and purchased homes, bringing demographic changes that could not be ignored. The ground had shifted under the feet of the *Sheff* remedies because the suburban schools of today no longer look as white as they did over twenty years ago.

WHY THE *PICS* DECISION DOES NOT (YET) APPLY TO *SHEFF*

When the *Sheff* plaintiffs and defendants were publicly discussing the limited outcomes of the four-year remedy with Connecticut state legislators in June 2007, the U.S. Supreme Court delivered its highly contested ruling in the Seattle/Louisville case. In its 4–1–4 decision, the Court held that school districts may take voluntary steps to promote racial diversity, but placed limits on classifying individual students solely by race to achieve this goal. Although Justice Kennedy, the swing vote, recognized racial diversity as a compelling interest and specifically approved of several of race-conscious measures (such as considering race when drawing attendance boundaries and recruiting students), he rejected both the Seattle and Louisville student assignment plans. Both districts considered the race of individual students as the sole factor in making "tie-breaker" decisions about the schools they would attend, thereby using race in a way that was not "narrowly tailored to its purpose."[32]

Amid the confusion and anxiety surrounding this complex decision from Washington, D.C., local advocates and officials in Connecticut asked whether or not it applied to the *Sheff* case. Dennis Parker, an American Civil Liberties Union attorney and long-term counsel for the *Sheff* plaintiffs, provided some clear answers. First, Parker explained that "*Sheff* is a court-ordered remedial case and not a voluntary one."[33] Unlike the Seattle and Louisville districts, which voluntarily decided to promote racial diversity, the Connecticut Supreme Court ruled in 1996 that the state constitution's equal education clause had been violated, and it required a remedy to address the needs of Hartford's schoolchildren. Hypothetically, the U.S. Supreme Court could issue a future ruling that a violation of Connecticut's state constitution would be insufficient grounds to meet federal court standards on race and schooling, but such a conflict between federal and state courts seems highly unlikely. Given the existing context, Connecticut's court-ordered remedy blocks federal intrusion into *Sheff*.

Attorney Parker pointed to a second reason why the Seattle/Louisville ruling does not apply to *Sheff.* Unlike desegregation plans overturned by the
U.S. Supreme Court for classifying students solely on the basis of race, Parker
explained to state legislators that in the *Sheff* remedy "there's no specific program that says that you have to achieve these goals by denying students the
opportunity to go to individual schools on the basis of their race."[34] Connecticut's policy and practices on interdistrict magnet schools support Parker's
claim. For example, the state law that established magnets specifically men-
tions their goal of promoting racial diversity and requires that newer magnets meet a racial target to qualify for state funds, but it does not consider the
race of individual students.[35] When students apply to Hartford-area magnet
schools they indicate their individual race on the form, but the lottery system is driven by students' place of residence. In HPS magnet school lotteries,
applications are divided into two categories: Hartford-resident versus non-
resident. In CREC magnets, where several districts cooperate to pay for their
allocation of seats, separate lotteries are run for applicants from each district.
"We've never had to use a lottery that was race based," explained Bruce Douglas, CREC's executive director.[36] Instead, magnet school planners avoid individual student race by using residence as a proxy.

But Connecticut policy underlying the Project Choice city-suburb transfer program is different, and its use of racial classification might not meet
the strict scrutiny standard of the Seattle/Louisville ruling if it were to be
challenged in federal court. Although Project Choice eligibility is open to
students of all races, statutory language specifically restricts the percentage
of white Hartford students who may participate. The law states: "Beginning
with the 2001–02 school year, the proportion of students who are not minority students to the total number of students leaving Hartford . . . to participate in the program shall not be greater than the proportion of students who
were not minority students in the prior school year to the total number of
students enrolled in Hartford . . . in the prior school year."[37] In other words,
white Hartford students may apply to Project Choice to leave Hartford (and
therefore increase racial isolation), but their numbers must be proportionate
(or lower) than the previous year.

Consider this hypothetical test case, which could happen only if a federal court intervened against Connecticut's constitutional basis for its court-
ordered *Sheff* remedy. The vast majority of Project Choice students are black
or Hispanic, but there is a small handful of white students who also use
the program to transfer out of Hartford Public Schools. All applications are
entered into the same database, for a race-neutral lottery. Looking back on

previous years, the number of white Hartford participants has been slowly declining from seven (0.65%) in 2006–07, down to six (0.55%) in 2007–08 (see table 5.2).[38] But imagine that, in 2008–09, the lottery selected at least two white Hartford applicants who both accepted the Project Choice transfer, thereby raising the number of whites to eight, while the base total remained constant. This increase in the proportion of white Hartford participants over the previous year would clearly violate the statute above. In order to comply with state law, would CREC (the Project Choice manager) be required to remove one of the white Hartford participants from the program solely on the basis of the individual's race? If so, would that white individual have a case against Connecticut on the grounds of the Seattle/Louisville decision?

If such a case went to federal court with no recognition for the state court-ordered remedy, then the Seattle/Louisville decision would force the question, Is the use of race in Project Choice "narrowly tailored" to its compelling interests? Most likely, the answer is no, for three reasons. First, like the Seattle case, the Connecticut statute supporting Project Choice uses a simplistic binary system of racial classification ("minority" versus "not minority"), which does not recognize multiple dimensions of diversity. Second, Connecticut does not yet have a strong body of evidence that it has considered race-neutral alternatives. In Project Choice, white student participation is restricted by a race-specific statute (unlike the magnet program, which uses residence as a proxy for race). No other student characteristics are considered, with the exception of their residence in the City of Hartford and a routine preference for siblings or No Child Left Behind transfers. Third, Project Choice's race-conscious plan does not affect a sufficient number of white students to be deemed "necessary" to achieve integration.[39] While only a hypothetical case (premised on an unlikely federal-state conflict), the exercise suggests that the Seattle/Louisville ruling may have placed one aspect of the *Sheff* remedy on shakier legal ground than previously realized.

TABLE 5.2: Project Choice Participants from Hartford, by Race, 2006–08

Year	Black	Hispanic	White	Other	Total	Percentage White
2006–07	858	208	7	4	1077	0.65
2007–08	862	217	6	6	1091	0.55

Source: Connecticut Department of Education, 2007, 2008.

WHY DID THE *SHEFF I* REMEDY FAIL?

Why did the *Sheff I* remedy fail to meet its goal of enrolling 30 percent of Hartford minority students in reduced-isolation settings by 2007? Competing interpretations arose among the wide range of stakeholders: the plaintiffs, defendants, legislators, and state education officials. For each of these parties, their diagnosis of the problem behind the original *Sheff I* remedy was informed by their desire to shape negotiations over the subsequent *Sheff II* remedy. Furthermore, as the policymaking process expanded simultaneously in the state's judicial and legislative branches, stakeholders clashed on whether the next remedy should be determined by a judge's order or political compromise.

Before the four-year settlement period ended, many observers pointed to logistical barriers that slowed progress toward the goal. On a practical level, state education officials lamented delays in new magnet school construction, which reduced the number of available seats. Many observers also called attention to the absence of a joint magnet office, a "one-stop-shopping" destination where applicants could submit one common application form to the twenty-two interdistrict magnet schools operated by CREC, HPS, and two suburban districts. Similarly, both magnet and Project Choice managers complained about the difficulty of arranging an efficient school bus system to prevent students' having long bus rides between city and suburban districts.[40]

Although every metropolitan desegregation plan faces logistical challenges, the absence of clear governance over the *Sheff I* remedy made these problems even worse in Connecticut. "Murky accountability" was the key problem identified by journalist Rachel Gottlieb Frank, who listed a long string of oversight changes during the 2003–07 settlement period, including "five state education commissioners, multiple reorganizations of the state Department of Education, four Hartford superintendents, a transition from State control over Hartford schools to local control, and the creation and disbanding of a magnet school office in Hartford."[41] Although the *Sheff v. O'Neill* lawsuit was filed by plaintiffs against the State of Connecticut, most of the responsibility for implementing the *Sheff I* settlement rested with the HPS and CREC, which managed the magnet schools, and with CREC, which managed Project Choice. Oddly, the Connecticut Department of Education played an indirect monitoring and funding role during most of 2003–07. "The overall process has no quarterback, no lead manager, no commander," Leonard Stevens, the plaintiffs' desegregation expert, complained in 2004. "The State permits the process to unfold virtually at will, limits its role to observation, unintrusive technical advice and distribution of state-level funding."[42]

Beyond governance issues, the *Sheff I* remedy also suffered from two significant flaws in its policy design. First, as noted above, Hartford-area magnet schools are somewhat ineffective policy tools for achieving racial balance. Although the *Sheff I* remedy specified numerical goals for the percentage of Hartford minorities in desegregated settings, the interdistrict magnet lotteries used urban/suburban residence as a proxy for race. Given the suburban minority students' high level of interest in magnets (over 40 percent of all magnet minority students reside in a suburb outside of Hartford), planners were surprised by how few of the magnet schools met the desegregation standard.[43] In the wake of the Seattle/Louisville ruling, advocates of voluntary desegregation plans should pay close attention to the negative example taught by *Sheff I*: this implementation of a perfectly legal, residence-based magnet lottery did not produce the intended racial-balance results.

A second major desegregation policy flaw was the legislature's failure to align the *Sheff I* magnet enrollment goals in with its own magnet funding requirements. When the *Sheff* plaintiffs and defendants agreed to the 2003 legal settlement, it called for all interdistrict magnet schools to meet a specific desegregation standard—to enroll fewer than 75 percent minority students within three years—in order to count toward the overall goal. However, Connecticut statutes continued to fund interdistrict magnets that violated this portion of the *Sheff I* remedy as long as they were established before July 2005.[44] As a result, several long-standing magnet schools continued to receive funding while enrolling 75 percent or more minority students. Connecticut's financial incentives for magnet administrators were not directly aligned with the goals of the *Sheff I* remedy.

On another policy level, the *Sheff I* remedy was burdened by powerful disincentives against suburban participation in magnet schools and Project Choice. Indeed, several observers have commented on suburban whites' fears about attending schools with black or Hispanic urban students. "Suburban parents have some trepidation about sending their children into the inner city," noted Tom Murphy, spokesperson for the Connecticut Department of Education. "Whether it's perceived or accurate, we are aware of it."[45] Nevertheless, white racism alone does not explain the failure of *Sheff I*. According to combined datasets, approximately eight hundred suburban whites applied to magnet schools located within the City of Hartford for 2006–07.[46] Similarly, for every suburban district that enrolls a small percentage of urban Project Choice students (such as Wethersfield, which enrolled only thirteen

Hartford minorities, or 0.3 percent of its total student population), there are other suburbs that enroll a greater share (such as Farmington, which enrolled ninety-five Hartford minorities, or 2.2 percent of its total student population). White racism exists, but it is not uniformly pervasive enough to fully justify the demise of *Sheff I*.

The most important suburban disincentives against magnet and Project Choice participation are those created by state policies. Local school board member and policy analyst David MacDonald identified the two-part problem behind magnet school funding. First, the typical state reimbursement for magnet school students during the *Sheff I* settlement did not cover the actual costs of providing this education. In 2003, the typical reimbursement rate for a suburban student in a CREC-managed magnet was about $5,000 per pupil, while the actual operating expense ranged between $7,000 and $10,000 per pupil. Suburban districts were expected to pay "tuition" to cover the $2,000 to $5,000 gap for each of their pupils, and when several districts refused or were unable to pay, CREC ran a multimillion-dollar deficit.[47] Second, when the Connecticut legislature modified the magnet funding formula in 2002, the outcome favored Hartford-managed host magnets, which created "a disincentive for school districts to develop a significant number of interdistrict magnet schools that have a balance of students from multiple districts," such as the CREC model.[48]

Project Choice also has been seriously hampered by state-level financial disincentives against suburban participation. Connecticut reimburses suburban districts only $2,500 per student transfer from Hartford, despite an average expenditure of $10,000 per pupil. As a result, school desegregation researcher Erica Frankenberg concluded, "Most districts report that they determine how many seats to offer for Project Choice students by looking at their projected enrollments by grade. . . . In other words, they will take [Hartford] students if it is convenient for them."[49] The state's financial incentive is so low that it only makes sense for suburban districts to accept Project Choice students into a handful of seats that would otherwise remain empty in an existing classroom. The funding fills in the margins, where they exist, but does not inspire more meaningful participation. Furthermore, suburban legislators and school board members are very aware that Project Choice is "a losing proposition" for them financially. "In communities that have a reputation for being fiscally conservative," Frankenberg warns, "Project Choice could be targeted" in local town budget disputes.[50]

Perhaps the most troubling disincentive against suburban participation in the *Sheff* remedy is the one caused by the federal No Child Left Behind

Act, whose original purpose was to reduce the racial achievement gap. Under NCLB, school districts experience increased pressure to maintain "adequate yearly progress" in subgroup test scores, but this federal pressure runs counter to the state's desegregation agenda. According to Connecticut law, for the purposes of standardized testing requirements, Hartford students who participate in the Project Choice transfer program "shall be considered residents of the school district in which they attend school," meaning the suburban district.[51] Given that Hartford minority student scores, on average, fall below NCLB cutoffs, suburban districts risk penalties in accepting Project Choice students. Furthermore, as Frankenberg points out, some suburban schools "have so few minority students that accepting a substantial number of Project Choice students might trigger an additional 'subgroup' that they would be held accountable for under NCLB."[52] For example, under NCLB regulations, the suburban district of Avon was not required to report African American students' scores as a subgroup in 2006–07 because there were slightly fewer than forty black students in grades three through eight combined that year. If the Avon School District increased its number of Project Choice minority students, it would risk crossing the forty-student threshold for black students, which would require them to report data for this subgroup. If an insufficient percentage of black students in Avon met the NCLB cutoff, then the entire district would lose its currently "perfect" status in achieving adequately yearly progress (see figure 5.2).[53] According to Frankenberg, one way to remove this suburban disincentive would be "to provide a waiver for an initial period in exchange for a school accepting a certain number of students," which is possible under the safe haven provision of NCLB.[54] But this safe haven provision would only mask the problem for a specific period of time, and suburban state legislators are very aware of this disincentive.[55]

Beyond these questions of policy disincentives, there have been persistent questions about whether a voluntary desegregation plan comprised of interdistrict magnets and city-suburban transfers could truly integrate Hartford schools with its surrounding suburban neighbors. By design, Project Choice can only serve a small proportion of Hartford minority students (currently 1,000 out of nearly 22,000), unless its goal shifts to "emptying out" all of Hartford's neighborhood schools, which has never been a realistic option. Similarly, constructing new magnet schools in Hartford can only go so far until it replaces all neighborhood schools. Both interdistrict magnets and Project Choice are also limited by transportation constraints across distance: students can only travel so far before the amount of time spent on buses conflicts with the broader mission. Hartford minority student attrition from

Adequate Yearly Progress (AYP) Status Data for the 2006-07 School Year

Based on 2007 Connecticut Mastery Test (CMT) results and the 2007 Connecticut Academic Performance Test (CAPT)

The tables below show this district's performance on the AYP indicators. A district fails AYP if there is a "No" under the AYP Target Met column for BOTH the CMT and the CAPT. Only students who were enrolled in this district for the full academic year were inleuded in these calculations.

4 - 00

Connecticut Mastery Test (CMT) Results (Grades 3 through 8)

| Subgroup | Participation Rate (95 % participation needed) | | | | | | | % At or Above Proficient | | | |
| | Mathematics | | | Reading | | | AYP Target Met? | Mathematics (74 % proficient needed) | | Reading (68 % proficient needed) | |
	Current	2 Year Avg.	3 Year Avg.	Current	2 Year Avg.	3 Year Avg.		AYP Calculation	AYP Target Met?	AYP Calculation	AYP Target Met?
Whole District	99.9	100	100	99.9	100	100	Yes	96.6	Yes	94.9	Yes
American Indian	Fewer than 40 students in this subgroup							Fewer than 40 students in this subgroup		Fewer than 40 students in this subgroup	
Asian American	100	100	99.3	100	99.5	99	Yes	99.9	Yes	99.7	Yes
Black	Fewer than 40 students in this subgroup							Fewer than 40 students in this subgroup		Fewer than 40 students in this subgroup	
Hispanic	100	100	100	100	100	100	Yes	99.1	Yes	99	Yes
White	99.9	100	100	99.9	100	100	Yes	97.2	Yes	95.3	Yes
Students with Disabilities	100	100	100	100	99.5	99.7	Yes	77.4	Yes	70.3	Yes
English Language Learners	Fewer than 40 students in this subgroup							Fewer than 40 students in this subgroup		Fewer than 40 students in this subgroup	
Economically Disadvantaged	100	100	100	100	100	100	Yes	90.5	Yes	88.7	Yes

Additional Academic Indicator: Writing — AYP Target Met? Yes

(continues)

FIGURE 5.2: (Continued)

Connecticut Academic Performance Test (CAPT) Results (Grade 10)

Subgroup	Participation Rate (95 % participation needed)							% At or Above Proficient			
	Mathematics			Reading			AYP Target Met?	Mathematics (69 % proficient needed)		Reading (72 % proficient needed)	
	Current	2 Year Avg.	3 Year Avg.	Current	2 Year Avg.	3 Year Avg.		AYP Calculation	AYP Target Met?	AYP Calculation	AYP Target Met?
Whole District	99.2	99.6	99.7	98.7	99.4	99.6	Yes	100	Yes	100	Yes
American Indian	Fewer than 40 students in this subgroup							Fewer than 40 students in this subgroup		Fewer than 40 students in this subgroup	
Asian American	Fewer than 40 students in this subgroup							Fewer than 40 students in this subgroup		Fewer than 40 students in this subgroup	
Black	Fewer than 40 students in this subgroup							Fewer than 40 students in this subgroup		Fewer than 40 students in this subgroup	
Hispanic	Fewer than 40 students in this subgroup							Fewer than 40 students in this subgroup		Fewer than 40 students in this subgroup	
White	99.1	99.6	99.4	98.6	99.3	99.2	Yes	100	Yes	100	Yes
Students with Disabilities	Fewer than 40 students in this subgroup							Fewer than 40 students in this subgroup		Fewer than 40 students in this subgroup	
English Language Learners	Fewer than 40 students in this subgroup							Fewer than 40 students in this subgroup		Fewer than 40 students in this subgroup	
Economically Disadvantaged	Fewer than 40 students in this subgroup							Fewer than 40 students in this subgroup		Fewer than 40 students in this subgroup	

Additional Academic Indicator: Graduation Rate	AYP Target Met?	Yes

Source: No Child Left Behind Report, Avon School District, 2006–07.

Project Choice is becoming a more serious issue, as participation rates grow higher in the outer-ring suburbs than the inner-ring suburbs.[56] As Leonard Stevens, the *Sheff* plaintiffs' desegregation expert, warned, "Integration programs by definition depend on a two-way flow of students; otherwise, students of one racial group bear a disproportionate share of the burden of traveling to get to integrated schools."[57]

THE INITIAL *SHEFF II* PROPOSAL—AND WHY IT COLLAPSED

In late May, 2007, as the four-year *Sheff I* remedy drew to a close, the plaintiffs and defendants negotiated a new settlement proposal, the first attempt to craft a *Sheff II* agreement. The new plan featured the ambitious goal of increasing the percentage of Hartford minority students in reduced-isolation settings from 22 percent (in 2008–09) to 41 percent (in 2011–12)—far above the level of 17 percent in the original remedy.[58] Most important, to achieve the numerical goal, the *Sheff II* proposal envisioned a dramatic change in implementation authority. The proposal outlined a "comprehensive management plan" for bringing existing interdistrict magnets into compliance, creating new school choice options and expanding Project Choice in the suburbs. "The responsibility for implementing [it] now rests clearly in the State Department of Education," *Sheff* attorney Dennis Parker explained, rather than with the Hartford Public Schools and CREC, which would continue to provide services but were not legally responsible under the 1996 *Sheff* decision.[59] Under Connecticut law, Attorney General Richard Blumenthal (representing the state as the defendant) submitted the proposal and its financial appropriation to the state legislature, which, during a 30-day period, could strike down the settlement with a three-fifths majority in both houses.

State legislators from both suburban and urban districts sharply critiqued the initial *Sheff II* remedy. State senator Thomas Gaffey, cochair of the education committee and a key Democratic leader behind the 1997 legislative response to *Sheff*, opened the public hearing on the 2007 proposal with a challenge to its supporters. "Prove to us how investing another $112 million in essentially the same model we've been following for the last decade will produce real results in easing racial isolation and enhancing student achievement for the school district of the City of Hartford," Gaffey insisted, raising a concern felt by many suburban lawmakers.[60] Representative Doug McCrory, an African American educator from Hartford, also expressed serious doubts. McCrory asked whether the *Sheff* remedy placed too much emphasis on achieving numerical desegregation goals rather than lifting minority student achievement, particularly given Connecticut's status as having the highest racial achievement gap in the nation. "We focus a lot on the deseg-regation part, but one part we refuse to talk about is the academic achieve-ment of children," McCrory began. "I don't want anyone to think that I'm not a supporter of *Sheff*," he continued, adding that many of his peers had excelled in their education by leaving the Hartford Public Schools for sub-urban districts or parochial schools. But McCrory clearly was enamored of recent examples of predominantly black and Latino charter schools whose students scored exceptionally well on the Connecticut Mastery Test (CMT). "If we can develop some [charter] schools in the Hartford region [that are] 95 percent minority, and those kids are kicking butt on CMTs and the academic levels are high and they're going to college, I think our children should be in those schools."[61]

But the strongest opposition to the *Sheff II* agreement came from an unex-pected political opponent: the City of Hartford. While *Sheff II* negotiations were underway between the plaintiffs and the attorney general, the City of Hartford received permission from the court to intervene in the litigation. Mayor Eddie Perez, the first elected Hispanic leader of a major Northeastern city, who also served as chair of its Board of Education, spoke at a public leg-islative hearing to stress "the unintended consequences of the financial bur-den that the first phase of the implementation had on the City of Hartford."[62] Although Hartford was not a party to the *Sheff I* settlement, that agreement required the city to pay up front to create eight new magnet schools, although the incomplete and delayed state reimbursement only covered 80 percent of the city's costs. Perez's newly appointed superintendent of Hartford Pub-lic Schools, Steve Adamowski, also criticized *Sheff II* on the grounds that "at this time it still has no specific plan" for realistically achieving its goal for 41 percent of Hartford minority students to be enrolled in reduced-isolation settings.[63]

Taken together, the legislature's skepticism about the costs and effec-tiveness of the *Sheff II* remedy, along with the City of Hartford's refusal to endorse it, caused a political derailment. Although the *Sheff* plaintiffs and the attorney general had negotiated an agreement in May 2007, the state legis-lature refused to act on it during the last few days of its regular session or its brief special session. Officially, the 30-day legislative review period had not expired and would not do so until the next regular session in spring 2008. *Sheff II* was going nowhere in the political process. As a result, in July 2007 the plaintiffs filed a motion to take the case back to court.[64]

Amid all of the controversy, one important piece of the *Sheff II* remedy was quietly approved by the legislature's June 2007 special session. The successful bill required that extra seats in magnet schools be filled by students whose districts did not participate in CREC magnet partnerships. For years, magnet advocates called attention to white suburban families who wanted to send their children to magnet schools but whose home district refused to participate by paying a share of the costs. The poster child was a white student from South Windsor, who wanted to attend the Greater Hartford Academy of Math and Science but was blocked by his home district. The boy's mother, Laurie O'Brien, lobbied the South Windsor Board of Education, the commissioner of education, and even the governor, but could not persuade anyone to let her son attend the magnet school, even after she offered to pay the cost. South Windsor refused to participate in interdistrict magnets, she concluded, because "towns want top intelligent students to stay in their towns because that keeps their [test] numbers up."[65] The new legislation now required magnets with open seats to give preference to students from nonparticipating districts, like South Windsor. The law also included a financial mandate: the home school district "shall contribute funds to support the operation of the interdistrict magnet school in an amount equal to the per student tuition, if any, charged to participating districts."[66] Identical language had appeared in the initial *Sheff II* proposal. In other words, Connecticut's magnet school law now had some (small) teeth: if a suburban family voluntarily wished to send their child to a magnet school, their decision would force their suburban district to pay a share of the costs. The law still supported the concept of voluntary desegregation, but if parents wanted to participate, it forced suburban districts to help fund it.

THE REDESIGNED *SHEFF II* PROPOSAL—AND WHY IT WAS APPROVED

When Connecticut Superior Court judge Marshall Berger opened the *Sheff v. O'Neill* hearing in November 2007, he faced attorneys for three separate parties. First, the *Sheff* plaintiffs, led by ACLU attorney Dennis Parker and his colleagues, filed the motion for a court-ordered remedy because eleven years had passed since the 1996 decision and the state legislature had failed to act on the *Sheff II* remedy the previous summer. The plaintiffs' witnesses testified about the limited progress achieved by the *Sheff I* remedy, plus the need for a stronger, comprehensive voluntary desegregation plan.[67] Second, Ralph Urban, the assistant attorney general defending the state, insisted that no court-ordered action was necessary and that incremental improvements to the existing magnet schools and Project Choice program were clear signs of progress. Finally, John Rose, counsel for the City of Hartford, played the odd role of the third-party intervener in this long-running litigation. While Hartford's chief complaint was the state's failure to fully reimburse its magnet costs, the city's leading witness, Superintendent Adamowski, strongly supported the plaintiffs' demand for a comprehensive desegregation plan with a special master, and pushed it further by calling for a metropolitan school district—a politically unpopular plan last raised in the 1990s.[68]

After two weeks of testimony and two additional months of deliberation, Judge Berger issued what appeared to be an anticlimactic ruling in January 2008. Technically, the initial *Sheff II* proposal was still pending before the legislature, since the 30-day review period had not officially expired when the session adjourned. Therefore, Judge Berger officially ruled that the initial *Sheff II* plan would become law thirty days after the legislature reconvened in spring 2008, if the resolution was not voted down or withdrawn by the attorney general.[69] But behind closed doors, negotiations continued over a revised *Sheff II* proposal that would address concerns raised in the courtroom and the legislature. In March 2008, the initial agreement was withdrawn and subsequently replaced in April 2008 with a revised agreement reached by the plaintiffs and the defendants.[70] The City of Hartford did not sign on to this version, nor did it actively oppose it.

Like its predecessor, the revised *Sheff II* remedy identifies specific goals for increasing the number of Hartford minority students in reduced-isolation settings over a five-year period. While the agreement begins with conventional percentage goals (starting at 19 percent in 2008–09), it now concludes with a demand-driven goal, where 80 percent of the applications by Hartford minority students for reduced-isolation settings must be met by 2012–13.[71] According to plaintiff attorney Dennis Parker, this is the only demand-driven school desegregation goal by law in the nation. At this point, it remains unclear what a demand-driven goal would look like in practice or if it might introduce unforeseen issues, such as a disincentive against marketing magnets and Project Choice by the State of Connecticut, which is legally obligated to meet 80 percent of the Hartford minority demand.

To help achieve the revised *Sheff II* goals, the settlement agreement includes a lengthy outline for a comprehensive management plan to be produced by the state by the end of 2008, which encompasses magnets, Project Choice, and other existing school choice programs such as charters and vocational-technical schools. The revised five-year operating cost ($125 million) is similar to the initial proposal's price tag ($112 million), but the revised plan also could result in an additional $483 million of construction costs and debt service for approximately five new magnet schools.[72] Overall, the second draft of *Sheff II* is much more robust than the first draft.

When the *Sheff* plaintiffs and defendants testified on behalf of the revised *Sheff II* remedy before the state legislature's education committee in April 2008, they encountered similar skepticism and doubts that had arisen nearly a year earlier. Suburban and urban legislators sharply questioned the witnesses about the costs and expected results, the role of academic achievement, and their concerns about acting on this resolution before the comprehensive management plan has been drafted. Most interesting was an exchange between education committee cochair Senator Gaffey and the new commissioner of education, Mark McQuillan, regarding the proper degree of governmental authority necessary to implement the desegregation agreement. Commissioner McQuillan suggested that suburban school superintendents had expressed more support for enrolling Hartford students through Project Choice. Senator Gaffey replied that suburban superintendents serve at the behest of their boards of education, which may not be as supportive. He then pointedly asked his witness, "Do you contemplate the need to seek additional authority?"

"At this point, no," Commissioner McQuillan replied, demurring the senator's offer for greater authority to pressure suburban districts to participate in school desegregation.[73] Perhaps this dance between the branches of state government is part of an elaborate diplomatic strategy to entice voluntary cooperation from reluctant suburbs. Given the context, Commissioner McQuillan can present suburban districts with a "choice": either increase participation in *Sheff* voluntarily or face mandatory participation requirements from the state legislature—or, if that fails, the plaintiffs will win an even stronger court order from Judge Berger. The outcome of this political calculus is unclear, but it would not be the first (or the last) time that Connecticut has grappled with the question of voluntary versus mandatory desegregation policymaking.

Nevertheless, the revised *Sheff II* remedy effectively became law in mid-2008. The house education committee voted 15–9 in favor, followed by a senate committee vote of 5–0. Neither full body of the legislature voted it down before the review period ended in May, and Judge Berger officially approved the agreement in June.[74] Judge Berger's role helps to explain why the first version of *Sheff I* failed while the revised version passed. To some degree, the 2008 settlement is a better designed plan than its 2007 predecessor, in part due to the multiple issues raised and considered in the courtroom. But, more important, Judge Berger's activity in the negotiations exerted significant indirect pressure on the legislature: if they did not approve the revised plan, that would have opened the door for the *Sheff* plaintiffs to return to Judge Berger's courtroom with a demand for stronger judicial action, most likely a court-appointed special master. Behind the legislature's vote in favor of a renewed voluntary desegregation plan is the veiled threat of a mandatory one.

CONTINUING MANDATORY-VOLUNTARY DESEGREGATION DILEMMA

"The notion that we're going to get a better result by voluntary programs is ridiculous," Senator Gaffey announced to the press at the beginning of Judge Berger's courtroom hearing on the failed *Sheff I* remedy in November 2007. "We need to shift away from the model of remedy that the State has been pursuing for years," he urged, suggesting that the commissioner needed more authority to require suburban desegregation, although it would be difficult to gain approval for this measure in the legislature.[75]

Gaffey acknowledged the continuing dilemma of mandatory versus voluntary desegregation that Connecticut has endured for nearly two decades. The state has weaved back and forth between demanding action on school integration and then implementing only weak policy tools to achieve that goal. The 1996 Connecticut Supreme Court ruled the existing system of school districting unconstitutional, but the 1997 legislature merely required each district to report on its progress toward racial and economic diversity while providing millions of dollars of interdistrict magnet and city-suburban transfer funding without mandating any goals for suburban participation. In 2003, the *Sheff* plaintiffs and state defendants agreed on a legal settlement with numerical goals and a timetable for partial desegregation in the metropolitan Hartford region, but no mandates for individual suburbs. Not a single suburban district is required to send students to interdistrict magnets or to accept Project Choice students from Hartford. The 2008 *Sheff II* settlement adds a stronger state role in designing and executing a comprehensive management plan, but the details over how this authority will be used remain unclear at this point in time. Voluntary methods still prevail, yet powerful disincentives remain in place.

Other than approving the five-year *Sheff II* remedy, the only significant change in state policy has been a quiet shift toward a demand-side mandate for suburban magnet funding. Although districts are not required to send students to magnet schools, as a result of the 2007 legislature, if a suburban family wishes to attend a magnet with available space, then the suburban district is mandated to pay the same share of costs borne by other suburbs that regularly participate in that magnet. Essentially, Connecticut has inserted a suburban funding mandate into an otherwise all-voluntary magnet desegregation program. Suburban dollars must follow the child to the magnet school.

A test of this policy recently arose in the form of magnet school tuition bills. The Greater Hartford Classical Magnet School, operated by the Hartford Public Schools, sent a $2,500 per-pupil tuition bill to suburban districts that was designed to cover the gap between the $6,730 state subsidy it receives and the approximately $10,000 actual cost of educating each pupil who attends the magnet school. In past years, the City of Hartford picked up the cost, but Hartford officials no longer intend to subsidize suburban participation. The practice is perfectly legal under the 2007 law, but this is the first time a Hartford-operated magnet has tested it. J. Callender Heminway, chair of the Board of Education in suburban Granby, told the press that he understood the reasoning but was unhappy with the decision. "From our perspective," Heminway observed, "I think it would have a terrible chilling effect upon the willingness of suburban districts to participate in the magnet program."[76] Will this new suburban funding mandate conflict with *Sheff*'s voluntary goal of attracting more white suburban participation to interdistrict magnets? Perhaps the next five years of the *Sheff II* settlement will provide an answer.[77]

Resegregation, Achievement, and the Chimera of Choice in Post-Unitary Charlotte-Mecklenburg Schools

Roslyn Arlin Mickelson, Stephen Samuel Smith, and Stephanie Southworth

The Charlotte-Mecklenburg Schools (CMS) is a system once widely considered the epitome of a successfully desegregated school district—an example for the nation of how desegregation could be accomplished in ways that fostered student achievement, interracial civility, political stability, and economic growth. CMS policies gave rise to the *Swann v. Charlotte-Mecklenburg Board of Education* litigation,[1] in which a landmark 1971 U.S. Supreme Court ruling allowed the use of busing, the limited use of numerical ratios (e.g., the proportion of black to white students in a school), along with other strategies, to achieve desegregation. In addition to facilitating desegregation nationally, the *Swann* ruling led the previously reluctant CMS to vigorously pursue desegregation, most notably through a mandatory busing plan that was generally considered one of the nation's most successful because of its high levels of racial balance and, initially at least, improved academic outcomes.[2] However, a legal challenge by white parents in the late 1990s led to the reopening of the case and a ruling by a federal district court that CMS was unitary. Following the Supreme Court's refusal in 2002 to review the lower court's unitary ruling, CMS implemented a race-neutral pupil assignment plan, under which the district has experienced considerable resegregation.

CMS's resegregation resulted from several factors. Although the race-neutral assignment plan was called the Family Choice Plan (FCP), in practice the plan allowed relatively little choice because it guaranteed students who chose to attend a neighborhood school a seat at that school. That guarantee, combined with residential segregation, led to increased resegregation in the schools. However, there were other factors that interacted with the home-school guarantee and residential segregation to foster post-unitary CMS's resegregation: various constraints on parents' choices, district policy on transferring to overcrowded schools, shifts in the local political situation, and the district's changing demographics.

In addition to discussing resegregation in post-unitary CMS, this chapter considers the school system's current relationship between segregation and academic achievement. Our discussion proceeds in five stages. The first provides background information on CMS and the community in which it is located. The second discusses the political and legal history of CMS in the aftermath of the 1999 district court decision that CMS was unitary. The third summarizes the main characteristics of the FCP and its effects on pupil assignment, achievement, and attainment. The fourth section relates the consequences of the FCP to CMS's political situation, and the fifth concludes the chapter by commenting on the implications of recent developments in CMS for the future of educational equity and excellence in Charlotte and in the nation.

Before turning our focus to CMS, it will be useful to provide a few additional prefatory comments about the broader implications of the district's recent experience. Given the importance of CMS in school desegregation history, a study of the causes and consequences of its recent resegregation is of considerable interest in and of itself. But a discussion of CMS resegregation acquires additional significance in light of recent national legal, political, and demographic developments. Although scholars disagree about the extent to which U.S. schools are resegregating, even those who challenge claims of wholesale resegregation acknowledge that progress toward segregation "has faltered since the early 1990s."[3] However these trends are characterized, there is little reason to think they will be reversed, especially in light of the 2007 Supreme Court decision striking down race-conscious pupil assignment plans in Seattle and Louisville. A series of previous court decisions, primarily in the 1990s, including the ruling in the reopened *Swann* case, made it increasingly easy for school districts to be released from court-mandated desegregation and to be declared unitary. But the Seattle and Louisville cases differed from the earlier ones because these two districts were not under court order to desegregate but had voluntarily initiated such policies.[4]

The Court's ruling against such race-based, voluntarily initiated policies have further increased the legal hurdles desegregation proponents have to deal with and thus increased the likelihood that desegregation progress will continue to falter, if not fully give way to increased resegregation. To facilitate understanding of how these national trends could affect academic outcomes, it is useful to understand how resegregation in CMS influenced academic outcomes in the district.

BACKGROUND

As its name suggests, CMS is a consolidated school system covering all 526 square miles of North Carolina's Mecklenburg County. Although the county's outlying areas contain six small towns, the city of Charlotte is the county's political and economic hub, especially because North Carolina's liberal annexation laws have allowed the city to annex many of the county's rapidly growing unincorporated areas. Charlotte has grown dramatically in the past thirty years, developing from a regional transportation, commercial, and financial center into an increasingly important actor in national and international affairs. Charlotte is home to two of the nation's largest banks—Bank of America and Wachovia—and is the nation's second-largest banking center. The city boasts National Football League and National Basketball Association franchises, and the NASCAR Hall of Fame is currently being built there as well.

Accompanying Charlotte's economic transformation has been significant growth in public school enrollment and significant changes in the district's racial and ethnic composition. These trends go back a quarter century. From the early 1980s (the heyday of the mandatory busing plan) to 2008,[5] enrollment went from approximately 72,000 to 132,000 students. The racial and ethnic composition of CMS also changed during this period. In the 1980s, blacks constituted 39 percent of CMS's enrollment, whites constituted 58 percent, and Hispanics, American Indians, and Asians constituted less than 3 percent.[6] By the 2008 school year, the percentage of black students (45%) had increased somewhat, but whites constituted only 35 percent of enrollment, while Hispanics constituted 15 percent, Asians 4 percent, and Native Americans 1 percent.

While the trends in these enrollment characteristics go back several decades, they have become increasingly noteworthy in the post-unitary era.

Between the 2000 school year, when the ruling was issued in the reopened *Swann* litigation, and the 2008 school year, CMS enrollment jumped by 32 percent, the white share of CMS enrollment dropped from 48 percent to 35 percent, and the Hispanic share increased from 4 percent to 15 percent.

A comparison with nearby school districts helps put these changes at CMS in a broader context.[7] CMS is bordered by five North Carolina counties containing a total of seven school systems, all of which, like CMS, saw public school enrollment increase in this eight-year period, which is what would be expected, given the Charlotte area's rapid economic development. Of these seven nearby districts, three experienced a greater rate of enrollment increase than CMS and four experienced less growth. While CMS is in the middle of the pack when it comes to enrollment growth, the same cannot be said of the shrinking of its white enrollment. As might be expected, given national trends in the demographic composition of U.S. schools, all eight of these districts (CMS and those nearby) saw the white share of enrollment drop. But CMS's drop of 28 percent was the largest of the eight districts; only one other dropped more than 20 percent. The available data do not allow us to discern to what extent the relatively larger drop in CMS's white enrollment can be attributed to developments largely endogenous to CMS and those exogenous to it (e.g., housing prices, tax rates, employment opportunities, and improved transportation). But whatever the cause, the drop almost certainly added to the obstacles CMS faced in pursuing desegregation. However, as we shall demonstrate, the implementation of the FCP triggered a marked increase in resegregation independent of this drop and other long-term trends.

DESEGREGATION HISTORY

As noted earlier, CMS policies gave rise to the landmark *Swann* litigation, and in the wake of the Supreme Court's 1971 decision in that case, CMS developed a busing plan that was generally considered among the nation's most successful. The plan attained high levels of racial balance, improved both black and white academic performance, contributed to a local political climate often praised for its tranquil and progressive race relations, and was a source of great civic pride. All of these developments helped fuel Charlotte's reputation as a good place to live and do business, thus contributing to its economic attractiveness and population growth. Ironically, the very growth the busing plan contributed to helped undermine the district's desegregation efforts, because this growth brought to Charlotte many middle-class whites from other parts of the country who were accustomed to smaller, more socio-economically and racially homogeneous school districts.[8] Moreover, many of these white newcomers settled in outlying parts of the county whose great distance from black neighborhoods made busing more difficult than it previously had been. The growth of these predominantly white outlying areas contributed to a drift toward resegregation that began in the mid-1980s.

It should be noted, however, that the development of these outlying neighborhoods was not something, like the weather, that is generally beyond the reach of conscious human effort to change. Rather, their development was greatly facilitated by decisions about the location of roads and other infrastructure that were made by county and city officials (but not school board members) more concerned with pursuing economic development in general than in pursuing economic development that would help CMS maintain its nationally lauded desegregation plan. In other words, *Swann* required CMS to pursue desegregation but it did not require local governments to build roads and infrastructure in ways that would help the district pursue its desegregation efforts. When development conflicted with desegregation, the former typically won, in part because developers and their allies had more economic and political clout than desegregation proponents. Moreover, even in the heyday of the mandatory busing plan, CMS faced financial difficulties that made it difficult to construct new schools in areas that would facilitate desegregation. Thus, despite the *Swann* mandate, in the 1980s and 1990s, CMS built a large number of schools in outlying, predominantly white areas, where land was less expensive than locations that would have been logistically easier to desegregate.[9]

Beginning in the late 1980s, public criticism of CMS became more widespread. Spearheaded by white newcomers, the criticism resonated with the growing national distemper over public education.[10] In an effort to placate such criticism, and in keeping with growing national sentiment in favor of giving families greater choice in the selection of the schools their children attended, CMS replaced crucial aspects of the mandatory busing plan with a controlled-choice system of magnet schools in 1992. The new choice policy was a major departure from the heavy reliance on mandatory busing that had characterized CMS's desegregation efforts since the 1970s. Under this plan, each magnet school sought a racial composition similar to that of the entire district (40 percent black and 60 percent nonblack).

However, a legal challenge by a group of white parents over CMS's use of race in pupil assignment led to a reopening of the *Swann* case and a six-week trial in 1999 in federal district court. The litigation involved three parties: the white plaintiffs challenging CMS's use of racial guidelines; black plaintiffs represented by the NAACP's Legal Defense and Education Fund (LDF), who sought to preserve the use of racial guidelines; and the defendant, CMS. However, unlike the situation in the original *Swann* litigation in which CMS had strongly opposed desegregation efforts, in the 1999 trial, a majority of board members sought to continue these efforts despite the strong opposition of a minority of board members. The board majority's support for desegregation resulted in CMS taking a position in the trial that was similar to that of the LDF. Indeed, given how school districts typically seek to be released from court orders requiring desegregation, CMS's determined fight to remain under these orders during the trial was unusual in the history of school desegregation. Hearing the case was Federal District Court judge Robert Potter, who had been active in Charlotte's antibusing movement of the 1960s and had been appointed to the bench by Ronald Reagan. Thus, it was perhaps not surprising that his September 1999 ruling declared CMS unitary and ordered it to stop pursuing desegregation.

The ruling triggered intense local struggle over a new pupil assignment plan, as well as legal appeals to the higher courts. However, even before the Supreme Court indicated in April 2002 that the declaration of unitary status would stand, CMS had adopted a new race-neutral, neighborhood school–based choice pupil assignment plan, the Family Choice Plan.

Turbulent Prologue to the New Family Choice Pupil Assignment Plan

The FCP resulted from the almost two years of political battles within CMS that had followed Potter's unitary ruling. For most of this time, the same board majority that sought to defend CMS's commitment to desegregation at the 1999 trial sought to maintain as much as possible of CMS's historical commitment to this effort. But these board members faced an uphill battle, for several reasons. Although the legal issues were not yet settled, the trends in the federal courts' desegregation rulings offered little hope that Judge Potter's declaration of unitary status would be reversed. The legal situation fueled local political developments. Fearing that uncertainty over a new pupil assignment plan would damage CMS's reputation, thus hurting efforts to attract capital to Charlotte and interfering with economic development, Charlotte's politically influential business elite pressured CMS to "move on"—in other words, to quickly resolve the uncertainty over the plan by adopting a new plan, any plan.

The superintendent also pressed the board to adopt a new plan quickly. He worried that continued uncertainty over pupil assignment would undermine citizen support for CMS and interfere with efforts to boost academic achievement and narrow racial differences in achievement. Although aware that other districts could claim little systematic success in educating children in schools with concentrated poverty and high minority enrollments, the superintendent felt that CMS had the resources to deal with the challenges posed by such schools if the community mobilized its resources appropriately. When he was specifically asked by a local journalist whether concentrating low-income children in inner-city schools made it harder to educate them, he replied, "I don't think it matters."[11] It was this optimistic answer about the educational prospects of high-poverty schools that helped explain why, in the battle over the specifics of the new assignment plan, the superintendent rejected proposals by desegregation advocates that CMS place a ceiling on the number of poor children (defined by eligibility for free or reduced-price lunch) accepted to their schools. Since such ceilings were race neutral, advocates of ceilings argued they were fully consistent with the court's ruling. The superintendent, however, worried that the victorious plaintiffs in the 1999 trial would claim that poverty ceilings were a proxy for racial balance and that the ceilings might weaken what he considered the more crucial aspects of the plan he was pushing—a guarantee of a seat in a neighborhood school and cohort continuity (i.e., maximizing the likelihood that students who so wanted could attend elementary, middle, and high school with the same group of students).

As a result of these multiple political pressures, the pro-desegregation board majority found itself fighting a rearguard action and increasingly having to settle for the promise of additional resources for schools adversely affected by likely resegregation.[12] Thus, as the board was crafting the details of a new pupil assignment plan, it was also debating how to supply additional resources to the schools it anticipated would become resegregated by race and socioeconomic status (SES).

In anticipation of the resegregation of the schools by race and SES, the board adopted what would be called the Equity Plan at the same time it developed the FCP. This plan's core provisions included the identification of high-poverty, low-performing schools as Equity Plus II schools (EPII). EPII schools were guaranteed smaller teacher-student ratios, teachers in them were to be paid a premium of several thousand dollars per year above their base salary and receive tuition for completing advanced degrees, and EPII schools were promised bond funds for renovations, additional learning equipment, and supplies. The final piece of the Equity Plan was the opportunity for parents to opt out of EPII schools and enroll their children in a higher performing school if they so choose. It was with these promises of increased resources that the board adopted, in July 2001 by an 8-to-1 margin, the FCP, despite being aware that doing so would almost certainly increase resegregation by student race and socioeconomic status.[13]

The FCP went into effect at the start of the 2003 school year. It was essentially a neighborhood school assignment plan with a race-neutral choice among generally nearby magnet schools. More specifically, the FCP offered (1) a guaranteed seat in a neighborhood "home" school, (2) maximum stability of school assignments over a student's educational career, (3) a guaranteed option for poor-performing or low-income students who attended schools with a high number of similar students to enroll in a high-performing school, (4) the option to choose from magnet schools with a variety of themes, and (5) maximum utilization of all school seat capacity. Starting in the 2004 school year (the second year under the FCP), students assigned to home schools that had a percentage of low-income students at least 30 percent above the systemwide average were allowed to move to the top of the list for admission to schools with a below-average poverty level if seats were available.[14]

Consequently, school choice in post-unitary CMS took two forms: (1) initial choice of either a guaranteed seat in a neighborhood home school or a magnet school, and (2) the choice to opt out of a low-performing school in accordance with CMS's Equity Plan.[15] Students who did not want to attend their home school could apply to other schools, but if a school lacked the capacity to accommodate all applicants, preference went to those for whom it was the home school. Admittance to magnet schools was determined by a lottery, but in keeping with the district court's unitary ruling, neither the lottery nor any other aspect of the pupil assignment plan took race into account.

Continued Turbulence and Decreased Public Support for CMS

The new FCP led CMS to abandon much of its goal to become a desegregated system in fact as well as in name. Therefore, it is ironic that the first years of the new plan saw increased white dissatisfaction with CMS—especially in outlying, predominantly middle-class white neighborhoods. Part of the reason for this is that the new assignment plan increased overcrowding at schools in these neighborhoods, but another reason is more political: the new plan's emphasis on neighborhood schools helped undermine allegiance to CMS as a countywide system in which all citizens were invested to some degree.

Exemplifying the dissatisfaction with CMS were movements in Mecklenburg's outlying northern and southern areas that sought to deconsolidate CMS and split it into three smaller districts. Anger at overcrowding in schools in these outlying areas was fueled by conservative activists' claim that suburban overcrowding existed largely because CMS was spending too much money on renovating and building schools in minority, central-city neighborhoods. Added to the dissatisfaction with overcrowding and the perceived misallocation of resources were complaints about discipline, safety, and the district's large size, many of the latter coming from newcomers to Charlotte who were accustomed to smaller districts in other parts of the country.[16] However, efforts to deconsolidate CMS failed because deconsolidation required approval by the state legislature, which has traditionally encouraged consolidation between a county district and any smaller districts within that particular county.

Although deconsolidation failed, the secessionist movement alarmed Charlotte's political and business leaders and led them in March 2005 to create a high-profile task force. Unlike similar task forces in CMS's history, this one was not funded or chosen publicly. Instead, local businesses contributed $500,000 to support the work of the task force, which was cochaired by one of Charlotte's most prominent black citizens, former mayor Harvey Gantt, and a white Bank of America executive, Cathy Bessant. The two cochairs exemplified the alliance between the business elite and Charlotte's black political leadership that had dominated local politics during the heyday of the busing plan, but the task force paid scant attention to the issues that had engendered the busing plan. While the task force report rejected deconsolidation, its first four recommendations called for the sweeping decentralization of CMS. These recommendations reflected the influence of this deconsolidation movement, which charged that the bureaucratic and remote CMS central office was insensitive to the concerns of parents in the district's predominantly white outlying areas. Also reflecting the influence of the secessionist movement was the task force's recommendation that CMS "modify its K–8 student assignment plan toward a fixed assignment based on residence."[17]

Just as the task force's recommendations indicated how the interests of whites in outlying areas were trumping CMS's historic commitment to desegregation, so, too, did school board elections reflect diminished black political influence in school board politics. This became apparent in 2003, when the incumbent board chair, a black, failed to win reelection, and even more so in 2007, when no black even appeared on the ballot—the first time since 1968 that no black candidate had sought election to the CMS school board.[18] Part of the reason for the lack of a black candidate was that a promising black candidate, who would have had strong appeal for whites, was unable to run for personal reasons. But a more important reason was that the 2003 defeat of the incumbent chair, and the defeat in subsequent years of prominent black candidates for at-large seats on the county commission, led many black activists to believe that an African American could not win a countywide election in Mecklenburg's current political climate.

ILLUSORY CHOICE, RESEGREGATION, AND ACADEMIC ACHIEVEMENT

Illusory Choice

Brick and mortar limits to choice

From the outset, "choice" under the FCP was largely a chimera. The foremost reason for this is that explosive growth, especially in outlying neighborhoods, meant that when CMS honored home school guarantees to all who sought them, few seats, if any, remained for potential transfer students from middle-ring or urban schools. When the new FCP went into effect, the school system's existing schools became the building blocks for the new neighborhood school–based FCP. Outlying schools' seating capacities were required to accommodate the students guaranteed the option of attending their neighborhood schools. The overcrowding problem in some outlying schools was so extreme that the school district capped their enrollment.[19] These enrollment caps blocked access to the high-performing suburban schools for families who wanted to opt out of their own low-performing/high-poverty schools, as CMS's EPII plan promised.

At the same time suburban schools were bursting at their seams, many inner-city schools initially became underutilized neighborhood schools.[20] Under- and overutilization patterns were related to the schools' racial composition. In the 2002–03 academic year, all but one of the thirty-nine underutilized schools were racially imbalanced minority schools.[21] Of the thirty-three overutilized schools, six (three elementary and three high schools) were racially identifiable as minority, thirteen were racially balanced, and fourteen were racially identifiable as white.[22]

Transfer options

According to CMS's 2001 Equity Plan, parents of students attending schools with concentrated poverty 30 percent over the district's average or schools that repeatedly fail to meet the North Carolina accountability program (ABC Plan) growth and performance goals can transfer their children to a lower-poverty, high-performing school.[23] In the second year of the Equity Plan's operation (2003–04), this option was available to students attending underperforming schools, yet few parents of the 9,600 eligible students had even inquired about the program as of January 2003, the end of the application period for the forthcoming school year.[24] Eighteen months later, just days before the beginning of the fall semester in August 2004, the parents of 8,200 students attending low-performing schools were informed of their child's eligibility to transfer to moderately more successful schools under a variety of policies, including CMS's Family Choice Plan, the Equity Plus II plan, North Carolina's ABC Plan, and NCLB provisions. Only 658 (8%) of the 8,200 eligible students accepted last-minute transfers to new schools.[25]

What kinds of schools did those who transferred choose? Only a handful of them got seats in the top-performing schools, many of which had been capped due to their extreme overcapacity problems. Of the 658 students who opted out of their low-performing schools, a majority transferred to schools with only moderately better records of test performance. A number of them chose magnet programs, but a substantial minority of the students transferred to other low-performing schools.[26]

We are not aware of any systematic data that would permit us to account for CMS's low number of applications to transfer. Anecdotal evidence from CMS and elsewhere suggests several possible explanations for why a majority of the eligible students did not apply to transfer to higher-performing schools. First, during the initial two years of the Equity Plan, the information available to parents of eligible students was not provided in a sufficiently timely manner to allow parents to investigate other schools and apply for a transfer during the window of time available.[27] Second, knowledgeable and motivated parents who wanted to transfer their children may have been discouraged because they were given few attractive alternatives, as most of the schools that were considered "good" were overenrolled. Their choices included a limited number of seats in moderate- or low-performing schools. CMS simply did not have the seat capacity in higher-performing schools to accommodate all the students eligible to opt out of their low-performing schools, as promised by the Equity Plan.[28] Third, there is anecdotal evidence from Maryland and Virginia suggesting that middle-class parents are the most likely to transfer their children when given the option.[29] Considering that most students attending low-performing schools are not middle-class, their parents' failure to seek transfers is consistent with the anecdotal evidence from other states.

By 2007, students who wanted to attend a school other than their home school the following year faced the following situation: of the nine nonmagnet school options available to families, the lowest-poverty school had a rate that was approximately 1.3 times the systemwide average, and the average of the poverty rates in these nine schools was approximately 1.8 times the systemwide average. Of the twenty-nine schools with magnet options, only two had poverty rates below the systemwide average.[30]

Additional indication of how little choice the FCP actually gave families came in 2004, when CMS dropped the word "choice" from the name of its pupil assignment plan.[31] The subsequent pupil assignment policy bore the modest title, Student Assignment Plan. The name change reflected the fact that once CMS returned to a neighborhood school–based assignment plan, choice essentially became an illusion. With so many white, middle-class, suburban families choosing to exercise their guarantee of attending their home school, there were few choices other than seats in high-poverty schools available to students who did not want to attend their home schools. The vast majority of CMS students—even those in chronically underperforming schools—had no option but to attend their neighborhood schools. Given this limited choice, it is hardly surprising that the new plan also led to an increase in resegregation by race and socioeconomic status.

Resegregation

Losing sight of desegregation

We shall shortly demonstrate how the new pupil assignment plan led to an increase in both racial and socioeconomic resegregation. However, before presenting the relevant data, we note that just as CMS acknowledged how little choice the new plan provided by changing the plan's name, so, too, did it acknowledge the reality of increased resegregation by changing the district's vision statement. From at least the early 1990s, the district's vision statement had included the lofty aspiration of being "the premier, urban integrated school system in the nation in which all students acquire the knowledge, skills, and values" necessary to live full, enlightened and productive lives." But in 2006, the district changed that statement to represent a much less ambitious vision, stating that the district "provides all students the best education available anywhere, preparing every child to lead a rich and productive life."[32] The revised statement made no reference to integration or even implied the commitment to diversity and racial justice that was inherent in the abandoned vision statement.

Racial isolation

We initially measured racial isolation using the index of racial dissimilarity. This index is independent of the racial composition of a district and indicates the proportion of a district's students that would have to be moved to ensure that the racial composition of each school in the district would be the same as the racial composition of the entire district. This index ranges from 0 (perfect racial balance) to 100 (complete segregation).[33] Dissimilarity indices can be computed for any two groups of students (e.g., Hispanics/blacks; Hispanics/whites, blacks/whites, etc.). Although it is important to consider segregation from multiethnic/multiracial and socioeconomic perspectives, there are good reasons to focus the discussion on resegregation between blacks and whites. The two groups are still the largest in CMS's increasingly diverse student population, and blacks and whites remain Charlotte's two most politically influential ethnic groups.

Using the racial dissimilarity index, figure 6.1 charts changes in black-white segregation in CMS elementary schools, which tend to provide a more sensitive measure of segregation than middle or high schools because their enrollments and attendance zones are typically smaller. As figure 6.1 indicates, black-white segregation drifted upward through the 1990s, jumped sharply in between the 2002 and 2003 school years, and has gradually increased since then. Although—as figure 6.1 also shows—the white share of the district enrollment trended downward during these same eleven years, this trend shows nowhere near the marked change between 2002 and 2003 that the data on racial dissimilarity shows. Because 2003 was the first year of the new pupil assignment plan, the marked increase in the racial dissimilarity index in 2003 indicates that the new pupil assignment plan contributed to resegregation independent of any resegregation that might be attributed to long-term resegregation trends and/or the declining percentage of the district's students who are white.

Socioeconomic isolation

CMS has also resegregated by socioeconomic status since the implementation of the FCP. Student SES is indicated by the dichotomous measure of whether or not the student is eligible for free or reduced-price lunch (FRL). Figure 6.2 offers data on the systemwide percentage of FRL students and displays trends in socioeconomic resegregation in CMS's elementary schools. It presents data

FIGURE 6.1: Elementary School Racial Segregation, 1998–2008

Source: North Carolina Department of Public Instruction.

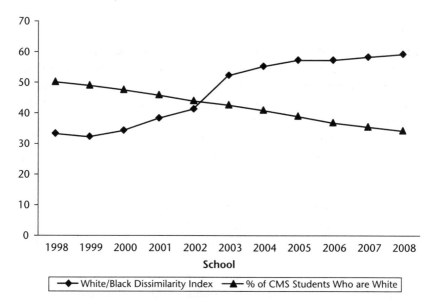

FIGURE 6.2: Elementary School Socioeconomic Segregation, 1998–2008

Source: Charlotte-Mecklenburg Schools.

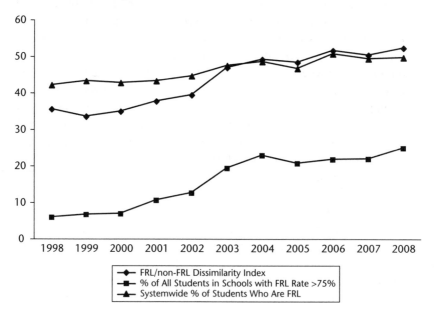

on the FRL/non-FRL dissimilarity index and the percentage of all elementary students in high-poverty schools (defined as schools whose FRL population is greater than 75 percent).

Prior to the implementation of the FCP in 2002, the percentage of students in high-poverty schools was increased only slightly, and it has been largely constant since the plan was implemented. However, the percentage of students in high-poverty schools jumped by approximately 75 percent. Moreover, as figure 6.2 indicates, the single sharpest increase in the FRL/non-FRL dissimilarity index occurred upon the implementation of the new pupil assignment plan. The magnitude of the jump in both measures of socioeconomic resegregation cannot be attributed to the systemwide increase in the percentage of FRL students, since that percentage increased only slightly between 2002 and 2003.

In sum, both racial and socioeconomic segregation increased in recent years. Figures 6.1 and 6.2 show that the new assignment plan resulted in large jumps in both types of resegregation in the 2003 school year, the first year CMS operated under the FCP. While both kinds of resegregation trended upward over the 11-year period displayed in both figure 6.1 and figure 6.2, there is no instance in either figure where resegregation jumped as markedly between any two school years as it did between 2002 and 2003. Therefore, these figures indicate that, independent of demographic trends, the implementation of the FCP increased resegregation by socioeconomic status and by race.

Our findings about resegregation, we should add, are consistent with those of Clotfelter, Ladd, and Vigdor, who measured K–12 racial segregation in North Carolina public schools using detailed 2005–06 administrative data from the North Carolina Department of Public Instruction.[34] Their research indicates that no other large district in North Carolina experienced an increase in segregation as dramatic as that at CMS in this period, and they conclude, as do we, that a district's choice plan appears to markedly increase segregation. They also examined racial segregation within schools by tracks and found that this also increased between the school years ending in 2001 and 2006. Within-school segregation is an important measure because it indicated that schools resegregated students by tracks even in racially balanced schools.[35]

Academic Achievement

We report selected elementary, middle, and high school achievement data by school year, student race, student SES, and by school SES composition.

Based on elementary or middle schools' percentage of students receiving free or reduced-price lunch, we divided schools into low-poverty (0 percent to 25 percent of their students on FRL), moderate-poverty (26 percent to 75 percent), and high-poverty (76 percent to 100 percent) categories. We divided high schools into low-poverty (0 percent to 25 percent of their students on FRL), moderate-poverty (26 percent to 55 percent), and high-poverty (56 percent to 87 percent) categories. Three alternative high schools, all with more than 87 percent FRL students, formed a fourth category of extremely high-poverty schools.[36]

Our investigation of school SES, racial composition, and student achievement uses publicly available data from the North Carolina Department of Public Instruction.[37] Using these data, we investigated post-unitary achievement trends in several ways. First, we examined fifth- and eighth-grade students' math and reading end-of-grade scores by race and FRL status at two points in time—in the 2002 school year (the last year that CMS operated under its mandatory desegregation plan) and in 2005 (three years after the implementation of the FCP). Because CMS used different tests each year, we converted math and reading scale scores to Z-scores so that we could compare across the different tests.

Table 6.1 indicates that during the first three years after receiving unitary status, CMS made modest progress in improving fifth- and eighth-grade math and reading proficiency scores of black, white, poor, and nonpoor students. With the exception of a small reading gain among Hispanic fifth graders, all other Hispanic scores worsened in reading and math. Importantly, the gains among poor students and blacks were greater than the gains among nonpoor students and whites, suggesting that since 2002, the gaps between black-white and free or reduced-price lunch and non-FRL students have narrowed slightly among fifth and eighth graders in both subject areas. The white-Hispanic gap in fifth-grade reading narrowed as well.

While the gains in fifth- and eighth-grade reading and math scores indicate that CMS's efforts to improve outcomes have been modestly effective for most students, the resegregation of the school system by race and SES raises the possibility that the overall gains in test scores may be unevenly distrib-

TABLE 6.1: Changes in Z-Scores for Math and EOG Scale Scores for CMS Students in Fifth and Eighth Grade, 2002–05

	Reading 2002	Reading 2005	Change 2002–2005	Math 2002	Math 2005	Change 2002–2005
Fifth Grade	(N=8246)	(N=8857)		(N=8349)	(N=8908)	
Receiving Free Lunch	–.534	–.452	+.082	–.525	–.447	+.078
Not Receiving Free Lunch	.413	.431	+.018	.414	.430	+.016
White	.499	.517	+.018	.511	.524	+.013
Black	–.437	–.405	+.032	–.477	–.457	+.020
Hispanic	–.368	–.318	+.050	–.293	–.200	+.093
Eighth Grade	(N=7703)	(N=9102)		(N=7719)	(N=9143)	
Receiving Free Lunch	–.606	–.496	+.110	–.551	–.510	+.041
Not Receiving Free Lunch	.343	.423	+.080	.314	.438	+.124
White	.512	.570	+.058	.494	.613	+.119
Black	–.489	–.397	+.092	–.507	–.472	+.035
Hispanic	–.421	–.464	–.043	–.360	–.388	–.028

Source: North Carolina Educational Research Data Center, Public Use Files, 2002–2005.

uted among students attending different kinds of schools. We investigated whether the SES of the schools students attended is correlated with their outcomes, net of students' own race and family background. Table 6.2 presents mean fifth- and eighth-grade end-of-grade (EOG) math and reading scale scores for students in the low-, moderate-, and high-poverty schools.

Table 6.2 shows that controlling for students' own race and SES, those who attend a low-poverty school do better in math and reading than their peers of similar racial and SES backgrounds attending either a moderate- or high-poverty school. The findings in table 6.2 indicate that in all cases, students from more privileged backgrounds score higher than their peers from less privileged ones. However, attending schools with high levels of student poverty has a negative relationship with achievement for all students, irrespective of their own race and SES. In fact, fifth-grade mean reading scores of FRL students in low-poverty schools (256.14) are higher than their counterparts in both moderate-poverty (254.33) and high-poverty schools (252.85). This pattern appears in all comparisons in table 6.2.

Next, we examined high school students' 2004–05 end-of-course (EOC) scale scores by students' race and free/reduced-price lunch status. Table 6.3 presents mean EOC scale scores in English I, biology, and Algebra I by high school poverty level. The results show that concentrated poverty in high schools is negatively associated with achievement. As one reads from left to right in any row in table 6.3, scores go from higher to lower, indicating that, irrespective of their own race or SES, students in schools with low poverty levels outperform their race and SES counterparts who attend schools with higher concentrations of poverty. In fact, low-income students who attend low-poverty schools scored higher in biology (53.25) than their more prosperous peers who attend schools with high levels of poverty (52.83); low-income students who attend low-poverty schools scored higher in Algebra I (53.49) than their more prosperous peers who attend schools with high levels of school poverty (52.77). In all subjects, FRL students in schools with low levels of poverty outperformed students in alternative schools who did not qualify for free or reduced-price lunch.

To further explore high school achievement in relation to school race and SES composition, we looked at 2004–05 CMS high school seniors' percentage of proficiency on EOC composites and the Advanced Placement exam pass rates. We contrast four racially imbalanced minority schools with high concentrations of poverty and with one of the racially imbalanced white high schools with very few students living in poverty.[38] In 2006, the four high-poverty minority high schools became the targets of a North Carolina

TABLE 6.2: Fifth- and Eighth-Grade CMS Reading and Math Test Scale Scores by Percentage of Students in School on Free or Reduced-Price Lunch (FRL) Status by Student SES and Race, 2005

	School Population 0–25% FRL		School Population 26–75% FRL		School Population 76–100% FRL	
	Reading	Math	Reading	Math	Reading	Math
Fifth Grade						
Student on FRL	256.14	260.44	254.33	258.56	252.85	257.87
Student not on FRL	262.55	269.52	260.06	265.68	256.97	262.16
Black	256.09	259.31	254.84	258.50	254.04	257.71
White	262.58	269.55	260.94	266.93	256.67	262.33
Hispanic	258.28	264.55	255.25	261.21	253.53	259.51
Eighth Grade						
Student on FRL	262.63	270.96	259.60	266.55	257.79	264.60
Student not on FRL	270.20	280.96	267.46	276.77	263.16	270.35
Black	262.89	270.71	260.73	267.03	258.61	264.99
White	270.56	281.29	268.71	278.73	264.58	272.69
Hispanic	266.14	276.44	259.69	267.67	256.97	264.65

Source: North Carolina Educational Research Data Center, Public Use Files, 2005.

TABLE 6.3: Mean Scale Score on Selected High School End-of-Course Tests in CMS by Student SES, Race by School Poverty Status, 2005

	0–25% Student Body on FRL (N of schools=6)	26–55% Student Body on FRL (N of schools=6)	56–87% Student Body on FRL (N of schools=5)	88–100% Student Body on FRL[d] (N of schools=3)
English 1[a]				
FRL	54.46	54.62	53.28	51.00
Not on FRL	62.11	59.56	55.73	50.78
White	62.81	61.13	56.53	58.23
Black	54.87	55.73	53.86	50.30
Hispanic	56.41	54.89	51.67	49.82
Biology[b]				
FRL	53.25	51.86	50.99	46.54
Not FRL	60.23	56.53	52.83	48.14
White	61.03	59.22	54.75	54.71
Black	52.79	52.34	51.05	46.01
Hispanic	55.28	53.22	51.24	48.00
Algebra 1[c]				
FRL	53.49	52.69	52.55	49.18
Not on FRL	57.81	54.87	52.77	53.06
White	61.03	59.22	54.75	54.71
Black	52.79	52.34	51.05	46.01
Hispanic	55.28	53.22	51.24	48.00

Source: North Carolina Educational Research Data Center, Public Use Files, 2005.

[a] English I, N= 3651 white, 4000 black, 692 Hispanic, 3278 Free Lunch

[b] Biology, N= 3691 white, 3821 black, 559 Hispanic, 2883 Free Lunch

[c] Algebra I, N= 4302 white, 4944 black, 862 Hispanic, 4120 Free Lunch

[d] Alternative Schools; all others are comprehensive high schools

state assistance team because their students repeatedly failed to score proficiently on EOC exams. Our comparisons among the five schools illustrate the outcomes and opportunities to learn in CMS's four highest-poverty, racially imbalanced minority high schools and its most highly regarded, racially imbalanced, white low-poverty high school, Myers Park. EOC proficiency rates are inexact indicators of a school's effectiveness, but they are widely used for high-stakes decisionmaking. AP exam pass rates are one indicator of a school's success in preparing its students for higher education. Table 6.4 shows that twelfth-grade students at Myers Park were far more likely to be proficient in their EOC subjects and to pass Advanced Placement exams than their peers at Harding, Wadell, Berry, and West Charlotte, the four the racially imbalanced minority, high-poverty high schools in our comparison.

Resources and School Composition

We also investigated the relationship between school resources and racial composition. There were two reasons for doing this. The first is that one of the critical pathways by which school composition influences outcomes is its association with the distribution of resources, especially teachers.[39] The second is that in an effort to deal with increased resegregation, CMS has, as indicated above, developed programs aimed at providing additional resources to schools heavily affected by resegregation.

TABLE 6.4: CMS Seniors' Proficiency, AP Passing Rate, and Selected Characteristics at Four Racially Imbalanced, Minority, High-Poverty High Schools and One Racially Imbalanced, White, Low-Poverty High School, 2005

School	% Proficient III EOG Composite	% AP Exam Pass Rate	% EOC Underqualified Teachers	% Math College Prep Math Courses	% Science College Prep Math Courses
Harding	55.5	29	31	40	65
Waddell	47.2	21	38	24	31
Berry	45.7	14	29	36	40
West Charlotte	34.5	0	40	21	23
Myers Park	81.2	56	9	48	68

Source: Roslyn Arlin Mickelson and Bobbie Everett, "Neotracking in North Carolina: How High School Courses of Study Reproduce Race and Class-based Stratification," *Teachers College Record* 110 (2008): 535–70.

Clotfelter and his colleagues examined whether the changes in CMS's segregation levels in recent years led to changes in resource disparities. Focusing on teacher characteristics, they found that whites are more likely than blacks to attend schools with the most highly qualified teachers. They report that between 2002 and 2006, disparities in CMS teacher resources grew more pronounced between black and white students and between high- and low-income students.[40] They concluded that resegregation was directly responsible for growing teacher resource disparities in CMS.

One could easily dismiss the apparent relationship between the school race and SES composition and EOC composite proficiency levels and AP pass rates found in table 6.4 as unremarkable reflections of the well-known relationships among achievement, family background, and race. However, our data—and Clotfelter's—suggest otherwise; that is, student performance is linked to opportunities to learn as well. Table 6.4 presents disparities in opportunity to learn that are linked to the high schools' racial and SES composition. Qualified teachers are essential to opportunities to learn, yet the racially imbalanced, minority, high-poverty schools have three or four times as many underqualified teachers (between 29 percent and 40 percent) as Myers Park (9 percent), the racially imbalanced, white, low-poverty school. Similarly, Myers Park offers 48 percent of its math and 68 percent of its science courses at the college preparatory level. With the exception of Harding University High School—designated as a college preparatory magnet high school—the racially imbalanced, minority, high-poverty schools offer proportionately fewer math and science courses at the college preparatory level. Differential proficiency levels and AP pass rates are likely related to curricular and teacher resource differences among the schools. Disparities in teacher quality parallel disparities in opportunities to learn in the school attended by the fifth- and eighth-grade students whose performance we analyzed earlier. For example, the percentage of inexperienced teachers (35.7%) at the high-poverty schools is greater than that at low-poverty schools (23.4%), with the moderate-poverty schools having a percentage of such teachers (32.4%) between the two other groups. Similarly, teacher turnover (27.8%) at the high-poverty schools is greater than that at the low-poverty schools (16.2%), with the percentage (22.3%) at the moderate-poverty schools falling in between. Additionally, when it comes to desirable teacher characteristics such as being fully licensed and having an advanced degree, the high-poverty schools have the lowest percentages of qualified teachers, the low-poverty schools have the highest percentages of such teachers, and the percentages for the moderate-poverty schools again fall between those of the two other groups.

Findings presented in tables 6.2, 6.3, and 6.4 indicate that achievement gains in CMS since 2002 are unevenly distributed. Students with less privileged backgrounds and those attending schools with concentrations of low-income (and minority) students score well below their peers at low-poverty schools. And the data on teacher characteristics and course offerings in table 6.4 illustrate how access to highly qualified teachers and rigorous curricula—stratified by a school's race and SES composition—tends to correlates with student outcomes.

High School Graduation Rates

Finally, we report recent data on CMS high school graduation rates. Swanson calculated 2003–04 graduation rates using the Common Core of Data, following the Cumulative Promotion Index method. He reported disparities in 2004 public high school graduation rates between urban students and their peers in suburban schools in the nation's fifty largest cities. He found that in 2004, CMS's graduation rate of 59.8 percent was 10.7 percent lower than the rate of the surrounding suburban districts. CMS's overall graduation rate was comparable to the average rate for the other urban school systems, and the surrounding suburban district's rate was slightly below the national average for suburbs.[41]

In 2007, CMS high school dropout numbers had increased sharply over 2006.[42] Although dropout rates remained lower at suburban schools attended by affluent, primarily white students, the dropout rate for white students in CMS had increased by 3.5 percent between 2006 and 2007. For blacks the rate increased by 9 percent, and for Hispanics by 11.5 percent. West Charlotte High School, a racially imbalanced minority school with high poverty levels, reported an increase of 46 percent in its dropout rate between 2006 and 2007. Moreover, the increases for blacks and Hispanics at CMS exceeded the state of North Carolina's increase for the two ethnic groups, while the CMS rate of increase for whites was lower than the state's.

Although Swanson's examination of CMS's 2004 graduation rates and the CMS report on its 2007 high school dropout rates are independent studies, the two sets of findings complement achievement data suggesting that, since 2002, the school system has not been successful in educating children who attend schools characterized by high levels of concentrated poverty. And because of the resegregation triggered by the district's pupil assignment plan, the students who attend the schools with concentrated poverty are overwhelmingly low-income students of color.

DISCUSSION

Our data indicate that since becoming unitary, CMS has, generally speaking, slightly improved EOG math and language performance for whites and blacks and language proficiency among Hispanics. During this period, CMS could justifiably point to other noteworthy accomplishments, many of which signified important national recognition of its students, teachers, and/or the district itself.[43] A handful of high-poverty elementary schools with award-winning principals or gifted magnet programs outperformed the predictions based on their students' demographic profiles.[44] Furthermore, the majority of the district's students benefited on a daily basis from the work of thousands of CMS employees who fulfilled their responsibilities with skill, care, and dedication, despite the legal and political turmoil with which the district was dealing.[45]

There are currently still striking SES and racial differences in opportunities to learn and in student performance in CMS schools. The district has experienced marked resegregation by SES and race/ethnicity since 2002. Levels of concentrated poverty in CMS elementary, middle, and high schools are negatively related to student performance. The findings also suggest that the resegregation has consequences for educational outcomes. The inequitable allocation of resources, especially of certified teachers, reflects the new racial and SES stratification in the schools.

CMS is clearly aware of these problems, and it has been taking steps to address them. Among other things, CMS has instituted a range of strategies to lure highly qualified teachers to high-poverty schools, including signing bonuses of $15,000. But despite these efforts, high-poverty schools have not successfully recruited highly qualified teachers.[46] In fact, some of the strategies employed to boost student achievement in underperforming schools have had the unintended consequence of undermining the recruitment and retention of highly qualified teachers at these schools. For example, because the current superintendent threatened to fire teachers who do not raise their students' EOG or EOC scores, a number of veteran teachers left underperforming schools for suburban and mid-ring schools where student performance is typically higher.[47] Aware of how these disincentives operate, the superintendent proposed in January 2008 to transfer—against a teacher's will if necessary—successful teachers to high-poverty schools. But only one board member—an African American retired teacher—voiced support for such transfers, and the superintendent subsequently withdrew the proposal, saying that "it had been made very clear to me" that a majority of board members were opposed to such transfers.[48] Thus, CMS's efforts to move especially talented teachers to high-poverty schools have produced, at best, mixed results. Thirty teachers agreed to transfer to high-poverty schools, but a majority of them were transferring from other high-poverty schools.[49]

As indicated by the discussion of teacher transfers, CMS faces a wide range of obstacles in trying to deal with the consequences of the court order declaring it unitary and the many other challenges it faces. Many of these obstacles, such as the legal ones, are shared with other districts that have been declared unitary and/or are trying to deal with the barriers that the Supreme Court erected to voluntary desegregation in the Seattle and Louisville districts. And, like many other urban districts, CMS must compete for teachers with nearby districts whose schools may not pose the challenging issues that many CMS schools do. But CMS faces political barriers as well as opportunities that many other urban districts do not face. Such barriers and opportunities arise from CMS's being a consolidated district that covers all of Mecklenburg County. This extensive area discouraged white flight during the heyday of mandatory busing and continues to give the district access to a diversity of financial and human resources that many urban districts lack.

Middle-class whites have had the advantages that middle-class white citizens typically enjoy in politics. But in Charlotte, these advantages were previously balanced somewhat by the pride long-time white Charlotteans had in CMS's desegregation accomplishments and in school board politics that facilitated the election of black board members. That situation has changed. As noted above, the 2007 school board election was the first since 1968 in which no African American sought a seat on the board, a graphic indication of how, in the years following the adoption of the race-neutral choice plan, there has been significant black political demobilization on education issues.

These political considerations strongly suggest that a necessary—but certainly not sufficient—condition to providing CMS with the political will and capacity to address the educational needs of all students, but especially low-income children of color, is a political remobilization of black Charlotteans and their traditional liberal white allies. To succeed, such remobilization would require coalitions with other peoples of color, especially from Charlotte's burgeoning Hispanic population. The ability of African Americans and Hispanics to ally on educational issues generally depends on the specifics of an issue,[50] but given the fact that disproportionately high percentages of black and Hispanic students are often found in the same CMS schools, there would appear to be a strong basis for alliances on policies that would provide additional resources for these schools and give students at these schools more options in pupil assignment.

CONCLUSION

Whatever the political and educational future of CMS might be, it is clear that its recent educational past is consistent with the vast corpus of research on school choice showing the limitations of race-neutral school choice policies for creating diverse schools.[51] CMS's recent history demonstrates why without race- and SES-conscious controls, the vast majority of school choice policies and practices cannot forestall resegregation by race and SES. CMS's material and spatial realities limited the viability of choice as an equitable and quality option for students consigned to low-performing schools. In fact, the race-neutral design of CMS's Family Choice Plan facilitated the resegregation of the school system. Given the Supreme Court's ruling in the Seattle and Louisville cases and the general tenor of federal court rulings over the last two decades, CMS's recent experience is important because it may well foreshadow the fate of other school systems that abandon efforts to create racially and socioeconomically diverse schools through race-conscious policies. Race-neutral choice as a strategy, like CMS's FCP, will likely increase the difficulties faced by local educators seeking to provide equity or excellence in public education.

CMS's recent experience is also consistent with the corpus of research indicating the need for caution—perhaps even precision—in anticipating the consequences of race-neutral choice plans for pupil assignment. To be sure, CMS began resegregating long before the district was declared unitary, and the decrease in the white share of the district's enrollment began well before the declaration of unitary status. But, as indicated by the marked jump in resegregation upon implementation of the race-neutral pupil assignment plan in 2003, the FCP increased resegregation independently of these long-term trends. Our data do not allow us to parse with any precision how much the various aspects of the race-neutral plan contributed to the resegregation because these various aspects reinforced each other. In other words, the neighborhood school guarantee combined with overcrowding at high-performing and/or predominantly white schools created a situation that limited the choices available to students whose home school was low-performing and/or segregated by race and/or socioeconomic status.

Whether one concludes that the chimera of choice in CMS has been an unrealized dream, an unintended consequence of the race-neutral plan, or a goal of the plan depends on one's perspective or, perhaps, level of cynicism. Whatever one's perspective, CMS's recent history shows that even though the choice plan was aimed at placating desegregation's opponents, anger at CMS in outlying, predominantly white areas became even stronger in the first years of the plan. Indicators of school excellence show uneven accomplishments, and markers of equity show striking disparities. Despite the catchy name and the politically appealing pairing of the words "family" and "choice," CMS's FCP offered little to no choice to the vast majority of families, including those who were entitled to transfer from their low-performing neighborhood school to a higher-performing one. Implementation of the FCP increased the resegregation of the district by race and socioeconomic status. It also increased the stratification of key resources and student achievement.

The reconstitution of the post-unitary CMS as a system with increasingly inequitable outcomes, schools segregated by race and socioeconomic status, and a community no longer invested in a single school system for all children is telling. The recent history of the Charlotte-Mecklenburg Schools, once emblematic of the possibilities of school desegregation, now foreshadows the probable nationwide consequences of resegregation after court-ended desegregation.

CHAPTER SEVEN

Neighborhood Schools in the Aftermath of Court-Ended Busing

Educators' Perspectives on How Context and Composition Matter

Claire E. Smrekar and Ellen B. Goldring

In the fall of 1998, the Metropolitan Nashville school board and the plaintiffs in a 42-year-old federal school desegregation suit agreed to court-granted unitary status for the district and a $206 million school improvement plan that reduced crosstown busing and created new magnet and neighborhood schools. The new plan radically changed student assignment policies in the Nashville schools by eliminating the court-ordered busing patterns that had driven school assignment policies since 1971. The earlier court plan established a satellite busing system that paired largely African American inner-city neighborhoods with mostly white suburban areas. Under this arrangement, many Metro students rode the bus for over an hour each way to school.

The unitary-status plan reorganized student assignment into eleven cluster feeder patterns (elementary-middle school attendance zones that feed to a common high school) designed to reduce the distance between students' homes and schools. The plan increased school choice to include magnet schools, enhanced option schools for high-poverty neighborhoods, and design-center programs. Enhanced option schools were intended to deliver extra support to students and their families. The main features of these schools included smaller class size (capped at fifteen) and an extended school year (originally forty extra instructional days, now reduced to twenty). These schools were designed to link closely with the attendance zone neighborhood and the surrounding community. "Enhanced" services included early education programs (preK), afterschool academic enrichment and tutoring, and social and health services. These resources were not guaranteed in the plan.

The school improvement plan called for phased-in implementation over a five-year period, and the 2003–04 school year marked the final year of that plan. During the years of implementation, significant changes in the district have included rezoning schools to reflect neighborhood attendance zones, transforming nine existing inner-city schools into extended-year enhanced option schools, and establishing new magnet school programs. The majority of the rezoning and reconfiguring in Nashville is now complete, although the district continues to modify some aspects of the plan, including attendance zones and magnet school operations.

The purpose of this chapter is to explore the consequences of a return to neighborhood schools for students in poverty following the end of court-ordered crosstown busing. These new policies for neighborhood schools reflect imperatives that privilege close proximity of home and school, often at the cost of socioeconomic and ethnic diversity. These trends raise important questions regarding the role and relative significance of "the total ecology of schooling"[1] in a postdesegregation (or postbusing) era that reproduces the corrosive conditions of neighborhood poverty in newly rezoned, socioeconomically isolated, high-poverty neighborhood schools.

In this chapter, we explore the ways that neighborhoods matter in the school lives of teachers and their students. Specifically, we examine enhanced option schools—new neighborhood school programs adopted as part of the new student assignment plan—that are located in inner-city neighborhoods and have been transformed to address the educational needs of students at risk of school failure due to poverty.[2] They serve children from the immediate neighborhoods in which they are located. As designed, enhanced option schools reflect the district's and the plaintiffs' concerns related to issues of equity (or inequity) in the aftermath of court-ended crosstown busing. With the imprimatur now firmly rooted in neighborhood schooling in Metropolitan Nashville, the enhanced option schools represent an effort to allocate additional resources to neighborhood schools comprised of students with the greatest academic and social needs—those children living in concentrated poverty. These students' school experiences and academic performance establish the test of equity for this district, which is now operating under a new set of imperatives geared toward achievement, accountability, and parental choice.

The significance of the success or failure of a school model linked to a promise of equity in a district declared unitary is important. Without court oversight, it is unclear if at-risk students who are returned to racially isolated neighborhood schools will receive the resources promised in the new student assignment plan that are intended to support high expectations for learning. Although legally repudiated in the 1896 *Plessy v. Ferguson* decision, the unequal distribution of dollars, facilities, and programs between white and black schools persisted following that landmark U.S. Supreme Court ruling. Almost sixty years later, *Brown* outlawed the doctrine of "separate but equal," and with it within-district funding inequity. Evidence from years of study, however, shows a continuing relationship between the percentage of minority students in a school and the financial resources allocated to it in terms of class size, age, condition of facilities, teacher-student ratios, and per-pupil expenditures.[3] Historically in the South, in "areas where blacks were more numerous, a greater share of school resources were diverted from the black schools to white schools, raising the resources in white schools and depressing them in black schools."[4]

Against the backdrop of a new student assignment plan and the decades of crosstown busing now ended by a grant of unitary status, our attention rests with the new schools designed to meet the needs of children "returned" to their neighborhood school after a sustained period of busing. We focus on the students the district considers to be at risk of school failure due to an array of conditions associated with poverty. Our conceptual lenses turn to the relationship between geographic and social space, and to the social processes and social structures in communities that have an impact on the educational experiences and opportunities of families and children. We ask, does neighborhood matter?

THE ECOLOGY OF NEIGHBORHOODS

Early work by sociologists at the University of Chicago highlights the conditions of disadvantage associated with particular structural factors in neighborhoods.[5] These early studies of urban environments underscore the deleterious effects of low-income, racially segregated neighborhoods on the social disorganization of community life, including the social instability that leads to high crime rates. An extension of this social disorganization model—known as social transformation theory[6]—underscores the impact of concentrated neighborhood poverty and social isolation on individuals who adapt to the limited economic opportunities and weak social ties found in inner-city neighborhoods. Residents in inner-city neighborhoods characterized by concentrated poverty and social isolation face limited access to quality schools and few opportunities to find well-paying, stable jobs. Social isolation restricts access to the social networks essential for individual economic advancement in a modern industrial society.

This study underscores the salience of these influences for children, their families, and the schools. These urban sociological models unpack the significance of sociodemographic conditions associated with neighborhoods that are characterized by liability or risk.

High-Risk Neighborhoods

The concept of a high-risk neighborhood is derived from the social and economic conditions that put individuals at risk of failure, or of encountering significant problems related to employment, education, self-sufficiency, or a healthy lifestyle. At-risk conditions include both environmental and community characteristics, such as crime and limited employment opportunities, and individual qualities, such as poverty and low educational attainment. The problems or failures encountered by those labeled at risk are oriented toward the future but linked to current conditions.

The understanding that interactions between particular environmental and individual characteristics may lead to a heightened risk of negative outcomes is rooted in the health and medical literature, and it is widely examined in studies of social stratification, educational inequality, and social policy. Common arguments in these sociological studies suggest that individuals "disadvantaged" by low socioeconomic status are more susceptible to adverse environmental or community conditions, such as unsafe housing and poor-quality schooling.[7] Decades of social science research provide compelling evidence that the extent and concentration of neighborhood poverty and the presence (or absence) of affluent neighbors are associated with an array of outcomes, including rates of teenage pregnancy and school dropout.[8] But policymakers and social scientists also underscore the finding that in socially depleted neighborhoods, residents are often constrained in their efforts to transmit positive values and productive norms because of a lack of community structure and effective social controls.[9]

Historically, neighborhoods have functioned as the social, political, and cultural webbing for families and children. This context links families and individuals to a set of norms, routines, and traditions. The social scripts embedded in the geography and culture of the neighborhood, if well known and well defined, become institutionalized practices for children and adults. Social actions flow from perceptions of safety and opportunity, expectations regarding appropriate parenting styles and child behavior, and norms regarding home maintenance and respect for property.[10] The neighborhood environment defines the formation of particular social networks among families and the levels of trust, familiarity, and face-to-face engagement among members.

Clusters of interlocking and corrosive conditions are persistent in high-risk neighborhoods and are evidenced by dense and dilapidated housing, a real and constant threat of violent crime, inadequate and inaccessible health care, a lack of employment opportunities that pay a living wage, and unreliable and limited public transportation.[11] These concrete indicators of poverty and social isolation give rise to an insidious and entrenched culture of fear, disconnection, and distrust in high-risk neighborhoods. Families may be paralyzed by fear of gangs and guns. Omnipresent drug traffic and a constant threat of victimization minimize opportunities for interdependence and delimit social interaction among community members. High mobility rates in these neighborhoods lead to blocks of unstable and abandoned housing. Researchers agree that these out-of-school environments constitute vital components that are deeply connected but external to students' experiences in formal school settings.[12]

What role do enhanced option schools play in mediating the impact of adverse conditions in high-risk neighborhoods? What are the implications of assigning kids to enhanced option schools when the neighborhood is high risk?

Social Capital Theory

This study is anchored to questions and concepts that relate to the development of social capital in schools that are nested in neighborhoods of concentrated poverty and served by enhanced option schools in Nashville. Social capital bridges human capital theory,[13] which underscores the economic value of individuals for collective purposes, and social organization theory. James S. Coleman defines social capital as "the norms, the social networks, and the relationships between adults and children that are of value for the child's growing up."[14] The critical elements of social capital include shared values, norms, and attitudes that help promote trust, facilitate open and fluid communication, and produce purposeful and meaningful activities that benefit students and adults alike. Social capital is sustained when there is "a sense of community" or a set of organizational and institutional affiliations (e.g., civic, religious, professional) that bind families in stable, predictable, and enduring social ties.[15] Intergenerational closure describes an element of social capital through which children know each other's parents and parents are in regular communication with each other. This overlapping social structure enables adults to "use their mutual obligations to aid them in raising their own children and establish good norms that reinforce each other's sanctioning of the children."[16] Neighborhood-based institutions, including youth organizations (e.g., the Boys and Girls Club), religious organizations (churches, synagogues, mosques), and recreation programs (afterschool sports), represent sources that produce social capital (including intergenerational closure) and thus are essential for enhancing the trust and communication—and a sense of community—among children and families alike in neighborhoods.[17]

METHODOLOGY

Site

This chapter is based on data from the Nashville school district, a teacher survey, and a subset of qualitative case studies that are part of a larger, multiple-methods research study of unitary status and implementation of the School Improvement Plan in the Metropolitan Nashville Public Schools. According to the district, total enrollment in the 2003–04 school year was 71,000 students; of this population, 48 percent were black, 40 percent were white, 8 percent Hispanic, and 3 percent Asian; fewer than 1 percent were American Indian. The poverty rate for the district in 2003–04 was 51 percent. This demographic portrait of the district's student population contrasts sharply with census data for the metropolitan area as a whole, in which whites comprise 65 percent of the total population, blacks make up 26 percent, and Hispanics, 5 percent. With a poverty rate of 19 percent, the Nashville public schools reflect a trend found nationwide across urban school districts, with a higher proportion of minority students and a higher poverty rate than the city as a whole.

Notably, as the new student assignment plan was implemented, there were substantial achievement gaps between students in enhanced options schools and other zoned, neighborhood schools in the district (excluding magnet schools). These gaps amounted to thirty-seven points on standardized achievement tests in reading and forty-eight points in math in 1999–00, and thirty-seven points in reading and forty-three points in math in 2002–03—perhaps evidence of slight progress in math, but the gap remains extremely wide.[18]

Data Collection

The quantitative data for our analysis come from Nashville district files for six school years: 1998–99 to 2003–04. In addition, as an ongoing effort to monitor Metro's progress in meeting the goals set forth in the unitary-status plan, teachers and staff members at all five of the initial enhanced option schools were surveyed at the end of the 2001–02 school year and again at the end of the 2003–04 school year. The same survey was issued at both points to measure potential changes over time. The survey covered areas that were considered part of Metro's commitment to educating at-risk students: the availability of enhanced services and the adequacy of resources. The overall response rates on the teacher surveys for the two school years were 90 percent (N=186 and N=167). Surveys were collected during faculty meetings, which resulted in a high response rate. For the purposes of this study, we present teachers' descriptive responses to survey questions that pertain to the availability of resources.

For the qualitative case studies, teachers, principals, and school staff members—counselors, reading specialists, Title I coordinators, social workers, nurses, family resource center directors, and school secretaries—were interviewed at each of the two enhanced option schools in our study. Interviews were also conducted with officials from an array of neighborhood-based organizations, including community centers, libraries, advocacy groups, medical clinics, child-care centers, and public housing. A total of seventy-five interviews were completed over eighteen months (data collection ended November 2004).

The two enhanced option schools selected for our case studies, Olive and Jefferson (pseudonyms), were established in the first and third years, respectively, of the student assignment plan (1999 and 2001).[19] This timing allowed us to explore relatively "mature" school reforms that had well-established enhanced option programs in place. At the time of the case study research (2003–04), these two schools were among eight enhanced option schools operating in the district (a ninth school opened the following year). The selection of these two schools creates contrasting case studies along demographic and school-size dimensions. Olive reflects the characteristics typical of the other enhanced option schools in terms of poverty rate and percentage of minority and white students, while Jefferson's enrollment is somewhat smaller (but not the smallest) and less poor (see table 7.1). This comparative

TABLE 7.1: Demographic Background of Students Enrolled in Enhanced Option Schools, Metropolitan Nashville Public Schools, 2003–04

Enhanced Option	Opened	% FRLP	% White	% Black	% Hispanic	% Asian	Enrollment
School A	2003	97	3	97	0	0	360
B (Olive)	1999	95	2	95	2	1	450
C	2003	94	17	82	2	0	330
D	1999	91	3	97	0	1	350
E	2003	90	1	98	1	0	250
F	1999	88	6	92	1	0	590
G	2001	84	10	89	1	0	305
H (Jefferson)	2001	79	21	71	4	4	340

Source: Metropolitan Nashville Public Schools, 2004

design was adopted in order to explore whether or not (even with relatively high levels of poverty and minority student enrollment at both schools) the differences in socioeconomic context and racial composition matter in terms of the nature and quality of social capital (and liability) in the enhanced option schools.

Olive Enhanced Option School opened in a new building on the site that the old Olive Elementary School building had stood for almost forty years. The grade configuration under the enhanced model was changed from kindergarten through second grade to preK through fourth grade—the grade-level configuration for all elementary schools in the district under the new student assignment plan. Jefferson had reopened as an enhanced option program in the existing building built more than thirty years earlier in a pod-style/open classroom arrangement (renovated in 2001 to a traditional "walls 'n' door" classroom arrangement). Jefferson's grade configuration changed from K–6 to preK–4.

ENHANCED OPTION SCHOOLS

The policy rationale behind enhanced option schools is tied to providing resources beyond those offered at other public schools in the district in order to help schools in areas of concentrated poverty meet the needs of their students more effectively—psychologically, socially, and academically. Much of this policy rationale is based on years of research indicating that schools with high concentrations of minority, poor, or low-achieving students tend to have higher percentages of less experienced, less qualified, and lower paid instructional staff than schools with low concentrations of these students.[20] This differing access to qualified teachers may subsequently lead to differences in instructional strategies; in fact, studies show that teachers with less experience and less knowledge are more likely to use ineffective instructional methods.[21]

Teacher Backgrounds

Districtwide data suggest that the enhanced option schools, on average, employ teachers with fewer years of experience than other schools in the district (see figure 7.1). Throughout the years of implementing the new student assignment plan, teachers at enhanced option schools had an average of one or two years less experience than the district average. These teachers had substantially less experience than those at the academically selective magnet schools in the district and less than teachers in other neighborhood schools whose students do not live in such concentrated poverty. Research suggests that teacher experience is related to student achievement. Some report that teaching experience improves reading test scores, while other research cautions that the benefits of experience may level off after five years and may depend on other factors, such as the quality and quantity of professional development and opportunities for continued learning and collaboration.[22] In addition, enhanced option schools are much more likely to employ nonwhite teachers. Although the percentage of minority teachers is increasing throughout the district, the percentage of nonwhite teachers in enhanced option schools is higher than the district average and 10 percent higher than the academic selective magnets. The research on the relationship between students and teachers' race are mixed and inconclusive.[23] The percentage of teachers who stayed at the enhanced option schools are close to or exceed the district average. In 2004, 69 percent of the teachers stayed at their enhanced option school, compared to 61 percent of the teachers districtwide who stayed at their schools. Seventy-one percent of academic magnet school teachers continued teaching in their schools.

Enhanced Services and Community Resources

Teachers in our sample of enhanced option schools were asked on the surveys what percentage of their students needed additional services in the areas of

FIGURE 7.1: Mean Experience by School Type

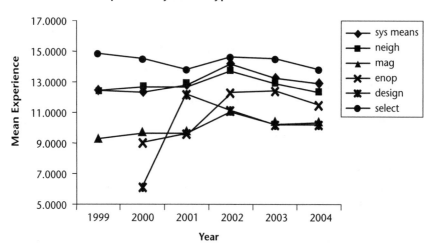

academic tutoring, mentoring, health services, and other social services. On average, the teachers reported that about 50 percent of the students are in need of these added supports. However, the important question is whether students who need these support services actually receive them. Teachers were asked, "About what percentage of your students in your most typical class who need support services actually receive them?" Teachers at enhanced option schools reported the highest percentage of students receiving social services of any school type. On average, enhanced option teachers reported that about 35 percent of students who need services receive them, compared to about 25 percent reported by other schools over both years. Thus, 50 percent of enhanced option students need support services and only about 35 percent actually receive them. While enhanced option schools are not meeting the needs of every child, they are better able to offer services to many more students than they would be if they attended any other type of school (see figure 7.2).

To facilitate additional academic and support services, enhanced option schools were allocated more personnel than other school types. This is clearly the case; about 17 percent of the total staff at enhanced option schools is designated for support services. Only about 7 percent of the staff of other school types is hired specifically to provide support to teachers and students, according to teacher reports. Furthermore, when teachers were asked if there were a curriculum/instruction specialist at their schools, teachers at enhanced

FIGURE 7.2: Percentage of Students Who Need Support Services Compared to Percentage of Students Who Receive Services

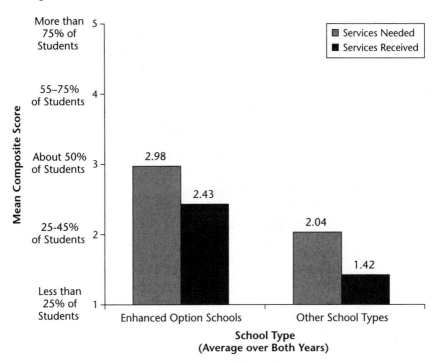

option schools reported "yes" at a higher rate than teachers at any other type of school in both years (57 percent in year one and 90 percent in year two). Additionally, teachers at enhanced option schools were more likely (in both years) to report that if their school had a curriculum specialist, they used them to help with lesson planning, lesson development, and other related activities.

Resource Adequacy

Even though a school may have additional resources, they might not be adequate to meet the needs of the student body. We asked teachers how adequate the resources are across a number of areas, such as reference materials in their classrooms (maps, science kits), supplemental texts and workbooks, supplies, and computers. In year one, enhanced option teachers rated these resources fairly consistently with other school types (mean = 2.66, or adequate). However, in year two, enhanced option schools rated the adequacy of resources as a 2.84, or mostly adequate. Their score was higher than any other school at any other period of time, and the growth from year one to year two was also larger in enhanced option schools than in any other school type. Thus, in 2001–02, enhanced option schools seemed to be average in their resource adequacy in comparison to other school types; however, this seemed to change over time, as is consistent with other reports of the increased resources from year one to year two in enhanced option schools.

In sum, based on teacher reports on surveys collected in our study, the enhanced option schools have more resources than other school types; these resources are intended to support academic goals for at-risk students. Teachers report enhanced services, more personnel, and adequate educational materials (books, computers). The greater need *is* met with the availability of more services. However, consistent with other research on schools that serve at-risk students, these schools have a higher number of less experienced teachers than other schools in the district.

Do these resource enhancements translate to supportive social structures and social processes in enhanced option schools? We now turn to an in-depth examination of how the in-school and out-of-school lives intersect for students and teachers at Olive and Jefferson enhanced option schools.

CASE STUDY: ENHANCED OPTION SCHOOLS

As part of the package of "enhanced" programs, both Olive and Jefferson offer an array of social and health services designed to provide "wrap-around" care to students and families. These extras include a school nurse (full-time), a family resource center (for outreach services, including food, clothing, housing, and utility assistance), and a home-school coordinator (to connect families to school through parent information meetings, home visits). Each school offers psychological counseling for Medicaid-eligible students (provided by local agencies or university-affiliated professional staff). The caseloads are limited to twenty to twenty-five children. Guidance counselors at each school provide additional individual and group counseling services to students.

Olive offers an afterschool academic and enrichment program (funded by the federal 21st Century Community Learning Center grant) that serves approximately fifty children for two hours each day, from 3:00–5:00 PM. The first hour focuses on homework and skill-building; the second hour may involve chess, dance, music, art, or sign language instruction. In the Olive neighborhood, afterschool tutoring and recreation programs are offered by the local public library that serves about fifteen youth each day, by the community center that serves up to fifty children each day, and by a faith-based youth-serving organization that serves dinner and provides tutoring, woodshop, basketball, and other recreation services to children and youth (including many middle school children). A church located outside of the community provides "inner-city ministry" one or two evenings a week; the church van transports children from the housing project to the church for dinner and an enrichment program.

Jefferson schoolchildren have access to a local Boys and Girls Club, although the programs tend to be geared to older, middle school–age children. The primary afterschool program is provided free of charge by a local faith-based organization located immediately across the street from the federal housing project in the Jefferson neighborhood.

Olive School has partnered with Family and Children's Services—a city social services agency—to provide "trauma debriefing" counseling services to children and their families who experience a loss of life and the subsequent grief due to a sudden illness, murder, assault, or suicide, or who witness a traumatic event, such as a shooting, beating, or arrest of a family member or loved one. At Jefferson, due to a unique arrangement with a local university medical center, students and their families have access to a medical clinic on the school site that is staffed by a part-time nurse practitioner, in addition to the full-time nurse. Both schools receive monetary and in-kind assistance (tutoring, mentoring) from local businesses, community centers, churches, senior centers, and universities.

In terms of academic achievement, both schools rank below (with some exceptions at Jefferson) district averages across categories (Below Proficient, Proficient, Advanced) on Criterion Referenced Tests (CRTs) in third-grade math and reading. Olive, however, ranks near the bottom for the district, with 65 percent and 55 percent of students testing Below Proficient in math and reading, respectively, compared to district averages of 24 percent and 23 percent.[24] Only 35 percent of the Olive third graders scored Proficient or above on math, compared to a 76 percent district average. At Jefferson, the academic performance is more mixed across subject matter and overall is more positive, with 31 percent Below Proficient in math (compared to the district average of 24 percent) and just 15 percent Below Proficient in reading (compared to a 23 percent district average). Some 69 percent of third-grade students at Jefferson scored at or above Proficient in math (seven percentage points below the district average), but 85 percent scored at or above Proficient in reading (compared to a district average of 79 percent).

Findings: The impact of enhanced services and resources

Our findings suggest that despite the layered services and additional pro-grams provided at enhanced option schools, the social disorganization of neighborhood conditions may overwhelm these schools' efforts to address the social and academic needs of children and their families.[25] As the guid-ance counselor at Olive observed, "We have so much here, and it still isn't enough." The neighborhood conditions include elements related to infra-structure, demographics, institutions, and social organization.[26] The neigh-borhood effects are context specific and directly impact the social relations and academic climate of the neighborhood's enhanced elementary school.[27] In the first case study examined here, conditions of poverty, high crime, dense public housing, high unemployment, drug and alcohol abuse—concen-trated in the neighborhood that engulfs the Olive School—provide the tem-plate for understanding how these structures link to social processes defined in the relationships between families and schools.

Jefferson Enhanced Option School represents a contrasting case study that explores the way neighborhood schools may be impacted by the social trans-formation and social reorganization associated with housing redevelopment and community revitalization in a community comprised mostly of work-ing-poor families and residents moving from welfare to work (and back to school for job training), and new residents living in a federal housing proj-ect—HOPE VI.[28] In 1992, Congress enacted the HOPE VI program to overhaul the nation's public housing policy. The reform legislation was prompted by a report commissioned by Congress that found two-thirds of all public hous-ing "severely distressed."[29] Since the landmark housing policy was enacted in 1992, HUD has awarded 237 HOPE VI grants to 127 cities, totaling $5.8 billion.[30] HOPE VI provides a critical context to "test" mixed-income public housing policy as a lever for reducing educational inequalities associated with concentrated poverty and social isolation.

Olive School Neighborhood

A slow and deliberate drive around the neighborhood that surrounds Olive Enhanced Option School confirms the bleak portrait painted by the census tract numbers. Olive sits amid urban poverty in a neighborhood defined by a sprawling, low-story public housing project built a half-century ago, a heavily trafficked arm of the interstate highway system, and a busy four-lane boule-vard pocked by broken sidewalks and discount tobacco and liquor stores. Ran-domly scattered industrial yards and aging commercial sites form the south-ern border. Many of the wood-sided homes that encircle the school—more

compact versions of the narrow "shotgun" homes built over fifty years ago—
are abandoned, condemned, or currently vacant. Abandoned cars, some with
burned-out front ends and cracked windows, dot this neighborhood landscape. The only green space can be found in the broad patches of lawn that
provide relief to the blocks of the public housing units. There are no banks,
laundromats, or competitively priced (chain) grocery stores in the area. These
are found only after a forty-five-minute city bus ride out of the area.

Almost all of the students at Olive reside in the two adjacent housing projects that border the school and extend side by side for four blocks northward.
The two housing projects comprise the largest public housing area in the city,
with over 2,300 residents. Police reports for the area indicate that a total of
576 serious criminal offenses (homicide, rape, robbery, burglary, auto theft,
etc.) were committed in 2002, one of the highest crime rates for housing
projects in the city. According to census block group data and public housing reports, approximately two-thirds of the residents live in poverty (see
table 7.2); almost a third of all households report receiving public assistance.[31]
More than 70 percent of the children in the community live in a single-
parent household. According to the school officials and community-based
organization staff members interviewed for this study, few (estimates range
from 20 percent to 35 percent) of the Olive community residents own an
automobile. According to these officials, most residents rely on friends, family, or neighbors for transportation, or take a city bus that requires excessive

TABLE 7.2: School Contexts

	Olive	Jefferson
Population	3,213	4,174
Poverty Rate	67%	16%
Median Income	$ 11,349	$ 26,725
Family Structure	71% single parent	26% single parent
Education Attainment (over-age 25 population)	58% no high-school diploma	39% no HS diploma
Crime Rate	One of the highest for public housing in the city	One of the lowest for public housing in the city
Ethnicity	92% African-American 3% White	27% African-American 66% White

Source: Smrekar and Goldring's (authors) data collection.

amounts of time spent in transfers across the city. The median income sits at $11,349 (less than half of the median income of the Jefferson School population zone). More than half of the population over twenty-five left high school early and does not hold a high school diploma. Out of almost 1,300 residents over twenty-five, only 31 (2.5%) have a college degree. The population is 92 percent African American and is considered one of the oldest surviving African American communities in the Nashville area, marked by the establishment of the original Olive School in 1898.[32]

In what ways does neighborhood matter in the social organization and social life of schools? Does the enhanced option model work to mediate the influence of social structures found in high-risk neighborhoods? Where is the social equity in these postbusing neighborhood schools?

Interviews with teachers and other school and community agency staff (about half of the interviewees are African American and half are white), coupled with repeated observations of parent and neighborhood groups meeting at Olive School, suggest that the social aspects of schooling—the degree of safety, order, and discipline, patterns of communication, interaction, and participation—are powerfully influenced by the social structures and processes found in the community.[33] In critical ways, these neighborhood conditions roll into Olive's school corridors and classrooms with a penetrating influence and effect, shaping the interactions, norms, and expectations of students, families, and school staff.

Fighting to survive

One Olive teacher comments on the children:

> They see a lot of fights, a lot of fights. . . . They talk about all the gambling and the throwing dice and the stuff that goes on out there, the betting. You know, I have had kids who come in late. I had a child last year who came in late because, she said, "Someone got shot outside my house and my mom didn't want me to leave until the cops were all gone." I think there is a lot of physicality. . . . They are used to being hit around, slapped.

The neighborhood portrait sketched above outlines the demographic, institutional, and infrastructural elements that shape social processes in the Olive community. These measures provide the guideposts for understanding the effects of a neighborhood and their penetrating reach into school life.[34]

The children at Olive School, aged five to ten, live in the social space defined by their neighborhood and their school, framed by four city blocks.

Their isolation is real; few families have ready and reliable transportation in this community. These children have learned to adapt to the social structures concentrated in their neighborhood, acquiring the skills needed to survive in a community fractured by drug and domestic violence, underemployment, and poverty. They often care for themselves and younger siblings; they watch a lot of television. They are accustomed to ducking away from the sounds of gunshot and gang warfare. As the Olive community center director observed, "These kids are street smart because they're on their own; nobody raises anybody here."

Researchers suggest that these neighborhood conditions trigger a protective response that provides a layer of resiliency for children and adults.[35] At Olive, the students' social scripts are defined by a survival tactic, a defensive posture characterized by quick anger, aggression, and a readiness to fight. Without exception, teachers identified the culture of survival as the orienting feature of their experiences with the children and parents at Olive. These teachers explained the backdrop of survival and the sources of social stress in this neighborhood:

> They come in from the weekend and tell me how this person has been shot, in the middle of the street, how they have to run in and take cover and everything. It is like a war, a battle over there in that neighborhood and they are trying to survive. That is why we have so many young children being, trying to be the adult, trying to lead, and the problems that we have here are because over there in the neighborhood, they are learning to survive.

> I have met two fathers in this classroom. I know of five that are in prison. I know of three [students] who know nothing about their father. I know one whose father is deceased, actually had two, the other little boy transferred. There are children in this building who have witnessed one parent murder another. There were children here whose parent was in prison for trying to kill one of their younger brothers or sisters. There are parents who come into this building who are high, drunk, who will ask you for money. There are children who get themselves up in the morning, who come in a bad mood if they woke themselves up late because they missed breakfast, five- and six-year-olds.

> These children see a lot of trauma. They see a lot, they know a lot of death. They know a lot of people getting shot and getting killed. A lot of them have relatives in jail, relatives on their way to jail. I had a little boy who saw a lot of domestic violence, so they see a lot of trauma. They talk about it a lot.

The conflicts and social stressors in the community become the battles in the classroom for focus, discipline, and, as one teacher put it, "separation of the survival skills from the classroom skills." But the children at Olive School do not—most likely cannot—separate their lives neatly and compactly into school and home. As another teacher noted, "They can't just switch their behavior immediately." In this social context, there is seamless integration of neighborhood and school. The neighborhood children comprise almost the entire population of schoolchildren. All experience the same neighborhood structures and neighborhood social processes. And the two social spaces are necessarily intermingled and interdependent. The distracting and disabling conditions in the neighborhood spill into the classrooms and corridors with regularity and frequency. School staff consistently noted the students' inclination to fight over what seem small or insignificant matters of disagreement or disrespect. Sometimes this physicality and disrespect is directed at teachers. Conflicts often start blocks away in the neighborhood and involve heated conversations or physical interactions that roll into the classroom. As a third-grade teacher observed, "They are with the same people all the time." Another teacher echoed this view, underscoring the pervasiveness of a survival culture: "They see nothing else, they know nothing else. They have no motivation to do anything else." An Olive teacher with thirty years of experience, most of it spent in inner-city schools, underscored the challenges of a neighborhood school in a neighborhood defined by social isolation and survival:

> We have about thirty-five blue signs all over [reading] "Quiet Zone." And I thought, I have never been in a school [with these signs], why would you have to have this? Well, they get out in the hallway and they start picking at each other or another class, because they all live in the same area. They have enemies and problems in that housing project and they come to school with it. I have interrupted several fights. I have pulled children off, little children and you think, gee. But it is like that is the mentality of survival. You start something up in the neighborhood and they continue it here at school.

Her colleague agreed:

> My main problem with this school is that these children all live together, they come to school together, they ride the church bus together, they are on the playground up there, they are together all the time. So any problems that they have up there follows them here or vice versa.

In a school bounded by an array of challenging neighborhood-level social processes and structures, the Olive "Mission Statement" reflects the ultimate expression of irony: "Olive School, where home, school and community go hand in hand." The statement unmistakably underscores the central dilemma for faculty and staff as they, too, struggle to survive.

Teacher-student interactions

How do teachers respond? How are social interactions between teachers and students defined? What is the nature and quality of these experiences? During numerous observations and extensive teacher and staff interviews conducted over the course of one year at Olive School, patterns of a survival mentality coupled with overt stress and fatigue were clearly evident among the faculty and staff. The school's front office was constantly filled with a half-dozen or more students sent by their classroom teachers to the principal for behavior issues. A long line meant a long wait. Shouting for order and discipline seemed commonplace as a behavior management tool. When asked, many teachers suggested that shouting was often the only way to discipline children at Olive, the only way to get their attention and maintain control. "There is a lot of verbal hostility toward the kids here," one teacher noted. On numerous occasions, teachers told chatty students who were walking in a broken, jagged line down the hallway to the cafeteria: "Shut your mouths. Walk on the blue tiles with your hands behind your back." This command, too, seemed commonplace, frequently and widely used by the faculty and staff. As one teacher lamented, "You find yourself saying things to [them] that you thought you would never say to children." Teachers described teaching fifteen kids—the cap under the design of the enhanced option model—not as a luxury, but as a necessity. "It feels like I have twenty-five kids on most days," noted one teacher, a sentiment echoed by many of her colleagues.

Each year, the conditions prove too difficult for many teachers and staff, many of whom depart after just a few years at Olive. In fact, the mobility rate among faculty and staff surpasses the mobility rate for the children at Olive. Almost half of the faculty and staff combined have left the school each of the past three years, whereas the student mobility rate stands at approximately 32 percent. Under these conditions, a "veteran" of Olive School may mean a teacher with only three years at the school. The teachers interviewed for this study had taught at least three years at Olive; some left Olive the next year, however, and some of the teachers interviewed had taught at Olive when the district was still under court-ordered crosstown busing.[36] The high teacher mobility rate seems to compound the level of stress for those who remain behind, creating a survivor's instinct and culture. The teachers noted that the instability of the staff diminishes the sense of community and undercuts any element of continuity in curricular development and programming for the school. While some teachers have left due to retirement, most have sought out other school settings that provide a more academic environment, one less behavior centered. One veteran teacher with four years at Olive noted that she was the only remaining teacher from her cohort. The issues of concentrated poverty and social isolation among the children discouraged her colleagues, she said. The academic challenges were overwhelming and too often displaced by a focus on discipline and behavior.[37] There seemed to be a mismatch between teachers' training and their reality. The veteran teacher recalled:

> A lot of them worried that their skills as a teacher would diminish if they stayed here, meaning, you can't do a lot of the things here that you have been trained to do. A lot of the creativity and things like that take a back seat because it is so skills-based and remedial; you are teaching way below the grade level here.

Her colleague, who works with all the teachers at Olive in her capacity as a curriculum specialist, underscored the challenges of working in an enhanced option school:

> The enhanced option idea is tremendous, but it is still tiring. Teachers are overwhelmed. Teachers are overworked with the different levels of children that we have in our rooms. We have a few that are at grade level. We have many that are not at grade level. It is our job to prove that we have wonderful students on our [achievement tests], and the task is astronomical. We just cannot bring all children to grade level. We work very diligently all year long trying to get it done. . . . We could do a better job, but we are also working very hard. Our faculty is just worn out.

Social isolation

One home-school coordinator stated:

> I think here sometimes the neighborhood attendance zone limits what our kids are exposed to and it is not good. It limits them because they all live together, they walk together, and they are not exposed to anybody new. They are not exposed to new experiences.

In 1998–99, before the court order was lifted and the district was declared unitary, Olive School was racially balanced, with a student composition that was 49 percent black, 30 percent white, 16 percent Hispanic, and 5 percent

Asian. Under the court order, elementary-age children from the Olive housing projects rode a bus to a school that was miles away from the neighborhood—one that was racially mixed, with a far lower rate of children receiving free and reduced-price lunch than the current Olive rate.

During the first year of the student assignment plan, when Olive reopened as an enhanced option school and after many crosstown busing routes were eliminated, the black population grew at Olive while the white population decreased by half, to about 17 percent. The Hispanic population remained the same, due to a bus route that transported Hispanic, Kurdish, and other English-language learner (ELL) children from privately owned apartment buildings approximately four to five miles away from the school (those students now attend a satellite ELL school some miles away). The percentage of children receiving free or reduced-price lunch stood at 82 percent in 1998–99 and rose to 88 percent in the first year of the new plan. Today, the rate of children receiving free or reduced-price lunch at Olive is 95 percent.

According to extensive interviews with teachers and school staff, this pre–unitary status mix of children produced a dramatically different set of norms, expectations, and social relations at Olive. Teachers observed far less aggressive behavior from children and less hostility between children and teachers. Teachers drew portraits of an earlier school climate characterized by diversity across culture and neighborhood spaces:

> I think that the integration, the mixture, was good. I think it had a positive effect that we don't have now because there is no mixture. It is just one type of child from the same socioeconomic background. And many of the ELL students came from poor areas too, and were coming from other countries, so they were struggling, but it was a different kind of struggle. Yes, it was economically motivated or they suffered economically, but the differences in what the children knew and what the children could learn, even with that language barrier, it was really neat to see them get together and see what they could learn from one another.

> The mix before [unitary status], we had all, black, white, Hispanic, we had a variety. And that really helped the children in the neighborhood. The other children were bringing ideas from their area [outside of the neighborhood] and the children were really excited. . . . Now, unless there is a program in their area that is taking them out, to venture out into other areas, we are the only source for those children and that is why we try to hold activities for them outside, have people coming in, take them on field trips to get them exposed because they need a lot of exposure.

The staff members at the family resource center echoed these views, as each considered the combined lack of racial and economic diversity in the school and in the neighborhood. As one social worker observed:

> I don't think neighborhood schools are bad, I just think because this neighborhood has so little diversity that the kids here aren't exposed to a lot. The main white people they are exposed to are their teachers and us. They don't have many white students or Spanish-speaking students. They don't see families who live in a home that they own or who have their own little yard.

The theme of isolation and lack of exposure ripped through the teachers' and resource center staff's assessments of the neighborhood's effect on the social and academic climate at Olive. They lamented the lack of a range of abilities, students' lack of exposure to the city around them, their lack of experience with items in nature, and their lack of exposure to other cultures. In these conversations, diversity emerged as a multifaceted concept well beyond elements of the black-white student racial balance that launched the busing order in the city. In the postbusing context, teachers and community workers seem to accept the reality of single-race schools. Issues of racial diversity were routinely and quickly dismissed in our interviews by more pointed references to a profound need for diversity in academic ability, culture, and, most vitally, social class. The issues of academic ability, culture, and class seem to merge to form a pivotal point from which the social relations flow in the school, forming the essential character of the place. These images were widely shared by teachers:

> With the integration of different cultures or different socioeconomic backgrounds, different races, just all the differences, you had a much more balanced classroom. It was easier to manage the discipline. Of course, when discipline is easier the other things come easier too. . . . They had something different to see and aspire to be or not aspire to be.

> I really believe if children come into a diverse classroom, they model each other. You'll find them looking and seeing the children who are getting the praise and they start to mimic that because they want to be noticed in the right way. . . . When you have a classroom that doesn't have that and so many are struggling . . . [She trailed off and shook her head.]

Diversity across social class—the stunning lack of diversity here—bored through teacher and staff reflections as each considered the problems plaguing Olive Enhanced Option School. They suggested that only rezoning would address the problems of isolation or, as one teacher noted simply, "I would like to see some of these kids go somewhere else, let them know that there is something else out there." She put it bluntly:

> I think it needs to be diverse, both economically and culturally. If we are living in diverse a nation and world, we need to have that here as well. They need to know what is going on out there—not just drugs, alcohol, prostitution, and new babies.

The principal of Olive School, a true veteran of the district with over thirty years of professional experience in inner-city Nashville schools, linked the neighborhood isolation and concentrated poverty conditions to the issue of role models and student aspirations:

> There are no role models to mimic. They are boys and girls who know each other, who know each others' parents and who do the same things, who solve problems the same way, who bring the same kinds of difficulties here to the building. That in itself is challenging because we all know that we grow from diversity and we just don't have that diversity here.

The problems of student behavior seem to coalesce for school and community staff around the need for models of "other"—other ways of acting, alternative goals, and higher aspirations for the students at Olive. The staff from the youth-serving organizations in the neighborhood noted that some kids resist being named a role model based on their outstanding academic achievement. When afterschool program coordinators unfurled an "honor roll banner" at their gym last fall, many students whose names appeared on the banner reacted angrily and insisted that their names be removed. Each account of the conditions of social isolation at Olive reflects the same pattern of negative peer influence—a feature that seems to permeate the social processes adopted by students in response to the social structures in the community.[38] How do the physical structure and defining characteristics of the neighborhood intersect with these social structures? How do the social conditions associated with public housing contribute to the social isolation of families in the Olive community?

Problem of housing

One family resource center staff member at Olive School noted:

> A lot of my clients want to move. Unfortunately they are not always realistic in what they can actually do. I see some sad discussions with clients.

They want out of housing, period. And that is not realistic. A lot of them still want to leave here. They don't feel safe. I talk to parents who want to leave here and go to another housing development. They feel that Olive is less safe than others.

Community and school officials agree that part of the problem of neighborhood structures and their deleterious effect on school life at Olive is rooted in the condition of the housing projects. Although currently undergoing some renovations, the Olive apartments represent some of the "most severe" conditions of public housing, as one veteran community volunteer characterized them, lacking public Laundromat facilities, proper maintenance, effective crime control, and adequate play areas. Many of the parents interviewed for the study who have lived in other public housing areas described Olive public housing as "the worst." Recently, the Family Resource Center coordinator called a parent meeting at the school to discuss a nonprofit group's initiative to build a new playground on the edge of the housing project, which evoked deep skepticism among the dozen or so Olive parents who attended. All said that a park or playground was a pressing need in the community, agreeing with a mother who noted that kids in the suburbs enjoy recreation opportunities at sprawling neighborhood parks and playgrounds: "Our kids don't get exercise so they could use that." But many of the parents expressed doubt that kids could be safe in a playground centrally located within Olive public housing, even with fencing and card-key access. After one parent commented that a playground "would be just one more place for drug dealers to sell drugs, urinate, use needles, and throw their used condoms," most of the mothers agreed that a new park was a waste of money because "the drug dealers will tear it up in a month." The meeting ended after another mother urged an alternative plan to a playground—a more vigilant crime watch.

The housing problem—or housing solution—represents a critical difference in the context that defines the social aspects of schooling experienced at the two enhanced option schools in our study. We return to this subject—and to the implications of neighborhood contexts socially transformed—when we examine the ways public housing reform (HOPE VI projects) intersects with school improvement in the case of Jefferson Enhanced Option School.

Parenting

The economic and social environments in the high-risk neighborhood that surrounds Olive Enhanced Option School militate against the development and sustainability of social capital. The reasons are underscored in the research literature on neighborhood effects. Neighborhoods like Olive often reflect their social and economic context: scarce economic resources, unstable social networks, limited social trust, and a perceived lack of consensus on parenting.[39] Although an array of afterschool programs, church-related youth groups, and recreation and civic programs for children, youth, and families exist, these efforts seem insufficient to meet the pressing demands of students and their families. Research studies of parenting practices in high-risk neighborhoods —community contexts bereft of social capital—describe parenting as highly private, protected, and isolated set of activities.[40] Under manifestly dangerous conditions, parents in high-risk neighborhoods manage risk and opportunity by adopting stringent child monitoring and youth control, or "lock-down" strategies. These individual patterns of confinement and insularity in childrearing and parenting reflect the larger, collective neighborhood dynamics.[41] As more and more parents adopt these defensive tactics, increasing numbers of neighbors are disconnected, social networks of support dissolve, and opportunities for constructive collective socialization disappear.[42] These parenting patterns define the social relations and social scripts adopted by families in the Olive neighborhood.

Jefferson School Neighborhood

The neighbors near the Jefferson Enhanced Option School include a senior citizens' center and the sprawling state fairgrounds. These landmarks form a right angle at the end of the busy four-lane boulevard that divides this mostly residential neighborhood. Intersecting streets dotted with modest two-bedroom "brick 'n' siding" homes built sixty to seventy-five years ago mark the north side of the boulevard. A federal housing project and dilapidated single-family dwellings dot the south side. Jefferson School was built in 1970 and reflects the futuristic pod designs that were popular then. These open classroom arrangements have only recently been renovated to provide walls and doors for each classroom. The school is bordered on the west side by a large grassy recreation field; a chain-link fence encloses almost the entire campus. The school backs up to the campus of the local public television station, which is dotted with satellite dishes. There are a number of small businesses in the area—electrical repair, plumbing, and home construction–related trades, but there are no major employers in the attendance zone. The main commercial area of the community is a mile down the main boulevard, where it intersects with a busy commercial street bordered by gas stations, fast food restaurants, antique shops and auto dealerships, grocery and liquor stores, and a Goodwill store.

According to interviews with veteran school staff members, community-based social service staff, and local residents, Jefferson is a community long divided by assumptions about social class and cultural differences between the families. The division is both geographic and socioeconomic; the "boulevard divide" separates the lower income, mostly African American residents who live in the federal housing on south side of the street and the residents living in the modest single-family homes on the racially mixed (black, white, Hispanic) north side. Those distinctions have begun to dissolve in the past few years with the demolition of the 1950s-era, physically deteriorating, crime-ridden public housing "barracks." With a HOPE VI housing revitalization grant from the federal Housing and Urban Development Department (HUD), the Nashville housing authorities built attractive new duplexes in their place, with playgrounds and modest landscaping that create far more usable green space in the public housing complex. As a result of the HOPE VI revitalization, residential density (and capacity) were reduced. Today, the number of residents in the public housing complex is 420 residents, or just 40 percent of the original public housing population.

Jefferson defines a neighborhood school. Since its inception in 1970, the school has enrolled the children who live within walking distance of the campus. Jefferson was never subjected to the crosstown busing patterns under the court order in Nashville because the neighborhood was, and still is, racially mixed, if not balanced. The racial mix has grown a bit more diverse over the past several decades, from about 70 percent white and 30 percent black in the 1970s to a neighborhood that is 66 percent white, 27 percent black, with Asian and Hispanic populations of about 4 percent each.[43] Historically, the neighborhood has reflected a stable, multigenerational quality with extended kin settling in the area once financial independent is reached. According to officials with the Metropolitan Housing Authority and representatives of local neighborhood groups interviewed for this study, this trend has held constant for both black and white families.

How do the Jefferson School and the larger neighborhood community differ from the Olive neighborhood and school population? The 2000 U.S. Census block group data for the Jefferson school zone indicate that about one out of six residents in the Jefferson zone is living in poverty (compared to two out of three in the Olive zone); fewer than 2 percent of households report receiving public assistance.[44] The HOPE VI public housing complex near Jefferson has one of the lowest crime rates among all public housing complexes, with a total of thirty violent crimes (homicide, rape, robbery, burglary, auto theft, etc.) reported in 2002 among a population base of 420 residents (about half the crime rate of the public housing complexes located near the Olive School).

According to school officials, about 70 percent of the Jefferson students live in single-parent homes (compared to over 80 percent at Olive). Most Jefferson School families have reliable automobile transportation, according to school and community officials. The median income for the Jefferson neighborhood is $26,725 (more than double the Olive level), while the median income of Jefferson School families, based on applications for the federal free and reduced-price lunch program, is only $17,235. A far higher percentage of the population over twenty-five holds a high school diploma in the Jefferson neighborhood, according to block group data. Large and significant generational differences exist between the two communities as well. About half of the population in the Olive community is under eighteen, compared to only about a quarter of the Jefferson community. The housing stock differs across the two neighborhoods, too. About 10 percent of all housing units near Jefferson—an area comprised of mostly privately owned or rented, single-family dwellings—are considered vacant or abandoned by city and federal officials.

It should be noted that the school populations at both Olive and Jefferson are poorer and have larger rates of single-parent households than the community at large, according to the block group census data (see table 7.2), reflecting a neighborhood population within each school zone that is somewhat older—and different—than the parent population of the schoolchildren at Olive and Jefferson.

In what ways does neighborhood matter in the social organization and social life of Jefferson School? Does the enhanced option model work to mediate the influence of social structures found in this high-risk neighborhood? Our comparative qualitative case studies of these two school communities suggest important differences in the neighborhood conditions and social processes that impact Olive and Jefferson schools. Our interviews with school and community-linked staff at Jefferson Enhanced Option School provide a vivid illustration of a school ecology characterized by an array of economic, social, and psychological needs. These demands and the associated coping strategies embraced by school staff suggest a school community deeply influenced by elements of neighborhood stability, diversity, and revitalization.

Needy

The guidance counselor at Jefferson leads a group counseling program that focuses on the psychological and emotional problems children are experiencing, mostly related to neglect, abandonment, and, sometimes, abuse. The counselor also provides one-on-one counseling; both programs are full to capacity, with about twenty to twenty-five students each. Another mental health professional provides counseling services to students on a contract basis through a local mental health agency; she has a long waiting list. About six years ago, the counselor surveyed fourth graders about their exposure to violence in their community. Over half reported that they had seen someone shot, not on television or in the movies, but in person in their neighborhood. On a field trip for fourth graders designed to "scare 'em straight" out of the world of drug dealing and gun violence, the teacher was stunned to observe students smiling and waving to their relatives behind prison bars. "It was not scary to them; it was familiar."

Teachers and school staff consistently characterized Jefferson students as "needy," and echoed the sentiment that a capped class size of thirteen to fifteen students still felt like teaching twenty-five on most days. Although the district reports a free and reduced-price lunch rate of 79 percent, teachers perceive a higher rate of need. Most students at Jefferson (70 percent, according to the school reports) live in single-parent households or live with a grandparent. As one teacher noted, the students come "with a lot of baggage." These teachers compare Jefferson to their previous (different) schools in the suburbs:

> We are inner city and some of our students seem like they are five students, because these kids come with a lot more baggage than most kids. Truthfully, my fourteen children that I have sometimes feel about the same as when I taught twenty-five children, just because you are doing so many other things other than just teaching. . . . I have crackers here [for] when they don't eat. I never had to deal with that as much at other schools as I am here, of taking care of basic needs of the kids. They are just not getting it elsewhere.

> This is totally different. The [former] principal said to me, your first year is going to feel like five years. And he was right. You have to learn where these kids are coming from. These students are totally different.

As the demographics suggest, most Jefferson families are low income with modest educational backgrounds. For some children, basic needs are met by teachers and the network of social (family resource center, home-school coordinator) and health (nurse and health clinic) services provided at Jefferson. Indeed, the service networks were referenced by teachers as defining social aspects of the school and, as many of them observed, as "absolutely needed."

The webbing that is provided by an almost seamless intersection of actions by the health clinic nurses, guidance counselor, family resource center staff, and home-school coordinator helps to enhance communication between families and the school, and between teachers and children. The teachers were emphatic about the need for social services at Jefferson and at other public schools impacted by poverty:

> The services are wonderful. Super. And it makes me upset to know that they are not provided in other schools. That seems like inequity in education to me.

> I came from a school where we may have had a nurse one day a week. You maybe had a social worker here or there. But at this school, we have nurses on call every day. We have nurse practitioners so they can actually do appointments. We have counselors, we have mental health services, we have family resource. I have never been in a school that had so many things that were here not just for the school, but for the parents and the community.

The principal compared the enhancements at Jefferson to conditions at her previous school, a setting that was comprised of a similarly needy population of children: "There, we had to hustle for services; here, it's as though someone dreamed up what kinds of things would help the school, and they're all here." Most faculty and staff members pointed to the crucial role of the nurse, whose quick actions and expertise could prevent small but persistent health concerns—lice, cuts, nose bleeds, fevers, stomachaches—from growing into larger issues of need, distraction, and longer periods of student absence from the classroom. These support systems allowed most teachers to set aside the conditions of social and economic need and to focus more centrally on conditions of academic need. This teacher explained the educational dilemma:

> These kids, their parents care about them, but they are not particularly well educated. Not well educated doesn't mean you don't care about your children. It just means that you have different things to offer. So they come with a love their parents have given them, but they don't always come with all the tools that they need.

Radical change

Against the backdrop of student needs, some of which teachers and staff characterized as persistent and profound, the school staff focused repeatedly on the diversity of students. This diversity is reflected in students' socioeconomic backgrounds—including parents' education levels and occupational status. Teachers repeatedly used the phrase, "We have a range here," to denote the occupational backgrounds of parents, from day-care and fast food restaurant workers to college students, to bank tellers and state office workers, to nurses and insurance brokers. This teacher's viewpoint typifies many others:

> I have everything from parents who are very affluent and have wonderful jobs who work with their kids every night, to kids who don't have much of a home life at all. A lot of times I'm feeding them breakfast because their parents aren't even getting them here. . . . They have to wake themselves up, take care of themselves. I have every range.

Although widely referenced as a quick and comparable measure, the school neighborhood clearly reflects far more complex conditions than the percentage of families participating in the free lunch program. In stark contrast to teachers at Olive, the Jefferson teachers painted a portrait of within-school differences in income and culture among families, not the sameness of struggle and isolation evidenced at Olive. The element of widespread parental employment is new, as is the fairly wide range of occupations, and both contribute in significant ways to the shape of social relations between families and school staff at Jefferson. These family and neighborhood conditions and the processes associated with them—for example, more parents engaged in supportive educational activities like homework—signals a shift at the school, where previously the majority of the student population were residents from the dense and dilapidated federal housing project three blocks from the campus. What changed?

During the 2000–01 school year, the new HOPE VI housing project opened on the site that previously housed what was considered among the worst of public housing in the city—a set of low-rise, block-like barracks plagued by high crime, chronic unemployment, and poverty. The new development features attractive, New England–style duplexes, landscaped with trees and trimmed lawns. In an effort to decrease the concentration of very low-income families and build sustainable communities, HOPE VI represents a new philosophy for federal public housing, with new requirements for qualifying residents, including a clean criminal record and a good rental and residence maintenance report. Most significantly, residents must be employed or in school (or both) for a total of forty hours per week. With guidance from public housing staff, residents complete a self-sufficiency plan designed to move them toward a budgeting process and savings plan that will lead, eventually, to home ownership within five years. The housing staff reviews the plans regularly for issues related to residents' progress and compliance. This transition to self-sufficiency is designed to break the cycle of intergenerational poverty and dependence on federal assistance.

A six-foot-high iron security fence encircles the new HOPE VI duplexes in the Jefferson community. Access requires residents' consent (electronic gate release) for a visitor to enter. A community center with child-care programs, a fully staffed health clinic, and a Boys and Girls Club sit adjacent to the duplex complex; these elements reflect the HOPE VI goals for improving neighborhood-level social supports. How has the new housing reshaped social structures in the neighborhood and school? The school staff characterized the change as a shift from a community once punctuated by poverty to one stabilized by economic security. The guidance counselor called it "a radical change" in school climate. The teachers were equally vocal:

> It has been a good thing. When I first started here, everybody walked to school. Very few parents had cars. And now, there are a lot of cars out here. So evidently people are getting jobs and getting some transportation. We have seen a change in our demographics here. And it seems to be for the better in this area.

> Things have changed here at Jefferson. Many of our parents are middle-class families. There doesn't seem to be a need for the basic things like clothing. There are a few children, but not like what we used to see.

The claims of a "different clientele" permeated the comments of teachers and staff who reported that the new, less densely populated housing project with employment and education stipulations for residents "really makes a difference." Teachers pointed to discernible shifts—all in the positive direction—in patterns of family-school interactions, parental expectations regarding student achievement, and levels of parent involvement. Although the condition of nearly full employment/full education makes contacting public housing complex parents less predictable or assured than in the past, when parents could easily be found at home, most teachers suggested that the uptick in employment and economic stability for the neighborhood equated with a positive change in social relations at the school site. These comments typify the teachers' impressions of significant social change:

> I have called and talked to more parents in the last two years than I have in the [prior] nine years of teaching, because you have to have their support. I

would say probably 90 percent of my parents are more than willing to come right over and help out and take care of the situation.

Those who live in the Jefferson public housing, you have to either be in school or you have to be in a jobs program. So I have never had as many working parents. I have never worked with as many working parents. Every year I have a mother who is in school. Last year I had a mother who was working on a master's degree. So, this is still a hardscrabble life for them. They still have a tough life. . . . I have a couple of kids whose parents are more comfortable and some I think probably have a harder time. But just by the virtue of the fact that everybody is working, that makes, I can't get over what a big difference everybody's parents working makes.

Why do conditions of employment or adult education (or both) among parents—the requirements for residence in the new public housing complex—trigger new patterns of social relations with teachers? What impact could these neighborhood changes have on the school climate? The teachers responded to these questions with descriptive portraits of the "new clientele's" use of time, parenting style, and work routines:

For one thing, if you are working, you sure as heck don't want to be called at work because your child is disobeying. So when they tell their child, "Get it together; I don't want your teacher having to call me at work," they have values. There is a value added to that. Then, if you are seeing your parent get up and go to work every day, that has got to have a [more] positive effect than leaving and your mother is still in her house slippers and coming home and your mother is still in her house slippers. I have seen a real difference in the attitude. The parents, some here think the parents here are hard, demanding of things. And they are, they are more demanding, but I think it is because they are working so hard themselves that they want the very best because they are working hard. It is as it should be.

CONCLUSION

Following the grant of unitary status in the Nashville public schools in 1998, the new student assignment plan ended crosstown busing and embraced the ideal of neighborhood schools to strengthen social ties between communities and their schools. The new student assignment plan anticipated the problems concentrated poverty would bring to new neighborhood schools; the new enhanced option schools were established with an array of academic and social supports.

We examined the resource levels in these schools and explored the impact of the social composition of these enhanced option schools on social capital development. Our findings suggest that despite smaller class size and an array of social and health support services on site, the penetrating and punishing effects of neighborhood poverty overwhelm these efforts. At Olive School, the problems associated with concentrated poverty are particularly acute. In the absence of any socioeconomic diversity among families, educators focus on survival. As the guidance counselor at Olive observed, "We have so much here, and it still isn't enough."

Our findings suggest that neighborhood context matters; concentrated poverty leads to concentrated disadvantage in the social and geographical space shared between high-risk neighborhoods and nearby schools. We turn to concepts of social capital and social networks as a way of underscoring and complimenting the literature on neighborhood effects in a broad attempt to better understand how poverty and shared social and geographical spaces coalesce to produce inequality.[45] These case studies represent communities bounded by discrete physical boundaries (census tracts, block groups, public housing complexes) that intersect with social relationships and social institutions (e.g., schools). We agree with Sampson et al. and Small and Newman that more qualitative case studies are needed to better understand how we move conceptually from neighborhood clusters to examining the intersection and impact of embedded structures, local perceptions, and shared social spaces.[46]

We conclude that policymakers must take account of neighborhood-level conditions that diminish the impact of "full-service" schooling efforts in high-poverty neighborhoods.[47] These initiatives will require more than a review of free-lunch percentages as a measure of neighborhood poverty. Our work suggests that these data often overlook the social health of a neighborhood school and the relative social stability of its community, as in the case of the Olive School. These efforts must be coupled with an urgency that matches the increasing momentum of districts to end court-ordered desegregation and shift to neighborhood schooling—leaving in the wake high-poverty, socially isolated schools. The case studies of Olive and Jefferson elementary schools expose the limitations of strategies focused exclusively on in-school supports that ignore the ecology of schooling and the realities of high-risk neighborhoods. We echo what Jean Anyon suggests in her book *Radical Possibilities*, that one of the most important education reforms must involve housing policy reform, and point to HOPE VI as a step in that direction.[48] Recent research suggests some caution and caveats associated with any single-pronged approach, whether the strategy involves in-school supports or a singular focus on moving families out of poverty. The Moving to Opportunity (MTO) program was designed to address the effects of concentrated urban poverty by moving families from inner-city public housing to neighborhoods with lower rates of poverty. Recent studies of MTO suggest that seven years after relocating to lower poverty neighborhoods, these children are doing no better academically than their counterparts who remained in traditional public housing.[49] In sum, lower poverty levels did not generate the academic growth that relocation to affluent or even mixed-income schools might produce.[50] These findings underscore the importance of significantly expanding the economic opportunities, social networks, and peer groups that are essential for making substantive improvement in the academic and social environments for children and their families who are locked in neighborhoods of corrosive, concentrated poverty.[51]

Consequences of Court-Ended School Desegration

Administrative Decisions and Racial Segregation in North Carolina Public Schools

Charles T. Clotfelter, Helen F. Ladd, and Jacob L. Vigdor

More than a half-century after the end of de jure segregation in American public schools, de facto segregation remains an extremely salient public policy issue, in part because prominent U.S. Supreme Court cases such as *Parents Involved in Community Schools v. Seattle School District No. 1* have kept the issue in the headlines.[1] Even as America's metropolitan neighborhoods become more racially integrated and as surveys reveal a general softening of racial attitudes in the population, segregation in public school systems has persisted and may in fact be on the rise.[2] As an illustration, 37.4 percent of black public school students in 2000–01 attended schools with 90 percent or more minority enrollment, up from 33.9 percent in 1991–92. Almost identical figures describe the segregation of Hispanic students in the nation.[3]

What factors explain the persistence and resurgence of public school segregation? While considerable research has been devoted to identifying the causal factors driving cross-sectional and time-series variation in residential segregation[4] and a number of studies have considered the extent and effects of school segregation,[5] comparatively little attention has been devoted to this particular question. This preponderance of attention to residential segregation over school segregation is somewhat surprising, considering the general interest in the consequences of school segregation and the potential for public policy to influence segregation in schools.

This chapter is intended to reduce this differential in scholarly attention by modeling school segregation as the outcome of centralized decisions made by a school or district administrator. The administrator's problem is to balance the competing interests of parents, teachers, and the judicial system, where each group has its own preferences regarding the racial composition of schools and classrooms. Parents, courts, and other actors may be motivated by perceptions of the relationship between racial composition and education quality, or by a desire to restrict the benefits of investments in particular schools to members of their own racial or ethnic group.[6] For simplicity, our model posits two groups with different preferences: those who want to minimize the level of interracial exposure in public schools, and those who oppose segregation and want to achieve racial balance in the schools.

The model suggests that recent increases in school segregation can be attributed to some combination of three basic trends: reduced judicial scrutiny, increased minority enrollment, and increased white tolerance. This last counterintuitive effect occurs when marginally more tolerant whites lend support to public schools only in exchange for administrative concessions, expressed or implied, regarding the racial composition of classrooms within schools. For example, white parents may enroll their children in a racially diverse public school only if the school establishes a tracking program that restricts the amount of interracial exposure within classrooms.

We test the model's empirical implications by examining new evidence on school segregation derived from a rich administrative dataset covering thousands of individual classrooms in roughly two thousand schools in all 117 North Carolina public school districts. Our empirical findings suggest that the forces determining segregation between schools differ from those determining segregation within schools. Specifically, consistent with an administrative effort to reduce the potential for segregation across schools, we find that the greater the racial diversity of a district, the lower the district's propensity to build new schools in response to population growth. This effect is stronger when growth increases the nonwhite share of the school-age population. At the same time, we find that schools in racially diverse districts that have managed to achieve low degrees of segregation across schools are more likely to employ academic tracking, a policy that exacerbates segregation across classrooms within schools. This finding suggests a pattern of substitution between two forms of segregation, within schools and across them, which we attribute to the tendency of courts to focus their attention on between-school segregation to the exclusion of within-school segregation.

Both between and within schools, we observe a tendency for segregation to be highest in racially diverse districts.

We begin this chapter with a brief background on school segregation in the United States and in North Carolina. We next outline our model, and then move on to examine policy choices that have the potential to influence racial balance between and within schools. The next part of the chapter reports the results of empirical tests of the model, and the final section presents our conclusions.

BACKGROUND

Beginning with the momentous *Brown v. Board of Education* case in 1954, hundreds of court cases and district desegregation plans profoundly affected public schools and their communities nationwide between 1954 and the early 1990s. After two decades of tortuous legal maneuvers, public protests, and resigned acceptance, southern schools became the most racially integrated in the country.[7] Beginning in the 1970s, school segregation in northern cities became an issue of intense debate, provoking a new generation of initiatives aimed at creating racial balance in public schools. Over the past decade, the policy environment for debates over school desegregation has changed, becoming increasingly constrained by a series of Supreme Court decisions that seemed to signal an end to the era of proactive efforts to integrate public schools.[8] Indeed, as federal courts appeared to become more reluctant to allow districts to use race in making student assignments, some observers feared that the public schools were headed into a period of resegregation.[9]

Measurement of Segregation

A number of studies have tracked the level of segregation across schools within districts over this time period.[10] Much less research has been devoted to measuring interracial contact within schools. To our knowledge, the most comprehensive attempt to measure within-school contact is Morgan and McPartland's examination of classroom assignments in 43,738 public schools in the fall of 1976.[11] Their study, which computed segregation indices for each school rather than each district, found a small amount of intraschool segregation in elementary and middle school grades and a more pronounced amount in high schools. These studies summarize racial balance across schools by computing one or more segregation indices for each district. In this chapter, we use two fairly common measures of racial segregation in schools.[12]

We briefly define each measure here and offer a more complete discussion in appendix 8A. The first measure of interracial contact is the exposure rate, E, which gives the racial composition of the school attended by the typical student of a given racial group.[13] For example, the measure of exposure of whites to nonwhites across the schools in a district is expressed as

$$E_k^* = \frac{\sum_j W_{jk} n_{jk}}{\sum_j W_{jk}},$$

(1)

where j indexes the schools in district k, W_{jk} indicates the number of white students in each school, and n_{jk} denotes the percentage nonwhite in each school. Analogous exposure indices can be calculated to measure the exposure across classrooms within a district, a measure we denote E_k, or across classrooms within a school, which we denote E_{jk}.

The exposure index can be somewhat misleading if used as a measure of the evenness of racial composition across classrooms, since the minimum possible index value varies with the nonwhite share in the relevant district or school. As a measure of evenness, we use a second, "gap-based" segregation index, also known as the normalized exposure index.[14] For example, to measure the degree of segregation across schools within a district, we calculate

$$S_k^B = \frac{n_k - E_k^*}{n_k},$$

(2)

which is basically the gap between a district's observed exposure rate and that which would result from a perfectly even racial distribution across classrooms. The superscript B denotes between-school segregation. We similarly calculate the amount of within-school segregation for each district, S_k^W, by measuring the average difference between an even distribution and the actual outcome in each school.

We can also calculate a within-school segregation measure for an individual school, which we denote S_{jk}. Most previous studies of within-school segregation do not rely on indices to measure such patterns. Gamoran and Oakes and Guiton, for example, have analyzed the pattern of placements of students into academic tracks and present evidence that students of different racial groups faced different probabilities of being assigned to academic tracks, holding constant their measured achievement levels.[15] Oakes and Mickelson have analyzed the effects of such placements on the racial composition of individual classes.[16] In particular, Mickelson's study of high schools in Charlotte-Mecklenburg reveals a marked degree of segregation in some courses. Meier, Stewart, and England present a related analysis of various means of discrimination in schools, including disproportionate placement in special tracks, and Schofield provides an earlier study of interracial contact within a public middle school.[17]

For a given nonwhite share, the segregation index is a linear transformation of the exposure index. In the theoretical model presented below, we model segregation levels S as administrative choice variables; the resultant levels of exposure depend on the outcome of various reactions to this administrative choice that determine the equilibrium nonwhite share, n. Given a value of n and the administrative choice of S, the equilibrium exposure rate $E = (1 - S)n$.

The North Carolina Data

Our fundamental empirical interest in this chapter is to observe and analyze both the assignment of students to schools and to classrooms within schools. To examine these classroom assignments, we are fortunate to have access to detailed unpublished administrative data from the North Carolina Department of Public Instruction, made available to us under strict conditions to ensure confidentiality of information on individual students and teachers. The nation's eleventh most populous state, North Carolina has a sizeable minority population and it features many urban and rural school districts. Although the state has a small but rapidly growing Hispanic population, African Americans remain the largest minority group by far. In 2000–01, the state enrolled some 1.3 million students in grades K–12, including students in charter schools. Charter schools were included with the districts in which they were located, although they were administratively independent of those districts. Detailed information on the dataset and our calculations are presented in appendix 8A.

Table 8.1 presents average values for classroom-level segregation indices calculated using enrollment data for each school district in North Carolina in 1994–95 and 2000–01.[18] Average between-school, within-school, and overall indices are presented for elementary schools based on fourth-grade data, middle schools based on seventh-grade data, and high schools based on tenth-grade data.[19] This table shows that students at higher grade levels are more racially stratified across classrooms in a district, even though the schools they attend are more integrated. At all grade levels, segregation has increased over time, both because schools themselves have become more racially stratified and because students of different races have become more separated within

TABLE 8.1: Classroom-Level Segregation in North Carolina School Districts, 1994–95 and 2000–01

	1994–95			2000–01		
	Total	Between Schools	Within Schools	Total	Between Schools	Within Schools
Grade Level	S_k	S_k^B	S_k^W	S_k	S_k^B	S_k^W
Elementary (4th Grade)	0.14	0.12	0.02	0.20	0.16	0.04
Middle (7th Grade)	0.18	0.09	0.09	0.23	0.11	0.12
High (10th Grade)	0.20	0.08	0.12	0.23	0.09	0.15

Source: North Carolina Department of Public Instruction, North Carolina Education Research Data Center; School Activity Report Data, 1994–95 and 2000–01.

Note: Authors' calculations. See text for segregation index formulas.

schools. Segregation within schools in elementary grades is low enough to be entirely attributable to random variation but it is markedly higher at the secondary level. We performed a simulation to estimate the degree of segregation that would be observed under complete random assignment of students to classrooms and schools. The degree of within-school segregation derived from our simulation actually exceeds the value observed for elementary students in North Carolina in 1994–95 and equals the 2000–01 value. Between-school segregation patterns and within-school segregation at the secondary level are inconsistent with the random assignment simulation. These patterns are consistent with those described by Morgan and McPartland in their national survey of enrollment patterns undertaken in 1976.[20]

Figures 8.1 and 8.2 illustrate the relationship between classroom-level segregation and other characteristics. Segregation tends to be highest in racially mixed districts, as shown in figure 8.1. For this figure, we calculated the segregation level for a district by taking the weighted average of first-, fourth-, seventh-, and tenth-grade observations, with weights equal to the enrollment at each grade level. The parabola shown on this graph is the result of a regression of segregation on percentage nonwhite enrollment in each district and its square. Predicted segregation levels reach their maximum when a district's enrollment is roughly 50 percent nonwhite. Districts that were overwhelmingly white or nonwhite tend to exhibit more modest levels of segregation.

FIGURE 8.1: Classroom-Level Segregation and Nonwhite Share, by School District

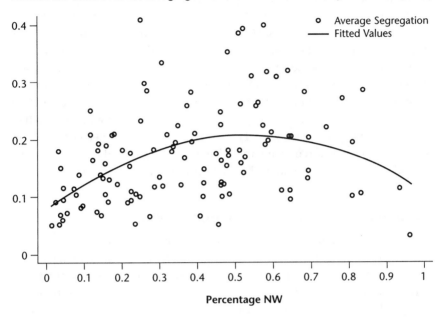

FIGURE 8.2: Classroom-Level Segregation and Residential Segregation, by County

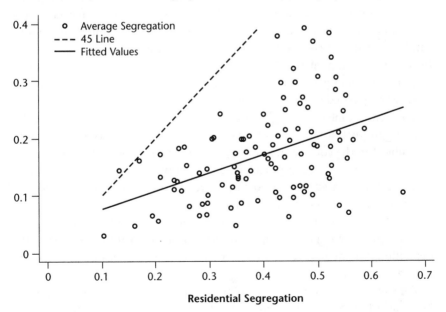

Figure 8.2 presents the relationship between classroom-level segregation in each of North Carolina's one hundred counties and a measure of residential segregation based on block-level data from the 2000 U.S. Census. For this figure, we created a set of classroom segregation indices across all classrooms in a county for those counties with multiple school districts. Classroom-level segregation tends to be higher in residentially segregated counties, but in ninety-nine out of one hundred counties, students are more integrated in their classrooms than in their neighborhoods. In North Carolina, the median individual lives on a block with 112 residents, roughly 20 percent of whom are school-aged children. Thus the number of school-aged children on the typical block closely resembles the number in the typical classroom.

A THEORETICAL MODEL OF SCHOOL SEGREGATION

We view the extent of racial balance across classrooms within a school or district as the result of a number of decisions made by administrators, parents, and, in some cases, students themselves. In this section, we model administrators as agents who choose a vector of policies that influence school segregation levels. These policies include capital investment decisions, such as the number of schools to build and where to build them; organizational decisions, such as whether to designate magnet schools; and purely instructional policies, such as whether to permit ability grouping in some subjects or how many and what type of electives to offer in middle schools and high schools. Another set of policies directly related to segregation, of course, pertains to student assignment to schools—how to assign students living in various neighborhoods to particular schools, and whether to depart from a method of geography-based school assignment.[21]

We view the measured segregation in a school district as the result of the school administrators' efforts to balance the wishes of various stakeholders, subject to the constraints inherent in the underlying racial composition of the community. This approach differs from one in which administrators make decisions based on their own preferences alone, for example, by aiming to minimize the degree of interracial contact or, alternatively, to achieve racially balanced schools and classrooms. The "objective function" used by the administrator might weight the utility of individual groups differentially, depending on the political or social power each group has to override the administrator's decision.

For simplicity, we divide stakeholders into two groups. One group prefers lower over higher rates of interracial exposure in schools. That this is a reasonable presumption to make is supported by Massey and Hajnal: "Over the past ninety years, segregation patterns in the United States have consistently evolved to satisfy one overriding principle—the minimization of white-black contact. What has changed over time is the level at which the segregation has occurred."[22] It is reasonable to suppose that this group consists primarily of a subset of white parents. The second group of stakeholders is comprised of institutions or groups who favor racial balance and oppose segregation. These stakeholders could be courts or other governmental bodies that could be expected to punish a district whose schools show an excessive degree of segregation, or they could be residents who would vote against school leaders whose policies exacerbate segregation. Among the opponents of segregation could also be advocacy groups such as the NAACP, whose efforts led to many of the court actions that effected desegregation in districts.[23] It is not necessary for any of the actors in this model to be extreme in their opposition to segregation or interracial exposure.

Our theoretical model, then, has administrators choosing a pattern of student assignments so as to minimize the costs to them from the two stylized sets of stakeholders: the costs to some white parents of increasing interracial exposure, and the costs to segregation opponents to increased school segregation. The more intensely the anti-exposure stakeholders oppose exposure, and the more political clout they have, the more administrators are likely to choose segregated student assignments. Similarly, the less fierce the opposition from integration advocates, the smaller the political price local administrators have to pay for segregated attendance patterns. Indeed, the growing reluctance of federal courts to intervene to promote school racial balance and the recent court decisions prohibiting race-specific student transfers in the service of diversity can be interpreted in the vocabulary of our model as a decrease in the costs to local administrators from proponents of interracial exposure.[24]

The decisions of local administrators will also be affected by the sensitivity of white households to changes in interracial exposure; that is, by the likelihood that white households will leave the school district or remove their children from public schools, rather than comply with administrative decisions. When there are few opponents of interracial contact or these opponents do not hold their views strongly, administrators could reasonably be expected to select policies that result in lower degrees of segregation. Virulent opposition to integration, by contrast, may lead administrators to make different decisions. This basic pattern need not always hold, however. For example, administrators may choose to ignore the wishes of a vocal but small faction, losing their support in the process but gaining favor among other constituencies. Were this faction to moderate its views, the administrator might react by bringing them into the fold. In other words, a moderation of intolerant views could lead to an increase in segregation if in the process administrators switch from ignoring those views to listening to them.

Between 1990 and 2000, 99 of North Carolina's 117 school districts experienced an increase in the nonwhite share of the school-age population. The median increase was four percentage points. For comparison, the median nonwhite share of the school-age population in 1990 was 29 percent. Increases in nonwhite share were concentrated in districts with low initial nonwhite share. The mean increase in nonwhite share was twice as high among the state's ninety-seven majority-white districts as among the twenty majority-nonwhite districts. A good deal of this increase can be attributed to a quintupling of the state's Hispanic population between census years. Our model suggests that administrators will respond to an exogenous increase in community nonwhite share by increasing segregation. The implications of changing community composition are more complicated, however, when changing composition also changes the weights placed on various constituent groups in the population. For example, in the special case where proponents of interracial exposure are nonwhite parents and antiexposure constituents are white parents, and the administrator attaches weights to each group proportional to their share in the population, the effect is theoretically ambiguous. This offers a potential explanation for the concave relationship between nonwhite share and segregation shown in figure 8.1.

In summary, the model offers three possible explanations for recent increases in classroom segregation. The first is a decreased propensity for white flight. The second is an increase in the nonwhite population, particularly in districts with a small initial nonwhite share. And the third is reduced opposition to segregation or, alternatively, a lessening of the weight placed on the preferences of those opposed to segregation.

Within-School versus Between-School Segregation

Although policies that influence segregation incorporate factors that operate at both levels, up to this point the model has not distinguished between- and within-school segregation. This distinction can be important to the extent that certain constituent groups care about one form of segregation but not the other. If opponents of segregation, for example, focus their attention exclusively on between-school segregation while opponents of exposure are most concerned with interracial contact at the classroom level, it may be possible for an administrator to satisfy both constituent groups simultaneously.[25] Such a scenario would appear to apply particularly to the opposition to segregation voiced by federal courts in the United States, which typically mandate remedies for reducing segregation between schools but pay less attention to what goes on within them.[26] A mandate to reduce between-school segregation might simply lead administrators to substitute segregation across classrooms within schools.

The empirically testable predictions of the model are clear in some cases but ambiguous in others. Factors enabling white flight or signaling decreased tolerance for interracial exposure have ambiguous effects on the predicted segregation level. Factors signaling decreased tolerance for segregation clearly predict lower segregation levels, other things being equal. Segregation will increase as administrators give greater weight to the preferences of exposure opponents and decrease as they attach greater weight to segregation opponents. A higher proportion of nonwhites in the population should generally increase segregation, except perhaps at relatively high levels. Finally, any incongruity in the levels at which constituent groups monitor segregation and exposure could lead to a scenario where the factors determining segregation between and within schools differ considerably from one another.

EXAMINING POLICY CHOICES

In this section, we focus our attention on two types of policy decisions that have the potential to influence racial balance between and within schools: school construction and policies related to academic tracking.[27]

District administrators can accommodate enrollment growth in one of two ways: by expanding the capacity of existing schools or by building new schools.[28] In general, choosing to expand existing schools rather than build new ones reduces the potential for between-school segregation. At the limit, a district could eliminate all differences in racial composition across schools by having only one school. More generally, in a state like North Carolina, where most school districts are coterminous with counties and older schools tend to be located in older city neighborhoods, a decision to expand existing schools generally has the effect of channeling a greater proportion of students toward central cities. In contrast, a decision to build new schools generally implies construction in suburban, predominantly white areas of a district.

A simple way to describe administrative policy relating to school size is to presume that each district adopts a "target" size for its schools (or, alternatively, for a representative school),

$$\text{Enrollment per School} = k(X), \tag{3}$$

where the function k takes as its argument a vector of district characteristics X. Factors generating variation in target school sizes across districts most likely derive from trade-offs between economies of scale in school construction and operation and the extra transportation costs of forcing students to attend more distant schools. Taking logs of (3), we write the equivalent relation:

$$\ln(\text{Number of Schools}) = \ln(\text{Enrollment}) - \ln k(X). \tag{4}$$

One practical problem with estimating equation (4) is the likelihood that the vector X includes many historical factors, such as past levels of enrollment and past racial discrimination, owing to the durability of investments in infrastructure. Economies of scale in school construction, difficulties in renting or selling excess schools, or political opposition to closing existing schools, for example, may lead districts with declining enrollments to operate more schools than otherwise equivalent districts with growing enrollments. Failure to control for historical components of X may result in biased estimates of the relationship between current district conditions and school construction decisions. To escape this bias, we first difference equation (4),

$$\Delta\ln(\text{Number of Schools}) = \Delta\ln(\text{Enrollment}) - \Delta\ln k(X), \tag{5}$$

which, under certain assumptions regarding the functional form of $k(X)$, will have the effect of dropping historical factors predating the first observation of $k(X)$ from the estimated equation.

The regression results reported in table 8.2 are based on equation (5), with two essential modifications. First, the school-age population in each district is used as a measure of size rather than public school enrollment, since the latter measure may be more endogenous to district policy choices, including school construction decisions. Second, the coefficient on that variable is not constrained to equal one, since district size itself may influence the school size decision. We also assume that the function $k(X)$ is exponential. The specifications analyze the determinants of relative change in the number of schools in each district.

Population growth is a strong predictor of school construction. The first result in table 8.2 shows that, on average, a 1 percent increase in a district's annual growth rate over the decade 1990–2000 is associated with a 2.7 percent increase in the number of schools between 1995 and 2001.

TABLE 8.2: Factors Influencing School Opening and Closing Decisions, 1995–2001

Independent Variable	Dependent Variable: Δ ln(number of schools, 1995–2001)				
Annual growth rate of school-age population, 1990–2000	2.737** (0.638)	2.941** (0.642)	5.683** (1.359)	5.591** (1.417)	8.687 (5.549)
Change in nonwhite share of school-age population, 1990–2000	—	−0.276* (0.152)	−0.344** (0.153)	−0.407** (0.176)	−0.259 (0.197)
Initial nonwhite share of school-age population (1990)	—	—	−0.073 (0.064)	−0.130* (0.076)	−0.065 (0.089)
Initial nonwhite share* annual growth rate	—	—	−8.861** (3.915)	−10.05** (4.065)	−8.389** (4.236)
Change in low-income household share of population, 1990–2000	—	—	—	0.270 (0.377)	−0.163 (0.503)
Change in high-income household share of population, 1990–2000	—	—	—	0.437 (0.754)	−0.173 (0.908)
Urban district	—	—	—	0.007 (0.023)	−0.008 (0.025)
Piedmont region	—	—	—	0.032 (0.028)	0.021 (0.030)
Coastal region	—	—	—	0.006 (0.030)	0.001 (0.031)
Initial low-income household share of population (1990)	—	—	—	—	−0.343 (0.268)
Initial high-income household share of population (1990)	—	—	—	—	0.202 (0.754)
Initial low-income share* annual growth rate	—	—	—	—	−12.43 (13.34)
Initial high-income share* annual growth rate	—	—	—	—	−4.482 (41.06)
N	117	117	117	117	117
R^2	0.138	0.162	0.199	0.227	0.252

Note: Standard errors in parentheses. Sample consists of all public school districts in the state of North Carolina. See appendix 8A for variable definitions and data sources.

* Denotes a coefficient significant at the 10 percent level, ** the 5 percent level.

Extrapolating the magnitude of this effect to a ten-year timeframe suggests that growing districts do not construct new schools at a rate sufficient to maintain average school size at initial levels. As districts become denser, administrators act to reduce net transportation costs by opening more schools and to take advantage of economies of scale by operating larger schools.[29] Does racial composition influence the decision to operate larger or more numerous schools? Our model suggests that the effect of a change in the racial composition on cost-minimizing segregation levels is ambiguous and depends on the relationship between the racial composition of the community and the weights administrators place on the preferences of those opposed to segregation. The first empirical evidence on this point is shown in the second regression, which adds a control for change in the nonwhite share of the school-age population between 1990 and 2000. Districts that became more nonwhite over this time period exhibited a marginally significant relative decrease in the number of schools operated. Relative to a district with stable racial composition, a district experiencing a ten percentage point increase in nonwhite share would be expected to operate roughly 3 percent fewer schools.

Stronger evidence of a link between race and school construction decisions appears in the third regression, which introduces a control for nonwhite share of the school-age population in 1990 and interacts that variable with the population growth measure. In this specification, the main growth effect and the effects of change in nonwhite share increase in magnitude and the coefficient of the change in nonwhite share attains significance at the 5 percent level. The interaction term is large, negative, and statistically significant. To consider the implications of this result, consider two districts identical except for racial composition, one of which is entirely white and the other evenly divided between white and nonwhite students. In response to a unit increase in the annual growth rate of the school-age population, the white district is predicted to open between four and five schools for every one opened in the evenly divided district. Racial heterogeneity, in other words, tends to suppress the impulse to build new schools when growth occurs. If population growth is accompanied by an increase in nonwhite share, of course the predicted response is even weaker. The exhibited tendency of racially heterogeneous districts to take actions that restrict the potential for greater between-school segregation is consistent with the theoretical model, wherein the weight attached to the preferences of segregation opponents increases with nonwhite share.

An alternative explanation for this result is that the racial composition of a district is a proxy for district wealth, and that districts that are more nonwhite and poorer have a harder time raising capital to build new schools when faced with population growth. The final regressions in table 8.2 check this possibility, first by introducing controls for changes in the income distribution in each district, and then by adding initial levels of the income distribution variables and interacting them with the growth measure. The income distribution variables are based on decennial census data and capture the share of households with income below \$20,000 in 1999 dollars, as well as the share of households with income above \$100,000 in 1999 dollars.[30] Controls for the distribution of income have little impact on the estimated interaction term between initial racial composition and population growth. The addition of interaction terms between initial income distribution and population growth reduce the precision of the main growth effect dramatically, and neither added interaction term is statistically significant. Although the addition of controls for changes and initial levels of income, plus interactions of initial levels with growth rate, renders statistically insignificant the effect of the change in nonwhite share, the coefficient is similar in magnitude to initial estimates. Overall, this evidence supports the view that the estimated effects of racial composition should be interpreted as the effects of race, rather than socioeconomic status.

If all administrative decisions in racially mixed districts were guided by a desire to limit the potential for classroom segregation, we would expect racially heterogeneous districts to avoid academic tracking of students within schools. To the extent that there are racial differences in the proportions of students assigned to each track, tracking will tend to increase racial segregation.[31] The results reported in table 8.3 suggest that the exact opposite pattern holds: as would be expected in scenarios where those opposed to segregation are more concerned with racial patterns between schools than within them, heterogeneous districts tend to employ greater degrees of tracking, except when segregation across schools is relatively high.

To analyze tracking decisions, we formed a tracking index based on administrative data on the racial composition of each English class in North Carolina secondary schools. These data identify the "academic level" of each class taught in each school, including standard, honors/advanced/ academically gifted, special education, and advanced placement categories, among others. Indexing academic levels t, with enrollment in each level e_t, the tracking index is calculated using the formula

$$\text{Tracking Index} = 1 - \sum_t \left(\frac{e_t}{\sum_t e_t} \right)^2. \tag{6}$$

TABLE 8.3: Factors Influencing Tracking Decisions, 2000–01

	Dependent Variable: Herfindahl-Style Tracking Index					
Independent Variable	Middle: 7th Grade			High: 10th Grade		
Nonwhite share of school-age population in district, 2000	0.058** (0.027)	0.106** (0.031)	0.080** (0.033)	-0.010 (0.060)	0.105** (0.051)	0.160* (0.077)
Same grade level between-school segregation in district, 2000–01	—	0.267** (0.121)	0.158 (0.114)	—	0.554* (0.310)	0.702** (0.341)
Nonwhite share* between-school segregation	—	−0.582** (0.288)	−0.397 (0.269)	—	−1.832** (0.924)	−1.867** (0.900)
Urban district	—	—	−0.009 (0.010)	—	—	−0.023 (0.024)
Piedmont region	—	—	0.012 (0.012)	—	—	−0.040* (0.021)
Coastal region	—	—	-0.006 (0.012)	—	—	0.010 (0.033)
ln(enrollment in grade)	—	—	−0.007 (0.007)	—	—	0.058** (0.010)
Private school market share in district (1990)	—	—	0.316* (0.158)	—	—	−1.132* (0.676)
District land area in thousands of square miles	—	—	−0.010 (0.018)	—	—	−0.001 (0.035)
District household income heterogeneity index	—	—	0.492 (0.916)	—	—	−0.632 (1.494)
N	527	527	527	356	356	356
R^2	0.012	0.019	0.041	0.0002	0.028	0.176

Note: Standard errors, corrected using the Huber-White procedure to reflect clustering at the school district level, in parentheses. Sample consists of secondary schools with at least twenty-four students enrolled in English courses in the relevant grade. See appendix 8A for variable definitions and data sources.

* Denotes a coefficient significant at the 5 percent level, ** the 1 percent level.

This index, which resembles a standard Herfindahl index or fragmentation indices common in recent public economics literature,[32] can be interpreted as the probability that two students randomly selected from a grade within a school will belong to different academic levels or tracks. When all students are enrolled in a single track, the index equals zero. As students are divided into more numerous small tracks, the index approaches one. The average tracking index among seventh-grade English students in academic year 2000–01 was relatively small, 0.036. Fewer than 20 percent of all public middle schools tracked seventh-grade English students. High schools were considerably more heavily tracked on average, with a mean index value of 0.602. More than 96 percent of North Carolina public high schools used some degree of tracking in tenth-grade English.

Simple bivariate tests of the relationship between district-level racial composition and the degree of tracking in a secondary school, shown in the first and fourth columns of table 8.3, show mixed results.[33] There is evidence of a significant link between the nonwhite share of a district's school-age population and tracking at the seventh-grade level, but not the tenth-grade level. This discrepancy in results disappears in the next set of regressions, which add controls for the level of between-school segregation in each school's district and the interaction of nonwhite share with segregation. These regressions reveal an intriguing and statistically significant pattern. In both middle and high schools, an increase in nonwhite share in a district with no between-school segregation leads to a significant increase in the use of tracking: a one-standard-deviation increase in nonwhite share predicts a one-third to one-half-standard-deviation increase in the tracking index. Among districts with a high degree of between-school segregation, however, the link between nonwhite share and tracking is either negligible or negative. These results suggest that pressure to implement tracking in racially heterogeneous districts is eased by the presence of segregation between schools.

Greater racial heterogeneity in a school district thus predicts the adoption of policies that limit the potential for between-school segregation and increase the potential for within-school segregation. As discussed above, such a pattern is consistent with a scenario in which opponents of segregation focus primarily on between-school measures, while opponents of exposure are most concerned with classroom-level measures.

Not all evidence in the tracking regressions supports the notion that between- and within-school segregation are substitutes. The significant, positive main effect of between-school segregation implies that between-

and within-school segregation covary positively in predominantly white districts. Such a pattern could arise, for example, if those opposed to segregation, including the courts, take little notice or have little standing in overwhelmingly white districts, allowing variation in the preferences of opponents of exposure to determine both between- and within-school segregation patterns. In majority-nonwhite districts, higher between-school segregation predicts lower degrees of tracking within each school.

The final regressions in table 8.3 add a number of covariates intended to capture variation in the feasibility of implementing tracking, regional patterns, and differences in the competitive environment schools face. More complete tracking is presumably more feasible in larger schools. Hence a control for the logarithm of enrollment in each school is added. To capture differences in the competitive environment, the regressions control for district land area and a lagged measure of private school market share.[34] A measure of income heterogeneity captures the potential demand for tracking stemming from wealthy parents' desire to limit their children's exposure to peers of low socioeconomic status. Across specifications, there are few consistent patterns among these additional control variables. None are significant with the same sign in both specifications. Incorporating these controls does not change the general pattern of coefficients among the variables of interest, although the coefficients of the between-school segregation control and interaction term become insignificant in the specification for middle schools. The magnitude and significance of coefficients in the high school regression increase.

The evidence presented in this section suggests that school and district administrators achieve a compromise between simultaneous pressures to integrate schools and limit interracial exposure. Relative to overwhelmingly white districts, racially heterogeneous districts build fewer schools in response to population growth. Opting for larger schools rather than a greater number of schools places limits on the amount of between-school segregation that can occur, especially in districts where new schools would otherwise have been built near new suburban neighborhoods that are occupied predominantly by white families. At the same time, the results imply that administrators in racially heterogeneous districts are more likely to resort to academic tracking in secondary schools, especially when between-school segregation is low. From an educational standpoint, these policy choices may have adverse consequences to the extent that small school size and interaction of students with varying ability would promote achievement for disadvantaged students.[35]

EXAMINING BETWEEN-SCHOOL AND WITHIN-SCHOOL SEGREGATION PATTERNS

While our analysis of policy choices uncovers some evidence consistent with our model, we cannot hope to identify and quantify all the policy decisions that might be sensitive to considerations of interracial contact within classrooms and schools, such as where to draw attendance zone boundaries and where to offer elective courses likely to appeal disproportionately to students of one racial group. The remainder of our empirical analysis therefore looks directly for evidence that segregation levels in North Carolina's districts and schools are influenced by the types of factors suggested by our model.

In table 8.4, we begin by explaining cross-sectional variation in between-school segregation for North Carolina districts in the 2000–01 school year. Our analysis focuses on three grade levels: fourth, seventh, and tenth, representing elementary, middle, and high schools. At each grade level, we begin by examining the basic relationship between segregation and the racial composition of the district and then add a number of additional controls that may capture variation in preferences, group political power, or availability of outside options.[36]

As in the preceding tables, racial composition is measured using decennial census measures of the entire school-age population in each district. At all grade levels, the results confirm the basic pattern shown in figure 8.1: districts serving racially heterogeneous populations tend to have higher between-school segregation levels than either predominantly white or predominantly nonwhite districts. The maximum predicted segregation level is associated with districts that are fairly close to 50 percent nonwhite.

Adding controls for a number of covariates reduces the magnitude and significance of the relationship between racial composition and segregation at all three grade levels. The set of introduced control variables includes regional and urban district effect; measures of district land area and lagged private school market share, which capture the ease of exit from each district; and three variables describing the income distribution in each district: the income heterogeneity index used in table 8.3, as well as measures of the relative density of high-income households in the white and nonwhite populations. These income measures could capture information about the distribution of preferences or political power by race in each district. The only control variable entering significantly in each regression, however, is the logarithm of the school-age population served in each district, as measured in the 2000 census.

TABLE 8.4: Explaining Segregation between Schools, 2000–01

Independent Variable	Dependent Variable: Between-School Segregation					
	Elementary: 4th Grade		Middle: 7th Grade		High: 10th Grade	
Nonwhite share of school-age population in district, 2000	0.387** (0.141)	0.314** (0.151)	0.290** (0.132)	0.163 (0.149)	0.248** (0.102)	0.136 (0.111)
Nonwhite share squared	−0.334* (0.177)	−0.246 (0.193)	−0.316* (0.167)	−0.222 (0.192)	−0.272** (0.129)	−0.178 (0.142)
ln(school-age population, 2000)	—	0.050** (0.014)	—	0.045** (0.014)	—	0.046** (0.010)
Urban district	—	−0.024 (0.021)	—	−0.012 (0.021)	—	−0.018 (0.016)
Piedmont region	—	−0.014 (0.021)	—	−0.006 (0.021)	—	$3.54*10^{-7}$ (0.016)
Coastal region	—	0.003 (0.023)	—	0.021 (0.023)	—	0.025 (0.017)
Private school market share, 1990	—	−0.071 (0.279)	—	−0.166 (0.284)	—	−0.356 (0.209)
Land area in thousands of square miles	—	0.057 (0.048)	—	0.059 (0.049)	—	−0.006 (0.036)
Household income heterogeneity index	—	−0.841 (1.864)	—	−1.661 (1.878)	—	−1.561 (1.395)
Share of white households with 1999 income over $100,000	—	0.163 (0.289)	—	0.248 (0.292)	—	0.275 (0.216)
Share of nonwhite households with 1999 income over $100,000	—	0.028 (0.399)	—	−0.400 (0.398)	—	−0.085 (0.295)
N	116	116	116	116	117	117
R^2	0.116	0.470	0.045	0.360	0.054	0.413

Note: Standard errors in parentheses. Unit of observation is the school district. Missing observations attributable to complete racial homogeneity within some grades in some districts. See appendix 8A for variable definitions and data sources.

* Denotes a coefficient significant at the 10 percent level, ** the 5 percent level.

Based on these results, it appears that the relationship between racial composition and school segregation is confounded with the positive correlation between segregation and the size of the district. The absence of a strong link between the racial composition of the district and between-school segregation aligns with the earlier finding that districts with a higher proportion of nonwhites tend to restrict the number of new schools created. In both cases, the evidence suggests that administrators resist pressure to increase between-school segregation in heterogeneous districts.

Table 8.5 essentially replicates, at the school level, the regression specifications of table 8.4, substituting a measure of within-school segregation—the extent to which the racial composition of English classes in each school departs from that of the school itself—as the dependent variable for each school. We focus on middle and high school grades in this table, since within-school segregation is uniformly low in the elementary grades. The first and fourth regressions in the table show that within-school segregation, like its between-school counterpart, tends to be higher in racially heterogeneous schools.[37] At the school level, evidence of a link between district racial composition and within-school segregation levels is uniformly strong and robust to the inclusion of control variables. Estimates for both middle and high schools suggest that the most segregated schools are generally found in districts where slightly less than half the underlying school-age population is nonwhite.

There is evidence of an asymmetric response of within-school segregation to district-level measures of income among white and nonwhite households. Among control variables, one factor entering significantly relates to the income distribution within the white and nonwhite population. Districts with larger shares of high-income white households tend to have more segregation within their middle and high schools. Higher nonwhite income is associated with no such effect; in fact, districts with more high-income nonwhite households tend to have significantly less within-high school segregation. There are several ways to interpret these results.

First, if white resistance to racial integration is based in part on differences in socioeconomic status between students of different races, larger income differences should lead to greater resistance. Second, the weight that administrators place on the wishes of respective factions may depend on the income levels of those factions. Third, these measures of relative affluence by race may simply reflect the degree of income inequality in a district, which may in turn influence tracking and decisions about the offerings of electives independently of racial considerations. This last possibility seems unlikely, how-

TABLE 8.5: Explaining Within-School Segregation across Schools, 2000–01

Independent Variable	Dependent Variable: School-Specific Segregation Index					
	Middle: 7th Grade			High: 10th Grade		
Nonwhite share of school-age population in district, 2000	0.500** (0.084)	0.363** (0.094)	0.339** (0.091)	0.346** (0.104)	0.428** (0.139)	0.433** (0.136)
Nonwhite share squared	−0.538** (0.115)	−0.471** (0.117)	−0.448** (0.112)	−0.440** (0.112)	−0.550** (0.155)	−0.557** (0.153)
ln(school-age population, 2000)	—	0.005 (0.009)	0.007 (0.010)	—	0.011 (0.012)	0.009 (0.012)
Urban district	—	0.014 (0.012)	0.016 (0.012)	—	−0.019 (0.024)	−0.019 (0.024)
Piedmont region	—	−0.012 (0.012)	−0.014 (0.013)	—	$1.75*10^{-4}$ (0.017)	0.001 (0.017)
Coastal region	—	−0.027* (0.015)	−0.027* (0.015)	—	0.028 (0.024)	0.028 (0.023)
Private school market share, 1990	—	−0.098 (0.172)	−0.119 (0.165)	—	0.029 (0.346)	0.030 (0.349)
Land area in thousands of square miles	—	−0.062** (0.026)	−0.062** (0.027)	—	−0.068* (0.039)	−0.071* (0.039)
Household income heterogeneity index	—	−3.244** (1.219)	−3.229** (1.224)	—	−2.260 (1.482)	−2.159 (1.514)
Share of white households with 1999 income over $100,000	—	0.362** (0.157)	0.308** (0.155)	—	0.472** (0.245)	0.536** (0.245)
Share of nonwhite households with 1999 income over $100,000	—	0.153 (0.261)	0.124 (0.264)	—	−0.832** (0.420)	−0.812** (0.427)
Herfindahl-style tracking index	—	—	0.195** (0.097)	—	—	0.077* (0.040)
N	544	544	544	378	378	378
R^2	0.071	0.119	0.156	0.029	0.070	0.101

Note: Standard errors, corrected using the Huber-White procedure to reflect clustering at the school district level, in parentheses. Sample consists of all secondary schools in North Carolina. See appendix 8A for variable definitions and data sources.

* Denotes a coefficient significant at the 5 percent level, ** the 1 percent level.

ever, since the estimated effect of income inequality, as measured by the heterogeneity index, on within-school segregation is neither consistent nor statistically significant. In these specifications, two additional factors appear as strong and often significant predictors of within-school segregation. Holding other factors constant, physically larger school districts, which presumably operate in a less competitive environment than smaller districts, tend to feature more racially mixed classrooms. The administrators in such districts apparently have less reason to satisfy the wishes of white parents concerned about interracial exposure than do administrators in smaller districts, which white families may threaten to leave. Heterogeneity in household income is associated with lower levels of within-school segregation, and significantly so among middle schools. This pattern casts further doubt upon the third explanation for the asymmetric response of segregation to white and nonwhite income proposed above.

The third and sixth regressions in table 8.5 add the Herfindahl-style tracking index analyzed in table 8.2 to the list of control variables. As posited above, greater degrees of tracking within a school are associated with higher levels of segregation at that school. This finding corroborates largely anecdotal evidence cited in debates over the merits of academic tracking.[38] The effect is strongest across middle schools, where a one-standard-deviation increase in tracking predicts a one-fifth-standard-deviation increase in within-school segregation. The addition of the tracking index has surprisingly little effect on other coefficients estimated in the regression. Thus, if we accept the notion that factors such as nonwhite share and the distribution of income affect administrators' choices of cost-minimizing segregation levels, the role of academic tracking as a mechanism influencing segregation appears to be relatively small. Other policy decisions, and perhaps decisions by other actors including parents and students, explain most of the link between district racial composition and within-school segregation.

Taken together, our evidence on the determinants of between-school and within-school segregation in North Carolina suggests that very different sets of forces operate at the two levels. Moreover, there is a rational explanation for the difference. Between-school segregation, which is the form most likely to be regulated by court order, is relatively insensitive to district-specific factors aside from sheer size. Recent school construction decisions in racially heterogeneous districts suggest that administrators try to limit the potential for segregation across campuses. Relatively less regulated within-school segregation, by contrast, shows a much stronger and more robust relationship to racial composition, the presence of geographically proximate alternative districts, and the distribution of income within a district. Evidence also suggests that districts substitute between the two forms of segregation.

CONCLUSIONS

While they are not high by national standards, segregation levels between and within North Carolina's public schools have increased in recent years. This chapter provides evidence to suggest that district and school administrators actively manage the degree of interracial contact in public schools in order to accommodate the competing desires of their constituents. The model introduced here posits that some stakeholders possess limited tolerance for exposure to nonwhites, and others exhibit limited tolerance for segregation. In this model, the factors determining the cost-minimizing distribution of racial composition across classrooms include the strength of preferences within stakeholder groups, the sensitivity of white flight responses to racial composition, and the underlying racial composition itself.

The model provides several non–mutually exclusive explanations for recent patterns in North Carolina. Decreases in judicial scrutiny almost certainly have the effect of leading to higher segregation levels, at least between schools.[39] In the model, weakening opposition to segregation, or reduced attention of administrators to those who oppose segregation, unambiguously predicts higher cost-minimizing segregation levels. Growth in North Carolina's nonwhite population, driven primarily by Hispanic immigration over the past decade, may also explain increases in segregation, depending on whether this growth has been accompanied by proportionate increases in the weight administrators assign to segregation opponents when making policy decisions. The model also explains why increased racial tolerance on the part of white households might not be sufficient to offset the forces leading to higher segregation. In our model, the impact on segregation of a lower probability of white flight or greater tolerance for interracial contact is theoretically ambiguous.

Future research into the mechanisms underlying continued school segregation might further exploit administrative data of the type we employ in this chapter. In particular, researchers might explore the provisions of school assignment and "controlled choice" plans or the course selection patterns of individual students to more accurately gauge the role that parental and student choices have in limiting interracial contact within classrooms at the secondary level. Data on individual students linked across years could provide information on how the probability of student exit from the public school system varies with interracial exposure. Understanding school segregation as an equilibrium phenomenon will yield critical insights, both to researchers interested in understanding racial attitudes and to policymakers interested in changing patterns of interracial contact in twenty-first-century public schools.[40]

APPENDIX 8A

DATA SOURCES AND VARIABLE DEFINITIONS

School Segregation Indices

We employ an index based on the exposure rate, which is defined here as the percentage of nonwhite students enrolled with the typical white student. Using data at the classroom level, denoted by subscript i, the district-level exposure rate can be defined more accurately than by using only school-level enrollment data. This more exact exposure rate is

$$E_k = \frac{\sum_j \sum_i W_{ijk} n_{ijk}}{\sum_j \sum_i W_{ijk}},$$ (A1)

where W_{ijk} and n_{ijk} are, respectively, the number of white students in the grade of interest and the percentage nonwhite in classroom i, school j. Unless the classrooms in each school are racially balanced at that school's racial composition, this classroom-based exposure rate will be lower than the school-based exposure rate defined above. That is, $E_k \leq E_k{}^* \leq n_k$.

We define the segregation index S as the percentage gap between the maximum exposure rate, n_k, and the actual exposure rate of whites to nonwhites. Classroom-level segregation, which incorporates differences both between schools and within schools, is

$$S_k = \frac{n_k - E_k}{n_k}.$$ (A2)

For a district in which all schools reflect the overall racial composition of students, $S_k{}^B$ takes on its minimum value of zero. By contrast, when schools are completely segregated, so that $E_k{}^* = 0$, the index takes on its maximum value of one. Analogously, S_k equals zero in a district in which all classrooms reflect the district's overall racial composition and one in a district where no students share a classroom with a member of a different race.

The difference between the school- and classroom-level segregation indices represents the classroom-level segregation in a district that can be attributed to disparities in racial composition within schools, rather than across them. This quantity can be expressed as

$$S_k^W = \frac{E_k^* - E_k}{n_k},$$ (A3)

where the superscript W denotes "within."

It is worth noting that S_k^W is a characteristic of a district and is not designed to answer the question, "How segregated are the classrooms in school j?" To address this school-level question, we simply define an index of segregation that can be applied to each school. Where n_{jk} is the proportion nonwhite in school j, this index is defined analogously to previous indices as:

$$S_{jk} = \frac{n_{jk} - E_{jk}}{n_{jk}},$$ (A4)

where the school's exposure rate, E_{jk} is

$$E_{jk} = \frac{\sum_i W_{ijk} n_{ijk}}{\sum_i W_{ijk}}.$$ (A5)

This measure is based on the gap between a school's racial composition and the exposure rate, where the relevant gap is based on the school's, rather than the district's, racial composition. We use this school-level measure of segregation in the chapter to test hypotheses about within-school segregation that make no reference to district-level segregation.

The central dataset used in this analysis, referred to as the School Activity Report (SAR), lists the set of all classes, or "activities," that meet in a given school, along with the number, grade level, and racial breakdown of students enrolled in each of them. We used the SAR database to examine racial balance in the classrooms of first-, fourth-, seventh-, and tenth-grade students.

The notion of classroom assignment is complicated by the fact that students at all grade levels ordinarily have instruction in more than one class over the course of a day or week, ranging from pull-out reading instruction and music in elementary schools to the dozens of classrooms among which high school students scurry each hour when the bell rings. Since we were most interested in interracial contact during academic instruction time, we chose to focus on the classes that most nearly approximated the basic academic instruction at each grade level. To ensure that our assignment of students to classrooms included all the members of a school, we checked the sum of enrollments from the SAR data against an independent statewide tally of school enrollments.[1]

At the elementary level, in most cases we were able to assign individual students to an "activity" that resembles the archetypal elementary classroom: a class where students receive instruction in multiple subjects from a single teacher. However, for approximately 17 percent of the first-grade population and 27 percent of the fourth-grade population, we were unable to make this assignment to a basic classroom. In these cases, we grouped students into classes using data on enrollment in other courses, such as music, reading, or math. We operated under the presumption that elementary students typically proceed through their daily schedule with a constant set of peers, unlike secondary students, who may have different peers in different classes, and our data were fully consistent with this presumption.

In grades seven and ten, we determined the racial balance of schools and districts by examining the racial composition of English courses.[2] English is a required course of instruction for secondary students in the State of North Carolina. Our calculations were complicated by the fact that not all schools have classes that can be easily classified as "English" and "not English." In 42 percent of schools containing a seventh grade, for example, we were best able to match independent data on the size of the grade in each school by counting all English courses, including reading courses and courses combining language arts with other subjects. For high schools, the best match to the validating dataset at the tenth-grade level was to combine all English-related courses, a combination that worked best in 83 percent of schools. Our methodology is described in greater detail in "Segregation and Resegregation in North Carolina's Public School Classrooms" by Clotfelter, Ladd, and Vigdor.[3]

School District Characteristics, 1990

We obtained information on the size and racial composition of the school-age population, proportion of households with low income (defined as less than $15,000 in the year prior to the census) and high-income (greater than $75,000), and private school market share from the School District Data Book.

Sixteen district consolidations occurred in North Carolina between 1990 and 2000; we merged 1990 data for districts that consolidated with one another during the subsequent decade.

School District Characteristics, 2000

We obtained information on the size and racial composition of the school-age population from block-level census data in Summary File 1A, aggregated to the school district level. These data were also used to compute the land area of each district. Data on the proportion of households with low income (defined as less than $20,000 in the year prior to the census) and high-income (greater than $100,000), as well as the household income heterogeneity index, were derived from block group–level census data in Summary File 3A, aggregated to the school district level. The household income heterogeneity index is calculated by computing the share of households in each of sixteen income brackets, ranging from less than $10,000 to greater than $200,000, and summing the squared group shares. The resulting value is then subtracted from one to generate a variable that equals zero when all households are in a single income bracket, and approaches one as households are divided more evenly across brackets.

Other Variables

We classified as urban all districts in counties that were 45 percent or more urban in 1990 and all city districts in any county with enrollments of at least 2,000 in 2001–02, not counting charter school enrollments. Our count of the number of schools in each district uses SAR data from 1995 and 2001, and excludes charter schools operating in each district. The tracking index is calculated according to the formula in equation (6), using SAR data.

CHAPTER NINE

The End of *Keyes*

Resegregation Trends and Achievement in Denver Public Schools

Catherine L. Horn and Michal Kurlaender

On June 21, 1973, the U.S. Supreme Court delivered an opinion that dramatically shaped the future of both the Denver public schools and the country's legal consideration of school desegregation. In essence, *Keyes v. School District No. 1, Denver, Colorado* afforded Hispanics the same kinds of rights to desegregation remedies as black students had previously gained through other court decisions. For Denver, the decision meant a directive to desegregate the district's schools. For the country, it meant that desegregation was no longer just an issue for southern schools and for African American students, and that it extended to whole districts, not just single schools.[1]

More than two decades later, the courts revisited *Keyes*, this time with a different outcome. Desegregation efforts of the mid-1960s and 1970s, largely a result of the enforcement of *Brown v. Board of Education* (1954) and related legislation, most notably the 1964 Civil Rights Act, became largely undone by the late 1980s.[2] The 1990s also brought a series of decisions made by "a Supreme Court reconstructed by the appointees of Presidents Reagan and Bush . . . limiting desegregation rights and triggering a flood of lawsuits designed to end desegregation in major U.S. districts."[3] It was in that context, then, that Judge Richard P. Matsch, who had presided over the district court's oversight of Denver's desegregation plan, declared in 1995 that "the vestiges of past discrimination by the defendants have been eliminated to the extent practicable"[4] and, with his decree, ended mandated desegregation in the Denver Public Schools (DPS).

The legal and demographic shifts that have taken place in the Denver Public School District over the last decade provide an opportunity to investigate changes in school racial/ethnic composition and achievement patterns by race. As a growing number of districts across the country face similar legal and demographic changes, the implications of Denver's experience have become increasingly salient. In particular, Denver's multiracial context is one that increasingly mirrors many urban school districts that were initially desegregated in an African American-white framework. Moreover, in considering how districts might respond to the 2007 voluntary school desegregation case, *Parents Involved in Community Schools v. Seattle School District No. 1*, which concluded "that the racial classifications employed in each of the school districts were not necessary to advance their asserted interests, and that the districts had not adequately considered race-neutral alternative policies,"[5] understanding the DPS desegregation and resegregation history may be useful.

This chapter describes shifts in the racial/ethnic composition of schools and the academic achievement trends of fifth-grade students in Denver's elementary schools. In the first section, we provide a brief review of the literature on the effects of school desegregation. In the second, we describe the original 1973 *Keyes* decision and the path to its conclusion in 1995. We also provide a descriptive analysis of the changes in the DPS racial/ethnic composition over the past several decades, with a particular focus on the years immediately before and after the end of court-ordered school desegregation. The third section presents a chronology of the standardized measures of academic achievement used by DPS, and also provides a descriptive longitudinal analysis of school-level math performance by race/ethnicity for elementary schools in the district. We focus on elementary schools because they were the first to be shifted back to a neighborhood zoning approach as a result of the end of busing and court-ordered school desegregation. The chapter concludes with a section on policy implications.

RESEARCH ON THE EFFECTS OF SCHOOL DESEGREGATION

Research on the effects of school desegregation has a long history, but it has recently received renewed attention due to the companion Supreme Court cases challenging the use of voluntary school desegregation in the Seattle and Louisville school districts. The court ultimately rejected the use of race-conscious school assignment for the explicit purpose of producing racial balance. Yet, the split opinion leaves some room for interpretation, suggesting that districts develop a "more nuanced, individual evaluation of school needs and student characteristics that might include race as a component."[6]

The earliest studies of school desegregation recorded various changes in achievement outcomes for African American students who moved from segregated to desegregated settings with white students. From this work, we know that black students who attend integrated schools have improved academic achievement, as measured most frequently by test scores.[7] However, the magnitude and persistence of these benefits and the conditions under which they are present have all been widely debated in educational research. In a review of ninety-three research studies looking at the effect of school desegregation on academic achievement, Crain and Mahard concluded that desegregation does enhance black achievement. They also concluded that the methodological approach taken by social scientists in measuring these benefits may have an impact on the size of the effects.[8] In another review of the same era, Cook concluded that desegregation had only a modest effect on reading achievement and no effect on mathematics.[9] A more recent study that analyzed test-score data from Texas found that higher-achieving blacks, as measured by test scores, benefited from a more diverse school racial composition; however, this effect did not extend to lower-performing blacks, whose test scores were not influenced by the school racial composition above and beyond other characteristics of school quality.[10]

Other studies of the impact of desegregation on student achievement have focused on individual life chances rather than test-score improvement. Overall, these studies suggest that desegregated schooling is associated with higher educational and occupational aspirations and, to a modest degree, attainment for African American students.[11] Schools with a substantial white enrollment can offer minority students greater educational and career options, due to the more developed social networks that represent white middle-class norms.[12] These advantages, coupled with the fact that segregated minority schools often suffer from a severe lack of resources, such as quality teachers, counselors, and other educational advantages, leads to an inferior opportunity structure.[13]

There are other important attitudinal and civic outcomes that have been associated—albeit not causally—with attending a diverse school. From a review of twenty-one studies, Wells and Crain concluded that desegregated experiences for African American students lead to increased interaction with members of other racial groups in later years.[14] Moreover, white students in integrated settings exhibit more racial tolerance and less fear of their black peers over time than their counterparts in segregated environments.[15] Whites being in close proximity to blacks in schools, workplaces, and neighborhoods leads to their likelihood of having cross-racial interactions and friendships.[16] Students who attend more diverse schools have higher self-reported comfort with members of racial groups different from their own, an increased sense of civic engagement, and a greater desire to live and work in multiracial settings relative to their more segregated peers.[17]

Although the majority of the achievement studies in the desegregation literature focus on African Americans, some have also looked at Latinos. Schofield reviewed several studies that looked at the impact of desegregation on Latino students and found that average achievement levels for Latinos are higher in desegregated schools than in segregated schools.[18] Moreover, since Latinos are frequently segregated in some of the poorest schools with very few resources,[19] the potential increase in achievement for Latino students—much like African American students—would likely be attributed to having access to the better educational resources present in desegregated or predominantly white schools.

It is important to note that previous research on school desegregation has also focused on the conditions deemed necessary for expected minority outcomes to be realized. These include desegregation in the earliest possible grades; heterogeneous instructional strategies; a critical mass of students from each racial group; a desegregated staff; interracial extracurricular activities; smaller learning environments; and specialized training of teachers and school staff.[20] Although often not directly tested in the empirical literature, these conditions suggest that school desegregation is about much more than simply raising achievement test scores. In fact, more than fifty years after the historic *Brown* decision, the role of school desegregation in improving the educational opportunities of students of color remains in serious question, as many school districts across the country are facing challenges to their school desegregation plans and witnessing rapid resegregation.[21]

THE HISTORY OF THE *KEYES* DECISION AND THE DENVER PUBLIC SCHOOLS' RACIAL/ETHNIC COMPOSITION

The story of Denver's school desegregation began in the late 1960s, in an integrated middle-class neighborhood called Park Hill.[22] It is important to note that at the time, the Denver Public School District was predominantly white; only 15 percent of the student body was black and an additional 20 percent "Hispano" (the term used at the time for Latinos).[23] The Park Hill neighborhood is an important part of the history of *Keyes* because it provided a catalyst for the original lawsuit.[24] In 1969, the district court agreed with a group of eight black Park Hill parents, who argued that deliberate racial segregation had been carried out by the school board through several mechanisms, including the construction of a new elementary school in the middle of the black community west of Park Hill, the gerrymandering of student attendance zones, the use of so-called optional zones, and the excessive use of mobile classroom units. Specifically, the school board had used what the Supreme Court ultimately described as "state-imposed segregation in a substantial portion of the district,"[25] which resulted in racially isolated schools throughout the district but particularly in East Denver schools.[26] Although the district court chose not to generalize the finding across the rest of the city, they did rule that many Denver schools were both separate and unequal. As a result, the district court called for the school district to create a desegregation plan for the entire city.

Appealing this decision in the Tenth Circuit Court of Appeals, DPS succeeded in having the portion of the decision that called for complete desegregation overruled, leaving Park Hill the only part of the district required to desegregate. Ultimately, however, the U.S. Supreme Court overturned the Tenth Circuit decision in *Keyes v. Denver School District* (1973). The Court found that (1) Hispanic and black students should not be considered as desegregating each other because the inequities they suffered from were similar; (2) proof of de jure segregation in a substantial portion of the school district is enough to assume that the entire district is similarly affected; and (3) the burden of proof should be on the school board to show that other portions of the city are not affected by similar policies, rather than the plaintiffs having to prove intentional segregation in each section of the district.[27]

In response to the Supreme Court decision, Tenth Circuit Federal Court of Appeals judge William E. Doyle ordered the Denver Public Schools to integrate. With assistance from desegregation expert John Finger,[28] Judge Doyle created a plan that relied on redrawing school boundaries and establishing "paired" schools, which meant that students would be transported for half a day to a school outside their neighborhood so that a more racially diverse student body was achieved.[29] In the original plan, of roughly 41,500 students in the district, 12,861 were attending paired schools.[30]

Reactions to court-ordered busing were mixed, but with the exception of a few "incidents,"[31] schools ran relatively smoothly once busing began.[32] In comparing the community response to the desegregation initiative in Denver to that in other cities across the country that were undergoing similar efforts, reporters often noted that Denver's implementation process was relatively smooth and less violently resisted. They typically attributed this to the fact that Denver "lacks a key ingredient found in, for example, Boston's troubles: a substantial number of lower-class whites. Many either moved to the suburbs years ago or are too old to have children in school."[33] However, reporters often noted that "if Denver's almost totally white suburbs were forced to accept minority students from inner city schools, there would almost certainly be trouble."[34]

In 1974, Colorado changed the state constitution with the Poundstone Amendment, a law that cut off school growth by prohibiting the annexation of lands surrounding the city. Because *Keyes* only covered schools located within the 1974 boundaries of Denver, the Poundstone Amendment effectively sealed off Denver from the surrounding suburbs and severely curtailed its ability to have any lasting and stable desegregation of its public schools.[35]

Emerging federal policies and a political shift during the early 1980s chipped away much of the civil rights foundation on which *Keyes* rested. President Reagan's first term in office brought sweeping changes by calling for less federal action in civil rights cases, for opposition to court-ordered busing, and for decisionmakers to be color-blind in their approach to race-related issues.[36] The foundation of the *Keyes* decision was more fully undermined when the U.S. assistant attorney general for civil rights said, "The Justice Department would no longer seek to desegregate an entire school district on the basis of segregation found to exist in just part of it."[37]

Within this context, in 1987, the district judge in Denver made the desegregation orders less stringent but refused to completely remove them.[38] Specifically, Judge Matsch identified four issues to which DPS still had to attend: integration levels at three elementary schools (i.e., Barrett, Harrington, and Mitchell); the student transfer policy; the district's plan to maintain a unitary system; and faculty integration. Five years later, in 1992, DPS sought a release from court-mandated busing, filing a motion with the district court to that end.[39] Around the same time, a $50 million settlement with the district was proposed by the plaintiffs. It would have upgraded early childhood education and community resource schools, and also have funded programs intended to lower the dropout rate and increase overall academic achievement in DPS. The district rejected this proposal, arguing that it was both cost prohibitive and an expansion of the required parameters of the initial desegregation order.[40]

In September 1995, Judge Richard Matsch, who had presided over the court order since 1976, lifted the busing mandate and eliminated racial integration as a decisive factor in determining school boundaries. In justifying the decision, Judge Matsch wrote, "The Denver now before this court is very different from what it was when this lawsuit began. . . . The current mayor of Denver is black. His predecessor was Hispanic. A black woman has been superintendent of schools. Black and Hispanic men and women are in the city council, the school board, the State Legislature, and other political positions."[41] He went on to say that "the vestiges of past discrimination by the defendants have been eliminated to the extent practicable" and that the district had "complied in good faith with the desegregation decrees."[42] In response, the school board voted for a return to neighborhood schools, a policy that would send students to the school nearest their home.[43] As a result, one-third of Denver's seventy-eight elementary schools and half of the eighteen middle schools became predominantly black or Hispanic almost immediately.[44]

The decision was met with mixed reactions from the community. On the one hand, opponents of busing saw it as a welcome end to an ineffective approach to "real" integration[45] and a way to boost academic performance.[46] On the other hand, supporters of busing worried that racial isolation and the attendant inequalities associated with it would recur.[47] Half a decade later, 100 percent of Latino students and more than 50 percent of black students in DPS were in schools that were majority minority.[48]

Demographic Shifts and Resegregation Patterns

Like many other large urban centers, a decline in white enrollment and an increase in the share of the Latino population, coupled with fixed boundaries, were largely responsible for the demographic transformation of Denver Public Schools.[49] Moreover, suburban districts immediately surrounding Denver grew rapidly in the 1980s, drawing in not just whites but middle-class blacks and Latinos.[50] The white share of the DPS student enrollment was dropping even before the *Keyes* ruling in 1973 (table 9.1), largely as a result of migration to the suburbs and increasing numbers of Latino students.[51] White enrollment in DPS declined from 66 percent of the total enrollment in 1967 to 20 percent by 2003, making attempts to desegregate within an urban center increasingly difficult. The drop in white enrollment was largely replaced by Latino enrollment, which rose from 20 percent to 57 percent during the same time period. Black and Asian shares of school enrollment also increased during this time, albeit at a slower rate than the Latino enrollment.

It is complicated to understand the full effects of the end of court-mandated desegregation on school racial/ethnic composition. First, the *Keyes* decision did not affect all Denver schools; some schools excluded from the case

TABLE 9.1: Change in Racial Composition in the Denver Public Schools, 1967–2006

Year	% White	% Black	% Latino	% Asian
1967	66	14	20*	—
1972	58	17	23	1
1976	48	21	29	1
1980	41	23	32	—
1986	37	22	36	4
1990	34	22	39	4
1994	29	21	45	4
1996	26	21	47	4
2000	22	20	53	3
2003	20	19	57	3
2004	20	19	57	3
2005	19	19	57	3
2006	20	18	58	3

* Latino included Asian and Native American in 1967

Source: DBS Corp., 1982, 1987; OCR data tapes from 1968–84; G. Orfield, R. George, and A. Orfield, "Racial Change in U.S. School Enrollments, 1968–84," paper presented at the National Conference on School Desegregation, University of Chicago, 1986; National Center for Education Statistics, Common Core of Data, 1990–2006.

(many heavily minority) never came under the court order and remain heavily minority today.[52] Second, notwithstanding court decisions and other district policies, the Denver metropolitan area, as noted above, was experiencing substantial demographic changes during this period. Given these and other temporal changes experienced by Denver Public Schools, it is difficult to draw any causal conclusions about the effect of the end of *Keyes* on resegregation patterns. Nevertheless, it is obvious from the dramatic changes in school racial composition that occurred in many of Denver's elementary schools that the district wasted no time in returning to neighborhood schools after being declared unitary. Thus, although, it is clear that demographic shifts contributed to the overall decline in white enrollment, they do not explain the dramatic changes in racial composition across schools in the period following the end of court-ordered busing.

Given the broader demographic shifts, how much did school racial/ethnic composition change with the end of court-mandated desegregation as a result of the 1995 decision? Most schools witnessed their biggest changes immediately following the 1995 ruling on unitary status, with the largest shifts in racial composition occurring in 1996 and 1997. Looking at the four-year changes between 1994 and 1998 (the year before the decision and the three years immediately after), we note shifts in several types of schools. Elementary schools in DPS experienced substantial (twenty percentage points or greater), moderate (between ten and twenty percentage points) and minimal (fewer than ten percentage points) shifts in the representation of white students from 1994 to 1998. (Similar shifts can be noted in Latino and black representation.) As such, we can identify a school with a substantial shift in white enrollment as one where the change has been more than roughly 300 percent of the district's overall demographic shift during the same time period.

About half of DPS elementary schools went through a noticeable change in white representation concurrent with the reversal of *Keyes*. The end of court-mandated busing, coupled with demographic changes, resulted in dramatic differences in the presence of whites at fourteen Denver schools in particular, eight of which experienced a decline in white enrollment of twenty to thirty-seven percentage points in the years immediately following *Keyes*. For example, white enrollment at Mitchell Elementary dropped by thirty-seven percentage points during the four-year period around the end of court-ordered school desegregation. In six other schools, the shift occurred in the opposite direction, with dramatic increases in white enrollment; consider Steele Elementary, which saw an increase in white enrollment of thirty-two percentage points from 1994 to 1998.

At a time when whites represented only about one-fifth of the DPS enrollment, twenty-eight schools impacted by *Keyes* witnessed moderate shifts in white representation immediately following the decision. This was, of course, accompanied by similar opposite shifts in Latino and black representation. Specifically, five elementary schools experienced an increase in white enrollment of ten to nineteen percentage points in the four years surrounding the decision, while another twenty-three experienced similar declines. For some schools, the shifts in white proportions were accompanied by differential patterns for Latinos and blacks. Thus, while it is apparent that whites were becoming more segregated from their peers of other racial groups, many African Americans and Hispanics were also becoming more isolated within their own respective racial/ethnic groups. In fact, despite an overall increase in Hispanic school enrollment, several schools experienced declines of over thirty percentage points in Hispanic enrollment during the four years surrounding the *Keyes* decision.

The Close Relationship between Race and Socioeconomic Status

There are many reasons why racial isolation may be harmful to students' educational experiences.[53] A primary reason is the close association between race and socioeconomic status, whereby predominantly minority schools are often disadvantaged relative to predominantly white schools.[54] This association is particularly important in Denver, where a school's percentage of white enrollment is highly correlated with the percentage of the school's population that is eligible for free or reduced-price lunch. Moreover, demographic trends in enrollment over the past two decades reveal a steady increase in the percentage of Denver students eligible for free or reduced-price lunch.[55] Previous research on school desegregation, and school quality more broadly, has been consistent in its conclusions that concentrations of poverty have negative educational consequences for all students, and that minority students are more likely to be enrolled in schools with high concentrations of economically disadvantaged students, as measured by eligibility for free or reduced-price lunch.

Figures 9.1 and 9.2 display scatterplots of the relationship between a school's percentage of white enrollment and its associated percentage of students eligible for free or reduced-price lunch in 1994 and 2000, respectively. These figures highlight that in both 1994 (before the district was declared unitary) and in 1998 (a couple of years later), most schools with a low white enrollment were also schools where the majority of the students were eligible for free or reduced-price lunch. Similarly, schools with higher white enrollment were also schools with more affluent students. When we compare the figures, several descriptive elements are particularly noteworthy. First, the variation in white enrollment shifts quite a bit in four years, so that in 1998 there are many more schools with lower concentrations of white students than there were in 1994. Second, looking at simple correlation coefficients, we also note how much stronger the association between white enrollment and free/reduced-price lunch eligibility had become in Denver during the period after the district was declared unitary. Thus, there were many more schools with very low white enrollments and correspondingly high levels of students eligible for free or reduced-price lunch in 1998 than there were in 1994. This of course is not necessarily a direct result of the end of mandatory

FIGURE 9.1: Correlation between Percentages of White School Enrollment and of Students Eligible for Free/Reduced-Price Lunch in Denver Public Schools in 1994

Source: Common Core of Data, 1994.

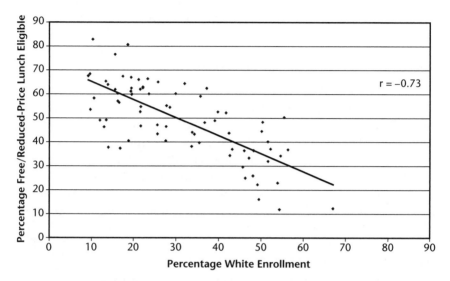

FIGURE 9.2: Correlation between Percentages of White School Enrollment and of Students Eligible for Free/Reduced-Price Lunch in Denver Public Schools in 1998

Source: Common Core of Data, 1998.

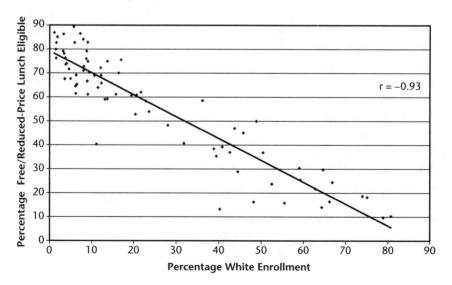

desegregation, but it is likely the result of some suburban migration among middle-class whites and minority families. All of this suggests that when we consider the influence of school racial composition on student outcomes, we cannot disentangle the role of socioeconomic status.

THE ACHIEVEMENT TRENDS IN DENVER PUBLIC SCHOOLS BY RACE/ETHNICITY

Data and methodological constraints make it difficult to draw any causal conclusions about the impact the end of *Keyes* had on achievement for different student populations in Denver Public Schools. Nevertheless, given the transformation of many of Denver's schools as a result of both demographic shifts (e.g., the overall rise in Hispanic representation and decline in white enrollment due to increased suburbanization) and the end of the district's mandatory desegregation plan, it is important to investigate achievement trends by race for the district during this time period, and more recently.

Data and Chronology of DPS Testing Policy

For more than fifteen years, DPS has administered the Iowa Test of Basic Skills (ITBS) to students in elementary grades one through five.[56] ITBS is a nationally normed test of student achievement across various grades and subject areas. The assessments are vertically scaled, allowing student growth to be tracked over time.[57] The ITBS scores have been used as a measure of academic progress and as a way to diagnostically assess strengths and areas for growth for students in individual schools. DPS began to phase out use of the ITBS in 2002, focusing its attention on a criterion-referenced test, the Colorado Student Assessment Plan (CSAP), which assessed student achievement against the State Model Content Standards.[58] At the elementary school level, CSAP is currently administered to grades three through five, and it tests students in math, reading, science, and writing.

We investigate two sets of test-score data to examine differential performance by race/ethnicity across schools over time. Because of a lack of clear substantive equivalence between the measured constructs in ITBS and CSAP and because of a lack of adequate data to prudently equate these two measures, this study separately utilizes school-level aggregated ITBS math data from 1994 to 2000[59] and available CSAP data from 2003 to 2007. We present only math scores, as they are typically less affected by English-language learner status.

ITBS Achievement Trends by Race

In describing the achievement trends of schools relative to the racial/ethnic shifts around the time of the reversal of *Keyes*, we first present two figures—the association between a school's average ITBS math percentile and its white enrollment in 1994, shortly before the end of court-mandated desegregation (figure 9.3), and in 1998, following the end of court-mandated desegregation (figure 9.4). In combination, they depict two important points. First, as noted earlier, there is evidence of much more segregation (as measured by percentage of white enrollment) in 1998 than in 1994, indicated by the "clumping" of schools in figure 9.4 in the zero-to-20 percent white enrollment band relative to the more dispersed spread of schools across a wider range of white enrollment in figure 9.3. In fact, in 1994, there were virtually no elementary schools with fewer than 10 percent whites enrolled; by 1998, that proportion had jumped to one-third of all elementary schools. Given that the reversal of *Keyes* shifted DPS back to a neighborhood-based school assignment plan, and because Denver displays significant residential segregation patterns, this is not surprising. Furthermore, in evaluating simple bivariate correlation coefficients, there is a substantially stronger association between white enrollment and average math test scores in 1998 than there is in 1994. Again, although the change in these associations cannot be directly attributed to the end of court-ordered school desegregation (since, as stated above, the district experienced other important temporal changes), it is important to note that just three years after the end of court-ordered school desegregation, the variation in aggregate school test scores is more strongly correlated with the presence of white students in the school ($r = .76$) than a mere four years earlier ($r = .44$).[60] Moreover, given the high association between the percentage of whites and percentage eligible for free and reduced-price lunch presented in figure 9.2, the association between percentage white and average test scores suggests that, in 1998, the percentage of whites in a school is a reasonable proxy for the socioeconomic status of the school (at least as measured by free/reduced-price lunch eligibility). These figures also provide an important context in which to understand changes in more recent CSAP scores, presented below, as they highlight that achievement, broadly described, has become more strongly associated with the percentage of whites in a school.

CSAP Achievement Trends by Race

In considering more recent achievement trends by race/ethnicity, the DPS CSAP fifth-grade math scores tell a story that is similar in many ways to that

FIGURE 9.3: Correlation between Average School Math Test Scores and White Enrollment in Denver Public Schools in 1994

Source: Common Core of Data, Denver Public Schools school-level ITBS data, 1994.

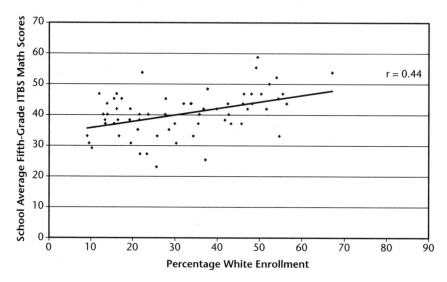

FIGURE 9.4: Correlation between Average School Math Test Scores and White Enrollment in Denver Public Schools in 1998

Source: Common Core of Data, Denver Public Schools School-Level ITBS Data, 1998.

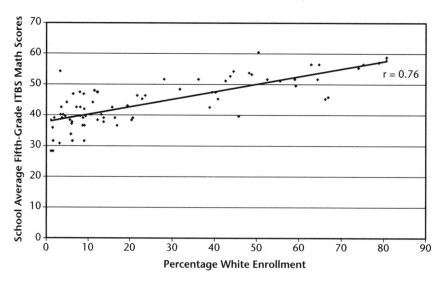

FIGURE 9.5: Percentage Proficient and Advanced on the CSAP, by Race, for Denver Public School District, 2003–07

Source: Colorado Department of Education, 2008.

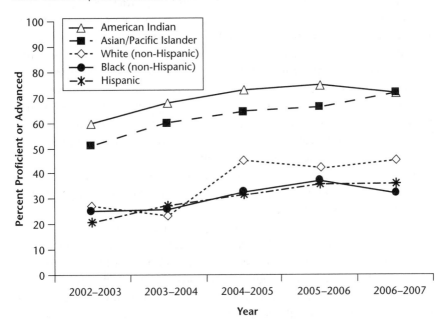

of the ITBS scores. Looking at figure 9.5, two important trends should be noted. First, the proportion of students scoring proficient and advanced on the fifth-grade math CSAP has minimally but steadily increased from 2003 to 2007 across all racial/ethnic groups. Despite these small increases, however, the figure also indicates a persistent gap between whites and Asians, on the one hand, and blacks and Latinos on the other. For example, in 2007, while 72 percent of whites and Asians scored at proficient or advanced levels on the fifth-grade math CSAP, only 32 percent of blacks and 36 percent of Hispanics scored as well. Such findings suggest that, at least at the district level, differential performance by race/ethnicity is pronounced.

CSAP Achievement Gap by School

In further examining differential performance across racial/ethnic groups, we turn next to investigate more current achievement trends by school. Again, several important trends are worth noting. First, the vast majority of schools have data only for one racial/ethnic group; in order for data to be made publicly available, a subgroup must have at least sixteen test-takers. The absence of data, then, suggests at least in part that schools are racially isolated. Second, within each racial/ethnic group, there is wide variation in proficiency levels across schools. The proportion of white students scoring Proficient and Advanced ranges from 18 percent to 97 percent; at twelve of the seventeen schools for which there is relevant data, more than 75 percent of their white students scored at least Proficient. For blacks, the proportion spans from zero to 50 percent; three of the eleven schools with available data had fewer than 20 percent of black students scoring Proficient or Advanced. For Hispanics, forty-three of the fifty-two elementary schools for which data are available had fewer than half scoring Proficient and Advanced, with an overall range among schools of 18 percent to 67 percent.

These findings correspond with much of the existing literature on the performance gap between racial/ethnic groups. In the more recent context of Denver's increasingly racially isolated schools, as is evidenced by even the availability of data on different racial/ethnic groups within a school, these trends reveal continued disparities in performance among racial/ethnic groups. For the schools that lack sufficient numbers of white and black and/or Latino test-takers, we note that the average white-Hispanic achievement gap across all schools (measured as the difference in the percentage of students scoring Proficient and above) is seven percentage points, while the average white-black achievement gap is eleven percentage points.

DISCUSSION AND CONCLUSION

Over the past several decades, federal courts have slowly abandoned their oversight of school district desegregation policies. They have declared that school districts, including those under decades-old federal court-ordered plans, are now unitary. In 1995, Denver schools became one such district, as Judge Matsch affirmed that the district had rid itself—to the extent possible—of the discrimination that the 22-year-old desegregation plan intended to address. The end of *Keyes v. School District No. 1, Denver, Colorado* is an important landmark in school desegregation history. The case was a critical one in that it established a precedent for the enforcement of *Brown* in northern school districts, as well as Hispanics' right to desegregation. More than ten years after the end of court-ordered desegregation, Denver presents an important case study for evaluating school racial/ethnic composition and achievement trends, following the end of mandated busing and amid rapid demographic transformation.

Although this study does not directly test the causal impact of the end of court-ordered school desegregation on achievement patterns, it nevertheless provides important descriptive findings about school resegregation patterns following the end of *Keyes* and about achievement trends, both right around the court decision and more recently. Specifically, changes in school desegregation polices, coupled with important demographic shifts in the school-age population in Denver, led to important changes in school racial composition in Denver Public Schools. A historic dataset of ITBS math percentile scores from 1994 to 2000 and more recent CSAP scores allows us to look descriptively at achievement patterns over time by race/ethnicity across schools. The role of school racial composition in predicting achievement differences is beyond the scope of this chapter; however, descriptive data clearly suggest that persistent gaps in performance continue to exist between whites and Asians relative to blacks and Latinos, and that these disparities differ across schools.

The end of court-ordered school desegregation came with an intense district focus on neighborhood schools. As such, the schools that had remained under the busing desegregation plan were transformed almost immediately, resulting in dramatic changes in school racial composition for about one-third of the district's elementary schools. Such changes of course occurred amid the district's otherwise changing demographics. Like many urban districts, Denver witnessed substantial declines in white enrollment and dramatic increases in Hispanic enrollment. Increased suburbanization transformed the metropolitan region, making city residents a small proportion of the otherwise growing metro area. At the time of the original court order, whites made up over two-thirds of the district enrollment; today they represent less than one-fifth of the district enrollment overall. However, despite their lower numbers, whites are also more racially isolated from their minority peers today than they were under desegregation.[61]

Following the end of court-ordered school desegregation, Denver's return to neighborhood schools was not without its challenges. Some school leaders felt the return to highly segregated schools left the district "back to where we started," while others critical of the treatment of minority students at the schools they were bused to found busing to be a "failed experiment."[62] Concurrent with demographic shifts, Denver Public Schools clearly witnessed a rise in the number of racially isolated schools in the district. Such isolation is likely the result of the district's focus on neighborhood schools and of demographic changes.

The impact of school racial composition on student achievement has been the subject of much debate and research.[63] From our descriptive look at aggregate achievement trend data, we note a consistent and substantial association between white enrollment in a school and average achievement scores, no doubt in large part as a result of the strong association between the percentage of whites in a school and the percentage eligible for free or reduced-price lunch. Of course, the available achievement data we present as school-level aggregates limit us analytically. In addition, as the chapter suggests, the findings presented are descriptive rather than causal in nature. Moreover, there are many important outcomes (e.g., educational and occupational attainment, and intergroup contact and racial attitudes) associated with school desegregation that this chapter does not address, but which previous research has suggested may be at risk for all students who are attending more racially isolated schools today than their peers in previous decades, when desegregation efforts were much more ardent. Despite the restrictions of the data, these descriptive findings are compelling, particularly for Latinos.

More than thirty years ago, *Keyes* recognized the need to consider Hispanics in determining whether a district suffered from explicit discrimination as a result of school segregation. This chapter reinforces the importance of that consideration. In recent years, the average Latino student attending a Denver public school is likely to experience substantial racial isolation in a school that is, on average, 75 percent Latino. Of course, additional research and much richer data are needed to fully understand the long-term implications of the end of court-ordered desegregation for all of Denver's students.[64]

CHAPTER TEN

Integrated Schools, Integrated Futures?

A Case Study of School Desegregation in Jefferson County, Kentucky

Kristie J. R. Phillips, Robert J. Rodosky, Marco A. Muñoz, and Elisabeth S. Larsen

HISTORICAL CONTEXT OF JEFFERSON COUNTY[1]

In Jefferson County, Kentucky, public schools have maintained remarkably low levels of segregation for the past three decades. In fact, it is one of the most successfully desegregated school districts in the nation.[2] By promoting and maintaining this level of desegregation, the school district initially faced severe opposition, but its integration efforts were later supported by residents of the county. These efforts aimed at maintaining racial integration came to be viewed with pride and as a landmark achievement for the Jefferson County school system. Jefferson County's unique history and strong, continued commitment to racial integration make it an ideal case to study the long-term effects of school desegregation on student outcomes.

The journey of integrating the Jefferson County school system began in 1956, in the aftermath of *Brown v. Board of Education* (1954). The Louisville Board of Education created a student assignment plan and an open transfer policy to aid integration, but the schools remained highly segregated for the following sixteen years. In 1972, parents and civil rights groups claimed the schools were unconstitutionally segregated and sued the Louisville Board of Education in federal court. The school district population was approximately half black and half white, but the racial composition of the schools failed to reflect this diversity. Forty of forty-six elementary schools and fourteen of nineteen middle and high schools were racially isolated, with over 80 percent of the students representing only one race.[3] To remedy this situation, the district court judge ordered the merger of the racially diverse (but geographically segregated) and financially struggling Louisville district with the predominantly white and affluent Jefferson County district, making the district one of the largest in the country. The judge also ordered the newly merged school districts to remedy de jure racial segregation by means of busing.

Resistance to Court-Ordered Desegregation

In 1975, the newly expanded district, Jefferson County Public Schools (JCPS), faced the challenge of integrating a population of roughly 80 percent white students and 20 percent black students against extreme opposition from parents and community members. The desegregation plan required a 12 percent to 40 percent black population for elementary schools and a 12.5 percent to 35 percent black population for secondary schools. To achieve this goal, the district adopted a complicated districtwide busing system, which reassigned 23,000 students based on their race and the first letter of their last names. White students were to be bused for two of their twelve years in the school district, while black students were to be bused for ten of their years. Twenty-five antibusing groups later arose in an attempt to thwart the proposed plan by conducting meetings, holding protests, and organizing boycotts. Private schools opened across the community to serve the onslaught of white families refusing to attend integrated schools, while districts in neighboring states and counties denied entrance to students from Jefferson County after a flood of calls from concerned parents. When the school year began, the protests turned violent, as protestors beat gas station owners for filling school buses and vandalized schools and buses, and the Ku Klux Klan increased its activity. A few days after school started, dozens of people were hurt and nearly two hundred people were arrested after two antibusing protests turned violent. After a few weeks, the violence subsided, and the protests diminished gradually over the next few years.

Voluntary Commitment to Integration

By 1978, the district court ended their active supervision of JCPS's desegregation plan due to the district's demonstration of compliance with the court order. However, the court left some parts of the desegregation decree in place. This decision mostly freed JCPS from their desegregation order, but the district chose to continue their efforts toward integration throughout the subsequent decades. As district demographics changed, the desegregation plan evolved as well. The 1984 plan created a new racial guideline of "10 percent above and 10 percent below the countywide average for the different grade levels" and redrew school boundaries so that students could attend the same schools throughout their entire middle school and high school experiences. This plan also marked the first introduction of magnet schools to the district.

In 1991, the district readjusted the plan to keep students from attending multiple elementary schools during their school career. This plan, entitled Project Renaissance, assigned elementary school students to a neighborhood school within a cluster of several elementary schools. Students could freely transfer within their cluster if they switched to a school that was predominantly a different race than their own. Middle school students could either attend their neighborhood school or a magnet school, while high school students could apply to any high school in the system and each high school would accept students based on racial compliance guidelines. Under this plan, schools had to achieve a level of 15 percent to 50 percent black students.

However, attacks against the Jefferson County integration plan began again in 1999, when six parents sued to remove the upper limit of 50 percent black from Central High, a historically black high school that served as a magnet school at the time. In 2000, the district court held that race targets at magnet schools were unconstitutional and dissolved the district's original desegregation ruling. However, JCPS continued to uphold the 15 percent to 50 percent guideline in their nonmagnet schools, an action that exemplified their dedication to maintaining a fully integrated school system.[4] Since the district's original desegregation order, racial integration has been at the forefront of district policies and educational priorities. As such, the district has conscientiously adopted policies intended to curtail the trend toward resegregation—a trend that has been widespread in the South as a result of the courts releasing districts from their desegregation orders.[5]

Court-Ordered Resegregation?

In spite of JPCS's emphasis on racial balance and many students' and parents' support of integration within the district,[6] some opposed these policies. The district's racial balancing policies came under national scrutiny when a student was denied entrance to his school of choice due to these policies. In August 2002, Crystal Meredith moved into the district and tried to enroll her son, Joshua McDonald, into their neighborhood school. The school was already at capacity because assignments had been made several months earlier. Therefore, the district assigned Joshua to another school within his cluster. However, the school to which he was assigned was ten miles away from his home. In an attempt to transfer her son to a school that was closer to home, Meredith requested that Joshua be allowed to attend school in another cluster. This request was initially denied because it would have upset the racial balance of the school's student body. Eventually the school admitted Joshua, but Meredith brought suit against the district over their use of race in determining students' acceptance to schools.[7] The Sixth U.S. Circuit Court of Appeals ruled against Meredith in October 2005, but the case was appealed to the U.S. Supreme Court. The Supreme Court combined the suit with a similar case from Seattle and named the case *Parents Involved in Community Schools v. Seattle School District No. 1 (PICS)*. In June 2007, the Supreme Court ruled that the use of individual student race to assign students to schools violates the constitutional guarantees of equal protection. Thus, Jefferson County's efforts to maintain the spirit of *Brown v. Board of Education* were ruled unconstitutional. This landmark ruling signals "a major shift in one of the country's most expansive and controversial attempts to right the wrongs of slavery and segregation."[8]

Today Jefferson County can no longer use the 15 percent to 50 percent guideline to create racial integration; however, the district remains committed to diversity in spite of the challenges raised by the 2007 Supreme Court case. Beginning with elementary schools in the 2009–10 school year, JCPS aims to implement a new student assignment plan that experts believe will withstand legal scrutiny and simultaneously keep schools from becoming racially or socioeconomically segregated.[9] The plan also extends to middle and high schools, although these changes are slated for the 2010–11 school year. Under the new student assignment plan, all schools must enroll at least 15 percent and no more than 50 percent of their student body from neighborhoods that have income and education levels below the school district average. In addition to neighborhood income and education levels, the district also considers the racial makeup of neighborhoods. Between 15 percent and 50 percent of students in each school much also come from neighborhoods with higher than average numbers of minorities. Because the new policy does not consider the race of students specifically, the plan does not violate the Supreme Court ruling. However, even with the multiple-factor policy described above, the district faces the possibility that racial balance may not be achievable to the extent it was in the past.[10] Today, JCPS faces the challenge of hitting a racial integration target without having the ability to set the most appropriate and most meaningful sights on their target. Integrating schools without being allowed to use race may prove difficult, but the district is determined to maintain its emphasis on racial balance and prevent resegregation.

WHY INTEGRATION?

After years of court orders, riots, changing student assignment plans, and elaborate busing strategies, the value of integration has come into question. In fact, such conditions have encouraged many parents across the United States to favor neighborhood schools even though neighborhoods tend to be racially and socioeconomically segregated.[11] JCPS, however, has chosen to embrace the social benefits of integration as they have been described in the academic literature. JCPS has recognized that schools are segregated because neighborhoods are segregated. As such, students of all races have limited exposure to students of racial and ethnic backgrounds that are different from their own—especially when the demographic makeup of their schools mirrors that of their neighborhoods. When neighborhoods are highly segregated by race and social class, few opportunities for regular interactions between racial groups exist. Attending an integrated school may be a child's only extended interaction with children who are different from them. These prolonged interactions have been demonstrated to increase students' level of comfort with other races and assist in breaking down racial stereotypes and prejudices. Ultimately, these experiences prepare students to live in a multicultural society.[12]

Nevertheless, less is known about the effects school integration has on the types of choices students make that might further promote integration later in life. Studies suggest that alumni of integrated schools credit their integrated educational environments for the level of comfort they feel when interacting with people of different races as adults.[13] However, these pro-integration attitudes may not necessarily translate into choices that place these individuals in more integrated settings. For example, people who attended integrated high schools may report increased comfort when interacting with people who are racially and ethnically different from themselves, but this may not indicate that they value diversity to the extent that they seek opportunities to work in an integrated environment or to live in an integrated neighborhood. Since residential segregation is at the root of the school segregation issue, it is possible that attending racially integrated schools would promote the desire to live in integrated neighborhoods. However, the direct relationship between the level of integration in students' schools and the ethnic diversity of their neighborhoods later in life has been understudied.

THE EFFECTS OF SCHOOL DESEGREGATION

Beginning with the 1954 *Brown v. Board of Education* decision and continuing to the 2007 *PICS* decision, the Supreme Court has put school racial integration and its implementation mechanisms at the forefront of educational debates. As such, researchers have spent several decades analyzing the effects of desegregation. Early research focused on the short-term effects of desegregation—specifically, student achievement and student interactions—to ascertain the effectiveness of fledgling programs and determine their viability for the future. Researchers have also focused on the long-term effects of school integration on student outcomes later in life. These outcomes include educational and occupational attainment, as well as occupational and residential integration. We discuss the findings from both areas of research.

Short-Term Effects

Early studies of desegregation produced discouraging results. For example, St. John's landmark 1975 study of the outcomes of desegregation reviewed over 120 studies of the effects of desegregation on achievement, attitudes, and behavior.[14] At that time, she concluded that desegregation could be considered neither a success nor a failure. Any reported academic gains were mixed or nonsignificant, and she found that self-esteem and aspirations for the future decreased for African American children. Crain and Mahard's 1983 meta-analysis of ninety-three desegregation studies also highlighted the vast differences among these studies. Some studies found dramatic achievement gains, while others saw only mild effects or none at all.[15] In this body of research, the level of academic achievement across studies strongly depended on the study's methodology itself, with the greatest achievement gains found in longitudinal, random assignment studies. These findings underscored the need to look at desegregation as a process and not necessarily a policy that would produce immediate effects.

Since these early studies were published, many researchers in both the social and education sciences have provided evidence of the benefits of racially desegregated schools. Most evidence supports integrated schools as avenues for improving student outcomes, such as enhanced learning, higher educational and occupational aspirations, and greater social interactions among members of different racial and ethnic backgrounds.[16] Nevertheless, the size of these short-term effects associated with school integration tends to be small.[17]

Studies that specifically address short-term effects other than student achievement typically find that integrated schools lead to patterns of interracial friendships and increased "racial comfort."[18] Specifically, students in integrated schools have greater levels of comfort discussing race-related issues and working in diverse groups. However, as the percentage of white students increases in the school, the level of racial comfort decreases. Furthermore, members of all other racial groups report higher levels of comfort with people of different racial and ethnic groups than do white students. This study demonstrates that while integrated schools may increase racial comfort, the results are not the same for all students.

Long-Term Effects

Research on the long-term effects of racial integration fundamentally assumes a much broader purpose for public education. While the research on the short-term effects of integration tends to focus on reducing achievement gaps by providing equitable educational opportunities, the research on the long-term effects focuses on students' lifelong social and academic orientations. While the aims of both types of research are important, studies of long-term effects fundamentally identify the purpose of public schooling as preparing students to interact in a diverse world, thereby highlighting the potential relationship between schools and society. As such, research assessing the potential long-term effects of integrated schools highlights the ways schools might change our current social structure—a structure that is often segregated and bears the vestiges of racism.

Long-term studies often address how school integration relates to the integrative experiences and social opportunities of students later in life. For example, studies have found that students who attended an integrated school typically demonstrated positive, long-term educational outcomes, such as increased educational attainment and participation in more advanced scientific and technical majors.[19] Dawkins and Braddock's meta-analysis found that elementary and secondary school desegregation had positive effects on the enrollment of African American students in predominantly white colleges and universities.[20] These students also were more likely to choose subjects like computer science, mathematics, or engineering than their peers from segregated schools. Wells and Crain mirror this finding, reporting that African American students at integrated high schools not only had higher educational and occupational goals, but these goals tended to be more realistically related to their educational background.[21] Their experiences with integration tended to make them more comfortable in choosing and participating at integrated universities, and attending integrated schools also introduced them to different avenues of study and potential career opportunities.

In addition to their effect on later educational outcomes, desegregated schools have also been found to increase student comfort in integrated workplaces. Students who attended desegregated schools were more likely to work in desegregated settings than students who attended segregated schools.[22] Not only were they more likely to accept integrated professions, they were more likely to have successful social interactions in their positions. In contrast, African Americans who attended segregated high schools reported less positive perceptions of and fewer social contacts with white coworkers than those who attended desegregated schools.[23] Findings also suggest that integrated high schools give students the opportunity to have repeated and meaningful interactions with students of other races, which influences their level of comfort in integrated workplaces and integrated communities.[24]

One recent criticism of the research on the long-term effects of integration is that these effects are typically only assessed for black students—as is true for the research outlined above. Few studies have analyzed the benefits of school integration for all students.[25] In fact, "while many Americans believe that desegregation has served black students well, and most do not believe that it has caused harm to whites, it is unclear whether they believe that whites have also benefited from desegregation policies."[26] Ironically, some researchers suggest that desegregation may provide the most valuable resource for white students, who are more likely than any other group to experience racial segregation.[27]

Only a handful of studies of the long-term effects of integration consider the possibility that integration may affect students from different racial backgrounds differently. These studies find that while all graduates expressed gratitude for their integrated educational experiences and the unique lessons about race they learned during their time at these schools, the specific benefits differed for each racial group. White graduates reported that integration taught them to break down stereotypes, to feel more at ease with people of different backgrounds, and to realize that their fears of minorities were unfounded. In contrast, students representing minority groups felt that integrated high schools prepared them for future discrimination, which contributed to their increased comfort when participating in integrated settings later on in life.[28]

School Integration and Residential Diversity

Because school segregation is usually the natural outgrowth of residential seg-regation, perhaps the strongest indicator of the lasting impact integrated edu-cation might have on society would be the relationship between integrated schools and the ethnic diversity of the neighborhoods in which students' choose to live later in life. In highlighting the challenges of social integration, one study reported that 75 percent of white graduates and 60 percent of all graduates from six different school districts reported living in racially segre-gated neighborhoods fifteen years after graduation.[29] Seemingly few students who attended integrated schools reported living in integrated neighborhoods later in life. However, this study relied on individual self-reports about lev-els of integration and did not consider location or relative differences in the racial composition of respondents' neighborhoods.

Researchers have also approached the relationship between school and residential integration by examining the changes in residential segregation in a large city after the schools in the city were desegregated. Several stud-ies have tracked the relationship between residential segregation levels and school desegregation patterns in specific cities over several decades. These studies generally report that as integration in schools increases, residential integration also increases.[30] However, Rivkin concludes that American neigh-borhoods remain highly segregated in spite of school integration efforts and that school integration has had little effect on residential integration.[31] While these macro-level patterns are important to consider, they fail to specifically address the racial contexts of students' schools and how those might predict students' residential choices later in life.

STUDYING THE EFFECTS OF SCHOOL INTEGRATION IN JCPS

While the research on school integration is both plentiful and varied, it also leaves room for improvement and expansion. First, studies of the long-term effects of integration have not yet used the level of integration in students' schools to predict the actual level of residential integration (as opposed to perceived integration) later in students' lives. Second, many of these studies focus on outcomes for African American students, although scholars con-tend that all students—especially white students—can benefit from attend-ing racially integrated schools. Third, because school integration is filtered through different histories and varied contexts, depending on the specific location of each school district, case studies are likely the best approach for researchers who want to determine the effects of integrated schools on student outcomes. Finally, little is known about how the recent *PICS* ruling might affect the trends that have been identified in the desegregation literature. It is the responsibility of researchers to continue exploring the effects of integrated schooling and discuss their results within the context of the race-neutral educational priorities described and set forth by the U.S. Supreme Court in *PICS*. Through the research we present in this chapter, we seek to shed light on three issues related to understanding how racial diversity in high schools may affect students' decisions about where to live later in their lives. We ask the following questions that address the potential long-term effects of attending a high school where racial integration has been at the heart of district educational priorities:

- Is the degree of racial integration in JCPS high schools related to the ethnic diversity of students' residential neighborhoods five years after high school graduation?
- If so, is this relationship similar for black and white students?
- What do these findings suggest for the present context of court-ordered racial neutrality?

Our research builds on the current literature by considering the following: We use student experiences in integrated schools to predict their decisions about the neighborhoods in which they will live. We address the effects of integrated schools within the context of one specific school district. We test our results for differential effects between black and white students. We then interpret these results within the framework of the current political trend of race-neutral student assignment.

METHODS

To understand the relationship between racial integration in schools and the subsequent residential patterns of students who attend these schools, we used three sources of data. First, we accessed contact and address information collected as part of a district-sponsored survey of 1997 graduates designed to track students five years after graduation. This information allowed us to measure the ethnic diversity of these former students' neighborhoods five years after they graduated from JCPS. Second, we examined twelve-year longitudinal cohort data available from JCPS, which tracked each student in the 1997 graduating class through their schooling experiences in JCPS from first grade (the 1985–86 school year) through their senior year of high school (the

1996–97 school year). This information included students' addresses while attending a school within the district, the schools each student attended, and other student background information. In addition to cohort data on seniors who graduated in 1997, data from the district also included information on all students in all schools from the 1985–86 school year to the 1996–97 school year. This longitudinal data provided by the school district facilitated the creation of accurate school-level indicators, such as the racial makeup of each school. Third, we used sociogeographic information describing students' residential neighborhoods, both when they were JCPS students and five years after graduation. This information is available from the U.S. Census Bureau via Geographic Information Systems (GIS) mapping software.

Analytic Sample

The district data included records for 5,249 students from the 1997 graduating class who enrolled in JCPS for their senior year. Of those students, 373 attended an alternative school designed for teens with special needs. Due to the small size and unique purpose of these schools, racial balancing was not their focus. As such, students who attended an alternative school during their senior year were dropped from all analyses. Of the 4,876 remaining students, the district did not have a valid residential address on file for 338 students while they were attending high school in JCPS. Additionally, addresses of graduates five years after graduation were either unavailable, invalid, or nonresidential (i.e., post office boxes or military addresses) for another 1,419 students. These students were also deleted, leaving 3,119 students for our analysis.[32]

Measures

To address the research questions outlined above, we employed several student background variables, measures of students' neighborhoods while they attended high school in JCPS and five years after graduation, and measures of the social characteristics of students' high schools. A description of each variable and its coding scheme are available in appendix 10A.

Ethnic diversity of former JCPS students' neighborhoods

To create our outcome measure—the ethnic diversity of students' residential neighborhoods five years after graduation—we matched 1997 JCPS high school seniors with their corresponding addresses in 2002 (five years after graduation). These addresses were then matched with census tracts and block groups (BGs).[33] Corresponding 2000 U.S. Census data describing the racial and ethnic composition of each BG were then used to calculate a measure of ethnic diversity.

We measure the diversity of former students' residences five years after high school graduation for several reasons. First, the five-year timeframe allows both the time and opportunity for former students to move away from home and pursue their first jobs and higher educational experiences. Second, this timeframe likely represents the first opportunities these former students have to make choices on their own about where to live and where to work. Within five years of high school graduation, most former students who pursued higher education had the opportunity to graduate from vocational or trade schools or from four-year colleges and universities. By measuring the diversity of former students' residences five years after high school graduation, we examine the early decisions they have made about where to live.[34] These early decisions are important because they are closest in time to students' high school experiences. They also provide a benchmark for the decisions these former students might make in the future about where they want to live.

We calculated ethnic diversity by using the ethnic fragmentation index,[35] which is used as a standard measure of diversity in empirical economics, sociology, criminology, and also in *U.S. News & World Report*'s college rankings.[36] This measure was calculated by subtracting from one the sum of the squared proportions of non-Hispanic/Latino whites, African Americans, Asians, Native Americans, and others. We then normalized this measure by dividing the product by .8, the maximum score possible. Once it is normalized, this measure ranges from 0 to 1, with high scores indicating a neighborhood that is racially and ethnically heterogeneous and low scores indicating a neighborhood that is racially and ethnically homogeneous. This index is often interpreted as the probability that two individuals who are randomly selected from the sample for which the index was created will represent two different ethnic groups.[37]

For former JCPS students, the ethnic diversity of residential neighborhoods five years after graduation ranges from 0 (completely homogeneous) to .94 (very diverse, where each ethnic group matched almost evenly).[38] The mobility of JCPS students partially accounts for this. While most JCPS students remain in Jefferson County (a racially fragmented region of Kentucky with few diverse neighborhoods), many leave the state and move to more diverse areas of the country (see figure 10.1).

FIGURE 10.1: Mapping Residential Addresses of JCPS Students Five Years after Graduation

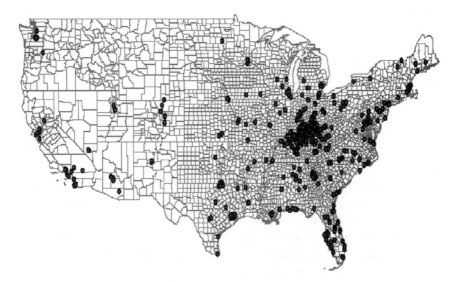

Student background variables

The JCPS district dataset included student background information for every year the student attended a school in the district. This information includes student race, gender, poverty status (whether or not the student participated in free or reduced-price lunch), and whether or not the student attended their zoned school. Student race was measured with a set of dummy variables indicating whether the student is white, black, or some other race, with white students used as the reference group. Student gender was coded 1 for female and 0 for male. Student poverty was coded 1 for students who had ever participated in the free or reduced-price lunch program during their JCPS experience and 0 for students who had never participated.[39]

Researchers who study school integration have raised the issue of potential selection bias that school choice might introduce in studies of the relationship between school racial composition and student outcomes.[40] For example, parents who value diversity would likely choose a school with a more diverse student body than the school they are zoned to attend. Similarly, other parents might value more homogeneous settings for their children when sending them to school. To address this selectivity issue, we identify students who were not attending their zoned school during their senior year of high school by using a dichotomous variable (coded 1 for choice school and 0 for zoned school). Every high school in the school district had a school choice component during the 1996–97 school year; therefore, controlled school choice was an important feature of high schools in the district. Nevertheless, given the district's commitment to racial balancing in each school, we do not anticipate that student choice will significantly impact the ethnic diversity of the neighborhood where students live five years after graduation. In other words, parents who sent their children to any school in JCPS during the time of our study were guaranteed an integrated school. Some schools were slightly less diverse than others, but we do not anticipate this to be a driving factor in parents' selection of schools—particularly at the high school level.

As an indicator of stability, we also included a measure of the number of years each student remained in the school district for their high school experiences. The measure ranges from one to four years. We also computed an indicator of whether or not the student lived in the same neighborhood (or BG) five years after graduation as they did during their senior year. About 40 percent of students remained in their same neighborhood five years after graduation. While this is not surprising, it may affect our results in nonrandom ways.[41] Therefore, we control for the influence of these students.

Neighborhood characteristics

While this chapter specifically aims to address the effect of the social composition of students' schools on later residential patterns, we understand that factors other than schools may contribute to these patterns. Sociologists have demonstrated that neighborhood characteristics predict a variety of outcomes for individuals.[42] To differentiate between the effects of students' schools and the neighborhoods where students lived while attending high school, we used student addresses recorded by the district during their senior year of high school to construct neighborhood measures. We matched these addresses with census tracts and BGs to construct measures of social advantage, economic deprivation, and ethnic diversity.

Social advantage was measured as a mean composite of the proportion of college graduates among adults who are at least twenty-five years old and the proportion of employed individuals with professional or managerial occupations ($\alpha = .95$). This factor allows for the consideration of the spatial concentration of "advantage" in terms of the potential pool of positive role models in the neighborhood.[43] Economic deprivation was also a mean composite of two items. It included the proportion of residents over age sixteen who were unemployed, as well as the proportion of individuals with incomes below the poverty level (α = .81). We included the jobless rate in our measure of economic deprivation because Wilson has emphasized its role in the creation of "the new urban poverty."[44] Joining these measures of unemployment and poverty allowed us to explore how material deprivation affects student outcomes.[45]

Similar to the outcome measure, we computed our measure of ethnic diversity in students' neighborhoods by using the ethnic fragmentation index. To be consistent in our measures of ethnic diversity, we also normalized this measure by dividing it by the maximum value (see appendix 10A for more information about this and all measures).

School characteristics

Researchers have vastly disagreed on the appropriate statistical measure to determine racial "integration."[46] As such, one can conclude that no single measure is completely adequate in measuring such a complex social phenomena. Kelly and Miller state that the best way researchers and policy analysts can present their data is with clarity and honesty about their assumptions.[47] In the spirit of their views, we identify two constraints we faced when creating measures of diversity for JCPS high schools. First, the level of ethnic diversity in each school is constrained by the racial makeup of the school district as a whole. The best JCPS can hope for when aiming to create diverse schools is to balance their schools according to the racial makeup of the district for any given school level. For example, JCPS enrolled about 70 percent white students and 28 percent black students at the high school level during the time of our study. Accordingly, an "integrated" school in the context of JCPS high schools would be a school that enrolled 70 percent white students and 28 percent black students. We cannot reasonably assume that the district can produce schools that are completely heterogeneous (50 percent black and 50 percent white, as defined by the fragmentation index) because it does not enroll enough minority students to accomplish this.

The index of dissimilarity is designed to measure the degree to which the racial composition of schools mirrors that of the district. For policy and legal analysis, this measure adequately highlights the degree to which district desegregation efforts create integration according to certain benchmarks (usually based on the racial makeup of the district as a whole). However, if we were to use the ever-popular index of dissimilarity, completely heterogeneous schools (as determined by the fragmentation index) would rank high on the dissimilarity index (indicating an unbalanced school) because they would have significantly different racial compositions than the district as a whole. In this study we are less interested in how closely a school's racial composition matches that of the school district and more interested in students' opportunities to experience diversity. As such, we do not want to flag completely heterogeneous schools as "imbalanced" (as would the index of dissimilarity) because such a school would create equal exposure to diversity for both racial groups. However, we also do not want to hold the district to the impossible standard of complete racial heterogeneity (meaning 50 percent black and 50 percent white in each school). To study the effects of attending racially diverse schools in JCPS, we developed a measure of integration that considers the balance between ethnic heterogeneity and racial dissimilarity within the context of a specific school district, as research suggests is appropriate.[48]

The school-level indicator most important to this study is our measure of school-level diversity. In an effort to consider the issues addressed above, we created a measure of the relative diversity of the school each student in our sample graduated from. We calculated each school-level measure by aggregating student-level data for the 1996–97 school year.[49] Because JCPS has maintained one of the most integrated school systems in the country,[50] most schools in the district have white-black ratios that are close to the district average. If a high school has more black students than the district average, the percentage of black students in any given school never exceeds 50 percent; therefore, the district does not have any racially isolated, all-black high schools.[51] When a school in this school district is "less diverse" than the district average, it tends to be more than 70 percent white. Therefore, we created a measure of diversity that considers the extent to which a school enrolls more white students than the district average. If a school enrolled more than 70 percent white students, we subtracted that percentage from the district average of 70 percent. In other words, if 75 percent of a school's student population was white, the school would receive a relative diversity score of .05, indicating that the school enrolled 5 percent more white students than the district average. JCPS's commitment to racial balancing is demonstrated in the fact that of the twenty-one high schools in the district, only ten schools tended to enroll more white students than the district average, with the highest percentage of white students in any high school being 79 percent. Because JCPS does not have any truly racially isolated schools, our analyses cannot address the extent to which hypersegregation in schools affects student outcomes, as has been an issue in many resegregated school districts that have been released from their court desegregation orders. Due to the conscientious efforts made by JCPS to create integrated schools, any results from this study will likely represent conservative measures of the effects of integration because the demographic differences between schools that mirror the district racial proportions and less diverse schools are slight.

Given the recent emphasis on socioeconomic integration as a replacement for racial integration,[52] we also included a measure of school poverty in our analyses. We calculated the percentage of students who participated in the free and reduced-price lunch program at each school as a measure of school poverty. This measure ranges from 10 percent to 65 percent and is adjusted to account for the underreporting of free and reduced-price lunch participation at the high school level (see appendix 10A). We also included school size in our analyses, which indicates the number of students enrolled in each school.

ANALYSIS

To address the extent to which the ethnic diversity of former students' residences is predicted by the level of racial integration in students' high schools, we use cross-classified models (HCM) in which students are cross-classified by neighborhoods and schools. The HCM framework accounts for the simultaneous nesting of students within neighborhoods and schools, even though neighborhoods are not necessarily nested within schools. Because student observations are not truly independent of one another when dealing with nested hierarchies, students who share the same neighborhoods and the same schools are likely to experience some shared variance. Multilevel models adjust for this non-independence of observations. However, a traditional hierarchical linear model (HLM) is insufficient in making use of the nesting structures inherent in our data. Many students within JCPS exercised school choices that took them away from their zoned school. As such, students were nested within neighborhoods and schools, but students who lived in the same neighborhood did not necessarily attend the same school. Traditional HLM modeling is a useful approach to data analysis when lower-level units are perfectly nested within higher-level units. In our datasets, however, the data were organized in a cross-classified design, where students were nested within neighborhoods and within schools, but neighborhoods are not necessarily nested within schools. HCMs are ideal for such data structures.[53]

We ran three separate models (see table 10.1). We first computed an unconditional (or null) model with no level-1, row, or column predictors. Second, we ran a full model with all student background variables in the level-1 portion of the model, neighborhood characteristics in the row level, and high school characteristics were entered at the column level. Third, we ran the full model with cross-level interactions between student race and school diversity. Specifically, we tested to see whether the effect of the relative racial diversity of schools is significantly different for black and white students.

The level-1 portion of our HCM analyses was estimated using the following equation:

$$Y_{ijk} = \pi_{0jk} + \pi_{ijk} \, STUDENT \, BACKGROUND_{ijk} + e_{ijk}, \tag{1}$$

where Y_{ijk} represents the ethnic diversity of the residential neighborhood five years after graduation for student i, who lived in high school neighborhood j and attended high school k, and π_{0jk} is the mean residential ethnic diversity of students who lived in neighborhood j during high school and attended high school k. $STUDENT \, BACKGROUND_{ijk}$ represents the regression coefficients relating to each of the seven students background variables included in the model. These variables include six dummy variables indicating whether or not a student is black, some other race, female, a free or reduced-price lunch participant, attending a nonzoned school, or living in the same census block group five years after graduation. An additional background variable measuring the number of years a student attended high school in the district was also included. Lastly, e_{ijk} is the random student effect, or the deviation of student ijk's diversity score from the cell mean.

The level-2 model, or between-cell model, for the intercept—which includes all row and column predictors—is as follows:

$$\pi_{0jk} = \theta_0 + (\gamma_{01} + c_{01k})NEIGHBORHOOD \, CONTEXTS_j + b_{00j} \tag{2}$$
$$+ (b_{01} + \beta_{01})SCHOOL \, CONTEXTS_k + c_{00k}$$

Within this equation, $NEIGHBORHOOD \, CONTEXTS_j$ refers to the coefficients associated with each of the three neighborhood context variables of JCPS students' residences during high school: social advantage, economic deprivation, and ethnic diversity. These variables are considered row-level predictors within the HCM framework. $SCHOOL \, CONTEXTS_k$ represents the coefficients associated with three school-level variables, which are relative diversity in the school, school poverty, and school size. These variables are considered column-level predictors within the HCM framework. Additionally, b_{00j} is the neighborhood random effect, and c_{00k} is the random effect associated with students' schools.

In the interest of parsimony, all other level-1 coefficients are fixed, as is detailed in the equation below:

$$\pi_{pjk} = \theta_p \tag{3}$$

In the equations presented above, we assume that the relationship between row and column predictors is random. That is, neighborhood effects are allowed to vary across schools, and school effects are allowed to vary across neighborhoods. By allowing this variation, we avoid underestimation of the standard error—which is a possibility when these associations are assumed to be fixed.[54]

RESULTS

Before discussing the results of our HCM analyses, we first highlight descriptive data that help contextualize our results (see appendix 10A). This study is unique in that it examines the diversity of students' schools as well as their neighborhoods and reports the effects of both. Many studies of the long-term effects of desegregation address the racial makeup of students' schools but do not provide information about the social contexts of students' neighborhoods. Since students' schools and neighborhoods are both likely to play an important role in their social experiences, it is important to examine both, as this chapter explains.

During high school, the students in our sample lived in neighborhoods with ethnic diversity ranging from 0 to .85 on the ethnic fragmentation index. The average level of fragmentation in students' high school neighborhoods was .27, indicating that about 85 percent of the neighborhood represented one race. As a whole, Jefferson County is about 75 percent one race (white), and the school district's population of high school students is about 70 percent white. Therefore, our data suggest that the average student in JCPS lives in a neighborhood that is less diverse than the county average (according to the U.S. Census) and less diverse than the school district where they attend school.

Students who attended more diverse high schools were also slightly more likely to live in more diverse neighborhoods (.28 on the ethnic fragmentation index) when compared to students who attended less diverse schools (.26 on the ethnic fragmentation index); however, this difference did not yield statistically significant results.[55] We also tested the correlation between the diversity in students' high schools and the diversity in their neighborhoods to

TABLE 10.1: Cross-Classified Model Predicting Ethnic Diversity of Students' Residence Five Years after Graduation

Variable List	Model 1: Null Model			Model 2: Full Model			Model 3: Interaction Model		
	coef	s.e.	p	coef	s.e.	p	coef	s.e.	p
Intercept	0.29	(.01)	***	0.16	(.02)	***	0.15	(.02)	***
Student Background Variables									
Student Race (ref = White)									
Black	—	—		0.06	(.01)	***	0.06	(.01)	***
Other	—	—		0.10	(.02)	***	0.10	(.02)	***
Student Gender (ref = Female)									
Female	—	—		-0.005	(.01)		-0.005	(.01)	
Student Poverty (ref = Paid Lunch)									
Student Participates in Free Lunch Program	—	—		0.001	(.01)		0.001	(.01)	
School Choice (ref = Zoned School)									
Student Attended a Non-Zoned High School	—	—		0.005	(.01)		0.005	(.01)	
# of Years Attended High School in the District	—	—		0.0001	(.00)		-0.001	(.00)	
Lives in Same Neighborhood 5 Years after Graduation	—	—		-0.03	(.01)	***	-0.03	(.01)	***
Student Neighborhood Characteristics									

	Model 1: Null Model			Model 2: Full Model			Model 3: Interaction Model		
	coef	s.e.	p	coef	s.e.	p	coef	s.e.	p
Social Advantage	—	—		0.06	(.03)	*	0.06	(.03)	*
Economic Deprivation	—	—		0.06	(.04)		0.06	(.04)	
Ethnic Diversity	—	—		0.39	(.02)	***	0.40	(.02)	***
High School Characteristics									
Relative Diversity of School	—	—		−0.14	(.01)	**	−0.16	(.01)	**
% Free & Reduced Lunch	—	—		0.04	(.04)		0.04	(.04)	
School Size	—	—		0.00002	(.00)		0.00002	(.00)	
Cross-Level Interaction Term									
Student is Black x Relative Diversity of School	—	—		—	—		0.07	(.22)	
Other Race x Relative Diversity of School	—	—		—	—		−0.12	(.66)	
Variance Components									
Row Level Variance Components:									
Intercept	0.09	(.01)	***	0.02	(.00)	***	0.02	(.00)	***
Level-1	0.18	(.03)		0.18	(.03)		0.18	(.03)	
Chi-square	1174.61			534.92			532.18		
df	518			512			512		

TABLE 10.1: (Continued)

	Model 1: Null Model			Model 2: Full Model			Model 3: Interaction Model		
	coef	s.e.	p	coef	s.e.	p	coef	s.e.	p
Column Level Variance Components:									
Intercept	0.03	(.00)	***	0.01	(.00)	***	0.01	(.00)	***
Chi-square	59.59			34.66			33.35		
df	20			14			14		
Covariance Components									
Deviance	−1244.29			−1699.48			−1703.77		
Number of Estimated Parameters	4			17			19		

***p < .001; **p < .01; *p < .05

N = 3,119 Students, 519 Neighborhoods (Block Groups), and 21 High Schools.

Source: Data in tables is derived from authors' research and calculations.

examine the extent to which high school diversity might be related to neighborhood diversity; however, no significant relationship between the two emerged.[56] Therefore, we can conclude that any HCM results that emerge in relation to school diversity and the diversity of students' high school neighborhoods are independent of one another.

Before discussing the effects of students' neighborhoods and schools on the ethnic diversity of their neighborhoods later in life, we report the results from the student portion of our full model (see table 10.1). Three student-level predictors yielded significant results. On average, black students lived in more heterogeneous neighborhoods five years after graduation than white students ($\beta = .06$, $p < .001$), as did students of other races ($\beta = .10$, $p < .001$). This finding is not surprising, given that whites tend to be the most segregated of all races.[57] Students who resided in the same neighborhood both during high school and five years after graduation tended to live in less heterogeneous neighborhood than students who moved away from the neighborhood where they lived while attending high school ($\beta = -.03$, $p < .001$).[58] Student gender, student poverty, attendance at a nonzoned high school, and the number of years a student attended high school in JCPS did not yield statistically significant results.

Two characteristics of students' high school neighborhoods were statistically significant. First, the social advantage composite was positively related to living in a more diverse neighborhood five years after graduation. Every one-unit increase in social advantage is associated with a six-unit increase in the ethnic diversity of students' residences after graduation ($\beta = .06$, $p < .05$). In terms of effect size, a one-standard-deviation increase in social advantage is associated with a 5 percent of one-standard-deviation increase in the ethnic diversity of a former student's residential neighborhood five years after graduation.[59] The ethnic diversity of students' high school neighborhoods also yielded statistically significant results. When students lived in a more heterogeneous neighborhood during high school, they tended to live in more diverse neighborhoods later in life. A one-unit increase in residential diversity during high school is associated with a thirty-nine-unit increase in the heterogeneity of their residential neighborhoods five years after graduation ($\beta = .39$, $p < .001$). The effect size associated with this coefficient is 37 percent. In other words, a one-standard-deviation increase in the ethnic diversity of a student's high school neighborhood yields a 37 percent increase in the standard deviation of the outcome variable. This represents the largest effect and the strongest predictor of the ethnic diversity of where students decide to live five years after graduation.

Figure 10.2 demonstrates the relationship between the ethnic diversity of students' high school neighborhoods and the levels of integration in the neighborhoods where they chose to live five years after graduation.[60] To demonstrate the range of possible outcomes for students, we present results for the lowest possible level of integration for students' high school neighborhoods alongside the highest possible level of integration recorded in our sample. When white students lived in a completely homogeneous neighborhood during high school (ethnic fragmentation = 0), they were likely to live in a neighborhood with a fragmentation score of .18 five years after graduation. If they lived in one of the most heterogeneous neighborhoods in Jefferson County, they were likely to live in a neighborhood with a fragmentation index score of .52 five years after graduation. This is a .33-point increase in the level of diversity in students' residential neighborhoods five years after graduation, an increase that exceeds the average of the fragmentation score for students' neighborhoods five years after graduation.

A similar trend exists for black students; however, they were likely to live in a neighborhood that was .06 points higher on the fragmentation index than white students, indicating that black students tend to live in slightly more diverse neighborhoods than white students five years after high school

FIGURE 10.2: Ethnic Diversity of High School Neighborhood & Residential Integration Later in Life

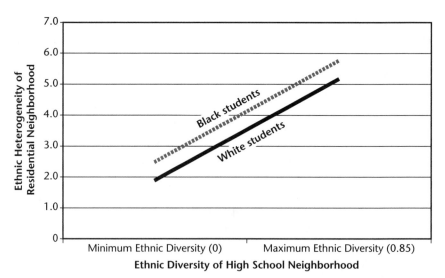

graduation. Nevertheless, this .06-point difference was not statistically significant.

Coefficients associated with our economic deprivation composite did not reach statistical significance. Given the recent Supreme Court decision in *PICS*, some scholars and policy analysts have suggested that socioeconomic integration might act as a proxy for racial integration. The lack of statistically significant results associated with our economic deprivation measure, coupled with the statistically significant results reported on our measure of ethnic diversity, indicates that socioeconomic integration may not have the potential to deliver the same kind of results as racial integration. From a social science perspective, one would not necessarily expect socioeconomic indicators to predict levels of racial integration later in students' lives; however, the recent *PICS* decision requires that scholars highlight the ways in which racial integration differs from socioeconomic integration and therefore is limited in its possible effects on maintaining diversity in schools and communities.

Of specific importance in addressing our first research question—is the degree of racial integration in JCPS high schools related to the ethnic diversity of students' residential neighborhoods five years after high school graduation?—we found that when high schools in JCPS are less diverse than the district average, the students who attend them tend to live in less heterogeneous neighborhoods five years after graduation. In fact, when a school exceeds the district average for percentage of white students enrolled, the ethnic diversity of the residential neighborhoods five years after graduation for students who attended that particular school decreases by an average of fourteen units ($\beta = -.14$, $p < .01$). This yields a 2 percent decrease in the standard deviation of residential ethnic diversity for every one-standard-deviation increase in relative school diversity. Thus, we conclude that the degree of racial integration in JCPS high schools is significantly related to the ethnic diversity of students' residential neighborhoods five years after graduation.[61]

Figure 10.3 highlights the relationship between the relative diversity of students' high schools and the levels of integration in the neighborhoods where they choose to live five years after graduation. To demonstrate the range of possible outcomes for students, we present results for the most diverse schools (70 percent white or less) and for each subsequent level of homogeneity within schools (i.e., percentage increase in the enrollment of white students up to 79 percent, the highest in the district). When white students attend schools that are at least as diverse as the district, they tend to live in neighborhoods that score .33 on the fragmentation index five years after high school graduation. For every 1 percent increase in white students attending a school, the level of diversity in students' neighborhoods later in life drops by about .0015 on the fragmentation index. A similar trend is observed for black students; however, five years after graduation, they live on average in neighborhoods that are .06 points more heterogeneous than white students. Once again, this difference is not statistically significant.

In addition to testing the effects of the relative diversity of high schools on the residential choices students make later in life, we also questioned whether or not this relationship is similar for black and white students. To address this question, we ran an HCM model using a cross-level interaction between black students and students of other races interacted with the relative diversity of student's schools (see table 10.1, Model 3). However, the interaction terms did not yield statistically significant results. As such, we conclude that the effects of attending a less diverse school (or, a school that enrolls a higher percentage of white students than the district average) are similar for black students, white students, and students representing other races and ethnicities.[62]

FIGURE 10.3: Relative Diversity of School & Residential Integration Later in Life

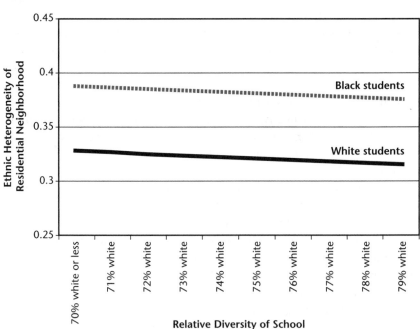

Two additional school-level measures were included in our statistical models—the percentage of students who participated in free or reduced-price lunch (school poverty) and the number of students in the school (school size). Neither of these measures yielded statistically significant results. The absence of statistically significant results associated with the school poverty measure is noteworthy because it is another socioeconomic indicator used in this analysis that does not create results that are similar to our school diversity indicator. Once again, this suggests that socioeconomic indicators and racial diversity measures may not behave similarly in predicting long-term outcomes for students. The *PICS* decision has left school districts with few other choices; however, this finding demonstrates the importance of fostering racial diversity in coordination with socioeconomic integration.

DISCUSSION AND CONCLUSIONS

We find that the two most important predictors of the ethnic composition of former students' residences five years after graduation are the ethnic diversity of the neighborhood where they grew up and the relative diversity of their high school. While the racial mix of the neighborhood where students lived while attending high school was the strongest predictor of the racial diversity in students' neighborhoods five years after graduation, the relative diversity of students' high schools was also significant. This finding is important because it is one of the few predictors of residential heterogeneity that can be addressed and manipulated through educational policy.[63] We also find that although black students and students of other races are, on average, more likely to live in more heterogeneous neighborhoods five years after graduation, the effect associated with the relative diversity of students' schools is similar for all groups of students. In other words, attending an integrated school does not seem to affect black students any differently than white students when predicting the heterogeneity of students' neighborhoods five years after graduation.

We suggest that the relationship between school diversity and residential heterogeneity later in life as observed in this study is likely a result of the value the JCPS students in our study place on integration—likely as a result of their exposure to integrated schools. While we did not test for this relationship specifically, our research compliments recent qualitative work on the long-term effects of school desegregation. This work indicates that individuals who experienced desegregated schools generally agree that racial diversity was an important part of their education because it taught them invaluable life lessons about living and working together.[64] Students who lived through desegregation also attributed changes in their worldviews to the diversity of their schools. They reported that diverse schools helped to reshape their views about race and to overcome their fears and distrust of people who were different. Because attending a desegregated school strongly influences the development of students' views and experiences about race, it seems only natural that students who experienced desegregation would be more comfortable living in racially diverse environments and more likely to seek out integrated opportunities. The benefits of integration that are observed over time (in this study and others) are important to consider when making and implementing educational policies. The trends we observe in this chapter can be quickly undone with a lack of emphasis and commitment to racial integration in schools.

Another important result emerged in our analysis in addition to the effects of school-level integration: we found no significant effect associated with the socioeconomic conditions of students' neighborhoods or high schools. This indicates that restructuring schools through socioeconomic integration alone will likely not result in long-term changes in students' choices about the racial integration of their future residences.

In the shadow of the Supreme Court's advocacy for race neutrality,[65] we reiterate that the nation's history of court-ordered school desegregation was necessitated by patterns of racism and discrimination. Vestiges of these patterns persist today in the form of geographic isolation and residential segregation.[66] In the presence of residential integration, school desegregation would be unnecessary. Nevertheless, residential areas remain segregated, and the Supreme Court has now limited the degree to which school districts can make racial integration a top priority. School districts like JCPS that want to maintain racial diversity in their schools now face the challenges of doing so through race-neutral student assignment plans.

One of the most popular methods of integrating schools through race-neutral student assignment is socioeconomic integration. However, research has clearly demonstrated that income and race cannot stand as proxies for one another. In other words, districts will likely not be able to accomplish racial integration by focusing on socioeconomic status (SES). In fact, Reardon, Yun, and Kurlaender assert that "absent some substantial decline in racial residential segregation, race-neutral assignment policies are unlikely to produce significant racial school desegregation."[67] Using multiple demographic factors that are correlated with race (in addition to SES) may improve the odds of creating racial integration in schools by means of race-neutral student assignment plans; however, researchers are skeptical about the degree of integration such multifactor policies would foster.[68]

Our study also raises questions about the value of socioeconomic integration when considering the long-term effects of school racial integration. While the relative diversity of students' schools was related to the racial heterogeneity of their residential neighborhoods later in life, our socioeconomic measures (both for students' neighborhoods and schools) did not yield statistically significant results. Within the context of JCPS, we see that race and SES are not good proxies for each other—especially when considering the long-term effects of integration. Most advocates of socioeconomic integration center their discussions around the short-term effects of integration: peer effects on student achievement, closing achievement gaps, and offering equitable educational opportunities to underprivileged children.[69] We do not dispute the value of socioeconomically integrated schools, nor do we suggest that racial integration is somehow more important than socioeconomic integration. We do argue that the two are not the same and therefore cannot produce the same results. We also argue that while the hypothesized short-term effects related to socioeconomic integration make reasonable sense, the types of long-term effects that have been demonstrated as products of racial integration in schools (such as comfort in working and interacting in diverse environments and living in more diverse neighborhoods) are unlikely results of socioeconomic integration.

Related to our findings about the relationship between school and residential diversity, research suggests that between 1970 and 1990, stable residential integration rose in the United States. Even though diverse residential areas are rare, a trend toward integration persists and was particularly evident between 1980 and 1990.[70] Interestingly, this rise in residential integration corresponds with the lowest levels of racial segregation in schools (particularly schools in the South that exercised compliance with court desegregation orders).[71] Suggesting that school desegregation causes these increases in residential integration is beyond the scope of this study; however, it raises a possibility that should be explored before dismissing racial integration in schools as a compelling national interest. It could be that the Supreme Court has ruled against integration just when we are beginning to experience its full potential in improving social issues such as residential segregation.

With the goal of upholding their current levels of racial integration, Jefferson County now aims to create racial integration in schools through race-neutral assignment plans. Because they understood the challenges inherent in this task, they incorporated race at the neighborhood level as part of their multifactor student assignment and school restructuring plan. Time will be the best judge of whether JCPS can maintain their record levels of school integration without using race as a factor in assigning students to schools. This study demonstrates that the decades of work in JCPS have been worthwhile. Their efforts further the extent to which former students choose to live in more heterogeneous neighborhoods later in their lives. As such, JCPS has engaged in the battle against the primary impetus for most race-based educational policies—the problem of residential segregation.

APPENDIX 10A: DESCRIPTION OF VARIABLES

	Mean	SD	Min	Max
Ethnic Diversity 5 Years Later	0.28	0.21	0	0.94
The sum of the squared proportions of Whites, African-Americans, Asians, Native Americans, and others subtracted from 1. This creates a measure ranging from 0 to .8. The measure is normalized by dividing by .8, 0 indicating a completely homogeneous neighborhood and 1 indicating a completely heterogeneous neighborhood.				
Student Race (White = reference group)	0.70	–	0	1
Groups: Black	0.28	–	0	1
Other	0.02	–	0	1
Student Gender				
Coded as: Male = 0	0.55	–	0	1
Female = 1	0.45	–	0	1
Student Participates in Free & Reduced Lunch Program				
Coded as: Non-Participant = 0	0.62	–	0	1
Participant = 1	0.38	–	0	1
Student Participated in High School School Choice				
Coded as: Attended Zoned High School = 0	0.48	–	0	1
Attended Non-Zoned High School = 1	0.52	–	0	1

	Mean	SD	Min	Max
Years in District	3.54	0.94	1	4
Total number of years a student attended high school in the school district.				
Same Neighborhood 5 Years After Graduation	0.40	0.49	0	1
Student lives in the same neighborhood 5 years after high school graduation that they lived in during high school.				
Social Advantage (2 item composite mean; " = .95)	0.25	0.17	0.01	0.70
Proportion of college graduates among adults age 25 and older & Proportion of employed persons with professional or managerial occupations.				
Economic Deprivation (2 item composite mean; " = .81)	0.27	0.12	0.09	0.82
Proportion of college graduates amoung adults age 25 and older & Proportion of employed persons with professional or managerial occupations.				
Ethnic Diversity	0.26	0.20	0	0.85
The sum of the squared proportions of Whites, African-Americans, Asians, Native Americans, and others subtracted from 1. This creates a measure ranging from 0 to .8. The measure is normalized by dividing by .8, 0 indicating a completely homogeneous neighborhood and 1 indicating a completely heterogeneous neighborhood.				
Relative Diversity of School	0.03	0.03	0	0.09
Percentage of white students above the average for all high schools (70%) in the district during the 1996–1997 school year.				
School Poverty	0.33	0.15	0.10	0.65
Percent of student body who qualify for free and reduced lunch during the 1996–1997 school year.				
School Size	1129.38	398.74	177	1700
Total number of students in the school during the 1996–1997 school year.				

N = 3,119 Students, 519 Neighborhoods (Block Groups), and 21 High Schools.

Source: Data in tables is derived from authors' research and calculations.

Racial Realities Across Different Places: Dual Directions in Recommitting to the Promises of *Brown*

Jerome E. Morris

From San Jose, California, to Charlotte-Mecklenburg, North Carolina, the authors of the preceding chapters present findings and insights from empirical research studies, political and legal analyses, and case studies that inform the challenges faced—and opportunities realized—in achieving the dual promises of racial integration and quality schooling represented in the passage of *Brown v. Board of Education*. Implicit in each chapter is the symbolic power of *Brown* in efforts to achieve the kind of social justice in U.S. public education that had been historically denied to racial and ethnic minorities, particularly African Americans. But how can the promise of *Brown* be realized in today's educational environment, as schools face the challenges of the twenty-first century, including declining judicial support for public school desegregation; the demographic shift of African Americans and Latinos into nontraditional geographic locations, thereby contributing to new patterns of predominantly minority schools and districts; and the growing belief among racial and ethnic minority groups that their gaining control of local neighborhood schools could prevent the further educational marginalization of their children?[1]

This concluding chapter addresses the overarching themes of the book, providing empirically based insights into how migratory patterns and the nexus of race, social class, and place will have to fashion the quest to achieve *Brown's* promises in profoundly different ways than in the previous fifty years. Rather than taking a unilateral approach that primarily emphasizes the importance of racially balanced schools, this chapter highlights the need to approach reform from dual directions, including a focus on creating racially balanced schools (as much as demographics allow) and classrooms, and on enhancing the schools that will continue to serve predominantly minority populations.

CAN JUDICIAL INTERVENTION MATTER?

In the summer of 2007, the U.S. Supreme Court issued a 5–4 ruling that struck down two cases (one from Louisville, Kentucky, and the other from Seattle, Washington) that involved the use of race to promote public school desegregation. In both cases, collectively referred to as *Parents Involved in Community Schools v. Seattle School District No. 1* (*PICS*) white parents whose children were denied admission to the schools of their choice sued, arguing that the measures these school districts took to achieve racial balance were unconstitutional. Their argument was supported by the Bush administration and the U.S. Department of Education.

Just what did this Court decision mean for the future of desegregation policy in the United States? If the Court had decided that the Louisville and Seattle desegregation plans were permissible, would there have been cause for celebration? Would it have changed the achievement disparity between African American and white students—an issue facing not only low-income blacks who attend urban schools but also middle-income black children who attend schools in suburban communities? Would it have chipped away at the root causes of de facto segregation in U.S. public schools, which include persistent racial stigmatizing and segregated housing patterns, caused in part by deeply held views about racial and ethnic minorities, specifically, the inequalities in income between whites and blacks in the United States?[2] As Koski and Oakes illuminate in their legal and political exploration of the history of desegregation litigation, school reform, and the courts in San Jose, California, decisions made by the Court may not necessarily mean the demise of present educational policies and reforms. Court decisions and judicial interventions may instead sow the seeds of educational reform. The passage of *Brown v. Board of Education* on May 17, 1954, arguably the most significant U.S. Supreme Court case of the twentieth century, illustrates this point.

Upon its passage in 1954, *Brown* brought about a renewed sense of hope for African American people, much as the election of Barack Obama as the first African American U.S. president has engendered a new sense of hope in millions of Americans across race, ethnic, gender, and social class divides. But the hope that was so luminous when *Brown* was passed unfortunately faded within only a few years. *Brown II*, passed in 1955, included the requirement that "all deliberate speed" should be employed in adhering to the mandates of the earlier ruling. This gave whites who resisted the Court's decision the opportunity to mount strategies to delay or circumvent its implementation.[3] In essence, *Brown*'s implementation was left in the hands of local white school boards, which continued to ignore the educational needs of African American children for more than a decade. Although it was the law, *Brown* was not implemented until more than fifteen years after its passage. The Court's decision provided a moral and legal foundation, but it would take the political organizing of community members, advocacy by civil rights organizations such as the NAACP, rulings by judges committed to the ideals of *Brown*, and leadership within school districts to ensure compliance with the mandates of the 1954 law.

The implementation of *Brown*, although instrumental in eradicating segregation between schools, placed the onus of desegregation on African American and Latino communities and brought about a new form of segregation: within school segregation, also referred to as second-generation segregation. Desegregation plans almost always involved the disproportionate busing of African American students to predominantly white schools, the closing of predominantly black schools, and, later, the creation of well-funded magnet schools to lure white students back into urban school districts.[4] Thus, desegregation plans were implemented in ways that ensured that whites were not inconvenienced and that they were the primary beneficiaries of a court case initially predicated on rectifying African American educational disenfranchisement.

As a number of the authors in this book have noted, second-generation segregation in the form of academic tracking and gifted education—both of which overwhelmingly favor white students—became the new inhibitors of quality schooling for racial and ethnic minorities. The second-generation segregation experienced by African American students who attend racially integrated schools has become a most troubling matter.[5] Compared to their white peers in the same schools, black students are more likely to be overrepresented in lower academic tracks and in special education,[6] underrepresented in gifted education,[7] and disproportionately subject to discipline at school.[8] Moreover, many of the causes of the inequities facing black students, particularly black males, have been traced to the deliberate actions of school officials.[9]

District administrators who were responsible for executing desegregation mandates became complicit in relegating *Brown*'s promise of quality schooling for African American and Latino students to the back burner. In chapter 8, Clotfelter, Ladd, and Vigdor provide an insightful analysis of the steps taken by district administrators in North Carolina to keep white students enrolled in the public schools by ensuring that they were enrolled in the high-level tracked classrooms. Thus, efforts to minimize segregation between schools often led to districts replacing it with within-school segregation. The North Carolina case study demonstrates how the racial politics of a district and stakeholders' power can influence the racial composition of schools or districts.

Racial-Ethnic Minorities' Perspectives on the Promises of *Brown*

Whereas the authors of the previous chapters focused a great deal on *Brown*'s promise of racially desegregated schools, African American and Latino groups (as some of the authors have described) were equally concerned about educational quality. Although *Brown* to many people might have represented the eradication of legalized segregation and the opportunity for racially integrated schooling, in African American and Latino communities it also represented the possibility that their children would receive quality schooling. The analyses of the implementation of desegregation measures in San Jose, California, and Denver, Colorado, strongly suggest that the scholarly and policy communities pay significant attention to the struggles for quality schooling beyond the traditional black/white dichotomy. Like the idea that African Americans' primary educational objective for their children was integrated schooling,[10] Latinos' desire for quality educational programs was misinterpreted as a desire primarily for integrated schooling.[11] Latinos were also concerned about quality schooling and about preventing their children's social, cultural, and educational marginalization in schools that were desegregated primarily on the surface. For example, members of the Latino community in San Jose bemoaned the closing of Wilson Middle School (their neighborhood middle school), and wanted it rebuilt. As Koski and Oakes explain in chapter 4:

> Wilson became the symbol of and rallying point for the growing dissatisfaction among Latinos with the district's perceived mistreatment of their children. Poor reading scores, poorly trained teachers, and almost no bilingual/bicultural education evidenced that educational mistreatment. But the litigation-conscious (certainly not integration-conscious) Board chose not to

rebuild Wilson, instead expanding the nearby Hoover site on the grounds that it did not want to exacerbate ethnic imbalance.

The Latino struggle for quality schooling in San Jose is reminiscent of the African American struggle in North Carolina, as chronicled by David Cecelski in *Along Freedom Road: Hyde County, North Carolina and the Fate of Black Schools in the South*.[12] For example, when some of the all-black schools were targeted for closure upon implementation of desegregation in Hyde County, African American students and families protested the closings and the subsequent placing of black children in the all-white school. Members of the African American community engaged in forms of civil disobedience, such as sit-ins and marches, while simultaneously withdrawing their children from the schools to educate them at home. African Americans' educational quest—like the Latinos' in San Jose—went beyond the one-dimensional desegregation plan that wrestled control of their children's schooling away from their communities and did little to ensure that their experiences within desegregated schools provided equitable educational opportunities—in other words, the plan created integrated spaces within desegregated schools.

Court decisions and judicial intervention can provide the legal and moral coercion to act, but the Courts have done little to ensure that the educational needs and concerns of African American and Latino community members have been met. Guaranteeing an equitable education has depended on the actions of activists and civil rights organizations within the African American and Latino communities, such as the NAACP and the Confederación de la Raza Unida. Furthermore, the San Jose desegregation case and its emphasis on the Latino educational experience serve as a prelude to understanding the challenges of creating racial balance and equitable education in schools across the United States. Some of the issues that began in San Jose more than thirty years ago are reemerging in other U.S. urban centers, most notably in the South.

Demographic Shifts and the Reshaping of School Desegregation

Through a collective analysis of the shifting landscape of public school desegregation policy and implementation in the United States, the authors in this volume capture how the nexus of race, social class status, and place shape the opportunities and outcomes of differently positioned social groups in U.S. society. Scholars now collectively refer to this area of research as "the geography of opportunity."[13] Where social groups live (e.g., the North, the Midwest, the South, suburbs, rural communities, or inner cities) has consequences for their social, economic, and political conditions,[14] thereby shaping their children's overall social development and educational outcomes.[15] Given the power of place to shape individuals' and groups' opportunities and outcomes, in what ways might the demographic shifts of African Americans and Latinos shape public school desegregation debates? Moreover, what does the increasing presence of racial and ethnic minority groups in new (and once exclusive) places mean for their social and educational opportunities?

In their analysis of national trends in school racial composition in the era of unitary status, An and Gamoran note that the increased presence in some school districts of African American students in majority "nonwhite schools" is not only a result of the declaration of unitary status but also of the increased presence of Latino students in new locales, such as urban centers in the South. In an apparent direct challenge to conventional arguments regarding the resegregation of the South that have been espoused by key desegregation scholars,[16] An and Gamoran highlight at least three demographic shifts that have occurred in the U.S. student population: (1) the white population and percentage of total population dropped in U.S. schools; (2) the Latino population and percentage of population increased; and (3) white students attending almost all-white schools decreased from 52 percent in 1993 to 39 percent in 2005. But there has been another shift that the authors have overlooked: the "return migration" of African Americans to the South represents a fourth demographic shift that has profound implications for the public school desegregation debate.[17]

Recent U.S. Census data reveal that the South had the largest net growth in black population between 1990 and 2000. Specifically, more than 3.6 million blacks migrated to the South during the 1990s, representing the largest internal migration of African Americans since the Great Black Migration during the early to mid-twentieth century.[18] In fact, two African Americans moved to the South for every one who left.[19] Eight of the top ten areas with the highest percentage of African Americans were located in the South. Moreover, although only 3 percent of U.S. counties are defined as majority black, ninety-one of the ninety-six predominantly black counties are located in the South.[20]

Thus, the southern United States is a critical geographical region for investigating the nexus of race and place, and the consequences of this in housing, school racial composition, and African American student achievement. But the U.S. South, as alluded to earlier, has also emerged as a new place to examine the public school desegregation debate beyond the black/white binary. For example, whereas more than 50 percent of Latinos have traditionally resided in the Southwest, the U.S. South is increasingly becoming a place that Latinos call home. As some of this book's authors have noted, these shifting patterns will advance the debate on school racial composition, and they will also influence how resources are controlled among groups that have traditionally been excluded.

Looking beyond their historical and contemporary presence in the South, over the past three decades, African Americans in large measure have moved out of urban centers and into suburban communities. For instance, in 1970, 60 percent of African Americans lived in central cities and 19 percent in suburban communities. In 2002, however, 51 percent of African Americans lived in metropolitan areas inside central cities and 36 percent lived in the suburbs.[21] In their chapter on *Sheff v. O'Neill*, Dougherty, Wanzer, and Ramsay capture the changing nature of urban areas and how African Americans' movement into suburbia in search of quality housing and schooling for their children has problematized notions of race and place, particularly in that conventional notions of "urban" can no longer euphemistically refer to African Americans.

Dougherty et al. note that a major flaw in the desegregation plan in Hartford, Connecticut (in particular, the interdistrict magnet lotteries) was its use of urban or suburban residence as a proxy for race. African Americans' increased presence in suburban communities contributed to the school district's inability to achieve its racial balancing goals. The plan was conceptualized with the assumption that white people would comprise the predominant population in the suburbs and African Americans would continue to reside primarily in the city. As Dougherty et al. write in chapter 5:

> When the *Sheff* case was filed in 1989, many people envisioned the "suburbs" as uniformly white towns and did not anticipate the growth of black and Latino student populations, particularly in inner-ring suburbs, during the 1990s and 2000s. . . . When Hartford-area magnet schools opened and began advertising for students, many planners anticipated that the suburbs would generate primarily white applicants. But when totaling all magnet enrollments in 2006–07, the share of suburban minority students (29%) surpassed that of suburban white students (25%).

In their formulation of new educational policies and reforms, policymakers and analysts must carefully consider how demographic patterns (such as the Great Black Migration, the return of blacks to the South, and the Latino Diaspora) are shaping housing patterns (construction of new ghettos and segregated residential areas) and, consequently, school racial patterns. As An and Gamoran assert, "Even if school districts fully integrated their schools, only a quarter of the total school segregation within states would be eliminated."

Thus, unitary status may not be the only culprit behind increased racial segregation in schools. Demographic and housing shifts have complicated the possibility of racial balance in public schools in certain sections of the country, especially in predominantly black metropolitan areas and counties in the South and Latino communities in the Southwest. The events surrounding desegregation in Denver and San Jose serve as a prelude to understanding the emerging challenges in creating racially balanced schools in other regions of the United States, particularly the influx of Latino families and students into urban communities and schools. Some of the issues that began in San Jose more than thirty years ago are present in new urban centers of the United States, particularly in the South. As Horn and Kurlaender note in chapter 9, which addresses resegregation trends and school achievement in Denver in the aftermath of *Keyes*, the increasing Latino population is becoming integral in the redefinition of minority status and in definitions and measures of school segregation.

Redefining "Minority" and Measures of Segregation and Quality Schooling

As noted earlier, the demographic shift of African Americans beyond the geographic areas in which they traditionally once lived and the increasing Latino population in different U.S. regions are reshaping the complexion of public schooling in the United States. These demographic shifts are also contesting the notions of "minority" and "segregated" that existed in the public and legal vernacular shortly after the *Brown* decision more than five decades ago, and, consequently, how such constructs are measured. Today, notions of minority have come to include various groups regardless of their socio-historical experiences in the U.S. Not all minority groups have had similar experiences in terms of their history and schooling; therefore, definitions of minority status have to be more complex and nuanced. Rather than uniformly applying the concept of minority to various racial and ethnic groups, the way educational anthropologists employ the concept in their research may offer more accurate ways to distinguish various groups in order to develop targeted educational reforms and policies.

Anthropologist John Ogbu asserts that the extent to which members of certain minority groups fail in mainstream schools can be linked to the different ways these groups enter society and approach schooling.[22] Using a cultural-ecological model to explain minority groups' school experiences, Ogbu developed a typology of ethnic groups based on each group's entry into the dominant society: voluntary or immigrant minorities, which include Asian Americans, recent African immigrants, and immigrants from the Caribbean; and involuntary or nonimmigrant minority groups, such as African Americans and Native Americans, and some Latino populations. These distinct definitions of minority may best describe these two groups, whose historical, social, and schooling experiences in the United States warrant judicial intervention and an educational remedy.

Over the past two decades, it is clear that there has been a shift in desegregation policy in the United States concurrent with an increase in predominantly minority public schools, which some scholars describe as the resegregation of public schools. Rather than viewing the increase in minority schools primarily as the result of court decisions that retreated from *Brown*, the authors in this book instead point to a confluence of forces. Court decisions, white resistance and outmigration from urban schools, and the demographic shifts and migration patterns of African American and Latino families are collectively reshaping the complexion of public schools in urban and suburban settings. This confluence of forces has created a racial and social class dynamic that differs significantly from that which existed before *Brown*, or even twenty years ago.

In addition to developing more nuanced definitions of minority status, definitions and measures of segregation must also be reconsidered in light of changing demographics. According to Clotfelter, Vigdor, and Ladd,[23] the common index of the proportion of black students attending majority nonwhite schools "may have lost much of its meaning as a measure of racial segregation." Definitions of segregation, as measured by the absence of white students, will miss the second-generation segregation of African American and Latino students that takes place within schools and classrooms. The courts have rarely responded to efforts to end the second-generation segregation that is taking place in desegregated schools. Therefore, definitions of "quality schooling" and "achievement" for populations that have been educationally disenfranchised historically have to be expanded, and they should not be contingent on the presence or absence of white students in the schools these disenfranchised children attend. A renewed interest in desegregation must occur, but it must focus on what takes place within schools and classrooms as well as between schools.

The Desegregation of Classroom Spaces: A Structural and Cultural Imperative

Whereas scholarly and policy discourses have focused primarily on creating equitable schooling opportunities for low-income and urban students in order to improve achievement, researchers are finding that middle-class and suburban African American students also do not achieve at expected levels. While low academic achievement is correlated with the percentage of economically disadvantaged and minority students in a school,[24] underachievement among black students in middle-class and predominantly white suburban schools have brought a number of issues to the fore. For example, in their study of fifteen urban and suburban school districts recognized for their academic reputations, well-established economic support of public schools, and locations near predominantly white universities, researchers affiliated with the Minority Student Achievement Network found that black students performed less well on measures of student achievement.[25] Ronald Ferguson's analysis aptly demonstrated how even highly touted school districts struggle with serious achievement disparities between African American and white students.

The second-generation segregation experienced by black students is further complicated by their reactions to desegregated school settings. Within predominantly white and racially desegregated schools, cultural processes and structures require that black students tactfully negotiate the intersection of academic identity with social identity based on race, class, and gender.[26] A growing number of researchers are beginning to explore how school settings and African American students' social identities shape their academic outcomes across different school contexts. For example, Tyson, Darity, and Castellino found that racialized peer pressure against African American students achieving well (i.e., "acting white") most likely occurs in schools where black students are grossly underrepresented in the most demanding courses.[27] Tyson et al. found that charges of acting white surfaced in Advanced Placement (AP) classes and resulted in animosity toward those few privileged black students in AP and honors courses. Institutional trends may also perpetuate inequalities and foster racialized peer pressure within predominantly white and racially diverse schools and classrooms.

Braddock's argument in chapter 1 becomes instructive in the overall effort to work against segregation between schools and within classrooms—which further militates against black student achievement. In his extensive review of the literature on school desegregation, Braddock illustrates the benefits of racial diversity for black students at schools that are predominantly but not overwhelmingly white. The schools that had the highest academic achievement and the smallest achievement gap "were between 61 percent and 90 percent white or Asian American and between 10 percent and 39 percent African American and Hispanic."

A renewed focus on creating equitable opportunities for students in desegregated schools will require a change in the organization of and practices in these schools. There is a major social benefit for all children when they interact with children from diverse populations, but the racial composition of classrooms is equally or more important than the racial composition of schools in ensuring the educational success of black and Latino students. Racially desegregated classrooms give African American and Latino students equitable access to the advanced subject matter they will need to enroll in colleges and universities. A greater presence of African American students in these classrooms may also mitigate against the animosity that some of them experience when they are the only African American student in an AP or gifted education program. Tyson and colleagues stress how integral institutional factors within schools—which often come to be interpreted as cultural forces—have been in cultivating racially identifiable attitudes toward the achievement of black children.

New Directions in Recommitting to *Brown*: Which Way?

The emergence of new racial realities in the United States requires new directions and strategies for bringing about *Brown*'s dual promises of racial integration and quality schooling. Given the critical insights presented by the authors in this volume, in which direction should educational policy move to fulfill the promises of *Brown*? Can policies that push for African American children to attend racially diverse schools ensure that the schools will recognize these children's culture in the schools and curriculum, and that the children will not be disproportionately tracked, disciplined, or placed in special education? Will the enhancement or financial support of urban and predominantly black or Latino schools through additional resources, rigorous academic curriculum, and facilities be sufficient? Several authors noted that some predominantly minority schools have shown improvement on certain measures of academic achievement, but can these schools provide quality schooling on a large scale?

While the exclusive enhancement of predominantly minority schools, as Smrekar and Goldring note, does not solve the structural inequities that these schools and their neighborhoods experience, it is apparent that dual directions must be taken in the quest to achieve *Brown*'s dual promises. Efforts to promote racial balancing in public schools must not be abandoned, given the long-term social and academic benefits of racially diverse schools. However, such schools must provide equitable schooling for all of their students. Meanwhile, millions of African American and Latino children will continue to attend schools that serve an overwhelmingly minority student population. Educators, researchers, and policymakers must research, understand, and improve the schools these children presently attend, and not where they believe the ideal setting for the children would be.

Finally, the authors in this book illustrate the complexity of various local situations while examining the shifting nature of desegregation policies and practices since the declaration of unitary status by some districts, and following the Supreme Courts' decision in 2007. While each chapter focuses on a unique geographic region and various periods of desegregation implementation in the U.S., collectively they offer the kind of panoramic analysis across cities and suburbs that points to the need to be mindful of the significance of migration patterns and demographic shifts across place and time. These patterns and shifts are not only shaping the complexion of schools and communities, but also the political landscape of public school desegregation. In the future, community members and political voices from these various racial and ethnic minorities will increasingly push for quality schooling, not just their children's enrollment in racially diverse schools, as a measure of the fulfillment of the promises of *Brown*.

Notes

FOREWORD

1. For nationally representative test-score comparisons by parental education level, see the appendix to chapter 8 of Ronald F. Ferguson, *Toward Excellence with Equity: An Emerging Vision for Closing the Achievement Gap* (Cambridge, MA: Harvard Education Press, 2007).

INTRODUCTION: UNITARY STATUS, NEIGHBORHOOD SCHOOLS, AND RESEGREGATION

Smrekar and Goldring

1. *Brown v. Board of Education of Topeka*, 347 U.S. 483 (1954).
2. *Brown v. Board of Education* (II), 349 U.S. 294 (1955).
3. *Green v. County School Board of New Kent County*, 191 U.S. 430 (1968).
4. *Swann v. Charlotte-Mecklenburg Board of Education*, 402 U.S. 1 (1971).
5. *Board of Education of Oklahoma City Public Schools v. Dowell*, 498 U.S. 237 (1991); *Freeman v. Pitts*, 503 U.S. 467 (1992).
6. U.S. Commission on Civil Rights, *Becoming Less Separate? School Desegregation, Justice Department Enforcement, and the Pursuit of Unitary Status* (Washington, DC: Author, September, 2007).
7. U.S. Commission on Civil Rights, *Becoming Less Separate?*
8. U.S. Commission on Civil Rights, *Becoming Less Separate?*, xii.
9. G. Orfield and C. Lee, *Racial Transformation and the Changing Nature of Segregation* (Cambridge, MA: The Civil Rights Project at Harvard University, 2006); G. Orfield and C. Lee, *Historic Reversals, Accelerating Resegregation, and the Need for New Integration Strategies* (Los Angeles: UCLA, The Civil Rights Project/Proyecto Derechos Civiles, 2007).
10. E. Frankenberg, C. Lee, and G. Orfield, *A Multiracial Society with Segregated Schools: Are We Losing the Dream?* (Cambridge, MA: The Civil Rights Project at Harvard University, January 2003).
11. Pew Research Center, *The Changing Racial and Ethnic Composition of U.S. Public Schools* (Washington, DC: Author, 2007).
12. Pew Research Center, *The Changing Racial and Ethnic Composition.*
13. R. C. Johnson, "MD District Plans Return to Neighborhood Schools," *Education Week*, November 29, 2000, 3.

14. E. Goldring, L. Cohen-Vogel, and C. Smrekar, "Schooling Closer to Home: Desegregation Policy and Neighborhood Contexts," *American Journal of Education*, 112, no. 3 (2006): 335–63.

15. Public Agenda Online, 1999, http://www.publicagenda.org.

16. R. Pride and H. V. M. May Jr., "Neighborhood Schools Again? Race, Educational Interest, and Traditional Values," *Urban Education*, 34, no. 3 (1999): 389–410.

17. E. B. Goldring, R. Crowson, D. Laird, and R. Berk, "Transition Leadership in a Changing Policy Environment," *Educational Evaluation and Policy Analysis*, 25 (2003): 473–88.

18. J. Morris, "Forgotten Voice of Black Educators: Critical Race Perspectives on the Implementation of a Desegregation Plan," *Educational Policy*, 15, no. 4 (2001): 595.

19. Goldring et al., "Schooling Closer to Home," 335.

20. *An Act to Amend Title 14 of the Delaware Code Relating to Neighborhood Schools*, Delaware Code, chapter 287 (n.d.), http://delcode.delaware.gov/sessionlaws/ga140/chp287.shtml.

21. Bill 3862 2003–2004, State of South Carolina, http://www.scstaehouse.net/sess115-2003-2004/bills/3863.htm.

22. U. Bronfenbrenner, *The Ecology of Human Development* (Cambridge, MA: Harvard University Press, 1979).

23. *Parents Involved in Community Schools v. Seattle School District No. 1*, 127 S. Ct. 2738 (2007).

24. NAACP Legal Defense and Educational Fund, *Still Looking to the Future: Voluntary K–12 School Integration* (New York: Author, 2008).

25. Orfield and Lee, *Historic Reversals*.

CHAPTER ONE: LOOKING BACK

Braddock

1. L. Guinier, "From Racial Liberalism to Racial Literacy: *Brown v. Board of Education* and the Interest-Divergence Dilemma," *Journal of American History*, 91, no. 1 (2004): 92–118.

2. S. A. Wells, J. Holme, A. Revilla, and A. Atanda, "How Society Failed School Desegregation Policy: Looking Past the Schools to Understand Them," *Review of Research in Education*, 28 (2004): 47–99; K. Welner, "Race-Conscious Student Assignment Policies: Law Social Science, and Diversity," *Review of Educational Research*, 76 (2006): 349–82.

3. J. D. Anderson, *The Education of Blacks in the South* (Chapel Hill: University of North Carolina Press, 1994).

4. E. Patterson, *"Brown* at Fifty: Fulfilling the Promise," *The Recorder*, May 14, 2004.

5. Briefs, Appendix to Appellant's, "The Effects of Segregation and the Consequences of Desegregation: A Social Science Statement," September 22, 1952, in *Brown v. Board of Education of Topeka Kansas*. 347 U.S. 483 (1954).

6. D. J. Armor, "Forced Justice: School Desegregation and the Law," in D. J. Armor, *Forced Justice: School Desegregation and the Law* (New York: Oxford, 1995).

7. J. H. Braddock, "School Desegregation and Black Assimilation," *Journal of Social Issues*, 41 (1985): 9–22; J. H. Braddock II and J. M. McPartland, "The Social and Academic Consequences of School Desegregation," *Equity and Choice* 4 (February 1988): 50–73; J. H. Braddock and M. P. Dawkins, "Long-Term Effects of School Desegregation on Southern Blacks," *Sociological Spectrum*, 4 (1984): 365–81; J. M. McPartland, "Desegregation and Equity in Higher Education: Is Progress Related to the Desegregation of Elementary and Secondary Schools?" *Law and Contemporary Problems*, 43, no. 3 (1978): 108–32; S. A. Wells and R. L. Crain, "Perpetuation Theory and the Long-Term Effects of School Desegregation," *Review of Educational Research*, 64 (1994): 531–56; S. A. Wells, "Reexamining Social Science Research on School Desegregation: Long- versus Short-Term Effects," *Teachers College Record*, 94, no. 4 (1995): 691–706; S. A. Wells, "The 'Consequences' of School Desegregation: The Mismatch between the Research and the Rationale," *Hastings Constitutional Law Quarterly*, 28, no. 4 (2002): 771–97; J. Schofield, "Review of Research on School Desegregation's Impact on Elementary and Secondary School Students," in J. A. Banks and C. M. Banks, eds., *Handbook of Research on Multicultural Education* (San Francisco: Jossey-Bass, 2001), 597–616; M. P. Dawkins and J. H. Braddock, "The Continuing Significance of School Desegregation: School Desegregation and African-American Inclusion in American Society," *Journal of Negro Education*, 63, no. 3 (1994): 394–405; J. H. Braddock and T. E. Eitle, "The Effects of School Desegregation," in J. Banks and C. M. Banks, eds., *Handbook of Research on Multicultural Education*, 2nd ed. (San Francisco: Jossey-Bass, 2003): 828–42.

8. J. M. McPartland and J. H. Braddock, "The Impact of School Desegregation on Going to College and Getting a Good Job," in W. Hawley, ed., *Effective School Desegregation* (New York: Sage, 1981), 141–54.

9. H. Levin, "Education, Life-Chances, and the Courts," *Law and Contemporary Problems*, 39, no. 2 (1975): 217–39; J. McPartland, J. Epstein, N. Karweit, and R. Slavin, "Productivity of Schools: Conceptual and Methodological Frameworks for Research" (Baltimore: Johns Hopkins University, Center for Social Organization of Schools, 1976).

10. C. Bankston and C. Caldas, "Majority African-American Schools and Social Injustice: The Influence of De Facto Segregation on Academic Achievement," *Social Forces*, 75 (1996): 535–52; J. Coleman et al., *Equality of Educational Opportunity* (Washington, DC: U.S. Government Printing Office, 1966); R. L. Crain and R. E. Mahard, "Desegregation and Black Achievement: A Review of the Research," *Law and Contemporary Problems*, 42 (1978): 17–56; R. A. Mickelson, "Subverting *Swann:* Tracking and Second Generation Segregation," *American Educational Research Journal*, 38, no. 2 (2001): 215–52; D. Pride and D. Woodard, *The Burden of Busing: The Politics of Desegregation in Nashville, Tennessee* (Knoxville: University of Tennessee Press, 1985).

11. T. D. Cook, "What Have Black Children Gained Academically from School Integration? Examination of the Meta-Analytic Evidence," in T. Cook et al., ed., *School Desegregation and Black Achievement* (Washington, DC: National Institute of Education, 1984), 6–42; R. Mahard and R. Crain, "Research on Minority Achievement in Desegregated Schools," in C. Rossell and W. Hawley, eds., *The Consequences of School Desegregation* (Philadelphia: Temple University Press, 1983), 103–25; N. St. John, *School Desegregation: Outcomes for Children* (New York: Wiley, 1975); Schofield, "Review of Research on School Desegregation's Impact on Elementary and Secondary School Students"; Wells, "Reexamining Social Science Research on School Desegregation."

12. Braddock, "School Desegregation and Black Assimilation"; Braddock and Dawkins, "Long-Term Effects of School Desegregation on Southern Blacks"; Braddock and McPartland, "The Social and Academic Consequences of School Desegregation"; Dawkins and Braddock, "The Continuing Significance of School Desegregation"; Schofield, "Review of Research on School Desegregations' Impact on Elementary and Secondary School Students"; Wells and Crain, "Perpetuation Theory and the Long-Term Effects of School Desegregation"; Wells, "Reexamining Social Science Research on School Desegregation"; Wells, "The 'Consequences' of School Desegregation."

13. McPartland and Braddock, "The Impact of Desegregation on Going to College and Getting a Good Job."

14. Crain and Mahard, "Desegregation and Black Achievement"; R. L. Crain and R. E. Mahard, "School Racial Composition and Black College Attendance and Achievement Test Performance," *Sociology of Education*, 51 (1978): 81–101; R. L. Crain and R. E. Mahard, "The Consequences of Controversy Accompanying Institutional Change: The Case of School Desegregation," *American Sociological Review*, 47, no. 6 (1981): 697–708; J. Prager and M. Seeman, *School Desegregation Research: New Directions in Situational Analysis* (New York: Plenum, 1986).

15. W. Hawley and S. Rosenholtz, *Achieving Quality Integrated Education* (Washington, DC: National Education Association, 1986).

16. Crain and Mahard, "The Consequences of Controversy Accompanying Institutional Change."

17. R. Mahard and R. Crain, "The Influence of High School Racial Composition on the Academic Achievement and College Attendance of Hispanics," paper presented at the annual meeting of the American Sociological Association, New York, 1980.

18. Schofield, "Review of Research on School Desegregations' Impact on Elementary and Secondary School Students."

19. T. D. Cook, "What Have Black Children Gained Academically from School Integration?"

20. Pride and Woodard, *The Burden of Busing*; K. Carsrud, "Does Pairing Hurt Chapter I Students?" Office of Research and Evaluation, Austin Independent School District, Austin, Texas, 1984.

21. M. B. Arias, "Compliance Monitor's Fifth-Annual Report Vasques v. San Jose (CA) Unified School District," Compliance Report, U.S. District Court, San Francisco, California, 1989.

22. A. Bennett and J. Q. Easton, "Voluntary Transfers and Student Achievement: Does It Help or Does It Hurt?" paper presented at the annual meeting of the American Educational Research Association, New Orleans, 1988; R. Gable and E. Iwanicki, "The Longitudinal Effects of a Voluntary School Desegregation Program on the Basic Skills of Program Participants," *Metropolitan Education*, 1 (1986): 76–7.

23. S. Mayer and C. Jencks, "Growing Up in Poor Neighborhoods: How Much Does It Matter?" *Science*, 243 (1989): 1441–45.

24. Mickelson, "Subverting *Swann*."

25. J. Ludwig, H. Ladd, and G. Duncan, "Urban Poverty and Educational Outcomes," in W. Gale and J. Pack, eds., *Brookings-Wharton Papers on Urban Affairs-2001* (Washington, DC: Brookings Institution Press, 2001), 147–201.

26. J. Rosenbaum, "Changing the Geography of Opportunity by Expanding Residential Choice: Lessons from the Gautreaux Program," *Housing Policy Debate*, 6, no. 1 (1995): 231–70.

27. Bankston and Caldas, "Majority African-American Schools and Social Injustice."

28. D. Grissmer, A. Flanagan, and S. Williamson, "Why Did the Black-White Score Gap Narrow in the 1970's and 1980's?" in C. Jencks and M. Phillips, eds., *The Black-White Test Score Gap* (Washington, DC: The Brookings Institution Press, 1998), 182–226.

29. J. Schiff, W. Firestone, and J. Young, "Organizational Context for Student Achievement: The Case of Student Racial Composition," paper presented at the annual meeting of the American Educational Research Association, Montreal, 1999.

30. S. Brown, "High School Racial Composition: Balancing Excellence and Equity," paper presented at the annual meeting of the American Sociological Association, Chicago, 1999.

31. H. Wainer, "Minority Contributions to the SAT Turnaround: An Example of Simpson's Paradox," *Journal of Educational Statistics*, 11 (1986): 239–44.

32. G. Anrig, "Educational, Standards, Testing and Equity," *Phi Delta Kappan* 66, no. 9 (1985): 623–25.

33. Schofield, "Review of Research on School Desegregations' Impact on Elementary and Secondary School Students."

34. H. B. Garard, "School Desegregation: The Social Science Role," *American Psychologist*, 38 (8) 1983: 869–77.

35. J. Epstein, "After the Bus Arrives: Resegregation in Desegregated Schools," *Journal of Social Issues*, 41 (1985): 23–43; J. Oakes, *Multiplying Inequalities: The Effects of Race, Social Class, and Ability Grouping on Opportunities to Learn Mathematics and Science* (New York: Macmillan, 1990); J. Oakes, "Two Cities: Tracking and Within-School Segregation," in L. Miller, ed., *Brown Plus Forty: The Promise* (New York: Teachers College Press, 1995); J. Oakes, *Keeping Track: How Schools Structure Inequality* (New Haven, CT: Yale University Press, 1985); R. Ferguson, "Teachers' Perceptions and Expectations and the Black-White Test Score Gap," in C. Jencks and M. Phillips, eds., *The Black-White Test Score Gap* (Washington, DC: The Brookings Institute Press, 1998), 273–317; Ferguson, "Teachers' Perceptions and Expectations and the Black-White Test Score Gap," 1998; R. Rist, "Student Social Class and Teacher Expectations: The Self-Fulfilling Prophecy in Ghetto Educa-

tion," *Harvard Educational Review*, 40 (1970): 411–52; R. Rist, *The Invisible Children* (Cambridge, MA: Harvard University Press, 1978).

36. Mickelson, "Subverting *Swann.*"

37. Wells et al., "How Society Failed School Desegregation Policy"; Coleman et al., *Equality of Educational Opportunity*.

38. Coleman, J. C., et al., *Equality of Educational Opportunity* (Washington, DC: Government Printing Office, 1966); D. Clement, M. Eisenhart, and J. Wood, "School Desegregation and Educational Inequality: Trends in the Literature," in National Institute of Education, ed., *The Desegregation Literature: A Critical Appraisal* (Washington, DC: National Institute of Education, 1976), 1–77.

39. Wells et al. "How Society Failed School Desegregation Policy."

40. Epstein, "After the Bus Arrives"; Oakes, *Keeping Track, Multiplying Inequalities*, "Two Cities."

41. Oakes, *Multiplying Inequalities*; U.S. Comission on Civil Rights, *Equal Opportunity and Nondiscrimination for Minority Students: Federal Enforcement of Title IV in Ability Group Practices* (Washington, DC: U.S. Comission on Civil Rights, 1999).

42. Oakes, *Multiplying Inequalities*.

43. R. Atanda, *Do Gatekeeper Courses Expand Education Options?* (Washington, DC: National Center for Education Statistics, 1999); Oakes, "Two Cities"; Oakes, *Multiplying Inequalities*.

44. Oakes, "Two Cities"; Mickelson, "Subverting *Swann.*"

45. J. H. Braddock, "Tracking and School Achievement," in V. Gadsden and D. Wagner, eds., *Literacy Among African American Youth: Issues in Learning, Teaching, and Schooling* (Cresskill, NJ: Hampton, 1995) 153–76; Oakes, *Keeping Track*, "Two Cities"; R. Slavin, "Achievement Effects of Ability Grouping in Secondary Schools," *Review of Educational Research*, 60 (1990): 471–99.

46. C. Weiss, "Improving the Linkage between Social Research and Public Policy," in B. Lynn, ed., *Knowledge and Policy: The Uncertain Connection* (Washington, DC: National Academy of Sciences, 1978), 23–81.

47. K. B. Clark, "Some Principles Related to the Problem of Desegregation," *Journal of Negro Education*, 23, no. 3 (1954): 339–47.

48. M. Halinan and S. Smith, "The Effects of Classroom Racial Composition on Students' Interracial Friendliness," *Social Psychology Quarterly*, 48, no. 1 (1985): 3–16; M. Hallinan and R. Williams, "Interracial Friendship Choices in Secondary Schools;" *American Sociological Review*, 54, no. 1

(1989): 67–78; R. Slavin, "Effects of Biracial Learning Teams on Cross-Racial Friendships," *Journal of Educational Pschology,* 60 (1979): 471–99; J. Schofield and W. Sagar, "Peer Interaction Patterns in an Integrated Middle School," *Sociometry,* 40, no. 21 (1977): 130–39.

49. T. Pettigrew and I. Tropp, "Does Intergroup Contact Reduce Prejudice? Recent Meta-Analytic Findings," in S. Oskamp, eds., *Reducing Prejudice and Discrimination: Social Psychological Perspectives* (Mahwah, NJ: Erlbaum, 2000), 93–114.

50. M. Patchen, *Black-White Contact in Schools: Its Social and Academic Consequences* (Lafayette, IN: Purdue University Press, 1982).

51. Schofield and Sagar, "Peer Interaction Patterns in an Integrated Middle School"; J. Schofield and W. Sagar, "Desegregation, School Practices and Student Race Relations," in C. Rossell and W. Hawley, eds., *The Consequences of School Desegregation* (Philadelphia: Temple University Press, 1983), 58–102; J. Schofield, "Promoting Positive Intergroup Relations in School Settings," in W. Hawley and A. Jackson, eds., *Toward a Common Destiny: Improving Race Relations in American Society* (San Francisco: Jossey-Bass, 1995), 257–89.

52. St. John, *School Desegregation;* W. Stephan, "School Desegregation: An Evaluation of Predictions Made in *Brown v. Board of Education,*" *Psychological Bulletin,* 85 (1978): 217–38.

53. M. Halinan and R. Teixeria, "Opportunities and Constraints: Black-White Differences in the Formation of Interracial Friendships," *Child Development,* 58 (1987): 13–58; Schofield, "Review of Research on School Desegregations' Impact on Elementary and Secondary School Students"; N. Sonleitner and P. Wood, "The Effect of Childhood Interracial Contact on Adult Antiblack Prejudice," *International Journal of Intercultural Relations,* 20, no. 1 (1996): 1–17; M. Hallinan, "Diversity Effects on Student Outcomes: Social Science Evidence," *Ohio State Law Journal,* 59 (1998): 733–54; Schofield and Sagar, "Desegregation, School Practices and Student Race Relations."

54. Schofield and Sagar, "Peer Interaction Patterns in an Integrated Middle School."

55. Halinan and Teixeria, "Opportunities and Constraints"; Hallinan and Williams, "Interracial Friendship Choices in Secondary School"; Schofield, "Promoting Positive Intergroup Relations in School Settings."

56. Halinan and Smith, "The Effects of Classroom Racial Composition on Students' Interracial Friendliness"; Halinan and Teixeria, "Opportunities and Constraints"; Patchen, *Black-White Contact in Schools.*

57. Halinan and Smith, "The Effects of Classroom Racial Composition on Students' Interracial Friendliness."

58. Halinan and Smith, "The Effects of Classroom Racial Composition on Students' Interracial Friendliness."

59. Sonleitner and Wood, "The Effect of Childhood Interracial Contact on Adult Antiblack Prejudice."

60. L. Sigelman, T. Bledso, S. Welch, and M. Combs, "Making Contact? Black-White Social Interaction in an Urban Setting," *American Journal of Sociology*, 101, no. 5 (1996): 1306–32.

61. J. H. Braddock and A. Gonzalez, "Social Isolation and Social Cohesion: The Effects of K–12 Neighborhood and School Segregation on Intergroup Orientations," *Teachers College Record*, forthcoming.

62. V. Saenz, H. Ngai, and S. Hurtado, "Factors Influencing Positive Interactions across Race for African-American, Asian-American, Latino, and White College Students," *Research in Higher Education*, 48, no. 1 (2007): 1–38.

63. R. L. Crain, "School Integration and Occupational of Negros," *American Journal of Sociology*, 75 (1970): 593–606; J. H. Braddock, M. P. Dawkins, and W. T. Trent, "Why Desegregate? The Effects of School Desegregation on Adult Occupational Attainment of African-Americans, Whites, and Hispanics," *International Journal of Contemporary Sociology*, 31 (1994): 271–83; U.S. Commission on Civil Rights, *Racial Isolation in the Public Schools* (Appendix C 5) (Washington, DC: U.S. Government Printing Office, 1967).

64. Crain, "School Integration and Occupational of Negros"; R. L. Crain and C. Weisman, *Discrimination, Personality and Achievement* (New York: Seminar Press, 1972).

65. J. H. Braddock, "Black Student Attendance at Segregated Schools and Colleges: More Evidence on the Perpetuation of Segregation Across Levels of Education," paper presented at the National Conference on School Desegregation Research, Chicago, 1986; Braddock and McPartland, "The Social and Academic Consequences of School Desegregation"; J. H. Braddock, J. M. McPartland, and W. T. Trent, "Desegregated Schools And Desegregated Work Environments," paper presented at the annual meeting of the American Educational Research Association, New Orleans, 1984; Braddock and Dawkins, "Long-Term Effects of School Desegregation on Southern Blacks"; Braddock, "School Desegregation and Black Assimilation"; Braddock and Eitle, "The Effects of School Desegregation"; J. H. Braddock and J. M. McPartland, "Social-Psychological Processes that Per-

petuate Segregation: The Relationship between School and Employment Desegregation," *Journal of Black Studies*, 19 (1989): 267–89; J. H. Braddock and J. M. McPartland, "Assessing School Desegregation Effects: New Directions in Research, Vol. 3," in R. Corwin, ed., *Research in Sociology of Education and Socialization* (Greenwich, CT: JAI, 1980), 209–82.

66. Matched on Standard Metropolitan Statistical Area location and public vs. private control. J. H. Braddock, "The Perpetuation of Segregation across Levels of Education," *Sociology of Education* (1980): 178–86.

67. Braddock and McPartland, "Assessing School Desegregation Effects."

68. Braddock, "Black Student Attendance at Segregated Schools and Colleges."

69. M. Dawkins, "Black Students' Occupational Expectations: A National Study of the Impact of School Desegregation," *Urban Education*, 18 (1983): 98–113.

70. Crain, "School Integration and Occupational of Negros"; Dawkins, "Black Students' Occupational Expectations"; Braddock, "Black Student Attendance at Segregated Schools and Colleges."

71. J. H. Braddock, R. Crain, J. McPartland, and R. Dawkins, "Applicant Race and Job Placement Decisions: A National Survey Experiment," *International Journal of Sociology and Social Policy*, 6 (1986): 3–24.

72. J. H. Braddock, J. M. McPartland, and W. T. Trent, "Desegregated Schools and Desegregated Work Environments," paper presented at the annual meeting of the American Educational Research Association, New Orleans1984; Braddock and McPartland, "Social-Psychological Processes that Perpetuate Segregation"; Braddock et al., "Why Desegregate? "; K. C. Green, "Integration and Attainment: Preliminary Results from a National Longitudinal Study of the Impact of School Desegregation," paper presented at the annual meeting of the American Educational Research Association, Los Angeles, 1982; K. C. Green, "The Impact of Neighborhood and Secondary School Integration on Educational and Occupational Attainment of College Bound Blacks," unpublished doctoral dissertation, University of California, Los Angeles, 1982.

73. Green, "Integration and Attainment," "The Impact of Neighborhood and Secondary School Integration."

74. Braddock and McPartland, "Social-Psychological Processes that Perpetuate Segregation."

75. Braddock et al., "Desegregated Schools and Desegregated Work Environments."

76. Braddock et al., "Why Desegregate?"

77. R. L. Crain, "The Quality of American High School Graduates: What Employers Say and Do about It," Report No. 354, Baltimore: Johns Hopkins University, Center for Social Organization of Schools, 1984.

78. Braddock, "Social Science Research and Educational Equity."

79. M. Fix and J. Passel, "U.S. Immigration: Trends and Implications for Schools," paper presented to the National Association for Bilingual Education's NCLB Implementation, New Orleans, 2003; G. Orfield and C. Sanni, "Resegregation in American Schools," The Civil Rights Project at Harvard University, Cambridge, MA, 1999.

80. R. Putnam, "*E Pluribus Unum*: Diversity and Community in the Twenty-First Century. The Johan Skytte Prize Lecture," *Scandinavian Political Studies*, 30, no. 2 (2007): 137–74; D. Bennett, "Segregation and Racial Interaction," *Annals of the Association of American Geographers*, 63, no. 1 (1973): 48–57; J. H. Braddock, "Diversity in K–12 Education: Implications for Individuals and Society," paper presented to the National Conference on High Poverty Schooling in America, Chapel Hill, North Carolina, October 2006.

CHAPTER TWO: TRENDS IN SCHOOL RACIAL COMPOSITION IN THE ERA OF UNITARY STATUS

An and Gamoran

1. C. T. Clotfelter, J. L. Vigdor, and H. F. Ladd, "Federal Oversight, Local Control, and the Specter of "Resegregation" in Southern Schools," *American Law and Economics Review*, 8 (2006): 347–89.

2. G. Orfield and C. Lee, *Racial Transformation and the Changing Nature of Segregation* (Cambridge, MA: The Civil Rights Project at Harvard University, 2006).

3. *Board of Education of Oklahoma City Public Schools v. Dowell*, 498 U.S. 237 (1991); *Freeman v. Pitts*, 503 U.S. 467 (1992); *State of Missouri v. Kalima Jenkins*, 115 S. Ct. 2038 (1995); G. Orfield and S. E. Eaton, *Dismantling Desegregation: The Quiet Reversal of* Brown v. Board of Education (New York: New Press, 1996).

4. J. Logan, D. Oakley, and J. Stowell, "Resegregation in U.S. Public Schools or White Decline? A Closer Look at Trends in the 1990s," *Children, Youth and Environments*, 16 (2006): 49–68.

5. G. Orfield and J. T. Yun, *Resegregation in American Schools* (Cambridge, MA: The Civil Rights Project at Harvard University, 1999).

6. Logan et al., "Resegregation in U.S. Public Schools or White Decline?"

7. Logan et al., "Resegregation in U.S. Public Schools or White Decline?"

8. S. F. Reardon and J. T. Yun, "Integrating Neighborhoods, Segregating Schools: The Retreat from School Desegregation in the South, 1990–2000," *North Carolina Law Review*, 81 (2003): 1563–96.]

9. Previous studies: Logan et al., "Resegregation in U.S. Public Schools or White Decline?"; Orfield and Lee, *Racial Transformation and the Changing Nature of Segregation*.

10. *Milliken, Governor of Michigan v. Bradley*, 418 U.S. 717 (1974).

11. R. W. Fairlie and A. M. Resch. "Is There 'White Flight' into Private Schools? Evidence from the National Educational Longitudinal Survey," *Review of Economics and Statistics*, 84 (2002): 21–33.

12. Reardon and Yun, "Integrating Neighborhoods, Segregating Schools."

13. Clotfelter et al., "Federal Oversight, Local Control."

14. For more information, see: Common Core of Data, "What Is the CCD?" National Center for Education Statistics, 2008, http://nces.ed.gov/ccd/aboutCCD.asp; Private School Universe Survey, "Overview," National Center for Education Statistics, 2008, http://nces.ed.gov/surveys/pss/index.asp.

15. Although the CCD provides school-level information for a comprehensive list of schools in the United States, information on school-level composition was not collected for all states across every year. There were five states (Missouri, South Dakota, Virginia, Georgia, and Maine) for which the CCD did not collect data on school racial composition in 1990–91. We therefore used data from the nearest year for which information was available: Missouri (1991–92), South Dakota (1992–93), Virginia (1992–93), Georgia (1993–94), and Maine (1993–94). Moreover, data for Tennessee was not collected for most of this decade. Therefore, we used data from 1998–99.

16. U.S. Department of Commerce, "Census of Population and Housing, 1990" [United States]: Summary tape file 1A [computer file]. ICPSR0-9575-v1. Washington, DC: Department of Commerce, Bureau of the Census [producer], 1991. Ann Arbor, MI: Inter-University Consortium for Political and Social Research [distributor], 1999; U.S. Department of Commerce, "Census of population and housing, 2000" [United States]: Summary file 1 [computer file]. ICPSR release. Washington, DC: Department of Commerce, Bureau of the Census [producer], 2001. Ann Arbor, MI: Inter-University Consortium for Political and Social Research [distributor], 2004.

17. The sources used were: Clotfelter et al., "Federal Oversight, Local Control";

B. F. Lutz, *Post* Brown vs. the Board of Education: *The Effects of the End of Court-Ordered Desegregation* (Washington, DC: Divisions of Research and Statistics and Monetary Affairs, Federal Reserve Board, 2005); G. Orfield and C. Lee, *New Faces, Old Patterns? Segregation in the Multiracial South* (Cambridge, MA: The Civil Rights Project at Harvard University, 2005).

18. S. F. Reardon and J. T. Yun, "Suburban Racial Change and Suburban School Segregation, 1987–95," *Sociology of Education*, 74 (2001): 79–101.

19. Reardon and Yun, "Integrating Neighborhoods, Segregating Schools."

20. Orfield and Lee, *Racial Transformation and the Changing Nature of Segregation.*

21. Logan et al., "Resegregation in U.S. Public Schools or White Decline?"

22. Logan et al., "Resegregation in U.S. Public Schools or White Decline?"

23. Tables of these results are available upon request.

24. Reardon and Yun, "Integrating Neighborhoods, Segregating Schools," 1571.

25. Orfield and Lee, *Racial Transformation and the Changing Nature of Segregation.*

26. *Milliken v. Bradley.*

27. The estimation of intercounty segregation includes both uni- and multidistrict counties. This measure was unadjusted because we compare school and residential segregation at the county level, and an accurate account of county-level segregation was needed.

28. Reardon and Yun, "Integrating Neighborhoods, Segregating Schools."

29. Reardon and Yun, "Suburban Racial Change and Suburban School Segregation."

30. Reardon and Yun, "Suburban Racial Change and Suburban School Segregation."

31. Reardon and Yun, "Integrating Neighborhoods, Segregating Schools."

32. Clotfelter et al., "Federal Oversight, Local Control."

33. Reardon and Yun, "Integrating Neighborhoods, Segregating Schools."

34. Fairlie and Resch, "Is There 'White Flight' into Private Schools?"; Reardon and Yun, "Integrating Neighborhoods, Segregating Schools."

35. Reardon and Yun, "Integrating Neighborhoods, Segregating Schools."

36. See Clotfelter et al., "Federal Oversight, Local Control" and Reardon and Yun, "Integrating Neighborhoods, Segregating Schools" versus Orfield and Lee, *New Faces, Old Patterns?*

37. A. Gamoran and B. P. An, "Effects of School Segregation and School Resources in a Changing Policy Context," paper presented to Research Committee 28 on Social Stratification and Mobility, International Sociological Association, Los Angeles, 2005.

38. The same districts were used for comparisons of all racial/ethnic groups. We identified comparable unitary and nonunitary districts using the following selection rules. First, nonunitary districts were in the same state as their matched unitary counterparts. Second, we matched nonunitary and unitary districts based on the diversity of the district as defined in appendix A, number of schools in the district, and district size. Each measure was averaged and taken from years 1987 and 1988. We allowed the measures between nonunitary and unitary districts to differ within 0.70–1.43 in magnitude. If there were no districts within a state that met these criteria, we chose nonunitary districts that most closely matched the unitary district. Third, because there were more nonunitary districts that matched to their unitary equivalents, we weighted the nonunitary districts to provide a 1:1 correspondence to their matched unitary districts.

39. Orfield and Yun, *Resegregation in American Schools*.

40. Reardon and Yun, "Suburban Racial Change and Suburban School Segregation."

41. Orfield and Yun, *Resegregation in American Schools*.

42. Orfield and Lee, *Racial Transformation and the Changing Nature of Segregation*.

43. Orfield and Lee, *Racial Transformation and the Changing Nature of Segregation*.

44. Clotfelter et al., "Federal Oversight, Local Control."

45. Clotfelter et al., "Federal Oversight, Local Control," 381.

46. Clotfelter et al., Clotfelter et al., "Federal Oversight, Local Control."

47. The research reported here was supported by the Institute of Education Sciences, U.S. Department of Education, through Award No. R305 C050055 to the University of Wisconsin–Madison, and by the William T. Grant Foundation. The opinions expressed are those of the authors and do not represent views of the supporting agencies.

Appendix 2A

1. S. F. Reardon, J. T. Yun, and T. M. Eitle, "The Changing Structure of School Segregation: Measurement and Evidence of Multiracial Metropolitan-Area School Segregation, 1989–1995," *Demography*, 37 (2000): 351–64.

CHAPTER THREE: THE POST-*PICS* PICTURE

Welner and Spindler

1. *Parents Involved in Community Schools v. Seattle School District*, 127 S. Ct. 2738, 168 L. Ed. 2d 508 (2007).

2. *Milliken v. Bradley*, 418 U.S. 717 (1974); *Washington v. Davis*, 426 U.S. 229 (1976).

3. R. L. Linn and K. G. Welner, eds., *Race-Conscious Policies for Assigning Students to Schools: Social Science Research and the Supreme Court Cases.* (Washington, DC: National Academy of Education, 2007).

4. G. Orfield and C. M. Lee, *Racial Transformation and the Changing Nature of Segregation* (Cambridge, MA: The Civil Rights Project at Harvard University, 2006), http://www.civilrightsproject.ucla.edu/research/deseg/Racial_Transformation.pdf.

5. L. Darling-Hammond, "New Standards and Old Inequalities: School Reform and the Education of African American Students," *Journal of Negro Education*, 61, no. 3 (2000): 237–49; L. Delpit, *Other People's Children: Cultural Conflict in the Classroom* (New York: New Press, 1996); J. B. Diamond, "Still Separate and Unequal: Examining Race, Opportunity, and School Achievement in 'Integrated' Suburbs," *Journal of Negro Education*, 75, no. 3 (2006): 495–505; J. Lee, "Racial and Ethnic Achievement Gap Trends: Reversing the Progress toward Equality," *Education Researcher*, 31, no. 1 (2002): 3–12; J. Oakes, *Keeping Track: How Schools Structure Inequality*, 2nd ed. (New Haven, CT: Yale University Press, 2005).

6. See Linn and Welner, *Race-Conscious Policies for Assigning Students to Schools*.

7. K. M. Borman, T. McNulty-Eitle, D. Michael, D. J. Eitle, R. Lee, L. Johnson, D. Cobb-Roberts, S. Dorn, and B. Shircliffe, "Accountability in a Post-Desegregation Era: The Continuing Significance of Racial Segregation in Florida's Schools," *American Educational Research Journal*, 41, no. 3 (2004): 605–31; E. A. Hanushek, J. F. Kain, and S. G. Rivkin, "New Evidence about *Brown v. Board of Education*: The Complex Effects of School Racial Composition on Achievement," unpublished manuscript, University of Texas, Dallas, 2006.

8. G. W. Allport, *The Nature of Prejudice* (Boston: Beacon Press, 1954); T. F. Pettigrew and L. R. Tropp, "A Meta-Analytic Test of Intergroup Contact Theory," *Journal of Personality & Social Psychology*, 90 (2006): 751–83.

9. M. P. Dawkins and J. H. Braddock II, "The Continuing Significance of Desegregation: School Racial Composition and African-American Inclusion in American Society," *Journal of Negro Education*, 63, no. 3 (1994): 394–405; M. Kurlaender and J. T. Yun, "Is Diversity a Compelling Educational Interest? Evidence from Louisville," in G. Orfield and

M. Kurlaender, eds., *Diversity Challenged: Evidence on the Impact of Affirmative Action* (Cambridge, MA: Harvard Education Publishing Group, 2001); A. S. Wells and R. L. Crain, "Perpetuation Theory and Long-Term Effects of School Desegregation," *Review of Educational Research*, 64, no. 4 (1994): 531–55.

10. Orfield and Lee, *Racial Transformation and the Changing Nature of Segregation.*

11. S. Fuhrman and M. Lazerson, eds., *The Institutions of American Democracy: The Public Schools* (New York: Oxford University Press, 2005); D. Ravitch, *The Troubled Crusade: American Education, 1945–1980* (New York: Basic Books, 1983).

12. Orfield and Lee, *Racial Transformation and the Changing Nature of Segregation*; M. A. Rebell, "Sleepless after Seattle? There's Still Hope for Equal Educational Opportunity," *Education Week*, February 13, 2008, http://www.edweek.org/ew/articles/2008/02/13/23rebell.h27.html.

13. J. Iceland et al., *Class Differences in African-American Residential Patterns in U.S. Metropolitan Areas: 1990–2000* (Washington, DC: U.S. Census Bureau, 2003); Some urban areas, however, have recently been showing greater white in-migration, while some suburban areas have been experiencing housing patterns resembling past urbanization, apparently connected to the crisis in housing and mortgages. See C. Dougherty, "The End of White Flight," *Wall Street Journal*, July 19, 2008; C. Leinberger, "The Next Slum?" *Atlantic Monthly*, March 2008.

14. See Linn and Welner, *Race-Conscious Policies for Assigning Students to Schools.*

15. *Johnson v. California*, 543 U.S. 499 (2005).

16. *Grutter v. Bollinger*, 539 U.S. 306 (2003); *Parents Involved in Community Schools v. Seattle School District No. 1*, 2007.

17. *Richmond v. J. A. Croson Co.*, 488 U.S. 469 (1989); *Adarand Constructors, Inc. v. Peña*, 515 U.S. 200 (1995); a set-aside reserves a specific percentage of opportunities for members of an underrepresented group.

18. *Hopwood v. Texas*, 78 F.3d 932 (5th Cir. 1996); *Podberesky v. Kirwan*, 956 F.2d 52 (4th Cir. 1994).

19. For example, *Eisenberg v. Montgomery County Public Schools*, 197 F. 3d 123 (4th Cir. 1999); *Tuttle v. Arlington County School Board*, 195 F. 3d 698 (4th Cir. 1999); *Wessmann v. Gittens*, 160 F.3d 790 (1st Cir. 1998).

20. *Wessmann v. Gittens.*

21. *Tuttle v. Arlington County School Board.*

22. *Eisenberg v. Montgomery County Public Schools.*

23. *Brewer v. West Irondequoit Central School District*, 212 F.3d 738 (2d Cir. 2000).

24. *Comfort ex. rel. Newmeyer v. Lynn School Committee*, 418 F.3d 1 (1st Cir. 2005) (en banc).

25. See K. G. Welner, "K–12 Race-Conscious Student Assignment Policies: Law, Social Science, and Diversity," *Review of Educational Research*, 76, no. 3 (2006): 349–82.

26. *Board of Education v. Dowell*, 498 U.S. 237 (1991); *Freeman v. Pitts*, 503 U.S. 467 (1992).

27. See Linn and Welner, *Race-Conscious Policies for Assigning Students to Schools*.

28. *Parents Involved in Community Schools v. Seattle School District No.1*, 426 F.3d 1162 (9th Cir. 2005) (en banc), 1180).

29. Welner, "K–12 Race-conscious Student Assignment Policies."

30. *McFarland v. Jefferson County Public Schools*, 416 F.3d 513 (6th Cir. 2005) (per curiam).

31. *Comfort ex. rel. Newmeyer v. Lynn School Committee; Parents Involved in Community Schools v. Seattle School District* (2005).

32. *McFarland v. Jefferson County Public Schools*, 330 F. Supp. 2d 834 (W.D.Ky. 2004), 859.

33. Welner, "K–12 Race-conscious Student Assignment Policies," 362.

34. *Comfort ex. rel. Newmeyer v. Lynn School Committee*, 18 (footnote omitted).

35. *Grutter v. Bollinger*, 328.

36. *Grutter v. Bollinger*, 331–32.

37. Put another way, in cases where no opinion garners five votes, the opinion that concurs with the judgment on the narrowest grounds is usually regarded as the most important. The most well-known example of this approach was, in fact, *Bakke* (1978), where Justice Lewis Powell's opinion for the Court largely held sway for twenty-five years. *Regents of the University of California v. Bakke*, 438 U.S. 265 (1978).

38. *Parents Involved in Community Schools v. Seattle School District* (2007), 2789–90.

39. *Parents Involved in Community Schools v. Seattle School District* (2007), 2791.

40. *Parents Involved in Community Schools v. Seattle School District* (2007), 2790.

41. A. Bhargava, E. Frankenberg, and C. Q. Le, *Still Looking to the Future: Voluntary K–12 School Integration: A Manual for Parents, Educators and Advo-*

cates (New York: NAACP Legal Defense and Education Fund, Inc. and UCLA, The Civil Rights Project/Proyecto Derechos Civiles, 2008), 29.

42. *Parents Involved in Community Schools v. Seattle School District* (2007), 2792, 2797.
43. Bhargava et al., *Still Looking to the Future.*
44. *Parents Involved in Community Schools v. Seattle School District* (2007), 2792.
45. *Parents Involved in Community Schools v. Seattle School District* (2007), 2792.
46. *Parents Involved in Community Schools v. Seattle School District* (2007), 2793.
47. *Grutter v. Bollinger*, 337.
48. *Parents Involved in Community Schools v. Seattle School District* (2007), 2793; *Grutter v. Bollinger*, 328.
49. J. E. Ryan, "The Supreme Court, 2006 Term: The Supreme Court and Voluntary Integration," *Harvard Law Review*, 121 (2007): 131–57.
50. M. J. Kaufman, "*PICS* in Focus: A Majority of the Supreme Court Reaffirms the Constitutionality of Race-Conscious School Integration Strategies," *Hastings Constitutional Law Quarterly*, 35 (2007): 1–40.
51. Bhargava et al., *Still Looking to the Future*, 29.
52. See Ryan, "The Supreme Court, 2006 Term."
53. Kaufman, "*PICS* in Focus," 13, n. 64 (internal citations omitted).
54. H. K. Gerken, "The Supreme Court, 2006 Term: Comment: Justice Kennedy and the Domains of Equal Protection," *Harvard Law Review*, 121 (2007): 104–30.
55. *Parents Involved in Community Schools v. Seattle School District* (2007), 2792 (internal citation omitted).
56. It is difficult to see, for instance, how the race-based data-collection could mitigate segregation without being able to apply that knowledge in designing race-based policies.
57. C. Gewertz, "Urban Leaders Assess Methods for Integrating Schools," *Education Week*, November 14, 2007, 9; Kaufman, "*PICS* in Focus."
58. Kaufman, "*PICS* in Focus."
59. Kaufman, "*PICS* in Focus."
60. Bhargava et al., *Still Looking to the Future*; W. Taylor and E. Darden, "Guidance to School Boards on Race and Student Assignment," Alexandria, VA: National School Board Association, 2008.
61. See K. C. West, "A Desegregation Tool That Backfired: Magnet Schools and Classroom Segregation," *Yale Law Journal*, 103 (1994): 2567.

62. Bhargava et al., *Still Looking to the Future*; Taylor and Darden, "Guidance to School Boards on Race and Student Assignment."

63. Bhargava et al., *Still Looking to the Future.*

64. Bhargava et al., *Still Looking to the Future.*

65. Bhargava et al., *Still Looking to the Future.*

66. R. Kahlenberg, *Rescuing* Brown v. Board of Education*: Profiles of Twelve School Districts Pursuing Socioeconomic School Integration* (New York: The Century Foundation, 2007); Kaufman, "*PICS* in Focus"; S. F. Reardon, J. T. Yun, and M. Kurlaender, "Implications of Income-Based School Assignment Policies for Racial School Segregation," *Educational Evaluation & Policy Analysis*, 28, no. 1 (2006).

67. R. D. Kahlenberg, *Economic School Integration*, Idea Brief No. 2 (New York: Century Foundation, 2000), http://www.tcf.org/Publications/Education/economicschoolintegration.pdf; Kahlenberg, *Rescuing* Brown v. Board of Education.

68. Kaufman, "*PICS* in Focus"; Reardon et al., "Implications of Income-Based School Assignment Policies."

69. Kaufman, "*PICS* in Focus," 16.

70. *Parents Involved in Community Schools v. Seattle School District* (2007), 2796–97.

71. A. Konz, "Temporary Desegregation Plan Approved," *The Courier-Journal* (Louisville, KY), February 1, 2008a, http://www.courier-journal.com/apps/pbcs.dll/article?AID=/20080201/NEWS01/802010411.

72. Konz, "Temporary Desegregation Plan Approved."

73. Konz, "Temporary Desegregation Plan Approved."

74. A. Konz, "Judge Refuses to Strike Down School Integration Plan," *The Courier-Journal* (Louisville, KY), March 12, 2008b, http://www.courier-journal.com/apps/pbcs.dll/article?AID=2008803121032.

75. E. Bazelon, "The Next Kind Of Integration," *The New York Times Magazine*, July 20, 2008, http://www.nytimes.com/2008/07/20/magazine/20integration-t.html.

76. A. Konz and C. Kenning, "Jefferson Wants Income, Race, Education as Criteria," *The Courier-Journal* (Louisville, KY), January 29, 2008.

77. Ryan, "The Supreme Court, 2006 Term."

78. Ryan, "The Supreme Court, 2006 Term," 148.

79. J. Tucker, "How High Court Ruling Will Affect Schools in S.F.," *San Francisco Chronicle*, June 29, 2007.

80. J. D. Glater and A. Finder, "School Diversity Based on Income Segregates Some," *The New York Times*, July 15, 2007.

81. As cited in Tucker, "How High Court Ruling Will Affect Schools in S.F."

82. *Parents Involved in Community Schools v. Seattle School District* (2007), 2797.

83. See *Parents Involved in Community Schools v. Seattle School District*, 2792.

84. School districts might also identify other compelling interests that could be furthered by a race-conscious student assignment policy, or they might define more precisely the benefits to be achieved by mitigating racial isolation. Michael Kaufman, for example, argues that school districts can or should have a compelling interest in teaching "racial literacy" (see Kaufman, "*PICS* in Focus," page 18, for an exposition of this concept).

85. *Parents Involved in Community Schools v. Seattle School District* (2007), 2792.

86. Ryan, "The Supreme Court, 2006 Term," 138.

87. Ryan, "The Supreme Court, 2006 Term."

88. M. C. Nussbaum, "The Supreme Court, 2006 Term: Foreword: Constitutions and Capabilities: "Perception" against Lofty Formalism," *Harvard Law Review*, 121 (2007): 4–97.

89. *Parents Involved in Community Schools v. Seattle School District* (2007), 2797.

90. See discussion in Nussbaum, "Constitutions and Capabilities"; Ryan, "The Supreme Court, 2006 Term."

91. See Ryan, "The Supreme Court, 2006 Term."

92. Gerken, "Justice Kennedy and the Domains of Equal Protection"; Ryan, "The Supreme Court, 2006 Term"; Bhargava et al., *Still Looking to the Future*.

93. Ryan, "The Supreme Court, 2006 Term," 139.

94. Bhargava et al., *Still Looking to the Future*; E. Heffter, "Some New Diversity Strategies Take Shape," *The Seattle Times*, June 29, 2007, http://seattletimes.nwsource.com/html/localnews/2003767422_tiebreakernext29m.html.

95. Bhargava et al., *Still Looking to the Future*.

96. *Parents Involved in Community Schools v. Seattle School District* (2007), 2791.

97. Nussbaum, "Constitutions and Capabilities," 93.

98. *Parents Involved in Community Schools v. Seattle School District* (2007), 2797.

99. Welner, "K–12 Race-conscious Student Assignment Policies."

100. *Parents Involved in Community Schools v. Seattle School District* (2007), 2768.

CHAPTER FOUR: EQUAL EDUCATIONAL OPPORTUNITY, SCHOOL REFORM, AND THE COURTS

Koski and Oakes

1. N. Glazer, "Towards an Imperial Judiciary?" *The Public Interest* (Fall 1975): 104–23; L. Graglia, *Disaster by Decree: The Supreme Court Decisions on Race and Schools* (Ithaca, NY: Cornell University Press, 1976); J. C. Yoo, "Who Measures the Chancellor's Foot? The Inherent Remedial Authority of the Federal Courts," *California Law Review*, 84 (1996): 1121–77.
2. J. L. Hochschild, *The New American Dilemma* (New Haven, CT: Yale University Press, 1984); J. S. Liebman, "Implementing *Brown* in the Nineties: Political Reconstruction, Liberal Recollection, and Litigatively Enforced Legislative Reform," *Virginia Law Review*, 76 (1990): 349–424.
3. P. J. Cooper, *Hard Judicial Choices* (New York: Oxford University Press, 1988); H. Kalodner and J. Fishman, eds., *Limits of Justice: The Courts' Role in School Desegregation* (Cambridge, MA: Ballinger, 1978); D. L. Kirp and G. Babcock, "Judge and Company: Court-Appointed Masters, School Desegregation, and Institutional Reform," *Alabama Law Review*, 32 (1981): 313–97; D. L. Kirp, *Just Schools: The Idea of Racial Equality in American Education* (Berkeley: University of California Press, 1982); Note, "Implementation Problems in Institutional Reform Litigation," *Harvard Law Review*, 91 (1977): 428–63; G. N. Rosenberg, *The Hollow Hope: Can Courts Bring About Social Change?* (Chicago: University of Chicago Press, 1991); K. Welner, *Legal Rights, Local Wrongs: When Community Control Collides with Educational Equity* (New York: State University of New York Press, 2001).
4. Rosenberg, *The Hollow Hope*.
5. Rosenberg, *The Hollow Hope*, 13.
6. J. A. Segal and H. J. Spaeth, "The Influence of Stare Decisis on the Votes of United States Supreme Court Justices," *American Journal of Political Science*, 40 (1996): 971–1003.
7. A. Chayes, "The Role of the Judge in Public Law Litigation," *Harvard Law Review*, 89 (1976): 1289–1316; Kalodner and Fishman, *Limits of Justice*; C. S. Diver, "The Judge as Political Power Broker: Superintending Structural Change in Public Institutions," *Virginia Law Review*, 65 (1979): 43–106; Kirp and Babcock, "Judge and Company"; M. G. Starr, "Accommodation

and Accountability: A Strategy for Judicial Enforcement of Institutional Reform Decrees," *Alabama Law Review*, 32 (1981): 399–440; M. A. Rebell and A. R. Block, *Educational Policy Making and the Courts* (Chicago: University of Chicago Press, 1982); M. W. Combs, "The Federal Judiciary and Northern School Desegregation: Judicial Management in Perspective," *Journal of Law and Education*, 13 (1984): 345–401; Rosenberg, *The Hollow Hope*; G. D. Brown, "Binding Advisory Opinions: A Federal Courts Perspective on the State School Finance Decisions," *Boston College Law Review*, 35 (1994): 543–68; Yoo, "Who Measures the Chancellor's Foot?"

8. Rebell and Block, *Educational Policy Making and the Courts.*

9. Diver, "The Judge as Political Power Broker"; Starr, "Accommodation and Accountability"; M. G. Yudof, "Implementation Theories and Desegregation Realities," *Alabama Law Review*, 32 (1981): 441–64.

10. Cooper, *Hard Judicial Choices*; T. Eisenberg and S. C. Yeazell, "The Ordinary and the Extraordinary in Institutional Reform Litigation," *Harvard Law Review*, 93 (1980): 465–517; Kirp and Babcock, "Judge and Company"; Yudof, "Implementation Theories and Desegregation Realities."

11. C. F. Sabel and W. H. Simon, "Destabilization Rights: How Public Law Litigation Succeeds," *Harvard Law Review*, 117 (2004): 1015–1101; J. S. Liebman and C. F. Sabel, "A Public Laboratory Dewey Barely Imagined: The Emerging Model of School Governance and Legal Reform," *Review of Law and Social Change*, 28 (2003): 183–304; see also Welner, *Legal Rights, Local Wrongs; When Community Control Collides with Educational Equity*; J. Oakes, K. Welner, S. Yonezawa, and R. Allen, "Norms and Politics of Equity Minded Change: Researching the 'Zone of Mediation'" in M. Fullan, A. Hargreaves, and A. Lieberman, eds., *International Handbook on Educational Change* (London: Klewer, 1998).

12. Liebman and Sabel, "A Public Laboratory Dewey Barely Imagined," 192.

13. San Jose Unified School District CBEDS Profile, 2006–07.

14. *Diaz v. San Jose Unified School District*, 412 F. Supp. 310 (N.D. Cal. 1976).

15. R. Wise, "A Balance of Races for Schools Here?" *San Jose Mercury and News* (San Jose, CA), October 23, 1966.

16. S. Hanson, "True Integration of City Schools Target of Study," *San Jose Mercury and News* (San Jose, CA), February 4, 1969.

17. Hanson, "True Integration of City Schools.

18. Hanson, "True Integration of City Schools.

19. *Diaz*, 412 F. Supp. 310.

20. "School Busing to Rid Racial Imbalance Opposed," *San Jose Mercury and News* (San Jose, CA), November 28, 1969.

21. "San Jose Unified Recall Looms Over Boardmembers," *San Jose Mercury and News* (San Jose, CA), April 17, 1970.

22. *Diaz*, 412 F. Supp. at 325.

23. J. Frein, "Schools Unvail Anti-Busing Poll," *San Jose Mercury News* (San Jose, CA), August 17, 1974.

24. L. P. Romero, "S. J. Couple Lent Names, Lost Friends Over School Suit," *San Jose Mercury News* (San Jose, CA), May 10, 1985.

25. "School Desegregation Complaint to be Heard Against San Jose," *Palo Alto/Peninsula Times-Tribune* (Palo Alto, CA), November 6, 1971.

26. "Schools Vow Fight," *San Jose Mercury News* (San Jose, CA), December 8, 1971.

27. J. Frein, "Schools Face Busing Threat in Rights Suit," *San Jose Mercury News* (San Jose, CA) July 20, 1974.

28. How "uncontrollable" the residential segregation was is an issue that Legal Aid did not attack. Housing discrimination in the form of low-income housing siting, restrictive covenants, lender red-lining, and zoning gerrymandering had long been practiced in the United States. More specific to this case, officials from the San Jose Unified School District, the City of San Jose, and Santa Clara County met several times in 1970 to discuss the link between residential and school segregation; see "City Hall Meeting on School Building," *San Jose Mercury and News* (San Jose, CA), February 3, 1970. At one such meeting, the officials recognized that residential zoning decisions affected school segregation and that low-income housing projects needed to be spread throughout the county to alleviate ethnic isolation. Whether the district, county, and city followed through on this suggestion is beyond the scope of this chapter, but may have been an issue that Legal Aid missed; an issue that could have paved the way for a *Milliken*-permitted metropolitan remedy that could have resulted in less busing across the length of the long and narrow district.

29. Consistent with the California Supreme Court's 1963 opinion in the Pasadena desegregation case, *Jackson v. Pasadena City School District*, the SBE issued regulations requiring school districts to consider racial balance issues in school attendance zone decisions and later to take steps to alleviate even de facto segregation; see *Jackson v. Pasadena City School District*, 59 Cal. 2d 876 (1963); *Crawford v. Board of Educ. of City of Los Angeles*, 17 Cal. 3d 280 (1976). San Jose largely ignored those regulations and was relieved altogether from complying with them in 1972 when a statewide voter initiative repealed the SBE's integration regulations; see *Diaz*, 412 F. Supp. 310.

30. *Diaz*, 412 F. Supp. 310.

31. *Diaz*, 412 F. Supp. at 336.

32. *Diaz v. San Jose Unified School District II*, 612 F.2d 411 (9th Cir. 1979).

33. *Diaz*, 612 F.2d at 415.

34. *Diaz v. San Jose Unified School District III*, 518 F. Supp. 622 (N.D. Cal. 1981). It is worth noting that although Peckham asked the lawyers to brief and re-argue the facts of the case in light of the Ninth Circuit opinion and the Ohio cases, Peckham refused to allow Legal Aid to introduce any new evidence of the district's failure to address the racial balance issue since the July 1974 trial.

35. "NAACP: SJ Needs Busing to Achieve School Balance," *San Jose Mercury News* (San Jose, CA), August 6, 1975.

36. D. Brignolo, "New Desegregation Guidelines Give Districts Broad Powers," *San Jose Mercury News* (San Jose, CA), April 17, 1978.

37. D. Brignolo, "SJ Inequality Ruling," *San Jose Mercury News* (San Jose, CA), March 5, 1980.

38. *Diaz v. San Jose Unified School District IV*, 705 F.2d 1129 (9th Cir. 1983).

39. *Diaz v. San Jose Unified School District V*, 733 F.2d 660 (9th Cir. 1984).

40. *Diaz*, 733 F.2d, at 675.

41. "Voluntary Desegregation," *San Jose Mercury News* (San Jose, CA), May 1, 1985.

42. *Diaz v. San Jose Unified School District VI*, 633 F. Supp. 808 (N.D. Cal. 1985).

43. A. Watson, "Cortines Vows to Quit if New Plan Is OK'd," *San Jose Mercury News* (San Jose, CA), November 17, 1985.

44. *Diaz*, 633 F. Supp. at 824.

45. A. Watson, "Desegregation Expert to Monitor S.J. Plan," *San Jose Mercury News* (San Jose, CA), March 13, 1986.

46. A. Watson, "Busing: All Present or Accounted For," *San Jose Mercury News* (San Jose, CA), Sept. 9, 1986.

47. A. Watson, "Desegregation Judge Scolds Schools," *San Jose Mercury News* (San Jose, CA), March 26, 1988.

48. H. Farrell, "Funds OK'd for S.J. Unified Desegregation," *San Jose Mercury News* (San Jose, CA), July 3, 1986.

49. J. Jacobs, "Filing for Deseg Dollars," *San Jose Mercury News* (San Jose, CA), November 22, 1993.

50. P. Yost, "San Jose Schools Refine Their Ethnic Balancing Act," Editorial, *San Jose Mercury News* (San Jose, CA), November 23, 1986.

51. Yost, "San Jose Schools Refine Their Ethnic Balancing Act."

52. A. Watson, "SJ Unified 'White Flight' Put at 3–6%," *San Jose Mercury News* (San Jose, CA), January 15, 1987.

53. A. Watson, "Mixing It Up: SJ Unified Is Integrating Faster Than Expected," *San Jose Mercury News* (San Jose, CA), March 27, 1987

54. A. Watson, "Hispanic Kids Benefit Little from S.J. Unified Integration" *San Jose Mercury News* (San Jose, CA), May 30, 1991; A. Watson, "Equal, but Separate: Five Years of Busing Have Mixed Kids in the Classroom, but They Have Done Little to Bring Their Worlds Together," *San Jose Mercury News* (San Jose, CA), June 2, 1991.

55. *Diaz v. San Jose Unified School District VII*, 861 F.2d 591 (9th Cir. 1988).

56. Watson, "Equal but Separate."

57. J. Oakes, K. Welner, and S. Yonezawa, *Mandating Equity* (Berkeley: California Policy Seminar, 1998); Watson, "Equal but Separate."

58. Watson, "Equal but Separate."

59. Watson, "Equal but Separate."

60. Watson, "Equal but Separate."

61. J. Oakes, *Keeping Track: How Schools Structure Inequality*, 2nd ed. (New Haven, CT: Yale University Press, 2005); A. Watson, "5 Years, $5 Million Fail to Integrate S.J. Schools," *San Jose Mercury News* (San Jose, CA), May 3, 1985; A. Watson, "Judge Scolds S.J. Unified Officials," *San Jose Mercury News* (San Jose, CA), December 13, 1985.

62. A. Watson, "Desegregation Judge Scolds Schools," *San Jose Mercury News* (San Jose, CA), March 26, 1988.

63. Watson, "Desegregation Judge Scolds Schools." The local newspaper similarly responded with an editorial defending the practice of ability grouping: "We see those problems as the result not of racial or ethnic differences, but of income differences that appear as ethnic differences because more minority students come from poor families"; "No News Is Good News. Numbers Are Encouraging on the Desegregation of San Jose Unified Schools," Editorial, *San Jose Mercury News* (San Jose, CA), February 19, 1988.

64. J. Oakes, "Ability Grouping, Tracking, and Within-School Segregation in the San Jose Unified School District," report prepared in conjunction with *Vásquez v. San Jose Unified School District*, No. 71-2130 RMW (N.D. Cal. 1993); Oakes, Welner, and Yonezawa, *Mandating Equity*.

65. A. Watson, "Hispanic Kids Benefit Little from S.J. Unified \ Integration," *San Jose Mercury News* (San Jose, CA), May 30, 1991; A. Watson, "Equal but Separate."

66. M. Guido, "S.J. Unified Settlement Agreement Would Reduce Forced Busing," *San Jose Mercury News* (San Jose, CA), January 15, 1994.

67. Guido, "S.J. Unified Settlement Agreement Would Reduce Forced Busing."

68. L. Murray, personal communication.

69. L. Murray, personal communication.

70. Guido, "S.J. Unified Settlement Agreement Would Reduce Forced Busing."

71. Guido, "S.J. Unified Settlement Agreement Would Reduce Forced Busing."

72. Guido, "S.J. Unified Settlement Agreement Would Reduce Forced Busing."

73. Consent Decree, *Vasquez v. San Jose Unified School District*, No. C-71-2130 RMW (N.D.Cal. 2004), 33.

74. Consent Decree, *Vasquez v. San Jose Unified School District*, 44.

75. L. Murray, personal communication.

76. S. Lubman, "'The Olive Branch Has Been Extended to Me.' S.J. Unified Chief Holds Off Ouster Bid Trustees Drop Resign or Be Fired Ultimatum," *San Jose Mercury News* (San Jose, California), January 25, 1996.

77. Oakes, Welner, and Yonezawa, *Mandating Equity*.

78. Lubman, "S.J. Unified Chief Holds Off Ouster."

79. Stipulation and Order Regarding Student Assignment, *Vasquez v. San Jose Unified School District*, No. 71-2130 RMW (N.D. Cal. Aug. 28, 1996).

80. District administrators predicted that within a few years, eleven of the district's twenty-eight elementary campuses would be more than 70 percent "minority," while five will be more than 90 percent "minority." (Oakes et al., *International Handbook on Educational Change*.)

81. L. Murray, personal communication.

82. M. B. Arias, *Five Year Summative Report for the Years 1986–1990, Vasquez v. San Jose Unified School District*, No. 71-2130 RFP (N.D. Cal. 1991).

83. The district reported that, in February 1997, it had 234 Spanish bilingual classrooms in grades K–5; see San Jose Unified School District, Status Annual Report for the 1996–97 Academic Year, *Vasquez v. San Jose Unified School District*, No. C-71-2130 RMW (N.D. Cal. Feb. 27, 1998).

84. M. B. Arias, "The Impact of Brown on Latinos: A Study of Transformation and Policy Intentions," *Teachers College Record*, 107 (2005): 1994. The board's racial/ethnic composition remained all white until 1992 when one Latino was elected. By 1996, however, the board became majority Latino—three Latinos, two whites.

85. Hon. R. M. Whyte to the parties, *Vasquez v. San Jose Unified School District*, No. C-71-2130 RMW (N.D. Cal. May 13, 2002).

86. L. Slonaker, "Integration Plan OK'd for Schools," *San Jose Mercury News* (San Jose, CA), August 23, 2003.

87. L. Slonaker, "Still Separate but Unequal Three Decades after the S.J. Uni-

fied School District Was Sued for Discrimination, Segregation Is Accepted as a Fact of Life. The Focus Has Switched to Providing Equal Opportunity," *San Jose Mercury News* (San Jose, CA), May 16, 2004.

88. L. Murray, personal communication.

89. Passing all of these courses with a grade of C or better is required for students to be considered for admission at all of California's four-year public universities. Students who received a D grade in one or more courses were still awarded diplomas, as they met the district's graduation requirement of passing those courses.

90. B. Lin, "A Dream Still Being Realized? Using San Jose Unified School District as a Case Study for the Effects of Structural Change on the College-Going Culture of Underrepresented Minorities," unpublished paper, University of California, Berkeley, 2007.

91. D. A. Sylvester, "San Jose Offers Minority Education Overhaul," *San Francisco Chronicle*, January 15, 1994.

CHAPTER FIVE: *SHEFF V. O'NEILL:* Weak Desegregation Remedies and Strong Disincentives in Connecticut

Dougherty, Wanzer, and Ramsay

1. *Missouri v. Jenkins*, 515 U.S. 70 (1995).

2. *Sheff v. O'Neill*, 678 A.2d 1267 (Conn. 1996) [Connecticut Supreme Court decision for plaintiffs, July 9, 1996], 1281.

3. J. L. Hochschild, *The New American Dilemma: Liberal Democracy and School Desegregation* (New Haven, CT: Yale University Press, 1984); C. H. Rossell, *The Carrot or the Stick for School Desegregation Policy: Magnet Schools or Forced Busing* (Philadelphia: Temple University Press, 1990); and D. Armor, *Forced Justice: School Desegregation and the Law* (New York: Oxford University Press, 1995).

4. *Sheff v. O'Neill*, Complaint in Superior Court, Judicial District of Hartford/New Britain, April 26, 1989.

5. Connecticut Department of Education, Public School Enrollment Data, by Race, October 1988 [in author's possession].

6. *Milliken v. Bradley*, 418 U.S. 717 (1974).

7. *Sheff v. O'Neill* 1996, 1274.

8. *Sheff v. O'Neill* 1996, 1289.

9. S. Eaton, *The Children in Room E4: American Education on Trial* (Chapel Hill, NC: Algonquin Books, 2007), 176–81.

10. *Sheff v. O'Neill* 1996, 1290.

11. R. Frahm, "Court Orders Desegregation: Rowland Rules Out Busing, Vows to Keep Local School Control," *The Hartford Courant* (Hartford, CT), July 10, 1996.

12. *An Act Enhancing Educational Choices and Opportunities*, Public Act 97-290, Connecticut General Assembly, June 26, 1997.

13. K. McDermott, G. Bruno, and A. Varghese, "Have Connecticut's Desegregation Policies Produced Desegregation?" *Equity & Excellence in Education*, 35, no. 1 (2002): 21.

14. *An Act Concerning . . . Interdistrict Public School Education Program, etc.*, Public Act 98-168, Connecticut General Assembly, June 4, 1998.

15. G. A. Bruno and K. A. McDermott, "The Unexamined Remedy," (report, Connecticut Center for School Change, Hartford, CT, June 1998); "Beyond the Unexamined Remedy: Moving Toward Quality, Integrated Schools" (report, Connecticut Center for School Change, Hartford, CT, July 2000). [Both documents in possession of the author.]

16. J. Dougherty, J. Wanzer, and C. Ramsay, "Missing the Goal: A Visual Guide to *Sheff vs. O'Neill* School Desegregation" [Plaintiff's exhibit 2 at the *Sheff* 2007 compliance hearing] (Hartford: Cities, Suburbs, and Schools Research Project at Trinity College, 2007), http://www.trincoll.edu/depts/educ/css/research/Sheff_Report_July2006.pdf.

17. *Sheff v. O'Neill*, 45 Conn Sup. 630 (1999) [Connecticut Superior Court decision for defendants, March 3, 1999], 657, 667.

18. *Sheff v. O'Neill*, Motion for Order Regarding Implementation of the Project Choice Program and the Interdistrict Magnet School Program in the Hartford Region, in Superior Court, Judicial District of New Britain, December 28, 2000.

19. *Sheff v. O'Neill*, Stipulation and Order, Superior Court at New Britain, January 22, 2003 [*Sheff I* Remedy].

20. *Approving the Stipulated Settlement Agreement in Sheff v. O'Neill*, Office of Legislative Reference report, House Resolution No. 9, Connecticut General Assembly, January 27, 2003; R. Frahm, "Legislators Approve *Sheff* Settlement," *The Hartford Courant* (Hartford, CT), February 26, 2003.

21. Dougherty et al., "Missing the Goal."

22. *Sheff v. O'Neill* 2003.

23. B. Q. Beaudin, "Interdistrict Magnet Schools and Magnet Programs in Connecticut: An Evaluation Report," (report, Connecticut Department of Education, Division of Evaluation and Research, Harford, CT, n.d.), http://www.sde.ct.gov/sde/lib/sde/PDF/Equity/magnet/cover_exec_toc.pdf, 28.

24. Dougherty et al., "Missing the Goal."

25. Dougherty et al., "Missing the Goal." See also McDermott et. al, "Have Connecticut's Desegregation Policies Produced Desegregation?," 25.

26. Dougherty et al., "Missing the Goal."

27. Dougherty et al., "Missing the Goal."

28. Dougherty et al., "Missing the Goal."

29. Dougherty et al., "Missing the Goal"; in his analysis of 2002–03 enrollment data from the beginning of the *Sheff I* settlement, Leonard Stevens notes that the actual number of Hartford minority students in desegregated settings was 6 percent, lower than the 10 percent official estimate; see L. B. Stevens, "Progress Toward Desegregated Education in Metropolitan Hartford: A Report to the Plaintiffs," March 2004, http://www.naacpldf.org/content/pdf/hartford/Sheff_Report_on_Progress.pdf.

30. This table is drawn from Dougherty et al., "Missing the Goal," revised to correct a small error (five students) in the total number of students, which raised the total meeting the *Sheff* goal from 16.9 percent to 17 percent. Hartford minority students in other public school choice programs are not included in this tabulation, but there were only two charter schools and two vocational-technical schools in metropolitan Hartford at this time.

31. Dougherty et al., "Missing the Goal."

32. *Parents Involved in Community Schools v. Seattle School District No. 1; Meredith v. Jefferson County Board of Education et al.* [Seattle/Louisville case], 551 U.S. (2007).

33. D. Parker, "Impact of the Supreme Court's Decision in Seattle & Louisville" (undated, probably 2007), http://www.sheffmovement.org/news/seattle-louisville.shtml, accessed May 2008.

34. Education Committee, *Public Information Hearing to Review Proposed* Sheff *Settlement*, Connecticut General Assembly, June 20, 2007[a].

35. *Grants for the Operation of Interdistrict Magnet School Programs*, General Statutes of Connecticut, chapter 172, section 10-264L, Supplement 2008[a].

36. R. Frahm, "A Ruling on Race: Court Rejects Diversity Plans; Little Effect Seen in Hartford," *The Hartford Courant* (Hartford, CT), June 29, 2007.

37. *State-Wide Interdistrict Pupil School Attendance Program*, General Statutes of Connecticut, chapter 172, section 10-266aa, Supplement 2008[b].

38. Connecticut Department of Education, *Summary of Open Choice Hartford Students in the Sheff Region, 2006–07 Academic Year* (June 2007) and *Summary of Open Choice Hartford Students in the Greater Hartford Region, 2007–08 Academic Year*, April 2008.

39. NAACP Legal Defense and Educational Fund, Inc., *Still Looking to the Future: Voluntary K–12 School Integration: A Manual for Parents, Educators, and Advocates* (2008).

40. R. Gottlieb Frank, "State Official Says Chronic Shortage of Money Works against 'Open Choice' Program," *The Hartford Courant* (Hartford, CT), November 8, 2007.

41. R. Gottlieb Frank and M. Perez, "Spotty *Sheff* Enforcement," *The Hartford Courant* (Hartford, CT), November 9, 2007.

42. L. B. Stevens, "Progress toward Desegregated Education in Metropolitan Hartford: A Report to the Plaintiffs," March 2004, http://www.naacpldf.org/content/pdf/hartford/Sheff_Report_on_Progress.pdf (see page 15).

43. Dougherty et al., "Missing the Goal."

44. General Statutes of Connecticut 2008a.

45. R. Gottlieb Frank, "A Shift of Views on *Sheff*: Case Returns to Court Amid New Skepticism," *The Hartford Courant* (Hartford, CT), November 5, 2007.

46. The source is the CREC and HPS magnet applicant data collected for the report by Dougherty et al., "Missing the Goal." The combined applicant total is 844, but dataset does not identify applicants who applied to more than one magnet.

47. D. MacDonald, "The Funding of Interdistrict Magnet Schools in Connecticut: A Failed Approach to Address the *Sheff v. O'Neill* Connecticut Supreme Court Ruling?" unpublished paper, Public Policy Studies, Trinity College, 2005, http://www.hartfordinfo.org/issues/wsd/education-funding/Magnet_School_Policy_Analysis.pdf, (see pages 11–12); L. B. Stevens, "Proposed Phase II Plan: *Sheff v O'Neill*," November 2007 [Plaintiff's exhibit 49 at Sheff compliance hearing], http://www.sheffmovement.org/resources.shtml (see page 10).

48. MacDonald, "The Funding of Interdistrict Magnet Schools in Connecticut," 16.

49. E. Frankenberg, *Improving and Expanding Hartford's Project Choice Program* (Washington, DC: Poverty & Race Research Action Council, 2007), http://www.prrac.org/pdf/ProjectChoiceCampaignFinalReport.pdf.

50. Frankenberg, *Improving and Expanding Hartford's Project Choice Program*, 70.

51. General Statutes of Connecticut 2008b.

52. Frankenberg, *Improving and Expanding Hartford's Project Choice Program*, 54.

53. Avon School District, "No Child Left Behind School Report: 2006–07 School

Year," Connecticut State Department of Education, http://www.csde.state. ct.us/public/cedar/nclb/dist_school_nclb_results/2006-07/01_99/04_ avon_district.pdf.

54. Frankenberg, *Improving and Expanding Hartford's Project Choice Program*, 54.

55. Education Committee, *Public Hearing on the Resolution Approving the Settlement Agreement in Sheff v. O'Neill*, Connecticut General Assembly, April 15, 2008.

56. Education Committee, *Public Hearing on the Resolution Approving the Settlement*, 19; Frankenberg, *Improving and Expanding Hartford's Project Choice Program*, 16.

57. Stevens, "Proposed Phase II Plan: *Sheff v. O'Neill*."

58. *Sheff v. O'Neill*, Stipulation and Order, Superior Court at Hartford, May 29, 2007a [initial proposal for *Sheff II* Remedy].

59. Education Committee, *Public Hearing on the Resolution Approving the Settlement*, 15.

60. Education Committee, *Public Hearing on the Resolution Approving the Settlement*, 2.

61. Education Committee, *Public Hearing on the Resolution Approving the Settlement*, 31, 44–45; ConnCAN, "The State of Connecticut Public Education: A 2007 Report Card for Elementary and Middle Schools," http: //www. conncan.org.

62. Education Committee, *Public Informational Forum on the* Sheff v. O'Neill *Stipulated Agreement and Implications of the U.S. Supreme Court Seattle/Louisville Decision for the* Sheff *Case and Other State Programs Regarding Racial Imbalance*, Connecticut General Assembly, July 12, 2007b, 4.

63. Education Committee, *Public Informational Forum on the* Sheff v. O'Neill *Stipulated Agreement*, 14.

64. *Sheff v. O'Neill*, Motion for Order Enforcing Judgment and to Obtain a Court-Ordered Remedy, Superior Court at Hartford, July 5, 2007[b].

65. R. Gottlieb Frank, "A Magnet School Dream Denied: Rules Bar South Windsor Student's Entry to Academy in Hartford," *The Hartford Courant* (Hartford, CT), November 13, 2004.

66. General Statutes of Connecticut 2008b, amended by *An Act Implementing the Provisions of the Budget Concerning Education*, Public Act 07-03, June Special Session, June 25, 2007.

67. In the interest of full disclosure, the lead author of this chapter was called on by the plaintiffs to serve as an expert witness regarding the "Missing the Goal" report at the *Sheff v. O'Neill* compliance hearing in November 2007.

68. *Sheff v. O'Neill*, Compliance Hearing opening arguments and testimony, Superior Court at Hartford, November 2007[c]; R. Gottlieb Frank, "Schools Chief Makes a Pitch: Adamowski Seeks Regional District," *The Hartford Courant* (Hartford, CT), November 15, 2007.

69. R. Gottlieb Frank, "Judge Sends *Sheff* Deal Back," *The Hartford Courant* (Hartford, CT), January 25, 2008.

70. *Sheff v. O'Neill*, Stipulation and Proposed Order, Superior Court at Hartford, April 4, 2008 [revised proposal for *Sheff II* Remedy].

71. *Sheff v. O'Neill* 2008.

72. Approving the Settlement Agreement in *Sheff v. O'Neill*, Fiscal Analysis file 737, House Resolution No. 16, Connecticut General Assembly, April 28, 2008.

73. Education Committee, Approving the Settlement Agreement in *Sheff v. O'Neill*, 2008.

74. C. Poitras and A. Levin Becker, "Sheff Plan Passes Legislative Committee Test," *The Hartford Courant* (Hartford, CT), April 23, 2008; A. Levin Becker, "Another Step in Hartford in *Sheff* Desegregation Case," *The Hartford Courant* (Hartford, CT), June 12, 2008.

75. Gottlieb Frank, "A Shift of Views on *Sheff*."

76. A. Levin Becker, "Hartford Magnet School Eyes Tuition Charges," *The Hartford Courant* (Hartford, CT), May 2, 2008.

77. This chapter was a collaborative effort between faculty and students from the Cities, Suburbs, and Schools research project (http://www.trincoll.edu/depts/educ/css) at Trinity College in Hartford, Connecticut. Jack Dougherty, associate professor of educational studies, took primary responsibility for researching and writing the policy analysis, which drew significantly from the school desegregation data collection and analysis by Jesse Wanzer (Class of 2008) and Christina Ramsay (Class of 2009) in the "Missing the Goal" Sheff progress report of 2007. We appreciate the comments received on earlier drafts of this chapter from Kathryn McDermott and Doug Reed. This interpretation does not necessarily represent the views of anyone other than the authors, who alone are responsible for any errors.

CHAPTER SIX: RESEGREGATION, ACHIEVEMENT, AND THE CHIMERA OF CHOICE IN POST-UNITARY CHARLOTTE-MECKLENBURG SCHOOLS

Mickelson, Smith, Southworth

1. *Swann v. Charlotte-Mecklenburg Board of Education*, 402 U.S. 1 (1971).

2. S. S. Smith, *Boom for Whom? Education Desegregation and Development in*

Charlotte (Albany: State University of New York Press, 2004). The chapter's discussion of CMS history draws heavily from this book.

3. J. Logan, *Resegregation in American Public Schools? Not in the 1990s* (Albany, NY: Lewis Mumford Center for Comparative Urban and Regional Research, 2004), 15.

4. We use the term "voluntarily initiated" rather than "voluntary" because the latter can have two meanings: the origins of a desegregation plan (i.e., court-ordered versus a voluntary district action) or the strategy used to pursue desegregation (e.g., mandatory busing as opposed magnet schools). For additional discussion of the relationship between these two meanings of voluntary, see: S. S. Smith, K. M. Kedrowski, J. M. Ellis, and J. Longshaw, "Your Father Works for My Father: Race, Class, and the Politics of Voluntary Mandated Desegregation," *Teachers College Record*, 110 (2008): 986–1032.

In twin cases involving voluntary desegregation in Seattle and Louisville (*Parents Involved in Community Schools v. Seattle School District No. 1* and *Meredith v. Jefferson County Board of Education*, 2007), a majority of the U.S. Supreme Court affirmed the nation's compelling interest in creating diverse schools and avoiding racially isolated schools. However, it also held that Seattle's and Louisville's particular race-conscious assignment plans were unconstitutional because they were not sufficiently narrowly tailored to satisfy a compelling state interest in the use of an individual student's race in assignment plans.

The Court's decision in these cases is an example of what Smith, Kedrowski, and Ellis have called a new politics of desegregation; see S. S. Smith, K. M. Kedrowski, and J. M. Ellis, "Electoral Structures, Venue Selection, and the (New?) Politics of School Desegregation," *Perspectives on Politics*, 2, no. 4 (2004): 795–801. In contrast to the civil rights era, when federal courts were more receptive to desegregation efforts than were local political arenas, changes in the federal judiciary, the decoupling of policy venues, and developments in local politics have combined to create a situation in which local venues currently tend to be more congenial.

5. We label school years by the calendar year in which they end. For example, 2008 refers to the 2007–08 school year.

6. Data are from the North Carolina Department of Public Instruction's (DPI) online database (http://149.168.35.67/WDS/ReportFolders/ReportFolders.aspx.), which uses only these five categories to report data. In keeping with the way this database reports data and for stylistic convenience, we use "white" as a proxy for "non-Hispanic white," even though the usage conflates ethnicity and race.

7. Four South Carolina school districts also adjoin CMS, but we exclude them to avoid extending the comparison to a different state with a different political culture and education system. Comparisons computed by authors from data obtained from CMS and the North Carolina Department of Public Instruction.

8. R. A. Mickelson and C. A. Ray, "Fear of Falling from Grace: The Middle Class, Downward Mobility, and School Desegregation," Research in Sociology of Education and Socialization, 10 (1994): 207–38.

9. Smith, Boom for Whom? The location of these new schools was a major issue in the reopened Swann litigation because it supported claims that CMS had not done what it was required to do under the original court orders and thus should not be declared unitary. But the courts ultimately rejected that claim.

10. C. A. Ray and R. A. Mickelson, "Restructuring Students for Restructured Work: The Economy, School Reform, and Noncollege-bound Youth," Sociology of Education, 66 (1993): 1–23.

11. Smith, Boom for Whom? 189. At best, the superintendent's comment was naive; at worst, disingenuous. He had previously hired Professor Gary Natriello to consult with CMS about high-poverty schools. At a September 28, 1999, televised meeting of the board, Natriello warned that concentrating low-income children in the same school made it extremely difficult and expensive to educate them [videotape of school board meeting in authors' possession].

12. The history of school desegregation—perhaps most famously in the Supreme Court's decision in Milliken II—is filled with occasions where desegregation proponents have been asked, pressured, told, and/or ordered to forsake desegregation in exchange for additional resources for segregated schools. The history of such quid pro quos indicates that they have been unsuccessful in addressing the goals of desegregation. Atlanta is one of the best-known examples of this lack of success. See G. Orfield and C. Askinaze, The Closing Door (Chicago: University of Chicago Press, 1993).

13. CMS EPII schools were later renamed Priority schools and, more recently, Focus schools. Events in CMS regarding post-unitary efforts to make high-poverty, minority-concentrated schools more equitable parallel those in another southern city that directed more resources to resegregated schools with high concentrations of poor students. As Phillips found in that city, such programs may have positive effects on the outcomes of students who attend them, but they do not completely medi-

ate the effects of the concentrated poverty and racial isolation of schools' neighborhoods. See K. Phillips, "Concentrated Poverty and Full-Service Schools: Mediating the Effects of Disadvantaged Neighborhoods on Student Participation and Engagement in School," paper presented at the annual meeting of the American Educational Research Association, New York, March 2008.

14. Charlotte-Mecklenburg Schools, Board Resolution, Charlotte, North Carolina, April 3, 2001.

15. North Carolina's ABCs of Public Education and the No Child Left Behind Act also allow students meeting these criteria to opt out of their low-performing schools.

16. E. Beshears, "Talk Builds of School Split for N. Meck—400 People Meet in Church and Are Asked to Sign Petition," *Charlotte Observer* (Charlotte, NC), February 18, 2005.

17. American Institutes for Research, Cross & Joftus, LLC, "Findings and Recommendations of the Citizens' Task Force on Charlotte-Mecklenburg Schools," (report, Foundation for the Carolinas, Charlotte, NC, December 14, 2005).

18. Since 1995, the CMS school board has been a hybrid, with three members elected at large from the entire county and six members elected from single-member districts. Members serve for four years, and elections are staggered so that the three at-large seats are on the ballot in one election (e.g., 2003 and 2007) and the six district seats are on the ballot two years later (e.g., 2005 and 2009). The boundaries of the six single-member districts are drawn so as to facilitate the election of blacks from two of the districts, and the 2009 school board election, like every election for districts since 1995, will almost certainly have black candidates for at least those two seats. Before 1995, all board members were elected at large and elections occurred every two years. There were thus a total of sixteen at-large elections from 1970 to 2007. With the exception of 2007, all of these elections had at least one black candidate on the ballot and frequently more than one. It thus seems safe to conclude that the 2007 election was characterized by significant black political demobilization in regard to school board politics. That black demobilization, combined with the intense mobilization of whites in outlying areas of the county, helps explain why CMS has recently been less responsive to blacks' political demands than in the past. For additional discussion of recent school board elections, see S. S. Smith, "Development and the Politics of School Desegregation and Resegregation," in H. Smith and W. Graves, eds., *Globalizing Charlotte: The*

Evolution of a Contemporary "New South" City (Athens: University of Georgia Press, 2009).

19. Overutilized schools have more students than their physical plants were designed to serve, necessitating the use of nonclassroom space, such as art or music rooms, for classrooms and the widespread use of mobile classroom units. Schools with underutilized seating capacity have fewer students than their physical plants were designed to serve.

20. Until the FCP was implemented, a number of inner-city schools were magnet or partial-magnet schools whose enhanced curricula attracted suburban students who preferred them to their assigned school. Once seats in neighborhood schools were guaranteed under the FCP, large numbers of white suburban students abandoned inner-city magnets for their neighborhood schools, leaving the inner-city schools underenrolled.

21. The meaning of "racially imbalanced" is not fixed. Historically, CMS schools that exceeded 15 percent of the district's black population were considered imbalanced black. Clearly, with the growth of the Hispanic and Asian population, using the district's black population to calculate racial balance makes no sense. Here we calculated imbalance summing black, Asian, Hispanics, and other ethnic minority students into one "minority" category.

22. R. A. Mickelson and S. Southworth, "When Opting Out Is Not a Choice: Implications for NCLB's Transfer Option from Charlotte, NC," *Equity and Excellence in Education*, 38 (2005): 249–63.

23. Consistent with North Carolina's New ABCs of Public Education framework, student achievement in grades three through eight is assessed by annual End-of-Grade (EOG) tests in reading, mathematics, and writing; see North Carolina Department of Public Instruction (NCDPI), *Evolution of the ABCs* (Raleigh, NC: Division of Accountability Services, 2004). High school students' achievement is assessed by End-of-Course (EOC) tests in several mandated subjects. EOG and EOC tests are aligned with the state's curricular standards in the tested subjects. Students' scale scores on EOG and EOC tests are rated at 4 if they exceed proficiency, 3 if they are proficient, 2 if their test performance is below proficiency, and 1 if their performance is not proficient. See "Determining Composite scores in the ABCs model revised," (report, North Carolina Department of Public Instruction, 2004), www.ncpublicschools.org/docs/accountability/reporting/2004memo/composite04.pdf, 10. According to the NCDPI website, subject-area tests, ranges of scores on tests, and proficiency cutoff levels for each new

test vary across the years this chapter covers (2002 through 2007). The use of new standardized tests requires the constant renorming of EOG and EOC tests and the development of new proficiency level cutoff scores. This series of new tests, norms, and proficiency levels makes it difficult to monitor overall change in proficiency levels by schools across time because scale scores cannot be compared between different tests. For these reasons, the chapter primarily offers cross-sectional data on student outcomes.

24. A. D. Helms, "Parents in Dark on 'Out' Choice," *Charlotte Observer* (Charlotte, NC), January 28, 2003.

25. A. D. Helms, "Only 658 of 8,200 Take CMS Transfers," *Charlotte Observer* (Charlotte, NC), August 24, 2004; P. Smolowitz, "Last Minute Transfers Leave Schools in Limbo," *Charlotte Observer* (Charlotte, NC), September 9, 2004.

26. Smolowitz, "Last Minute Transfers Leave Schools in Limbo."

27. A. D. Helms, "Parents in Dark"; A. D. Helms, "Only 658 of 8,200 take CMS transfers"; Smolowitz, "Last Minute Transfers Leave Schools in Limbo."

28. A. D. Helms, "In Demand Schools Shut Choice Door," *Charlotte Observer* (Charlotte, NC), March 23, 2003.

29. M. Glod, "High Achievement Leaving Schools Behind," *Washington Post*, November 10, 2004.

30. Computations based on data from Charlotte-Mecklenburg Schools, *Open Seat Option 2007–2008*, http://www.cms.k12.nc.us/studentassignment07-08/information/PDF/NewChoiceForm2007-08OpenSeat.pdf.

31. A. D. Helms, "Becoats Resigns from CMS," *Charlotte Observer* (Charlotte, NC), January 29, 2004.

32. Charlotte-Mecklenburg Schools, *Strategic Plan 2010: Educating Students to Compete Locally, Nationally, and Internationally* (Charlotte, NC: Author, 2006), 7; P. Smolowitz, "CMS Board Backs New Focus. Approval Expected for Mission Emphasizing Academic Achievement," *Charlotte Observer* (Charlotte, NC), January 26, 2006.

33. There is a wide range of opinion about what constitutes "high" or "low" levels of racial balance, but a good working definition comes from the national database on racial balance in districts that is currently maintained at Brown University's American Communities Project: "A value of 60 (or above) is considered very high . . . values of 40 or 50 are usually considered a moderate level of segregation, and values of 30 or below are considered to be fairly low"; see http://www.s4.brown.edu/schoolsegregation/index.htm.

34. C. Clotfelter, H. F. Ladd, and J. L. Vigdor, "School Segregation under Color-Blind Jurisprudence: The Case of North Carolina," Working Paper Series SAN 08–02, Terry Sanford Institute of Public Policy, Duke University, 2008.

35. Clotfelter et al., "School Segregation under Color-Blind Jurisprudence"; R. A. Mickelson, "Subverting *Swann*: First- and Second-Generation Segregation in the Charlotte-Mecklenburg Schools," *American Educational Research Journal*, 38 (2001): 215–52.

36. We believed collapsing the three alternative high schools into the same category as the comprehensive high schools with between 56 percent and 76 percent poverty would mask important distinctions between the two types of schools and needlessly distort the reported mean achievement in the high-poverty school category. Consequently, we added a fourth category for our high school analysis.

37. Our data sources include the NCDPI Public Use Files, available from the NCDPI website, http://www.ncpublicschools.org/, the North Carolina Educational Research Data Center at Duke University, http://www.childandfamilypolicy.duke.edu/ep/nceddatacenter/data.html, and the Charlotte-Mecklenburg Schools, www.cms.k12.nc.us/.

38. The composite of EOC tests was computed from ninth-grade Algebra I and tenth-grade writing scores. The composite score data were taken from NCDPI Assessment Team Reports that investigated these high schools as part of the state's evaluation of all failing high schools. Our comparisons rely on data in the Rebuttal Report critiquing NCDPI's Assessment Team Reports on the failing high schools. K. Godwin and R. A. Mickelson, *Analysis and Critique of NDCPI Assessment Team Reports: Consultant Report to the North Carolina Center for Civil Rights* (Chapel Hill: University of North Carolina at Chapel Hill Law School, 2006). The NCDPI's reports do not discuss all CMS high schools.

39. 39.Clotfelter et al., "School Segregation under Color-Blind Jurisprudence"; H. Lankford, S. Loeb, and J. Wyckoff, "Teacher Sorting and The Plight of Urban Schools: A Descriptive Analysis," *Educational Evaluation and Policy Analysis*, 24 (2002): 37–62.

40. Clotfelter et al., "School Segregation under Color-Blind Jurisprudence."

41. C. Swanson, "Cities in Crisis: A Special Analytic Report on High School Graduation," Editorial Projects in Education Research Center, 2008, http://www.americaspromise.org/uploadedFiles/AmericasPromiseAlliance/Dropout_Crisis/SWANSONCitiesInCrisis040108.pdf.

42. A. D. Helms, "CMS Dropouts Surge," *Charlotte Observer* (Charlotte, NC), February 8, 2008.

43. Editorial, "CMS Grads Rake in Awards," *Charlotte Observer* (Charlotte, NC), July 14, 2007; "The Top of The Class," *Newsweek*, May 28, 2007; Smolowitz, "Last Minute Transfers Leave Schools in Limbo"; B. Schiffman, "The Best Education in the Biggest Cities," *Forbes*, February 13, 2004, http://www.forbes.com/2004/02/13/cx_bs_0213home.html; S. Lyttle, "Educators Honor CMS Middle Schools," *Charlotte Observer* (Charlotte, NC), March 5, 2005; S. Lyttle, "130 CMS Teachers Earn Certification—Charlotte-Mecklenburg Now Has 516 Who Are Board Certified," *Charlotte Observer* (Charlotte, NC), January 1,2003; "2003–04 Record: Highs and Lows," *Charlotte Observer* (Charlotte, NC), August 1, 2004.

44. A. D. Helms, "High Poverty; High Achievement," *Charlotte Observer* (Charlotte, NC), January 9, 2008.

45. All three authors' children graduated from or currently attend CMS schools.

46. A. D. Helms, "Hiring Still Lags at Poor Schools," *Charlotte Observer* (Charlotte, NC), January 23, 2008.

47. A. D. Helms, "CMS May Go Beyond Moving Teachers," *Charlotte Observer* (Charlotte, NC), January 25, 2008.

48. A. D. Helms, "Gorman Cuts Plan to Shuffle Teachers," *Charlotte Observer* (Charlotte, NC), January 31, 2008.

49. A. D. Helms, "7 Struggling Schools Gain 20 Top Teachers," *Charlotte Observer* (Charlotte, NC), August 5, 2008.

50. K. J. Meier, P. D. McClain, J. L. Polinard, and R. D. Wrinkle, "Divided or Together: Conflict and Cooperation between African Americans and Latinos," *Political Research Quarterly*, 57 (2004): 399–409.

51. R. A. Mickelson, S. Southworth, and M. Bottia, "School Choice and Segregation by Race, Class, and Ability," in G. Miron and K. Welner, eds., "School Choice: Evidence and Recommendations," Great Lakes Center for Education Research and Practice, 2008, http://www.greatlakescenter.org.

CHAPTER SEVEN: NEIGHBORHOOD SCHOOLS IN THE AFTERMATH OF COURT-ENDED BUSING

Smrekar and Goldring

1. U. Bronfenbrenner, *The Ecology of Human Development* (Cambridge, MA: Harvard University Press, 1979).

2. Metropolitan Nashville Public Schools, School Board Minutes, January 28, 1998, and June 23, 1998.

3. L. Hertert, "Resource Allocation Patterns in Public Education: An Analysis of School-Level Equity in California," unpublished dissertation, University

of Southern California, 1993; J. Necochea and Z. Cline, "A Case Study Analysis of Within District School Funding Inequities," *Equity and Excellence in Education*, 29, no. 2 (1996): 69–77; L. Picus, "Estimating the Determinants of Pupil/Teacher Ratio: Evidence from the Schools and Staffing Survey," *Educational Considerations*, 21, no. 2 (1994): 44–55; P. C. Sexton, *Education and Income: Inequalities of Opportunity in Our Public Schools* (New York: Viking Press, 1961).

4. D. Card, and A. Krueger, "School Resources and Student Outcomes: An Overview of the Literature and New Evidence from North and South Carolina," working paper-5708, National Bureau of Economic Research, 1996, 18.

5. C. Shaw and H. McKay, *Juvenile Delinquency and Urban Areas* (Chicago: University of Chicago Press, 1942); C. Shaw and H. McKay, *Juvenile Delinquency and Urban Areas. A Study of Rates of Delinquency in Relation to Differential Characteristics of Local Communities American Cities* (Chicago: University of Chicago Press, 1969).

6. W. J. Wilson, *The Truly Disadvantaged* (Chicago: University of Chicago Press, 1987).

7. K. L. Alexander and D. R. Entwisle, "Schools and Children at Risk," in A. Booth and J. Dunn, eds., *Family-School Links* (Mahwah, NJ: Lawrence Erlbaum, 1996); G. Natriello, E. McDill, and A. M. Pallas, *Schooling Disadvantaged Children* (New York: Teachers College Press, 1990).

8. L. B. Schorr, *Common Purpose* (New York: Doubleday, 1997).

9. Wilson, *The Truly Disadvantaged*.

10. F. Furstenberg, "How Families Manage Risk and Opportunities in Dangerous Neighborhoods," in W. J. Wilson, ed., *Sociology and the Public Agenda* (Newbury Park, CA: Sage Publications, 1995): 231–57.

11. D. Massey and N. Denton, *American Apartheid: Segregation and the Making of the Underclass* (Cambridge, MA: Harvard University Press, 1993); Wilson, *The Truly Disadvantaged*.

12. A. Booth and J. Dunn, "Preface," in A. Booth and J. Dunn, eds., *Family-School Links* (Mahwah, NJ: Lawrence Erlbaum, 1996); Natriello et al., *Schooling Disadvantaged Children*.

13. T. Schultz, *The Economic Value of Education* (New York: Columbia University Press, 1963).

14. J. S. Coleman, "Families and Schools," *Educational Researcher*, 16 (1987): 36.

15. R. Putnam, "Bowling Alone," *Journal of Democracy*, 6, no. 1 (1995): 65–78.

16. J. Coleman, "Social Capital in the Creation Of Human Capital," *American*

Journal of Sociology, 94 (1988): 95–120; G. Grant, "Fluctuations of Social Capital in an Urban Neighborhood," in D. Ravitch and J. Viterritti, eds., *Making Good Citizens* (New Haven, CT: Yale University Press, 2001), 104.

17. S. B. Heath and M. W. McLaughlin, *Identity and Inner City Youth: Beyond Ethnicity and Gender* (New York: Teachers College Press, 1993); R. Putnam, "Community-Based Social Capital and Educational Performance," in Ravitch and Viterritti, *Making Good Citizens,* 58–95.

18. A. Gamoran, B. An, and C. Smrekar, "We Have So Much and It Still Isn't Enough: School Resources and Student Achievement after Court-Ended School Desegregation," paper presented to the annual meeting of the American Educational Research Association, Montreal, April 2005.

19. Other schools were converted to enhanced option programs during those years as well. In the 1999–2000 school year, the district reopened three schools as enhanced option programs (including Olive); two years later, two more schools were converted to enhanced option status (including Jefferson). In 2003–04, three existing schools were converted to enhanced option programs. In subsequent years, the district launched the last enhanced option school program, making a total of nine in the district.

20. J. C. Baratz, "A Quest for Equal Education Opportunity in a Major Urban School District: The Case of Washington, DC," Committee for Civil Rights Under Law, Washington, DC, 1975; J. Oakes, T. Ormseth, R. M. Bell, and P. Camp, *Multiplying Inequalities: The Effects of Race, Social Class and Tracking on Opportunities to Learn Mathematics and Science* (Santa Monica: RAND, 1990); G. Orfield and H. Mitzel, "The Chicago Study of Access and Choice in Higher Education," Committee on Public Policy Studies, University of Chicago, 1984.

21. M. S. Smith and J. O'Day, "Research into Teaching Quality: Main Findings and Lessons for Appraisal," report prepared for the meeting of the Working Party on the Condition of Teaching, Paris, France, 1988.

22. J. E. Rockoff, "The Impact of Individual Teachers on Student Achievement: Evidence from Panel Data," *American Economic Review,* 94, no. 2 (2004): 247–52; L. Darling-Hammond, "Teacher Quality and Student Achievement: A Review of State Policy Evidence," Center for the Study of Teaching and Policy, University of Washington, 1999.

23. A. J. Wayne and P. Youngs, "Teacher Characteristics and Student Achievement Gains: A Review," *Review of Educational Research,* 73 (2003): 89–122.

24. Tennessee State Department of Education, "2003 State Report Card."

25. Shaw and McKay, *Juvenile Delinquency and Urban Areas*; Wilson, *The Truly Disadvantaged.*

26. F. Furstenberg and M. E. Hughes, "The Influence of Neighborhoods on Children's Development: A Theoretical Perspective and Research Agenda," in J. Brooks-Gunn, G. Duncan, and J. Aber, eds., *Neighborhood Poverty: Context and Consequences for Children*, Vol. 1 and 2 (New York: Russell Sage Foundation, 1997).

27. R. Sampson, "The Neighborhood Context of Investing in Children: Facilitating Mechanisms and Undermining Risks," in S. Danziger and J. Waldfogel, eds., *Securing the Future* (New York: Russell Sage Foundation, 2000).

28. Wilson, *The Truly Disadvantaged*.

29. S. Popkin, B. Katz, M. Cunningham, K. Brown, J. Gustafson, and M. Turner, "A Decade of HOPE VI: Research Findings and Policy Challenges," Urban Institute, 2004, http://www.urban.org/uploadedpdf/411002HOPEVI.pdf.

30. Office of Housing and Urban Development, "HOPE VI Program Authority and Funding History," 2007, http://www.hud.gov/offices/pih/programs/ph/hope6/about/fundinghistory.pdf.

31. U.S. Bureau of the Census, *Census 2000 Tract Data* (Washington, DC: Author, 2002).

32. Per an internal school improvement plan filed with the Metropolitan Nashville Public Schools in 2003.

33. A. S. Bryk, V. E. Lee, and P. B. Holland, *Catholic Schools and the Common Good* (Cambridge, MA: Harvard University Press, 1993); J. Coleman and T. Hoffer, *Public and Private High Schools: The Impact of Communities* (New York: Basic Books, 1987).

34. Furstenberg and Hughes, "The Influence of Neighborhoods on Children's Development"; Wilson, *The Truly Disadvantaged*.

35. M. Wang, G. Haertel, and H. Walberg, "Educational Resilience in Inner Cities," in M. Wang and E. Gordon, eds., *Educational Resilience in Inner-city America: Challenges and Prospects* (Hillsdale, NJ: Lawrence Erlbaum, 1993), 45–72.

36. All of the teachers at Olive are female; about half of the faculty/staff is African American and half is white.

37. These findings are reinforced in responses from our teacher surveys. Enhanced option teachers face institutional fatigue, a decline in the academic press and professional climate over time compared to other teachers in other schools. In addition, teachers in enhanced option schools are much more likely than other teachers to indicate that their school and the neighborhood are not safe.

38. Sampson, "The neighborhood context of investing in children."

39. Coleman, "Families and Schools."

40. Coleman, "Families and Schools."

41. Furstenberg, "How Families Manage Risk and Opportunities in Dangerous Neighborhoods"; Wilson, *The Truly Disadvantaged*.

42. J. Brooks-Gunn, G. Duncan, and J. Aber, eds., *Neighborhood Poverty: Context and Consequences for Children*, Vol. 1 and 2 (New York: Russell Sage Foundation, 1997); Wilson, *The Truly Disadvantaged*.

43. About 60 percent of the faculty/staff are white and about 40 percent are African American. There is one male teacher at Jefferson.

44. U.S. Bureau of the Census, *Census 2000 Tract Data*.

45. M. L. Small and K. Newman, "Urban Poverty after *The Truly Disadvantaged*: The Rediscovery of the Family, The Neighborhood, and Culture," *Annual Review of Sociology*, 27 (2001): 23–45.

46. R. Sampson, S. Raudenbush, and F. Earls, "Neighborhoods and Violent Crime: A Multi-Level Study of Collective Efficacy," *Science*, 277 (1997): 918–24; Small and Newman, "Urban Poverty after *The Truly Disadvantaged*."

47. J. Dryfoos, *Full-Service Schooling* (San Francisco: Jossey-Bass, 1994).

48. J. Anyon, *Radical Possibilities* (New York: Routledge, 2005).

49. Brooks-Gunn et al., *Neighborhood Poverty*.

50. Brooks-Gunn et al., *Neighborhood Poverty*.

51. The funding for this research was supported with a generous grant from the W. T. Grant Foundation.

CHAPTER EIGHT: ADMINISTRATIVE DECISIONS AND RACIAL SEGREGATION IN NORTH CAROLINA PUBLIC SCHOOLS

Clotfelter, Ladd, and Vigdor

1. *Parents Involved in Community Schools v. Seattle School District, No. 1*, 127 S.Ct. 2738 (2007).

2. G. Orfield and S. E. Eaton, *Dismantling Desegregation: The Quiet Reversal of* Brown v. Board of Education (New York: The New Press, 1996); J. C. Boger, "Willful Colorblindness: The New Racial Piety and the Resegregation of Public Schools," *North Carolina Law Review*, 78 (September 2000): 1719–96; S. Reber, "Court-Ordered Desegregation: Successes and Failures in Integrating American Schools Since *Brown*," unpublished manuscript, Harvard University, 2002; C. T. Clotfelter, H. F. Ladd, and J. L. Vigdor, "Segregation and Resegregation in North Carolina's Public School Classrooms," *North Carolina Law Review*, 81 (2003): 1464–1511; E. L. Glaeser and J. L. Vigdor, "Racial Segregation: Promising News," in B. Katz and

R. Lang, eds., *Redefining Urban and Suburban America: Evidence from Census 2000*, Vol. 1 (Washington, DC: Brookings Institution Press, 2003), 211–34.

3. E. Frankenberg, C. Lee, and G. Orfield, "A Multiracial Society with Segregated Schools: Are We Losing the Dream?" (Cambridge, MA: The Civil Rights Project at Harvard University, 2003), table 29; Not all studies lead to the conclusion that segregation has increased in recent years. For a discussion, see J. Logan, "Resegregation in American Public Schools? Not in the 1990s," report from Lew Mumford Center for Comparative Urban and Regional Research, University at Albany, State University of New York, April 26, 2004. It is true, however, that no measure of school segregation suggests that it has fallen as rapidly as residential segregation over this time period.

4. D. S. Massey and N. A. Denton, *American Apartheid: Segregation and the Making of the Underclass* (Cambridge, MA: Harvard University Press, 1993); G. J. Borjas, "To Ghetto or Not to Ghetto: Ethnicity and Residential Segregation," *Journal of Urban Economics*, 44 (1998): 228–53; D. M. Cutler, E. L. Glaeser, and J. L. Vigdor. "The Rise and Decline of the American Ghetto," *Journal of Political Economy*, 107 (1999): 455–506; P. Bayer, R. McMillan, and K. Rueben, "What Drives Racial Segregation? Evidence from the San Francisco Bay Area Using Micro-Census Data," mimeograph, Yale University, 2002.

5. U.S. Commission on Civil Rights, "Racial Isolation in the Public Schools," Government Printing Office, Washington, DC, 1967; J. S. Coleman et al., "Trends in School Segregation, 1968–73," paper No. 722-03-01, Urban Institute, Washington, DC, August 1975; R. Farley and A. F. Taeuber, "Racial Segregation in the Public Schools," *American Journal of Sociology*, 79 (1974): 888–905; G. Orfield, "Housing Patterns and Desegregation Policy," in Willis Hawley, ed., *Effective School Desegregation: Equity, Quality, and Feasibility* (New York: Sage Publications, 1981): 185–221; S. G. Rivkin, "Residential Segregation and School Integration," *Sociology of Education*, 67 (October 1994): 279–92; C. T. Clotfelter, "Public School Segregation in Metropolitan Areas," *Land Economics*, 75 (November 1999): 487–504; S. G. Rivkin, "School Desegregation, Academic Attainment, and Earnings," *Journal of Human Resources*, 35 (2000): 333–46; G. Orfield and N. Gordon, "Schools More Separate: Consequences of a Decade of Resegregation," unpublished paper, Harvard University, July 2001; E. A. Hanushek, J. F. Kain, and S. G. Rivkin, "New Evidence about *Brown v. Board of Education*: The Complex Effects of School Racial Composition on Achieve-

ment," working paper #8741, National Bureau of Economic Research, Cambridge, MA, 2002.

6. As in A. Alesina, R. Baqir, and W. Easterly, "Public Goods and Ethnic Divisions," *Quarterly Journal of Economics*, 114 (1999): 1243–84; A. Alesina, E. L. Glaeser, and B. I. Sacerdote, "Why Doesn't the US Have a European-Style Welfare State?" *Brookings Papers on Economic Activity*, 2 (2001): 187–25; M. J. Gugerty and E. Miguel, "Ethnic Diversity, Social Sanctions, and Public Goods in Kenya," unpublished manuscript, University of California, Berkeley, 2002; E. F. P. Luttmer, "Group Loyalty and the Taste for Redistribution," *Journal of Political Economy*, 109 (2001): 500–28; J. L. Vigdor, "Community Composition and Collective Action: Analyzing Initial Mail Response to the 2000 Census," *Review of Economics and Statistics*, 86 (2004): 303–312.

7. G. Orfield, *Public School Desegregation in the United States, 1968–1980* (Washington, DC: Joint Center for Political Studies, 1983).

8. *Board of Education of Oklahoma v. Dowell*, 498 U.S. 237 (1991); *Freeman v. Pitts*, 503 U.S. 467 (1992).

9. Orfield and Eaton, *Dismantling Desegregation*; Boger, "Willful Colorblindness."

10. See, for example, Farley and Taeuber, "Racial Segregation in the Public Schools"; Coleman et al., "Trends in School Segregation, 1968-73"; R. Farley, T. Richards, and C. Wurdock, "School Desegregation and White Flight: An Investigation of Competing Models and their Discrepant Findings," *Sociology of Education*, 53 (July 1980): 123–39; Orfield, "Housing Patterns and Desegregation Policy"; Rivkin, "Residential Segregation and School Integration," 1; Clotfelter, "Public School Segregation in Metropolitan Areas"; Orfield and Gordon, "Schools More Separate."

11. P. R. Morgan and J. M. McPartland, "The Extent of Classroom Segregation within Desegregated Schools," unpublished manuscript, Johns Hopkins University, Center for Social Organization of Schools, August 1981.

12. F. James, "A New Generalized 'Exposure-Based' Segregation Index," *Sociological Methods and Research*, 14 (1986): 301–16; S. F. Reardon, "Methods of Measuring Diversity and Segregation in Multi-Group Populations: With Examples Using Racial School Enrollment Data," unpublished draft, Harvard Graduate School of Education, September 1998.

13. Sometimes denoted $_xP_y$ in the sociological literature, for the exposure of members of group x to members of group y.

14. S. F. Reardon, J. T. Yun, and M. Kurlaender, "Implications of Income-Based School Assignment Policies for Racial School Segregation," *Educational Evaluation and Policy Analysis*, 28 (Spring 2006): 49–75.

15. A. Gamoran, "Access to Excellence: Assignment to Honors English Classes in the Transition from Middle to High School," *Educational Evaluation and Policy Analysis*, 14 (Fall 1992): 185–204; J. Oakes and G. Guiton, "Matchmaking: The Dynamics of High School Tracking Decisions," *American Educational Research Journal*, 32, no. 1 (1995): 3–33.

16. J. Oakes, "Ability Grouping, Tracking and Within-School Segregation in New Castle County Schools," report to the U.S. District Court for the District of Delaware in the case of *Coalition to Save Our Children v. State Board of Education, et al.* December 9, 1994 (corrected January 1, 1995); R. A. Mickelson, "Subverting *Swann*: First- and Second-Generation Segregation in the Charlotte-Mecklenburg Schools," *American Education Research Journal*, 38 (2001): 215–52.

17. K. J. Meier, J. Stewart, and R.E. England, *Race, Class, and Education: The Politics of Second Generation Discrimination* (Madison: University of Wisconsin Press, 1989), 82, 98–99; J. W. Schofield, *Black and White in School: Trust, Tension, or Tolerance* (New York: Praeger, 1982).

18. Table 8.1 and the remainder of statistical evidence shown in this chapter classifies students as either white or nonwhite. The basic insights derived from table 8.1 are also applicable to segregation between whites and blacks, between whites and Hispanics, and between Hispanics and blacks. See Clotfelter et al., "Segregation and Resegregation in North Carolina's Public School Classrooms," for a comparison of calculated indices using alternative racial groupings.

19. For further analysis of school segregation patterns in North Carolina, including statistics for individual large districts and regions of the state, see Clotfelter et al., "Segregation and Resegregation in North Carolina's Public School Classrooms."

20. Morgan and McPartland, "The Extent of Classroom Segregation within Desegregated Schools."

21. In a more realistic model, the ultimate degree of exposure and segregation in a district would depend both on the administrator's policy choices and circumstances beyond the administrator's direct control. Administrators can use policy to influence the decisions made by parents, students, and others, but from the administrative perspective, some degree of noise will tend to create divergence between the intended and realized segregation levels. The model presented in the current paper could be extended to consider the optimization of expected social welfare, incorporating this uncertainty. Such an extension would have little impact on the comparative statistics we derive. The formal model is available from the authors on request.

22. D. S. Massey and Z. L. Hajnal, "The Changing Geographic Structure of

Black-White Segregation in the United States," *Social Science Quarterly*, 76 (September 1995): 539.

23. R. L. Crain et al., *The Politics of School Desegregation: Comparative Case Studies of Community Structure and Policy-Making* (Chicago: Aldine Press, 1968).

24. *Parents Involved in Community Schools v. Seattle School District, No. 1.*

25. In a model where the two groups cared exclusively about segregation and exposure at different levels, administrators would choose corner solutions, perfectly integrating schools, for example, but allowing rampant within-school segregation.

26. Federal courts have paid attention to especially egregious cases of within-school segregation, however. See, for example, *People Who Care v. Rockford Board of Education, School District No. 205*, 111 F.3d 528 (1997).

27. The most obvious policy tool administrators may use to influence segregation is the assignment of students to schools. With detailed panel data on the geographic location of school attendance zone boundaries in each district, we could analyze how administrators changed zone boundaries in response to changes in the racial distribution of the population over time. For a study taking advantage of data on attendance zone boundaries, see S. E. Black, "Do Better Schools Matter? Parental Valuation of Elementary Education," *The Quarterly Journal of Economics*, 114, no. 2 (1999): 577–99.

28. Analogously, administrators can respond to reductions in enrollment by either closing schools or reducing the size of each school.

29. In this analysis, changes in (log) population are equivalent to changes in (log) density, since district boundaries are fixed. There were several school district consolidations in the period under study; for purposes of this analysis, we carried the consolidations backward to keep the number of districts constant over time.

30. The respective cutoff points for the initial year, 1990, are $15,000 and $75,000. The Consumer Price Index rose by roughly one-third between 1989 and 1999.

31. In table 8.6, we provide evidence that tracking does indeed increase classroom segregation.

32. Alesina et al., "Public Goods and Ethnic Divisions"; Vigdor, "Community Composition and Collective Action."

33. In these regressions, the unit of observation is the individual school, while nonwhite share is measured at the district level. Standard errors have been adjusted to reflect the potential correlation of error terms within districts. Schools with exceptionally small enrollment—twenty-three or fewer students, representing the bottom 10 percent of all schools—in the grade of interest are omitted from the sample, since tracking may be

infeasible when enrollment is small. Results are robust to changes in the sample selection criteria.

34. The use of lagged private school market share measures is intended to address the concern that private school enrollment is a function of current policy decisions.

35. V. E. Lee and J. B. Smith, "Effects of High School Restructuring and Size on Early Gains in Achievement and Engagement," *Sociology of Education*, 68 (1995): 241–70; R. B. Pittman and P. Haughwout, "Influence of High School Size on Dropout Rate," *Educational Evaluation and Policy Analysis*, 9 (1987): 337–43; D. N. Figlio and M. E. Page, "School Choice and the Distributional Effects of Ability Tracking: Does Separation Increase Inequality?" *Journal of Urban Economics*, 51 (May 2002): 497–514.

36. One observation is dropped from our fourth- and seventh-grade specifications. In our fourth-grade segregation data, one district (Clay County) is dropped because the entire student body in that grade was white in 2000–01. In our seventh-grade data, one district (Clinton City) is dropped because the entire student body in that grade was nonwhite in 2000–01.

37. Because most of the control variables listed in table 8.5 are measured at the district level, the new estimates effectively give greater weight to districts with a larger number of secondary schools. Standard errors in table 8.5 have been corrected according to the Huber-White procedure to allow for the possibility of correlation in error terms within districts.

38. T. Loveless, *The Tracking Wars* (Washington, DC: Brookings Institution, 1999); Oakes, "Ability Grouping, Tracking and Within-School Segregation in New Castle County Schools"; J. Oakes, "Tracking in Secondary Schools: A Contextual Perspective," *Educational Psychologist*, 22, no.2 (1987): 129–53.

39. For an analysis of recent federal court decisions, see Boger, "Willful Colorblindness."

40. We are grateful to Thomas Ahn, Roger Aliaga, Carrie Ciaccia, and Robert Malme for research assistance, to the North Carolina Education Research Data Center and the North Carolina Department of Public Instruction for providing data, to Robert Cooper, William Spriggs, and seminar participants at Georgia State University and the 2002 APPAM meetings for helpful comments, and to the Spencer Foundation for financial support. The views reflected here are those of the authors and do not necessarily reflect those of any organization. Contact us at Box 90245, Duke University, Durham, North Carolina 27708.

Appendix 8A

1. Enrollment based on activity reports might not exactly match enrollment figures from the independent data source (membership reports) because these surveys were undertaken on different dates in the fall.
2. It could be argued that, owing to the significant number of students for whom English is not the first language, English classes may be subject to more segregation than those of other academic subjects. To explore this possibility, we employed an analogous approach, based on math courses rather than English courses, to calculate segregation within schools. Because it has no effect on the distribution of students across schools, this alternative approach has no effect on between-school segregation. Within-school segregation based on math courses is, however, less than that based on English courses, especially in grade 10, where the alternative approach yields an average index of 0.11 for the state, compared to the basic calculation of 0.15. We continue to use the indices based on English courses because English is required for all students, but we note the difference made by this decision.
3. C. T. Clotfelter, H. F. Ladd, and J. L. Vigdor, "Segregation and Resegregation in North Carolina's Public School Classrooms," *North Carolina Law Review*, 81 (2003): 1464–1511.

CHAPTER NINE: THE END OF *KEYES:* Resegregation Trends and Achievement in Denver Public Schools
Horn and Kurlaender

1. G. Orfield, and S. Eaton, *Dismantling Desegregation: The Quiet Reversal of Brown v. Board of Education* (New York: New Press, 1996).
2. M. Kurlaender and J. Yun, "Is Diversity a Compelling Educational Interest? Evidence from Louisville," in G. Orfield, ed., *Diversity Challenged: Evidence on the Impact of Affirmative Action* (Cambridge, MA: Harvard Education Publishing Group, 2001), 111–42.
3. G. Orfield and J. Yun, *Resegregation in American schools* (Cambridge, MA: The Civil Rights Project at Harvard University, 1999), 4.
4. "Court Oversight of Denver Schools Is Ended," *New York Times*, September 13, 1995.
5. *Parents Involved in Community Schools v. Seattle School District No. 1*, 127 S. Ct. 2738 (2007).
6. *Parents Involved in Community Schools v. Seattle School District No. 1*, 10.
7. R. Crain, "School Integration and Occupational Achievement of Negroes," *American Journal of Sociology*, 75, no. 2 (1970): 593–606; R. L. Crain and R. Mahard, "The Effect of Research Methodology on Desegregation Achieve-

ment Studies: A Meta Analysis," *American Journal of Sociology*, 88, no. 5 (1983): 839–54; J. W. Schofield, "Review of Research on School Desegregation's Impact on Elementary and Secondary School Students," in J. A. Banks and C. A. M. Banks, eds., *Handbook of Research on Multicultural Education* (New York: Simon & Schuster Macmillan, 1995); J. W. Schofield, "Maximizing the Benefits of a Diverse Student Body: Lessons from School Desegregation Research," in Orfield, *Diversity Challenged*, 99–110.

8. Crain and Mahard, "The Effect of Research Methodology on Desegregation Achievement Studies"; Crain and Mahard found that studies using an experimental design with random assignment tended to have stronger treatment effects than studies with a weaker control group, such as white students or achievement-test norms. Moreover, they identified several other methodological problems in much of the desegregation research, mainly that experiencing desegregation (the "treatment" social scientists are measuring) means many different things depending on the context of the school, district, individual, or family options for schooling, etc. These factors are difficult to control for and to compare across a set of studies but are nevertheless critical for understanding the conditions necessary for desegregation benefits to occur.

9. T. Cook, *What Have Black Children Gained Academically From School Integration? Examination Of Meta-Analytic Evidence* (Washington, DC: National Institute of Education, 1984).

10. E. Hanushek, J. Kain, and S. G. Rivkin, "New Evidence about *Brown v. Board of Education*: The Complex Effects of School Racial Composition on Achievement," working paper w8741, National Bureau of Economic Research, 2002, https://www.nber.org/papers/w8741.

11. J. H. Braddock and J. McPartland, "More Evidence on Social-Psychological Processes That Perpetuate Minority Segregation: The Relationship of School Desegregation and Employment Segregation," report no. 338, Johns Hopkins University, Center for Social Organization of Schools, 1983; R. Crain and C. Weisman, *Discrimination, Personality, and Achievement* (New York: Seminar Press, 1972); M. P. Dawkins and J. H. Braddock "The Continuing Significance of Desegregation: School Racial Composition and African-American Inclusion in American Society," *Journal of Negro Education*, 63, no. 3 (1994): 394–405; Schofield, "Review of Research on School Desegregation's Impact on Elementary and Secondary School Students"; W. Trent, "Outcomes of School Desegregation: Findings from Longitudinal Research," *Journal of Negro Education*, 66, no. 3 (1997): 255–57.

12. M. Dawkins, "Black Student's Occupational Expectations: A National

Study of the Impact of School Desegregation," *Urban Education*, 18 (1983): 98; J. W. Hoelter, "Segregation and Rationality in Black Status Aspiration Process," *Sociology of Education*, 55 (1982): 31; Schofield, "Review of Research on School Desegregation's Impact on Elementary and Secondary School Students"; Schofield, "Maximizing the Benefits of a Diverse Student Body."

13. Schofield, "Review of Research on School Desegregation's Impact on Elementary and Secondary School Students."

14. S. A. Wells and R. L. Crain, "Perpetuation Theory and the Long-Term Effects of School Desegregation," *Review of Educational Research*, 64, no. 4 (1994): 531–55.

15. J. Schofield, "Unchartered Territory: Speculations on Some Positive Effects of Desegregation White Students," *Urban Review*, 13, no. 4 (1981): 227–41.

16. M. T. Hallinan, "Classroom Racial Composition and Children's Friendship," *Social Forces*, 61 (1982): 56–72; M. T. Hallinan and S. Smith, "The Effect of Classroom Racial Composition on Students' Interracial Friendliness," *Social Psychology Quarterly*, 48, no. 1 (1985): 3–16; M. Jackman and M. Crane, "Some of My Best Friends Are Black . . . Interracial Friendship and Whites' Attitudes," *Public Opinion Quarterly*, 50 (1986): 459–86.

17. Kurlaender and Yun, "Is Diversity a Compelling Educational Interest?"; M. Kurlaender and J. Yun, "School Racial Composition and Student Outcomes in a Multiracial Society," paper presented at the annual meeting of the American Educational Research Association, Chicago, April 2003.

18. Schofield, "Review of Research on School Desegregation's Impact on Elementary and Secondary School Students"; see also M. B. Arias, "The Context of Education for Hispanic Students: An Overview," *American Journal of Education*, 95, no. 1 (1986): 26–57.

19. R. R. Valencia, ed., *Chicano School Failure and Success: Research and Policy Agendas for the 1990s* (New York: The Falmer Press, 1991).

20. W. D. Hawley, ed., *Effective School Desegregation: Equality, Quality, and Feasibility* (Beverly Hills, CA: Sage Publications, 1981).

21. G. Orfield and C. Lee, Brown *at 50: King's Dream or* Plessy's *Nightmare?* (Cambridge, MA: The Civil Rights Project at Harvard University, 2004).

22. J. J. Fishman and L. Strauss, "Endless Journey: Integration and the Provision of Equal Educational Opportunity in Denver's Public Schools. A Study of *Keyes v. School District No. 1*," *Howard Law Journal*, 32, no. 4 (1989): 627–728.

23. C. Jencks, "Busing: The Supreme Court Goes North," *New York Times*, November 19, 1972, SM40.

24. Fishman and Strauss, "Endless journey."

25. "Denver Districting Is Unconstitutional," *New York Times*, June 23, 1973, 42.

26. "Thousands Are Bused in Denver as School Desegregation Begins," *New York Times*, August 21, 1974, 32.

27. *Keyes v. School District no. 1, Denver, Colorado.* 413 U.S. 189 (1973). Throughout this chapter, the terms "Hispanic" and "Latino" are used interchangeably, as are the terms "black" and "African American." The case had profound implications on the legal consideration of integration in northern cities because it extended the principle of de jure segregation (successfully used in southern cases) to the actions of the school and excluded discussions of de facto segregation conditions that were the typically described conditions in the North; see E. Jenkins, "Race Ruling Called Pattern for the North," *New York Times*, June 23, 1973, 26.

28. D. Lembke, "Denver Busing Case May Set U.S. Pattern," *Los Angeles Times*, March 24, 1974, F1.

29. "Denver Schools Told to Integrate," *New York Times*, April 9, 1974, 28; this plan responded to the rejected district plan that suggested closing twelve schools and merging two high schools.

30. J. Sterba, "Denver School Busing Succeeds: Social Mixture Called a Factor," *New York Times*, October 26, 1974, 34.

31. It should be noted, however, that this process was not totally without resistance. For example, on February 22, 1974, almost half of the Denver Public School students were held out of class for a one-day boycott called by the Citizens Association for Neighborhood Schools (Lembke, "Denver Busing Case May Set U.S. Pattern"). In fact, in September 1974, Judge Doyle went so far as to grant a restraining order to stop the associations from promoting such boycotts; see "U.S. Judge Bars Boycotts of Denver School Busing," *New York Times*, October 11, 1974, 42. Moreover, some white parents did protest forced busing, including holding signs that read, "no one asked us what we want"; arsonists set fire to city school buses, and a bomb was exploded on the porch of Wilfred Keyes, the lead plaintiff in the case. See J. Brooke, "Court Says Denver Can End Forced Busing," *New York Times*, September 17, 1995, 16.

32. Sterba, "Denver School Busing Succeeds."

33. Sterba, "Denver School Busing Succeeds," 34.

34. Sterba, "Denver School Busing Succeeds."

35. C. Lee, *Denver Public Schools: Resegregation, Latino Style* (Cambridge, MA: The Civil Rights Project at Harvard University, 2006).

36. Orfield and Eaton, *Dismantling Desegregation.*

37. R. Pear, "Rights Policy: New Outlook," *New York Times*, December 14, 1981, A21.

38. M. Stevens, "DPS: Integration Order Met: Schools to Ask Court to Stop Its Supervision," *Denver Post*, January 17, 1992, A1.

39. M. Stevens, "DPS Desegregation Trial Scope Debated," *Denver Post*, May 6, 1992, 1B. A unitary school system is one in which the school district has demonstrated to have eliminated a racially segregated dual school system. Courts determine whether a district has established unitary status on the basis of several factors, such as faculty assignment to schools, quality of education, extracurricular activities across different racial/ethnic groups, and other criteria.

40. M. Stevens, "Busing Settlement Rejected," *Denver Post*, May 15, 1993, 1A.

41. As quoted in Brooke, "Court Says Denver Can End Forced Busing," 16.

42. As quoted in "Court Oversight of Denver Schools Is Ended," *New York Times*, September 13, 1995, B7.

43. B. Weberrocky, "Denver Schools Expect New Year to Bring Turmoil as Busing Ends Neighborhood Schools, Budget, Contract Talks to Keep District Hopping," *Rocky Mountain News* (Denver, CO), January 1, 1996, A16.

44. Lee, *Denver Public Schools*; Weberrocky, "Denver Schools Expect New Year to Bring Turmoil."

45. T. R. Witcher, "What Will Happen When Denver's Model of Integration, Manual High, Returns to the Old Days of Segregation?" *Denver Westword*, January 23, 1997.

46. Weberrocky, "Denver Schools Expect New Year to Bring Turmoil."

47. Weberrocky, "Denver Schools Expect New Year to Bring Turmoil."

48. G. Orfield and C. Lee, *Why Segregation Matters: Poverty and Educational Inequality* (Cambridge, MA: The Civil Rights Project at Harvard University, 2005); C. Clotfelter, *After* Brown*: The Rise and Retreat of School Desegregation* (Princeton, NJ: Princeton University Press, 2004).

49. Orfield and Lee, Brown *at 50*.

50. Brooke, "Court Says Denver Can End Forced Busing."

51. Brooke, "Court Says Denver Can End Forced Busing,"; The move to the suburbs was part of a larger metropolitan suburbanization pattern; in the 1990s, the city of Denver "gained about 31,000 people . . . (after having lost residents during the 1980s), but the counties that make up the Denver metropolitan area gained 284,000 people—about nine times as many"; see

B. Katz and J. Bradley, "Divided We Sprawl," *The Atlantic Monthly*, (December 1999): 26–42. In addition, some argue that white departure to the suburbs was also partly an effort to keep students out of perceived struggling urban schools; for example, see O. Gillham, *The Limitless City: A Primer on thw Urban Sprawl Debate* (Washington, DC: Island Press, 2002).

52. Stevens, "DPS: Integration order met"; Lee, *Denver Public Schools*.

53. R. L. Linn and K. G. Welner, eds., *Race-Conscious Policies for Assigning Students to Schools: Social Science Research and the Supreme Court Cases* (Washington, DC: National Academy of Education, 2007).

54. R. B. Kahlenberg, *All Together Now: Creating Middle Class Schools through Public School Choice* (Washington, DC: Brookings Institution Press, 2001); Orfield and Lee, Brown *at 50*.

55. National Center for Education Statistics, "Common Core of Data," U.S. Department of Education, 2004, http://www.nces.ed.gov/ccd/pubschuniv .asp.

56. For the purpose of this study, an elementary school is one with students in grades K–5.

57. Riverside Publishing Company, "Iowa Test of Basic Skills Forms A and B," 2006, http://www.riverpub.com/products/itbs/details.html#levels.

58. "Annual Report on the Colorado Student Assessment Program in Student Performance in Reading Comprehension Third Grade and Reading and Writing Fourth Grade Spring 1998," Colorado Department of Education, 1999.

59. Percentile scores have been transformed into equal-interval normal curve equivalents for all relevant calculations.

60. The values represent Pearson correlation coefficients from a simple bivariate relationship between average school math test scores and percentage white enrollment in a school.

61. Lee, *Denver Public Schools*; Clotfelter, *After* Brown.

62. C. Hendrie, "A Denver High School Reaches Out to the Neighborhood It Lost to Busing," *Education Week*, June 17, 1998.

63. Linn and Welner, *Race-conscious Policies for Assigning Students to Schools*.

64. We are grateful to the Piton Foundation for funding this work. We thank Chungmei Lee for her assistance throughout, Gary Orfield and Alan Gottlieb for their helpful feedback, and Dan Jorgensen and Norman Alerta from the Denver Public Schools for their assistance in helping us obtain the data. Conclusions and mistakes are our own.

CHAPTER TEN: INTEGRATED SCHOOLS, INTEGRATED FUTURES?

Phillips, Rodosky, Muñoz, and Larsen

1. Unless otherwise cited, all historical information regarding the historical context of JCPS comes from D. Young, Y. Jackson, and T. Isaacs, eds. *Annotated Newspaper Clippings: History of Desegregation in Jefferson County* (Louisville, KY: Jefferson County Public Schools Materials Production Department, n.d.).

2. *Parents Involved in Community Schools v. Seattle School District No. 1, et al.*, No. 05-908, 551 U.S. (2007); M. Kurlaender and J. T. Yun, "Is Diversity a Compelling Educational Interest? Evidence from Louisville," in G. Orfield, ed., *Diversity Challenged: Evidence on the Impact of Affirmative Action* (Cambridge, MA: Harvard Education Publishing Group, 2001).

3. *Parents Involved in Community Schools v. Seattle School District.*

4. *Parents Involved in Community Schools v. Seattle School District.*

5. G. Orfield, E. Frankenberg, and L. M. Garces, "Statement of American Social Scientists of Research on School Desegregation to the U.S. Supreme Court in *"Parents v. Seattle School District* and *Meredith v. Jefferson County,"* *The Urban Review*, 40, no. 1 (2008): 96–136.

6. Kurlaender and Yun, "Is Diversity a Compelling Educational Interest?"; T. Wilkerson, *Student Assignment Survey: Summary of Findings* (Louisville, KY: Wilkerson & Associates, 1996).

7. *Parents Involved in Community Schools v. Seattle School District.*

8. L. B. Blackford, "U.S. Supreme Court Strikes Down Plan: Major Shifts Seem Likely in Desegregation Efforts," *Lexington Herald-Leader* (Lexington, KY), June 29, 2007.

9. A. Konz, "JCPS Adopts New Assignment Plan," *Courier-Journal* (Louisville, KY), May 28, 2008.

10. See S. F. Reardon, J. T. Yun, and M. Kurlaender, "Implications of Income-Based School Assignment Policies for Racial School Segregation," *Educational Evaluation and Policy Analysis*, 28, no. 1 (2006): 49–75.

11. R. A. Pride and H. V. May Jr., "Neighborhood Schools Again? Race, Educational Interest, and Traditional Values," *Urban Education*, 34, no. 3 (1999): 389–410; E. Frankenberg, C. Lee, and G. Orfield, *A Multiracial Society with Segregated Schools: Are We Losing the Dream?* (Cambridge, MA: The Civil Rights Project at Harvard University, 2003); E. Frankenberg and C. Lee, *Race in American Public Schools: Rapidly Resegregating School Districts* (Cambridge, MA: The Civil Rights Project at Harvard University, 2002); G.

Orfield and S. E. Eaton, eds., *Dismantling Desegregation: The Quiet Reversal of* Brown v. Board of Education (New York: The New Press, 1996).

12. J. J. Holme, A. S. Wells, and A. T. Revilla, "Learning through Experience: What Graduates Gained by Attending Desegregated High Schools," *Equity and Excellence in Education*, 38 (2005): 14–24; M. Killen and C. Stangor, "Children's Social Reasoning about Inclusion and Exclusion in Gender and Race Peer Group Contexts," *Child Development*, 72, no. 1 (2001): 174–86; H. McGlothlin and M. Killen, "Children's Perceptions of Intergroup and Intragroup Similarity and the Role of Social Experience," *Applied Developmental Psychology*, 26 (2005): 680–98; T. F. Pettigrew and L. R. Tropp, "A Meta-Analytic Test of Intergroup Contact Theory," *Journal of Personality and Social Psychology*, 90, no. 5 (2006): 751–83; J. W. Schofield, "Review of Research on School Desegregation's Impact on Elementary and Secondary Students," in J. A. Banks and C. A. McGee Banks, eds., *Handbook of Research on Multicultural Education* (San Francisco: Jossey-Bass, 1995); A. S. Wells, J. J. Holme, A.T. Revilla, and A. K. Atanda, "A Study of Desegregated High Schools and the Class of 1980 Graduates," 2005, http://faculty.tc.columbia.edu/upload/asw86/ASWells041504.pdf.

13. Wells et al., "A Study of Desegregated High Schools."

14. N. H. St. John, *School Desegregation: Outcomes for Children* (New York: Wiley, 1975).

15. R. L. Crain and R. E. Mahard, "The Effect of Research Methodology on Desegregation-Achievement Studies: A Meta-Analysis," *The American Journal of Sociology*, 88, no. 5 (1983): 839–54.

16. R. K. Godwin, S. M. Leland, A. D. Baxter and S. Southworth, "Sinking *Swann*: Public School Choice and the Resegregation of Charlotte's Public Schools," *Review of Policy Research*, 23, no. 5 (2006): 983–97; P. Gurin, "The Compelling Need for Diversity in Higher Education: Expert Testimony in *Gratz et al. v. Bollinger et al.,*" *Michigan Journal of Race & Law*, 5 (1999): 363–425; D. N. Harris, *Lost Learning, Forgotten Promises: A National Analysis of School Racial Segregation, Student Achievement, and "Controlled Choice" Plans* (Washington, DC: Center for American Progress, 2006); R. A. Mickelson, "Segregation and the SAT," *Ohio State Law Journal*, 67 (2006): 157–99; R. A. Mickelson, "Subverting *Swann*: First- and Second-Generation Segregation in the Charlotte-Mecklenburg Schools," *American Educational Research Journal*, 38, no. 2 (2001): 215–52; R. A. Mickelson and S. Southworth, "When Opting-Out Is Not a Choice: Implications for NCLB from Charlotte, North Carolina," *Equity & Excellence in Education*, 38 (2005): 1–15; Schofield, "Review of Research on School Desegre-

gation's Impact"; J. W. Schofield, "Maximizing the Benefits of Student Diversity: Lessons from School Desegregation Research" in Orfield, *Diversity Challenged*; A. S. Wells and R. L. Crain, "Perpetuation Theory and the Long-Term Effects of School Desegregation," *Review of Educational Research*, 64, no. 4 (1994): 531–55.

17. T. Cook et al., *School Desegregation and Black Achievement* (Washington, DC: U.S. Department of Education, 1984); E. A. Hanushek, J. F. Kain, and S. G. Rivkin, "New Evidence about *Brown v. Board of Education*: The Complex Effects of School Racial Composition on Achievement," working paper, National Bureau of Economic Research, 2002.

18. M. Kurlaender and J. T. Yun, "Measuring School Racial Composition and Student Outcomes in a Multiracial Society," *American Journal of Education*, 113 (2007): 213–42; Schofield, "Maximizing the Benefits of Student Diversity."

19. O. Ashenfelter, W. J. Collins, and A. Yoon, "Evaluating the Importance of *Brown v. Board of Education* in School Equalization, Desegregation, and the Income of African-Americans," working paper, National Bureau of Economic Research, 2006; M. A. Boozer, A. B. Krueger, and S. Wolkon, "Race and School Quality Since *Brown v. Board of Education*," in M. N. Baily and C. Winston, eds., *Brookings Papers on Economic Activity Microeconomics, 1992* (Washington, DC: Brooking Institution Press, 1992), 269–338; M. P. Dawkins and J. H. Braddock, "Continuing Significance of Desegregation: School Racial Composition and African-American Inclusion in American Society," *Journal of Negro Education*, 63, no.3 (1994): 394–405; Wells and Crain, "Perpetuation Theory and the Long-Term Effects of Desegregation"; Am. S. Wells et al., "Brief of Profs. Amy Stuart Wells, Jomills Henry Braddock II, Linda Darling-Hammond, Jay P. Heubert, Jeannie Oakes, and Michael A. Rebell and the Campaign for Educational Equity as *amici curiae* in Support of Respondents," brief for *Parents Involved in Community Schools v. Seattle School District No.1 et al.* (2006).

20. Dawkins and Braddock, "Continuing Significance of Desegregation."

21. Wells and Crain, "Perpetuation Theory and the Long-Term Effects of Desegregation."

22. Wells and Crain, "Perpetuation Theory and the Long-Term Effects of Desegregation"; Dawkins and Braddock, "Continuing Significance of Desegregation"; J. H. Braddock and J. M. McPartland, "Social-Psychological Processes that Perpetuate Racial Segregation: The Relationship Between School and Employment Desegregation," *Journal of Black Studies*, 19, no. 3 (1989): 267–89; A. S. Wells, J. J. Holme, A. T. Revilla, and A. K.

Atanda, "How Desegregation Changed Us: The Effects of Racially Mixed Schools on Students and Society," 2004, http://faculty.tc.columbia.edu/upload/asw86/ASWells041504.pdf; Wells et al., "Brief of Profs."; Holme et al., "Learning through Experience"; Orfield et al., "Statement of American Social Scientists."

23. Braddock and McPartland, "Social-Psychological Processes that Perpetuate Racial Segregation."

24. Holme et al., "Learning through Experience"; Killen and Stangor, "Children's Social Reasoning about Inclusion and Exclusion"; Orfield et al., "Statement of American Social Scientists"; Pettigrew and Tropp, "A Meta-Analytic Test of Intergroup Contact Theory"; Wells et al., "How Desegregation Changed Us."

25. Kurlaender and Yun, "Measuring School Racial Composition and Student Outcomes in a Multiracial Society."

26. Kurlaender and Yun, "Measuring School Racial Composition," 214.

27. Orfield et al., "Statement of American Social Scientists."

28. Wells et al., "How Desegregation Changed Us"; Holme et al., "Learning through Experience"; Wells et al., "Brief of Profs."

29. Wells et al., "A Study of Desegregated High Schools."

30. D. E. Mitchell and M. Batie, "The Contributions of School Desegregation to Housing Integration: Case Studies in Two Large Urban Areas," paper presentation at the annual meeting of the American Educational Research Association, San Francisco, 2006; D. M. Pearce, R. L. Crain, and R. Farley, *Lessons Not Lost: The Effect of School Desegregation on the Rate of Residential Desegregation in Large Central Cities* (Washington, DC: U.S. Department of Education, 1984); S. F. Reardon and J. T. Yun, "Suburban Racial Change and Suburban School Segregation, 1987–95," *Sociology of Education*, 74, no. 2 (2001): 79–101.

31. S. G. Rivkin, "Residential Segregation and School Integration," *Sociology of Education*, 67, no. 4 (1994): 279–92.

32. Crucial to the research questions at hand is the extent to which missing data affected the racial composition of our analytic sample. To identify the extent to which our sample may differ from the population of JCPS students, we compared the racial and social composition of the analytic sample with the district as a whole, all high schools in the district, as well as the graduating class of 1997. The racial composition of our sample is nearly identical to the class of 1997, and all high schools in the district. Our sample does not mirror the racial composition of all students in the district, largely because there are more private school choice options in

Jefferson County at the elementary level than there are for middle and high school students. Our sample is also similar in composition of students who participate in free and reduced-price lunch for the class of 1997 and all high schools in the district. Nevertheless, it is important to note that participation in free and reduced-price lunch tends to be underreported at the high school level. We address this issue in our sample by indicating whether or not a student has ever participated in free or reduced-price lunch while attending a school within the district. Additionally, we examined the race and free- and reduced-price-lunch status of students who dropped out of JCPS during high school. We found that students who dropped out of JCPS during the years of our study reflect the racial and socioeconomic makeup of the high schools in the district. These comparisons demonstrate that our sample accurately represents the population of high school students in JCPS.

33. A census block group (BG) is "a cluster of census blocks having the same first digit of their four-digit identifying numbers within a census tract." See U.S. Bureau of the Census, *Census 2000: Geographic Terms and Concepts*, A–8. In other words, a BG is the smallest geographic area for which economic information is available. A typical BG is about 1,500 people and describes a small geographic area defined by main roads and streets. Census data is made available electronically at the block group level and can be manipulated using Geographical Information Systems (GIS) mapping software. Using block groups allows for the most accurate measures of each former student's residential neighborhood. Much research utilizing census data uses areas defined by zip codes as the basic unit of analysis, which encompass much larger geographic areas. Because I use BGs, my measures are much more precise and more specifically detail the extent to which former JCPS students are exposed to diversity in their neighborhoods. See I. G. Ellen, "Stable Racial Integration in the Contemporary United States: An Empirical Overview," *Journal of Urban Affairs*, 20, no. 1 (1998): 27–42. When using data aggregated at the zip code level, one runs the risk of assuming that a geographic area defined by the zip code is racially diverse when various racial and ethnic groups may actually be isolated in certain geographic areas within the zip code. Within such contexts, a measure of ethnic diversity is less meaningful because it fails to describe the extent to which residents are exposed to neighbors who are racially or ethnically different from themselves.

34. By examining the early decisions former students make about where to live, we fail to examine decisions about where to live that former stu-

dents might make later in their lives. For example, it's possible that former students value the opportunity to live in a diverse neighborhood early in their lives, but they might make different decisions when their ability to purchase larger homes in more expensive neighborhoods increases. Whether or not former students have school-aged children may also impact their decision about which neighborhoods to live in. We are unable to access these possibilities within the scope of our paper, but we agree that these issues are important and should be studied. We also believe that studying former students' early decisions about where to live provides an important benchmark for future studies that make use of similar data to access how former students' residential decisions might change or remain stable over time and how those decisions might be influenced by attending an integrated high school.

35. This measure is also referred to as the Absolute Diversity Index. See M. Y. S. Tam and G. W. Bassett Jr., "Does Diversity Matter? Measuring the Impact of High School Diversity on Freshman GPA," *The Policy Studies Journal*, 32, no. 1 (2004): 129–43.

36. J. L. Vigdor, "Interpreting Ethnic Fragmentation Effects," *Economics Letters*, 75 (2002): 271–76; P. E. Bellair, "Social Interaction and Community Crime: Examining the Importance of Neighbor Networks," *Criminology*, 35 (1997): 677–703; R. J. Sampson and W. B. Groves, "Neighborhood and Delinquency: An Assessment of Contextual Effects," *Criminology*, 24 (1989): 667–99; B. D. Warner and P. Wilcox Rountree, "Local Social Ties in a Community and Crime Model: Questioning the Systemic Nature of Informal Social Control," *Social Problems*, 44 (1997): 520–36; P. Meyer and S. McIntosh, "The USA Today Index of Ethnic Diversity," *Journal of Public Opinion Research*, 38 (1992): 56.

37. W. Easterly and R. Levine, "Africa's Growth Tragedy: Policies and Ethnic Divisions," *Quarterly Journal of Economics*, 112 (1997): 1203–50.

38. No JCPS student lived in a perfectly heterogeneous neighborhood five years after graduation; therefore, no one received the maximum score of 1 on the ethnic fragmentation index.

39. The data provided by the district includes only measures of whether or not a student *participates* in free or reduced-price lunch, as opposed to students who *qualify* for the program. As such, our measure of student poverty is underestimated at the high school level. For example, in 1997, 59 percent of elementary students participated in free or reduced-price lunch, 47 percent of middle school students, and only 33 percent of high school students. To adjust for this under-representation, we ana-

lyzed observations from every year the student was enrolled in JCPS. If a student ever participated in the free- or reduced-price-lunch program, we coded them as participants in our study. We also used all information available for each student in our sample to correctly determine the race and gender of each student. In the case of discrepancies from year to year, we assigned students to the modal category.

40. R. L. Crain and R. E. Mahard, "School Racial Composition and Black College Attendance and Achievement Test Performance," *Sociology of Education*, 51, no. 2 (1978): 81–101.

41. Students who live in the same census block group both during high school and five years after graduation are likely to be students who did not attend college, students who lived at home while obtaining higher education, or students who moved back home after completing a college or vocational degree. In all cases, these students are likely to be systematically different in terms of employment opportunities, financial and social resources, and personal tastes and preferences than students who live outside of the neighborhood they lived in during high school.

42. J. Crane, "Effects of Neighborhoods on Dropping Out of School and Teenage Childbearing," in C. Jencks and P. E. Peterson, eds., *The Urban Underclass* (Washington, DC: Brookings Institution Press, 1991); J. Crane, "The Epidemic Theory of Ghettos and Neighborhood Effects on Dropping Out and Teenage Childbearing," *American Journal of Sociology*, 96, no.5 (1991): 1225–59; J. D. Morenoff and M. Tienda, "Underclass Neighborhoods in Temporal and Ecological Perspective: An Illustration from Chicago," *Annals of the American Academy of Political and Social Science*, 551 (1997): 59–72; C. R. Shaw and H. D. McKay, *Juvenile Delinquency and Urban Areas* (Chicago: University of Chicago Press, 1969).

43. Morenoff and Tienda, "Underclass Neighborhoods in Temporal and Ecological Perspective."

44. W. J. Wilson, *When Work Disappears: The World of the New Urban Poor* (New York: Albert Knopf, 1996).

45. See J. W. Ainsworth, "Why Does It Take a Village? The Mediation of Neighborhood Effects on Educational Achievement," *Social Forces*, 81, no.1 (2002): 117–52.

46. See J. E. Farley, "Residential Interracial Exposure and Isolation Indices: Mean versus Median Indices, and the Difference It Makes," *The Sociological Quarterly*, 46, no.1 (2005): 19–45; P. Kelly and W. Miller, "Assessing Desegregation Efforts: No 'Best Measure'," *Public Administration Review*, 49, no. 5 (1989): 431–37; C. H. Walberg, D. J. Armor, and H. J. Walberg,

School Desegregation in the 21st Century (Westport, CT: Praeger Publishers, 2002).

47. Kelly and Miller, "Assessing Desegregation Efforts."

48. See Ellen, "Stable Racial Integration in the Contemporary United States"; P. Nyden, M. Maly, and J. Lukehart, "The Emergence of Stable Racially and Ethnically Diverse Urban Communities: A Case Study of Nine U.S. Cities," *Housing Policy Debate*, 8, no. 2 (1997): 491–534; J. Saltman, *A Fragile Movement: The Struggle for Neighborhood Stabilization* (New York: Greenwood, 1990).

49. These measures were then checked for accuracy against student aggregates for the same schools in previous years. No discrepancies or anomalies were found. In other words, all school-level characteristics were similar from one year to the next.

50. Frankenberg et al., *A Multiracial Society with Segregated Schools*.

51. One historically black magnet high school slightly exceeds 50 percent black students but is still considered racially heterogeneous (and, therefore, diverse).

52. *Parents Involved in Community Schools v. Seattle School District No. 1*.

53. S. W. Raudenbush and A. S. Bryk, *Hierarchical Linear Models: Applications and Data Analysis Methods* (Thousand Oaks, CA: Sage Publications, 2002).

54. Raudenbush and Bryk, *Hierarchical Linear Models: Applications and Data Analysis Methods*.

55. Independent sample t-tests were used to test the statistical significance of these differences.

56. To test for correlation between the racial diversity of students' schools and neighborhoods, we used the ethnic fragmentation index to measure both school and neighborhood diversity. Once the measures were converted to the same scale, the Pearson Correlation yielded a value of .145, indicating a low level of correlation between the two measures.

57. K. Jost, "Racial Diversity in Public Schools," *CQ Researcher*, 17, no. 32 (2007): 745–68.

58. We also ran models that excluded students who lived in the same neighborhoods during high school and five years after high school. When excluding these students, we found similar results; however, the effect associated with the ethnic diversity of students' high school neighborhoods diminished and the effect associated with the relative diversity of students' schools increased. We report our results on the model including all students in our sample.

59. Effect sizes are determined by multiplying the coefficient by its standard deviation and then dividing the product by the standard deviation of the dependant variable.

60. Values in all figures were calculated using the regression coefficients for the average male, non-free and reduced-price lunch, non-choice students who did not live in their high school neighborhoods five years after graduation. Separate values were calculated for white and black students. Neighborhood and school-level effects were multiplied by their averages (listed in appendix 10A) to measure the experience of the average student.

61. We also ran a model with testing for a possible interaction between the relative diversity of students' schools and the diversity of the neighborhoods they lived in during high school. These interactions did not yield statistically significant results; therefore, we argue that within the context of JCPS, residential diversity and school diversity act additively yet independently of each other in influencing the level of diversity in former students' neighborhoods later in life.

62. Aside from the interaction term specifically designed to test a specific research question, the results between the full model (Model 2) and the interaction model (Model 3) are nearly identical. As such, we report on the findings from the full model.

63. We would extend caution in the interpretation of our results. While we have demonstrated a relationship between the relative integration of students' schools and the ethnic diversity of their residences later in life, this relationship is one of correlation—not necessarily causation. We also cannot report on whether or not these students end up living in more diverse neighborhoods because they are in transition, because they enjoy living in diverse settings, or for other reasons. Research should explore these issues in more depth.

64. Wells et al., " A Study of Desegregated High Schools and the Class of 1980 Graduates."

65. *Parents Involved in Community Schools v. Seattle School District No. 1.*

66. J. R. Feagin and B. M. Barnett, "Success and Failure: How Systemic Racism Trumped the *Brown v. Board of Education* Decision," *University of Illinois Law Review*, 2004, no. 5 (2004): 1099–130; J. R. Logan, B. J. Stults, and R. Farley, "Segregation of Minorities in the Metropolis: Two Decades of Change," *Demography*, 41, no. 1 (2004): 1–22.

67. Reardon, Yun, and Kurlaender, "Implications of Income-Based School Assignment Policies for Racial School Segregation," 68.

68. Reardon et al., "Implications of Income-Based School Assignment Policies for Racial School Segregation."

69. Jost, "Racial Diversity in Public Schools"; R. D. Kahlenberg, *All Together Now: Creating Middle-Class Schools through Public School Choice* (Washington, DC: Brookings Institution Press, 2001).

70. Ellen, "Stable Racial Integration in the Contemporary United States"; R. Farley and W. H. Frey, "Changes in the Segregation of Whites from Blacks During the 1980s: Small Steps Toward a More Integrated Society," *American Sociological Review*, 96, no. 5 (1994): 23–45.

71. See G. Orfield and C. Lee, *Historic Reversals, Accelerating Resegregation, and the Need for New Integration Strategies* (Los Angeles: UCLA, The Civil Rights Project/Proyecto Derechos Civiles, 2007).

CONCLUSION: RACIAL REALITIES ACROSS DIFFERENT PLACES: DUAL DIRECTIONS IN RECOMMITTING TO THE PROMISES OF *BROWN*

Morris

1. Recently in Omaha, Nebraska, legislators passed a law allowing schools to function in a way that would permit schools that are predominantly white, predominantly black, and predominantly Latino. One of the sponsors, Ernie Chambers, who was the only black senator in the state, argued that the schools in Omaha were already segregated because the school district no longer engaged in busing and students attend neighborhood schools that were already racially segregated. This law was challenged by the NAACP as state-sponsored segregation. Moreover, some scholars note that having black-led governments or school systems may not result in an improvement in the conditions for African Americans—particularly those who are lower income; see J. R. Henig, R. C. Hula, M. Orr, and D. Pedescleaux, *The Color of School Reform: Race, Politics, and the Challenge of Urban Education* (Princeton, NJ: Princeton University Press, 1999); A. Reed Jr., "The Black Urban Regime: Structural Origins and Constraints," in M. P. Smith, ed., *Power, Community, and the City: Comparative Urban and Community Research* (New Brunswick, NJ: Transaction, 1988), 138–89; C. N. Stone, *Regime Politics: Governing Atlanta, 1946–1988* (Lawrence: University Press of Kansas, 1989).

2. For example, according to the Pew Wealth Study, the median net wealth of African Americans is $6000, compared to the median net wealth of white households, which is $88,000; see R. Kochhar, *The Wealth of Hispanic Households, 1996 to 2002* (Washington, DC: Pew Hispanic Center,

2004). And, according to William Darity, a professor of African American studies and economics at Duke University, "If African Americans saved all of their income (for a decade)—that is, if we didn't eat, pay any bills, but saved every cent of income, we could not close the wealth gap." See the following article on the Black Commentator.com, "Wealth of a White Nation: Blacks Sink Deeper in Hole," October 21, 2004, http://www. blackcommentator.com/110/110_cover_white_wealth.htm.

3. C. J. Ogletree, *All Deliberate Speed: Reflections on the First Half-Century of* Brown v. Board of Education (New York: W.W. Norton & Company, 2004).

4. V. Dempsey and G. Noblit, "The Demise of Caring in an African American Community: One Consequence of School Desegregation," *The Urban Review*, 25, no. 1 (1993): 47–61; V. G. Morris and C. L. Morris, *The Price They Paid: Desegregation in an African American Community* (New York: Teachers College Press, 2002); V. Siddle Walker, *Their Highest Potential: An African American School Community in the Segregated South* (Chapel Hill: University of North Carolina Press, 1996).

5. K. J. Meier, J. Stewart Jr., and R. E. England, *Race, Class, and Education: The Politics of Second-Generation Discrimination* (Madison: University of Wisconsin Press, 1989); R. A. Mickelson, "Subverting *Swann*: First- and Second-Generation Segregation in the Charlotte-Mecklenburg Schools," *American Educational Research Journal*, 38, no. 2 (2001): 215–52; R. A. Mickelson, "The Incomplete Desegregation of the Charlotte-Mecklenburg Schools and Its Consequences, 1971–2004," in J. C. Boger and G. Orfield, eds., *School Resegregation: Must the South Turn Back?* (Chapel Hill: The University of North Carolina Press, 2005), 87–110; B. D. Tatum, *Why Are All the Black Kids Sitting Together in the Cafeteria? And Other Conversations about Race* (New York: Basic Books, 1997).

6. J. H. Braddock, *Tracking: Implications for African American students* (Baltimore: The Johns Hopkins University, Center for Research on Effective Schooling for Disadvantaged Students, 1989); J. Oakes, *Keeping Track: How Schools Structure Inequality* (New Haven, CT: Yale University Press, 1985); S. R. Lucas, *Tracking Inequality: Stratification and Mobility in American High Schools* (New York: Teachers College Press, 1999); S. R. Lucas and M. Berends, "Race and Track Location in U.S. Public Schools," *Research in Social Stratification and Mobility*, 25 (2007): 269–87; Mickelson, "Subverting *Swann*."

7. D. Y. Ford and J. J. Harris III, *Multicultural Gifted Education* (New York: Teachers College Press, 1999); J. E. Morris, "African-American Students

and Gifted Education: The Politics of Race and Culture," *Roeper Review*, 24, no. 2 (2002): 59–62.

8. J. E. Morris and E. B. Goldring, "Are Magnet Schools More Equitable? An Analysis of the Disciplinary Rates of African-American and White Students in Cincinnati Magnet and Nonmagnet Schools," *Equity & Excellence in Education*, 32, no. 3 (1999): 59–65; C. R. Monroe, "Understanding the Discipline Gap through a Cultural Lens: Implications for the Education of African American Students," *Intercultural Education*, 16, no. 4 (2005): 317–30.

9. A. Ferguson, *Bad Boys: Public Schools in the Making of Black Masculinity* (Ann Arbor: University of Michigan Press, 2000); C. R. Monroe, "Understanding the Discipline Gap through a Cultural Lens: Implications for the Education of African American Students," *Intercultural Education*, 16, no. 4 (2005): 317–30.

10. J. E. Morris, "Race, Ideology, and Research: A Counter-Narrative to the Historical and Contemporary Representation of Predominantly Black Schooling," *Teachers College Record*, 110, no. 4 (2008): 713–32; J. E. Morris, *Paradox, Peril, and Promise: Schooling in Urban Black America* (Teachers College Press, forthcoming).

11. L. Slonaker, "Still Separate but Unequal Three Decades after the S. J. Unified School District Was Sued for Discrimination, Segregation Is Accepted as a Fact of Life: The Focus Has Switched to Providing Equal Opportunity," *San Jose Mercury News* (San Jose, CA), May 16, 2004.

12. D. S. Cecelski, *Along Freedom Road* (Chapel Hill: University of North Carolina Press, 1994).

13. X. Briggs, ed., *The Geography of Opportunity: Race and Housing Choices in Metropolitan America* (Washington, DC: Brookings Institution Press, 2005).

14. Briggs, *The Geography of Opportunity*; J. E. Morris, *Context and Social Setting as Factors in Shaping How Black Students Negotiate Identity and Schooling: A Social Science Memo*, paper presented at workshop sponsored by the American Sociological Association, Washington, DC, June 2006; J. E. Morris and C. R. Monroe, "Why Study the U.S. South? The Nexus of Race and Place in Investigating Black Student Achievement," *Educational Researcher* (in press); J. L. Rury and J. E. Mirel, "The Political Economy of Urban Education," *Review of Research in Education*, 22 (1997): 49–110; W. R. Tate, "Geography of Opportunity": Poverty, Place, and Educational Outcomes," *Educational Researcher*, 37, no. 7 (2008): 397–411; A. S. Wells, *Why Space and Place Matter in Education: Developing a New Understand-*

ing of Separate and Unequal in a Post-Desegregation Era, paper presented to the American Sociological Association, Washington, DC, June 2006; W. J. Wilson, "The Role of the Environment in the Black–White Test Score Gap," in C. Jencks and M. Phillips, eds., *The Black–White Test Score Gap* (Washington, DC: Brookings Institution Press, 1998), 501–10.

15. J. W. Ainsworth, "Why Does It Take a Village? The Mediation of Neighborhood Effects on Educational Achievement," *Social Forces*, 81, no. 1 (2002): 117–52; Briggs, *The Geography of Opportunity*; J. Brooks-Gunn, G. J. Duncan, P. Klebanov, and N. Sealand, "Do Neighborhoods Influence Child and Adolescent Development?" *American Journal of Sociology*, 99 (1993): 353–95; S. Catsambis and A. Beveridge, "Does Neighborhood Matter? Family, Neighborhood, and School Influences on Eighth Grade Mathematics Achievement," *Sociological Focus*, 43 (2001): 435–458; C. L. Garner and S. W. Raudenbush, "Neighborhood Effects on Educational Attainment: A Multilevel Analysis," *Sociology of Education*, 64 (1991): 251–62; J. E. Rosenbaum, S. DeLuca, and T. Tuck, "Crossing Borders and Adapting: Low-Income Black Families in Suburbia," in Briggs, *The Geography of Opportunity*, 150–75.

16. Boger and Orfield, *School Resegregation*.

17. Morris and Monroe, "Why Study the U.S. South?"

18. U.S. Census Bureau. *March 2000 Population Survey* (Washington, DC: Author, 2000); M. Tamman and E. Suggs, "Atlanta Is Top Magnet for Blacks: 460,000 Moved to Area in '90s," *The Atlanta Journal and Constitution*, Stacks, News Section, A1, July 8, 2001.

19. U.S. Census, *March 2000 Population Survey*.

20. J. McKinnon, *The Black Population 2000: Census 2000 Brief* (Washington, DC: U.S. Census Bureau, 2001).

21. U.S. Census Bureau, *Annual Demographic Supplement to the March 2002 Current Population Survey* (Washington, DC: Author, 2002); also see U.S. Census Bureau, *American Housing Survey* (Washington, DC: Author, 2005), table 5-1.

22. J. U. Ogbu, *Minority Education and Caste: The American System in Cross-Cultural Perspective* (New York: Academic Press, 1978).

23. C. T. J. Clotfelter, L. Vigdor, and H. F. Ladd, H. F., "Federal Oversight, Local Control, and the Specter of "Resegregation" in Southern Schools, *American Law and Economics Review*, 8 (2006): 347–89.

24. While most schools that serve low-income and minority students reflect low-academic achievement, some urban schools defy this pattern (see J. E. Morris, "Can Anything Good Come from Nazareth? Race, Class, and Afri-

can-American Schooling and Community in the Urban South and Midwest," *American Educational Research Journal*, 41, no. 1 (2004): 69–112.

25. R. F. Ferguson, *Ed-Excel Assessment of Secondary School Student Culture Tabulations by School District and Race/Ethnicity: Responses from Middle School, Junior High and High School (2000–2001 School Year)* (Cambridge, MA: Harvard University, John F. Kennedy School of Government, Wiener Center for Social Policy, 2002).

26. P. Carter, *Keepin' It Real: School Success beyond Black and White* (New York: Oxford University Press, 2005); S. Fordham, "Racelessness as a Factor in Black Students' School Success: Pragmatic Strategy or Pyrrhic Victory? *Harvard Educational Review*, 5, no. 8 (1988): 54–84; R. G. Fryer, "'Acting White': The Social Price Paid by the Best and Brightest Minority Students," *Education Next*, 6 (2006): 53–59.

27. K. Tyson, W. Darity Jr., and D. Castellino, "It's Not a Black Thing: Understanding the Burden of Acting White and Other Dilemmas of High Achievement," *American Sociological Review*, 70, no. 4 (2005): 582–605.

About the Authors

Brian P. An is a PhD candidate in the department of sociology at the University of Wisconsin–Madison. His research focuses on educational inequality, college access, and college persistence. His dissertation examines the impact of dual enrollment programs on college persistence.

Jomills Henry Braddock II is professor of sociology at the University of Miami. He has written extensively on equal educational opportunity, educational diversity, and the impact of athletics in educational contexts. His work has appeared in journals including *Sociology of Education, Harvard Educational Review, Journal of Social Issues, Journal of Negro Education, Phi Delta Kappan,* and *Review of Research in Education.*

Charles T. Clotfelter is the Z. Smith Reynolds Professor of Public Policy Studies and professor of economics and law at Duke University. His research involves the economics of education, public finance, the economics of gambling and state lotteries, tax policy and charitable behavior, and policies related to the nonprofit sector.

Jack Dougherty is an associate professor and director of the Educational Studies Program at Trinity College in Hartford, Connecticut. He and his undergraduate students have launched the Cities, Suburbs, and Schools Research Project, which investigates how private real estate markets and public school politics shaped metropolitan Hartford during the twentieth century.

Ronald F. Ferguson is faculty director of the Achievement Gap Initiative at Harvard University. An MIT-trained economist, his teaching and research at Harvard's Kennedy School of Government focus on economic development and education. His most recent book is *Toward Excellence with Equity: An Emerging Vision for Closing the Achievement Gap,* from Harvard Education Press.

Adam Gamoran is professor of sociology and educational policy studies at the University of Wisconsin–Madison, and director of the Wisconsin Center for Education Research. His areas of interest include the sociology of education, organizational analysis, social stratification, and resource allocation in school systems.

Ellen Goldring is professor of education policy and leadership at Peabody College, Vanderbilt University, and is an investigator with the National Center on School Choice and The Learning Sciences Institute. Goldring's research focuses on improving schools, with particular attention to educational leadership, and access and equity in schools of choice.

Catherine L. Horn is an assistant professor at the University of Houston. Her work addresses issues related to high-stakes testing, higher education access, affirmative action, and diversity. Horn's publications include coedited special volumes of *Educational Policy* and *Expanding Opportunity in Higher Education* (with P. Gándara and G. Orfield), both of which analyze the educational access and equity crisis in California.

William S. Koski is the Eric and Nancy Wright Professor of Clinical Education, professor of law, and professor of education (by courtesy) at Stanford University. He directs the Youth and Education Law Project, a legal clinic devoted to ensuring equal educational opportunities. He has published articles on educational equity and adequacy, the politics of judicial decisionmaking, and teacher assignment policies.

Michal Kurlaender is an assistant professor in the School of Education at the University of California–Davis. Her areas of research include access and persistence in higher education for underrepresented groups, K–12 school desegregation and integration, and bringing innovative quantitative methods to bear on issues of education policy.

Helen F. Ladd is the Edgar Thompson Professor of Public Policy Studies and Economics at Duke University. Her current research focuses primarily on education policy, including school accountability, parental choice and market-based reforms, charter schools, school finance and teacher labor markets. Her most recent book is *The Handbook of Research on Educational Finance and Policy* (coedited with E. Fiske).

Elisabeth S. Larsen is an advanced graduate student in the Department of Sociology at Brigham Young University. She is currently studying the sociology of education, and her research emphases include school desegregation and school choice.

Roslyn Arlin Mickelson is professor of sociology and adjunct professor of public policy, information technology, and women's studies at the University of North Carolina at Charlotte. With funding from the National Science Foundation, Mickelson has investigated school reform in the Charlotte-Mecklenburg Schools since 1988.

Jerome E. Morris is an associate professor of education and director of the Race, Class, Place, and Outcomes Research Group at The University of Georgia's Institute for Behavioral Research. His scholarship focuses on the sociology and anthropology of education, and prior and ongoing research investigations have specifically targeted communities, schools, families, adolescents, and school reform and policy.

Marco A. Muñoz is an evaluation specialist in the Accountability, Research, and Planning Department of the Jefferson County Public Schools in Louisville, Kentucky. He serves as an adjunct faculty member at the University of Louisville, where he teaches research methods, statistics, measurement, and evaluation. Muñoz received the American Evaluation Association's Marcia Guttentag Award in 2001 for his contribution in school district evaluation.

Jeannie Oakes is director of education and scholarship at the Ford Foundation. Oakes's research addresses the impact of education policies on the opportunities and outcomes of low-income students of color. Her recent books include *Beyond Tracking: Multiple Pathways to College, Career, and Civic Participation* (coedited with M. Saunders), from Harvard Education Press. Oakes is a member of the National Academy of Education.

Kristie J. R. Phillips is an assistant professor of sociology at Brigham Young University. Her current research interests include school choice, school desegregation, and the social contexts and organization of education. Her research combines elements of sociological theory, social geography, and education policy.

Christina Ramsay will complete her bachelor's degree with a dual major in educational studies and psychology from Trinity College in May 2009. As a member of the Cities, Suburbs, and Schools Research Project, she coauthored *Missing the Goal: A Visual Guide to* Sheff v. O'Neill *School Desegregation* (with J. Wanzer). Her current research is a qualitative study of Hartford family members' perceptions of the Project Choice program.

Robert J. Rodosky is the executive director of the Accountability, Research, and Planning Department for the Jefferson County Public Schools in Louisville, Kentucky, a district of 97,000 students that includes Louisville and its suburbs.

Stephen Samuel Smith is a professor of political science at Winthrop University. He served as an expert witness for the NAACP's Legal Defense and Educational Fund in the reopened *Swann* litigation, and he is the author of *Boom for Whom? Education, Desegregation, and Development in Charlotte*, and many articles and chapters dealing with urban politics and education.

Claire Smrekar is an associate professor of public policy and education at Peabody College, Vanderbilt University and an investigator with the National Center on School Choice. Her work involves qualitative research studies related to the social context of education and public policy, with specific reference to the impact of desegregation plans and choice policy on families, schools, and neighborhoods.

Stephanie Southworth is a PhD candidate in public policy at the University of North Carolina at Charlotte. Her research interests include, race, ethnicity, gender, and organizations and inequality. She is currently conducting a longitudinal study of the impact of the organizational characteristics of schools on academic achievement in North Carolina schools.

Eleanor R. Spindler is a PhD candidate in educational foundations, policy, and practice at the University of Colorado at Boulder. Her research interests include equity in public schools, racial segregation, and program evaluation. She is currently assisting in an evaluation of Denver's alternative teacher compensation program.

Jacob L. Vigdor is associate professor of public policy studies and economics at Duke University and a Faculty Research Fellow at the National Bureau of

Economic Research. He has written extensively on the subjects of education policy, racial segregation, and political economy.

Jesse Wanzer completed his bachelor's degree with a dual major in educational studies and psychology from Trinity College in 2008. As a member of the Cities, Suburbs, and Schools Research Project, he coauthored *Missing the Goal: A Visual Guide to* Sheff v. O'Neill *School Desegregation* (with C. Ramsay). He also coauthored *Mapping the Gap* with the Connecticut Coalition for Achievement Now.

Kevin G. Welner is director of the Education and the Public Interest Center and associate professor at the University of Colorado at Boulder, where he specializes in educational policy, law, and program evaluation. Welner has received AERA's Early Career Award and the Palmer O. Johnson Award for best article.

Index

Note: Page numbers followed by *f*, *m*, or *t* indicate figures, maps, and tables, respectively.